The Alpine Journal 1986

3

Volume 91 No 335

The Alpine Journal 1986

Incorporating the Journal of the Ladies' Alpine Club & Alpine Climbing

A record of mountain adventure and scientific observation

Edited by John Fairley

Assistant Editors:
Phil Bartlett and Geoffrey Templeman

assisted by Maurice Bennett,
Margaret Clennett, Ashley Greenwood,
Robin Robinson and Frank Solari.

The Alpine Club, London

4

Address all editorial communications to
the Hon Editor direct at:
51 Cholmeley Crescent
London
N6 5EX

Address all advertising communications to
the Business Manager
Peter Ledeboer
28 Shrewsbury House
Cheyne Walk
London SW3 5LW

Address all sales and distribution
communications to
West Col Productions
Goring, Reading
Berks RG8 9AA

Back numbers:
apply to the Alpine Club or for 1969 to
date to West Col Productions

SBN — 900523 52 2
ISSN 0065-6569

Designed by John Fairley
Printed in Great Britain by Swindon Press Ltd. Swindon, Wilts, SN2 6DU
Distributed by West Col Productions, Goring, Reading, Berks, RG8 9AA

The Alpine Club, 74 South Audley Street, London W1Y 5FF

Contents

6

Illustrations

In Memoriam

Sir Anthony Keith Rawlinson, KCB, 1926–1986

Sir Anthony Rawlinson, the forty-fourth president of the Club, was killed in a fall from Crib Goch on Snowdon on 22 February 1986. He was the first president to die in office and the first to be killed in the mountains. The club has suffered a grievous loss by his untimely death.

Anthony was born on 5 March 1926 and was the only son of Dr A E J Rawlinson, later Bishop of Derby. He had a brilliant academic career. He was a King's Scholar at Eton, and was Captain of the School in 1944. After completing his national service in 1944–47 as a lieutenant in the Grenadier Guards, he went up to Oxford on an open scholarship in classics. He obtained a first in Classical Mods and a second in Greats, the latter a few weeks after a near-fatal fall on Ben Nevis.

He then went into the civil service in the Ministry of Labour, transferring to the Treasury in 1953. He served for a time (1958–60) as private secretary to the chairman of the Atomic Energy Authority, and in 1972 became a deputy secretary, serving in Washington as Economic Minister and Head of the United Kingdom Treasury and Supply Delegation at the British Embassy. During this period he was also the UK executive director of the International Monetary Fund and the IBRD. On his return to London he was a deputy secretary, then second permanent secretary in the Department of Industry (1975–6) and then returned to the Treasury as a second permanent secretary. In that post his responsibilities included public expenditure control and the implementation of the switch to cash planning and budgeting. In 1983 he became permanent secretary of the Department of Trade, which soon after was combined with the Department of Industry. He remained as joint permanent secretary of the combined department until his retirement in 1985. He was then appointed chairman of the Gaming Board. In his long and distinguished career as a public servant, he earned the respect and admiration of his colleagues. As one of them has put it – 'In all that he did, as a civil servant or otherwise, he acted with clarity of mind and expression, meticulous attention to accuracy and to detail, robust firmness, and unswerving integrity and commitment.' He was appointed CB in 1975 and KCB in 1978.

Anthony's mountaineering career was equally distinguished. Throughout his life he kept detailed diaries of his expeditions to the hills, including in many instances notes on routes and times, equipment and expenses. His first accounts are of walking in and around Buttermere in 1937 when he was eleven, and for the next ten years he walked and scrambled in the Lakes, mostly based on family holidays in Buttermere, where he met and joined up with Claude Elliott, later to be his headmaster at Eton. In 1947 he attended his first OUMC meet at Brackenclose, with MHW, among others. He was a tall, slim, slightly gangling figure, clad as most of us were in those days in ex-army camouflage anorak, patched breeches, tricounis or tennis shoes, but in his case also sporting a shapeless black felt hat with the front brim turned up, in better days the property of his father, the bishop. In spite of some good times on that meet, the main impression of climbing carried away by the beginners was of rain, cold,

1   *Sir Anthony Keith Rawlinson, KCB.*

darkness and dirt and some doubted if it was for them. But this discouragement could not survive meeting Anthony next term, in the more civilized setting of his rooms at Christ Church. The enthusiasm for the mountains, the sense of fun, the glee with which he recalled the discomfort of reaching for holds submerged in rainwater, the pleasure at having done such classic climbs as the Needle, the planning for the next meet and the next season — they were all too infectious, and this meeting marked the start of a 20-year partnership.

He was soon one of the leading members of the OUMC. Indeed, it was always difficult to imagine Anthony not being a leading member of whatever group he joined. Not that he put himself forward, but in any company he stood out as a man of character, with an incisive mind and above all a man of goodwill. Moreover, he had a long apprenticeship in the hills behind him, an experience deepened by his interest in mountaineering history and literature. He was always willing to help, and was in due course treasurer, then president of the OUMC. For the next four years he climbed intensively with OUMC friends, and continued to climb with the same group for many years afterwards.

The OUMC was going through a good period. After the wartime interruption, British climbers were again in the Alps, keen to re-establish themselves, aiming not so much at first ascents as at 'first British' or 'first guideless'. Anthony played a large part in this effort. Standards were rising fast, due to men like Tom Bourdillon and Hamish Nicol. 'Practice for the Alps' was one of the ostensible reasons for the somewhat elitist OUMC Easter meets on Ben Nevis. Anthony was on three of these, doing most of the classics of those days, and finally attempting Zero Gully with Hamish, using old-fashioned ice-axes and tricounis. Their spectacular fall of some 240m did not dampen Anthony's enthusiasm, though it laid him low for some weeks.

He was elected to the Alpine Club in January 1951 — during the presidency of Claude Elliott — proposed by Jack Longland and seconded by David Cox, both of them later to become presidents of the Club. His 'list' at that time was long and detailed and in effect constituted the alpine record of the OUMC of the day. Typically, it consisted of classic traverses, meticulously researched and organized, with Anthony doing most of the research and much of the leading. Notable were the Ferpècle on the Dent Blanche, the Täschhorn by the Teufelsgrat, which then had quite a reputation, and the Mer de Glace face of the Grépon.

In the summer of 1951 he took part in the first guideless British ascent of the NW ridge of the Aiguille de Blaitière. This was a Ryan-Lochmatter route, and it was in keeping with Anthony's feeling for tradition that the first of his contributions to the *AJ* described this and two other Ryan-Lochmatter routes, the E ridge of the Dent d'Hérens and the Cresta Santa Caterina on the Nordend, both climbed in 1952. The latter was in some respects his best season and on return to England he was selected as one of the four reserves for the forthcoming expedition to Mount Everest. In fact he never visited the Himalaya, but this did not seriously disturb him because he was above all a traditionalist, who was steeped in alpine history and literature and found his greatest pleasure in following in the footsteps of the great alpine pioneers of the past, particularly in the Valais.

It was in 1953 that he did one of his most notable climbs, the fourth ascent (first British) of the Tronchey arete of the Grandes Jorasses, most of which he led, with Dick Viney, Ted Wrangham, Mike Harris and Ralph Jones. This was in a real sense a pioneering effort, with considerable problems of route finding on difficult rock. One has only to read Viney's account (*AJ59*, 323) to see what a source of strength Anthony was in a difficult situation. Another epic, with MHW in 1955, was the SW ridge of the Fou. The climb itself was straightforward, but the descent over the Ciseaux and Blaitière was in thunder, lightning, blizzard and cold. Anthony's patience and competence were unfailing.

His diaries continue to record a steady stream of climbs. The traverse of the Meije, the S face of the Pavé, the Ryan-Lochmatter on the Plan, visit after visit to Zermatt, completing his list of the classics with the E–N traverse of the Weißhorn (1967) and repeating many of his earlier ascents. The Dolomites, Tarentaise, Saas, Bernina, Bregaglia. 1965 is worth particular mention. He represented the Club as an observer on a course for prospective guides and porters in the Val d'Aosta (*AJ70*, 262). Anthony was already a friend of Toni Gobbi, chief guide of Courmayeur, and did much to strengthen the Club's links with Italian climbers. Unfortunately bad weather precluded any notable climbs on the course, but he relished the chance of working with first-class guides.

In later years he rather lowered his sights, being unwilling to risk holding up his companions on the classic traverses he enjoyed so much. But he maintained his active mountaineering. The Washington posting provided opportunities to walk in New England and Colorado. There were frequent holidays in Skye, Ben Nevis, North Wales, and in the Lakes which remained his first love. Recently he enjoyed walking and scrambling holidays in and around the Alps, with parties of old friends.

In addition to his record as a mountaineer, it is right that we should pay tribute to the other contributions he made to the sport. He was president of the OUMC; in 1955–59 editor of the Climbers Club Journal; in 1963–66 he was honorary secretary of the Alpine Club and in 1972–73 a vice-president. He served for many years on the Committee of Management of the Mount Everest Foundation and was chairman in 1970–71. In 1966, as honorary secretary of the Club and having been a founder-member of the ACG, he played a large part with JHEJ in negotiating the merger of the two clubs, thus fusing the modern and the traditional strands of mountaineering.

In January 1986, Anthony began his term of office as President. In the space of a few weeks he had already demonstrated his great enthusiasm for the job, the freshness of his ideas and of his plans for the future of the Club. The Committee will miss his clear direction of their deliberations and the Club is the poorer for his loss.

Above all, Anthony enjoyed his mountains, and the fun which is to be derived from climbing. He had a great capacity for friendship — and indeed most of his close friends were those with whom he had climbed. His death leaves us all distressed and deprived, but we retain many happy memories of days spent in his company. The Club's sympathy is extended to the close-knit family which he leaves behind, to the three sons of whom he was so proud; and particularly to Mary, who although unable to accompany Anthony into the high mountains never allowed that to interfere with his pursuit of the sport which gave him and his many friends so much pleasure.

J H Emlyn Jones and *Michael Westmacott*

Valedictory Address

Roger Chorley
(Read before the Alpine Club on 2 December 1985)

It is thirty-three years since I was last required to address the Club and on that occasion I had the brashness of youth and the inestimable aid of the lantern slide on my side. I also had something of practical interest to recount. Now, many years later, you have done me the honour of electing me your President, an unexpected pleasure. As the time approached to perform my task tonight I reflected that an exhaustive — and indeed to the audience an exhausting — account of the Club's affairs and the doings of its members is pretty boring fare. On the other hand, if one were to devote oneself to more philosophical matters, one inevitably wondered, being 36th in a long line of distinguished predecessors, whether there was anything new to be said. It was no comfort that one of my predecessors, Tom Longstaff, avoided the task by the simple expedient of entertaining us — his was the first meeting of the Club I attended — in his inimitable way with reminiscences. How much more worthwhile that was!

C E Matthews, who inaugurated the tradition in 1880, had no doubts. He said, you will recall, that his colleagues surely had the right to expect something more from their President, than that he should slink away like the Ghost from the battlements at Elsinore, feebly muttering: 'Adieu, adieu, adieu, remember me.' 'The President,' he said, 'is intimately acquainted with the traditions of Alpine government. He watches keenly the state of Alpine morals . . . He has sources of information open to him which are not always accessible to ordinary mountaineers.' And so on; it is heavy stuff and clearly he had in mind a state-of-the-nation address. For my part I want to descend to a rather more mundane level. I have a particular theme I want to develop and I can do no better than take my cue from Grove's valedictory address 100 years ago. 'How extraordinary does it seem,' he says, 'when we think of the year 1857, to contrast the facilities for world travel which then existed with those that exist now . . . and as facilities for going far have increased, so it has become cheaper and cheaper, . . . world travel . . . is no longer reserved for a few rich and adventurous men.'

Grove, you will observe, was talking of world travel, not Alpine travel. But it is pertinent to my purpose to start with Alpine travel and to start at the beginning. Next year marks the bicentenary of perhaps the most important event in our sport, the first ascent of Mont Blanc. It also, as it happens, marks the centenary of the first ascent of the Napes Needle by Haskett Smith, and the jubilee of the first ascent of Nanda Devi by Tilman and Odell in 1936. I shall come back to these anniversaries later.

Now one scarcely needs to be a student of Alpine history to observe that the Paccard/Balmat ascent of Mont Blanc did not inaugurate a great surge of mountaineering activity. It is true that the third ascent, by de Saussure, was in the following year. But between 1786 and 1851, the year of Albert Smith's well-known ascent, Mont Blanc was climbed only 37 times. It is not hard to see why, or rather why ascents of Mont Blanc subsequently became routine affairs. The reason does not lie, as has been suggested by some historians, with the publicity created by Albert Smith's lectures at the Egyptian Hall. Rather it was that Smith caught a tide, the tide of a break-through in accessibility – the age of the railway.

It is worth reminding ourselves just how dramatic the advent of the railway was, and it will not surprise you that I will be drawing a parallel later with air travel access to the greater ranges. As it happens, Albert Smith made his first visit to Chamonix in 1838, when he was a medical student in Paris, and it took him five hard travelling days to get there, including 78 hours non-stop by diligence to Geneva. And it took Frederik Clissold, who climbed Mont Blanc in 1822, 16 days from London before he reached Chamonix. By 1851 one could travel from London via Paris to Chalons-sur-Saône by rail, and Albert Smith could record, in 1853, that the traveller 'may sit down to his dinner, looking out at the sunset on Mont Blanc, on the third day of his departure from London.' The journey was a little complicated because at Chalons one had to take a boat to Lyons, then overnight by diligence to Geneva, ('the 'Berlines,' I think, are the quickest') with a further change there and at Sallanches. 'Of course,' he says, 'I only recommend this route to those who have youth and health, and are much pressed for time.' By the end of the 1850s the railways had penetrated to Geneva and the journey time to Chamonix could be reduced to two rather full days. The Visp-Zermatt railway was opened in 1891, and my edition of Whymper's guide to the valley of Zermatt, having recommended the Night Express from London, goes on to say, 'If this is taken, you should be landed at Zermatt in the following afternoon, in time to settle down for dinner.'

This, of course, needs to be put into the context of what nowadays we call holiday entitlement. Arnold Lunn's analysis of the composition of the Club in those days shows it to have been predominantly made up of professional men, and my grandfather Edward Hopkinson and his brothers, who in that respect were probably fairly typical members of the Club, would seem to have taken generally between two and four weeks' holiday. (I deduce this from his manuscript notes in the flyleaf of his 1885 *Baedeker*.) Without the railways one would scarcely want to spend three or four weeks getting to and from the Alps unless one could spend at least three or four weeks in the Alps. With the railways cutting travel times to two or three days in total, a three-to-four week, or even a two-week, period in the Alps became attractive and within the compass of a normal holiday. The Pilkington brothers, when they made with Gardner the first guideless ascent of the Meije in 1879 — another landmark in mountaineering — did so in a three-week holiday from Manchester. Lawrence Pilkington remarked rather defensively many years later that they weren't able to wait for the mountain to get into ideal condition as his brother had to get back to work. The saving in travel time, and also, but to a lesser extent, on costs which I will come to later, resulted in a quite disproportionate change in demand; a barrier was broken. The practicability of a regular Alpine holiday had arrived.

It is not surprising then that in the ten years to 1865 over 80 first ascents or pass crossings were made, not to mention the scores of other climbs. It is difficult to believe that, but for the railways, Whymper's famous engraving of members of the Alpine Club outside the Monte Rosa Hotel in 1865 would have had more than a fraction of the score or so who can be identified. The Golden Age of Alpine mountaineering was the railway age.

The other technological change that occurred at the same time was the steamship, and this is no doubt what Grove had in mind, although he and a number of other leading members of the Club at the time seemed to be more interested in the Caucases than, for example, the Himalaya, perhaps because one could go by railway to Odessa. Nevertheless, while travel times to India were vastly reduced by the steamship, we have had to wait nearly 100 years before the Himalaya could be considered to be a holiday playground. The boat journey to India took two weeks, and that, together with crossing India and long approach marches, meant that one needed at least a three-month trip in order to have four weeks or so in the mountains. Grove may have been right on the grounds of cost that world travel was no longer reserved for a few rich and adventurous men, but one did have to have more time than even the pre-Golden Age Alpine explorers. Shipton and Tilman's famous expedition of 1934, which solved the problem of getting into the Nanda Devi Sanctuary, and hence was the essential precursor to the successful ascent of 1936, cost them only £130 a head, but it took six months. Moreover, although £130 was considered amazingly modest at the time, it was no negligible sum for it was equivalent to nearly £2000 in today's £'s.

The ascent of Nanda Devi, or for that matter any of the other expeditions which we would regard as being notable in the development of Himalayan mountaineering and in particular lightweight expeditions, were a necessary but not a sufficient condition to opening up the Himalaya to holiday mountaineers, in the same way as the Alps in the 1860s and 1870s. As with the Alps, what mattered was being able to have a useful period of time in the Himalaya within the compass of a normal holiday. While the normal holiday for a professional man may not have changed greatly from 100 years ago — perhaps four to six weeks rather than three to four — at lower income levels the change has been proportionately much greater: between 1870 and 1979 overall average hours worked per person declined by nearly 50%. It is true that those who lived or were stationed in India were able to indulge in extended holiday mountaineering. And it is true that Imperial Airways opened a seven-day train and 'plane service to Karachi as early as 1929, but it was expensive. Shipton's cargo steamer cost £30 return, Imperial £260 — equivalent to more than £3000 today. It is also true that Campbell Secord, one of the most innovative of mountaineers, got himself to Gilgit in five days from London in 1947. But all this was exceptional, and it was not until the 1950s that travel times to the sub-continent were down to under 24 hours.

The other major factor in all this is cost — the massive change in travel and total holiday costs and how these costs relate to changes in incomes. Information on how much it cost to get to the Alps before the railways is scarce, but it is generally well established that the railways greatly reduced travel costs. Information on railway fares is, however, available; for example, Whymper's

Zermatt guide, which I have already referred to, advertises the first-class fare from London to Chamonix at £5:18s:10d., the second-class fare being £4:2s:4d.; this was for 1911. It is a notoriously hazardous task trying to adjust for inflation over such a long time-span, but estimates which have been made suggest an inflation factor of about 25 times, and on that basis the £4:2s:4d. fare would be £100, and this is perhaps double the cost of an individual's share of two people motoring to Chamonix today.

Total holiday costs are even more difficult to compare, but here the flyleaf of my grandfather's *Baedeker* again comes in handy, because he recorded how much he spent. His costs were typically £30 for a three-week holiday. This would have included a certain amount of guiding at 6s:8d. a day (an unbelievable £8 a day at present £'s), and would have been hotel-based; valley-based camping is a mainly post second world war phenomenon. So these costs, which work out at around £750 at today's prices, could not have been reduced significantly and would be of the order of three times as much as the cost of a fairly basic three-week Alpine holiday today.

Although travel to the Himalaya has been revolutionized by the aeroplane, air travel costs to the Himalaya were more expensive than by sea up to about 1960. Before then, if time was a problem, you had to go by air. Since 1945 air travel costs per passenger seat-mile have fallen by a factor of four. And due to the quirks of fare structures, ticket prices in certain instances have fallen even further. For example, when I went to Nepal in 1957, the round-trip fare was about £250 to Delhi, only about half today's standard economy fare which, as we all know, can usually be significantly discounted through 'bucket shops'. But my £250 is the equivalent of £2000 in today's £'s. It is true that porter rates have increased in real terms, but then for many areas much of the portering has been replaced by buses and trucks, and in any case today's generation are much more economical in the use of porters, thanks to modern food and gear and the tremendous, and welcome development of Alpine style climbing. In the 1950s it cost about £400-£600 a head for a lightweight expedition, that is to say £3000-£5000 at today's prices. Now you can do a basic climbing trip for £800-£1000, and a lightweight expedition for under £2000. To put it another way, it is now possible to spend a four-week holiday in the Himalaya for only a little more than the cost of my grandfather's three-week holiday in the Alps a hundred years ago. Moreover, while the costs we are particularly interested in have fallen steeply, economic progress has also continued in other fields; all in all there has been a roughly threefold increase in real incomes.

Of equal importance to the speed and cheapness of air travel to the sub-continent has been the more recent development of road building in the Himalaya — ironically usually for strategic reasons. (Much of the road building in Switzerland carried out between 1820 and 1860 was also for strategic purposes.) The recent opening of the Karakoram Highway from Islamabad to Hunza and beyond has brought Gilgit and Skardu to within a couple of days' bus journey — at a nominal fare in Western terms — of Islamabad. It is of course true that from 1948 both Gilgit and Skardu could be reached by air. But even that was (and still is) an uncertain, albeit memorable, affair. In 1954 we waited the best part of a week at Rawalpindi for favourable weather, and that would not seem to be untypical, but what a tremendous flight it was when we finally snaked up the Indus Gorge, with Nanga Parbat building itself a further 4500m above us. Now with the road, the delightful valleys and 6000m peaks to the west of the Hunza river, the 7000m peaks of the Batura to the north, and the great glacier systems and peaks of the Karakoram proper to the east, all this vast and magnificent area is only three or four days from Islamabad and only a day more from London. The Chogolungma glacier and its mountains are now only two days from Skardu, and as members know, it was the base for the first Alpine Club Himalaya climbing meet this summer. The Baltoro and Biafo glaciers are only a few days further and organized treks are now available to Concordia.

I must pass on to the Central Himalaya merely noting in passing that most of the mountain valleys in Zanskar, Kishtwar, Kulu, Spiti, and Lahul are now readily accessible. The roads here have opened up a region of thousands of square miles and hundreds of fine, 5000-6000m peaks. One thinks, for example, of the Kishtwar Shivling, and the tremendous new route put up by Renshaw and Venables in 1983, and notes that they were on the mountain in only five days from roadhead.

In Garwhal roads now penetrate into the heart of the massif, for example anyone who wants to repeat Chris Bonington and Jim Fotheringham's magnificent route on the western peak of Shivling can be at the foot of the mountain in four days from Delhi — two days bus and two days walking.

Road building in the mountain regions of Nepal has been rather less. Nevertheless the new road north from Kathmandu to Tibet has brought the Langtang Valley and its peaks to within a few days of the capital. Further west, Pokhara is accessible by both road and air, which brings the Annapurna Sanctuary to within a week from London. The Lukla airstrip has provided easy, if erratic, access to Sola Khumbu for a number of years, but perhaps more important, the road east from Kathmandu now takes one as far as Jiri; and one can now drive to Lhasa from Kathmandu.

The picture which emerges from this imperfect and rather anecdotal evidence is, I think, fairly clear: there has been since 1960 a revolution in accessibility to the greater ranges:

— the number of mountaineers who can afford to go to the Himalaya is vastly greater than the numbers who could afford to go to the Alps 100 years ago. The total number of mountaineers is also of course very much greater.
— their holiday entitlement is probably a month compared with perhaps three weeks for their greatly better-off — in relative terms — ancestors;
— there are now numerous Himalayan centres which can be accessed rapidly by road;
— travel times to these centres are only two or three days longer than the 24 hours it took to get to the Alps 100 years ago.

And this revolution has been accompanied by a diffusion of knowledge which in turn has brought a feeling of familiarity; we are, if you will, comfortable with the Himalaya.

In short it is now possible for the average mountaineer — and it is the average mountaineer who is my concern tonight — to take his annual holiday in the Himalaya, and to an increasing extent he is doing so as a matter of course. He will not climb as many peaks as he would in the Alps, but with luck he will get in several 5000-6000m peaks. He will be able to enjoy and explore big mountain country — both mountains and valleys — in the same way as the founding fathers of our sport did over 100 years ago. For the ordinary mountaineer air travel and roads have done for the Himalaya, and for that matter for the Andes, what the railways did for the Alps. I must apologise here to the devotees of the Andes that I have not included this great range in my survey; it is simply that there is not time to cover both adequately. I confine myself to observing that all the points I have made about Himalayan accessibility and costs apply equally, but that in addition there is a welcome freedom from red tape and the heights of the mountains make them more amenable to the holiday mountaineer.

At the same time this same prosperity has had its effects on our traditional playground, the Alps. The enchanting view of the Vale of Chamonix painted by William Pars in 1770 is now a ghastly metropolis complete with motorway, and in the summer months there are some 2000 people actively climbing each day; Zermatt in the summer and winter seasons is now one of the larger Swiss cities. There is no need for me to dilate on overcrowded huts, or overcrowded paths or even queueing for climbs. Nor do I wish to enter into that favourite debating topic of whether the Alps are now played out, although one's impression is that the number of new routes of quality has dropped off. Suffice it to say that at the same time and for the same reason that the Himalaya are now able to beckon, at least some of the charm and some of the challenge that have drawn us to the Alps for all these years, have gone.

It is difficult to envisage the same dramatic changes in Himalayan accessibility over the next 30 years as have occurred over the last 30 years, but there is little doubt that there will be a steady trend of improvement. In particular, new roads will open up more and more centres, and the number of people — I am not here thinking only of Britons — with sufficient holidays and sufficient incomes to go there will increase steadily. All of these have important consequences for the new playground countries, for mountaineering in general, and for the Club in particular. I would like briefly to touch on each of these.

The Himalaya may be a large place — there are over 1300 peaks of 6000m or above in Nepal alone — but the local economies are fragile and poor, certainly more so than the Alpine regions were a century ago when tourism was taking off. Moreover the Alpine regions did not suffer from the twin problems of the population explosion and deforestation. Nevertheless I do not myself believe that the additional burden of mountaineers is a significant problem except in the case of mammoth expeditions, and I doubt whether these will grow in number, or in the case of particularly sensitive honeypots such as the Nanda Devi Sanctuary. Sad though it is, one must surely applaud the Indian Government's decision to close it in 1983. Even if the number of climbing parties were to double or treble from the current level of 200 or so a year, when spread across the Himalaya they would still be tiny. The more sensitive problem is surely the growth of the trekking industry which is now big business — 50,000 trekking permits a year in Nepal.

This brings me to my second point, the increasing importance of our sister organizations in the proper development of mountaineering in the greater ranges. We must foster our contacts with them; with our long experience and traditions I would hope we could be of some assistance to them in exercising a large and difficult responsibility. We must also, I suggest, encourage their authorities to ease the red tape involved in getting to the mountains. I have in mind permits, peak fees, and mandatory liaison officers. If holiday mountaineering is to develop, with all the benefits it could bring to these isolated communities, then it would seem sense to do away with permits and fees for peaks under, say 6000m, and the need for liaison officers. Pakistan has done this, which was the main reason we selected the Chogolungma glacier for the AC meet this year. Nepal has recently increased the number of peaks which require only a trekking permit, which is encouraging, and it is to be hoped that the Indian Authorities will move in this direction. If we are to have an AC meet next year in the Indian Himalaya, as we would like to, it will certainly be necessary to secure flexible arrangements.

I turn now to what this growth may mean for mountaineering in general. Here there are perhaps two quite different points. First, however easy the access may become, the mountains are much bigger. The development of drugs may help with acclimatization or altitude-related problems, equipment will continue to improve, and today's generation will pass on its experience to tomorrow's. But there is no getting away from the fact that these mountains are much more dangerous because of both scale and altitude.

My second, rather different, point is the sad thought that, just as some of the charm of the Alps, and certainly of the valleys, has been destroyed by the very people who came to enjoy it, so inevitably will this happen in the greater ranges. When I first landed at Kathmandu in 1957 Wilfred Noyce looked out of the plane window and said with a note of horror, 'My God, they've tarmacked the runway'; one wonders what he would say today. More recently someone said to me, 'You don't need a map to get to the Everest base camp, just follow the trash.' Perhaps I am too pessimistic, the less grand parts of the Alps do still have a wonderful charm, and so perhaps it will be with the Himalaya. They are a big place.

Finally, what does all this mean for the Club? We call ourselves the Alpine Club, and from time to time in the last century the Club debated whether it should confine its interest to the Alps, but we never did so — the strong lead from people like Grove, Conway and Freshfield saw to that. Nevertheless, our essential background was the Alps, and only a few of our members had any sort of experience of the greater ranges. To go on an expedition to the Himalaya was something special; indeed for many people you didn't just 'go', you were 'selected'. If it was Everest it was a bit like being invited to join the MCC touring party to Australia. All that, I am glad to say, has changed and now, or perhaps it will be tomorrow, the average member of the Club will think no more of going to the Himalaya or to the Andes than he does of going to the Alps. Perhaps this will make the Club more cohesive — there won't be those

grand people who have 'been on an expedition' and those who have only been to
the Alps. So I see this progression as being a healthy development which we
should encourage. One means of encouragement is the Himalayan or Andean
meet. I would like to see them as a regular feature in the annual calendar of the
Club's activities. The 20 or so members who visited the Chogolungma glacier
this summer may not have climbed so many peaks as on an alpine meet;
nevertheless they climbed several and crossed some passes; it was a genuine
climbing meet of members, and I suggest in the annals of the Club it was in its
way a small but important historical event.

There are two other fields where the Club can be and is in fact being active.

Thirty years ago, when one was climbing actively, it was easy to know what
was going on in the Himalaya; it was mostly British and one knew most of the
people. Today, with several hundred parties visiting the Himalaya each year —
I prefer the word parties rather than expeditions — from a variety of nationalities, the scene is very different. The latest issue of that invaluable publication,
the Himalayan Club Newsletter, runs to nearly 40 closely printed pages with
only the briefest climbing details. How, in these circumstances, does one keep
abreast, not of the major events, but of the detail — if you will — of the 6000m
peaks and below. Our Journal cannot, nor should it attempt to, be the
repository of such detail.

It was from this problem that the notion of a Himalayan index emerged. I
found that Peter Lloyd, who was at that time Chairman of the Mount Everest
Foundation, was thinking along similar lines. It seemed clear that what was
wanted was some form of index to enable someone planning his annual holiday
to find out for any particular area what had been done, by whom, and when,
and with reference to the literature — published and unpublished — which
would be held by the Alpine Club Library. For the historian it was tempting to
draw an analogy with John Ball's — our first President — Alpine Guides which
were published in 1864 and reissued as a new edition by the Alpine Club
opening a subscription list after his death in 1889. This was a case of the Club
taking an initiative *pro bono publico*. Further thought suggested that Himalayan
guidebooks were not the appropriate solution. Nevertheless, it is interesting to
note *en passant* the number of commercially published trekking guides which
have appeared in the last few years. The concept was for a computerised data
base which would provide the essential information and references. A feasibility
study was carried out by a working party consisting of George Band, Stephen
Town, David Baldock and Bob Lawford. They examined the idea in some
depth, fleshed it out and endorsed it. By happy coincidence Michael Westmacott agreed to take on the task of directing the operation in addition to
becoming Chairman of the Alpine Club Library. We then set about the task of
raising the necessary funds. So far we have raised nearly £10,000, helped
considerably by a $5000 contribution from the American Alpine Club. The
Club has itself contributed the computer system which was needed for our own
administration and for the Library. But we still need to find another £5000 and
ideally rather more.

None of those who have been involved in the exercise have any illusions that
it is an ambitious undertaking — but so were John Ball's Alpine Guides. The

important point, it seems to me, is that we must not try to be all encompassing (for example, to try to cover all ascents). The essential task is to provide references — to the literature and to archive material — and to build as we go. The essence of a computer data base is its flexibility.

The Library as a comprehensive repository of books, journals, and unpublished material, is an essential component. I would here like to digress for a moment to pay tribute to the stewardship of Sir Douglas Busk, its Chairman from 1972 to early this year. When in 1970 in my capacity as Honorary Treasurer, I proposed on behalf of the Committee that the Library should be organized as a separate body with charitable status, that we needed a professional librarian to look after our unique collection, and that we should raise money, there were a few Thomas's who doubted whether the scheme would work. That it has worked is largely due to two outstanding chairmen, Edwin Herbert (Lord Tangley) and Douglas Busk, who between them raised large sums of money to secure it; nor must I forget the enormous practical help and advice given by two others, Bob Lawford and Frank Solari. But the Library, in spite of these efforts, is not adequately secure; it is not properly endowed and needs more money. We are the custodians of a unique heritage and I ask you to support the joint appeal for the Library and the Himalayan Index.

The Himalayan Index is one way that the Club can fulfil its traditional role of providing a lead in the mountaineering world. Another way is by holding symposia. In the 1970s the Club organized two important symposia on Mountain Medicine and Avalanches. Following that precedent and in line with the general thesis that we should support and encourage mountaineering in the greater ranges, we have held two successful symposia at Plas y Brenin. The first was in March 1984, organized by Charles Clarke and Audrey Salkeld, under the title of 'Lightweight Expeditions to the Great Ranges'. Ten papers were delivered, and lively discussions ensued. Listening to it, I was struck by the wealth of practical information — of know-how — on all aspects of the lightweight expedition, from 'Costs and How to Avoid Them' by Ron Rutland to 'The Risks and How I See Them' by Don Whillans. That symposium mainly focused on the Himalaya, so Al Rouse volunteered to organize a follow-up on the Andes. This was held last week-end, also at Plas y Brenin, and was a great success. I came away with two thoughts. First, we should organize a meet in Peru, perhaps in the Cordillera Vilcanota, in 1987. Second, that we should have at least annually joint ACG and AC meets.

What I have had to say to you tonight has been rather prosaic — how changing accessibility has influenced how and where we practise our sport, and why today in a very real sense the world is our oyster, and how, more importantly, it is more and more the oyster of the ordinary members of the Club. That is a good thing and not only in its own right but because it also enhances that common factor that brings us together. Thirty years ago Edwin Herbert delivered one of the most thoughtful valedictory addresses in our long tradition. You will recall — there will be many here tonight who were present then — how he sought to analyse what it was — the values and traditions — that make the sport of mountaineering what it is. One of the factors he

identified was what he termed 'the essential mountain experience' — that
something that most of us would be hard put to explain and which most of us
would see no reason why it required to be explained anyway. But it is that
experience, which in our different ways we all know, that, in Herbert's words,
'really binds together the members of the Club . . .' It is a catholic experience:
Ruskin who fulminated against the climbers who looked upon the Alps as
soaped poles in a bear garden, was as much a member of the Club as Albert
Smith whom he derided. And it has given us a literature which no other sport
can equal. It links Haskett-Smith's remarkable solo ascent of the Napes Needle
to those other two first ascents whose anniversaries we will soon be celebrating — Mont Blanc and Nanda Devi. And it links the ordinary members of the
Club with, to use Grove's words, the young braves of the ACG. It is that
'something' which can be experienced as much in our own hills as in the Alps or
greater ranges. Perhaps the last word should be indeed on our own hills, from
Geoffrey Young, in reflective mood at the end of a unique Alpine career, 'For
me, too, our own hills, within the measure of my walking, are as lovely and as
full of surprise as they ever were.'

The Siachen Indo-British Expedition 1985

Stephen Venables & Dave Wilkinson
Plates 2–10

Preliminaries   *Stephen Venables*
I first heard about the East Karakoram expedition in October 1984. A brief note in the Alpine Club newsletter announced that the club had been invited to send a team on a joint Indo-British expedition to the E Karakoram in 1985. Hopes for a gentle Summer in the Swiss Alps receded as I started to dream about the remote Nubra valley, the Shyok river, the mighty Siachen glacier, the Saser Kangri — remote, mysterious names.

Three months later, in February 1985, a team had chosen itself — Jim Fotheringham, Tony Saunders, Dave Wilkinson and myself. When Henry Osmaston joined the team in April plans were still disconcertingly vague. It was not until May that the IMF told us that we would be climbing with Harish Kapadia and the Bombay Mountaineers. At first, Harish had rejected our first choice of objective — Saser Kangri II — and wanted to explore the area around the junction of the Siachen and Teram Shehr glaciers, 80km further west. He changed his mind when he discovered that Base Camp would be next to a massive encampment of tin huts — the forward base of Indian military operations on the Siachen Glacier. He also discovered that the army's claim to have climbed 'Rimo' in 1984 was misleadingly vague; if they had climbed anything it was Rimo IV. Rimos I, II & III, all over 7000m, remained unclimbed. The army had approached the group from the Rimo Glacier, to the NE. To the SW of the group lay the Terong valley, which had only been visited once, in 1929, by Dr Visser's party on Dr Longstaff's advice:

> 'When it is desired to survey this unknown corner, will the party please proceed five miles up the Siachen Glacier and take the first turning on the right.'

Visser had followed his advice and explored most of this unknown corner — a large complex glacier system — but his report in the *GJ* was brief and he published no photos of the valley.

We quickly agreed that the Terong basin would make an ideal objective. Now that the army had built a road right up to the Siachen snout, access would be easy. It was an enticing valley, ringed by numerous unclimbed peaks.

On arrival in Bombay it was immediately clear that we would be climbing with a delightful group of people: Harish, Muslim Contractor, Dhiren Toolsidas and Zerksis Boga met us at the airport and a few days later we met Arun Samant and the sixth Indian member, Meena Agrawal, whom we had already met in London.

After four days of shopping, packing and being entertained by the Himalayan Club, six of us boarded the Frontier Mail for the long journey to Jammu, continuing by road to Srinagar. Arun and Meena later flew to Delhi, where they met Jim and Tony for the flight to Leh. Henry was not free until mid June and hoped to join us at Base Camp. The whole team apart from Henry finally assembled in Leh on 6 June.

Five days later we left Ley. We set off in a hired truck on the long climb to the Kardung la, across the Ladakh range, and down nearly 3000m to the Shyok river. This we crossed and we continued along the rough road up the left bank of the Nubra River to Panamik where we stopped for luxurious hot baths and an overnight stay at the Dak Bungalow. Panamik has always been an important staging post on the ancient trade route to the Karakoram Pass and the fields were now grazed by mules and yaks, which would soon be carrying loads over the Saser la to Daulat Beg Olde, near the Karakoram Pass. Nowadays, of course, there is no traffic across the pass itself, for it is on the heavily patrolled frontier between India and China.

In the morning we continued, past the improbable entrance to the Saser la, through the village of Warshi (which boasts just three inhabitants) and on into army territory, bumping dustily across boulder-fields which filled a wide plain enclosed by towering slabs of red granite.

My propensity for sleeping stopped me from seeing the last most spectacular part of the journey and I awoke to find the lorry parked three miles from the snout of the Siachen glacier. As we unloaded our truck, an army lorry appeared with lunch. Later, a jeep came bouncing across the sandy plain, recalling film images of Montgomery visiting the troops at Alamein. The officers who emerged from the jeep were extremely friendly, welcoming and impeccably vague about military operations, only admitting that 'those chaps over there are being a bit of a nuisance,' nodding in the direction of Pakistan.

Porters are hard to come by in the Nubra valley, particularly so now that most likely candidates are employed by the army, and we had only found nine men, in addition to our three Bhotias from Kumaon — Harsinh Senior, Harsinh Junior and Pratapsinh. But the colonel said that he could spare some of his men for one day and at 2am next morning a total of nearly 20 men assembled to collect their loads. A sudden announcement that the Ladakhis would only carry 20kg meant repacking all the loads. In the pre-dawn blackness of 14 June our beautifully prepared loads were torn apart. The cacophonic chaos of shouting in Kumaoni, Hindi, Gujurati, Ladakhi and English made the Tower of Babel seem like a polite drawing-room tea party.

Three days later all the loads had been relayed up to the Terong valley. Meena and I came up with the last carry, eager to see Longstaff's 'first turning on the right'. It was a spectacular sight. From the Siachen glacier we looked *down* into the valley, where the Terong glacier had receded out of sight leaving a flat valley floor of gravel flats through which flowed the Terong river before it was swallowed up under the ice of the Siachen.

In the course of its wanderings, the river abuts against high granite cliffs on both sides of the valley, so, after leaving our first camp on the left bank, we had to ford the river to the right before continuing to the snout of the Terong glacier. Now we only had nine Ladakhi and three Bhotia porters. Progress ferrying loads to Base Camp (*c.* 4300m) was slow and it took ten days to move only 18km. But one advantage of the delays was that we all felt very fit and acclimatised. Here we paid off the Ladakhis and set off for Advance Base, sited at 5000m beside a lake at a bifurcation of the N Terong glacier. All climbers did two carries before settling into Advance Base, our home for the next 23 days. It was kept supplied with loads from Base Camp by Pratap and the Harsinhs.

Tony and Jim had made the first reconnaissance to Advance Base and had caught a glimpse of Rimo. The rest of us, during two days of carrying up the glacier, had seen only mysterious hints of icefalls and buttresses disappearing into murky cloud. At last our turn came during our first evening at Advance Base on 25 June. Briefly, the clouds lifted to reveal soaring buttresses, plastered coldly with new snow. There was more snowfall during the night, but in the morning another brief clearing allowed us to see the panorama at the head of the glacier. It was dominated by Rimo I and Rimo III, both massively architectural, aloof and frightening. Then the clouds descended and we remained at Advance Base for two days of rain and snowfall.

Reconnaissance

Every few hours we assembled in Jim's stone-walled kitchen to discuss plans. One of the expedition's aims was to climb one of the Rimo peaks; but because we had no photographs to guide us (apart from one rather foggy picture of the far side of the group) the expedition was both an attempt and a reconnaissance. Both had to be squeezed into three weeks. In order to 'rub our noses' on the SW flanks of Rimo I and to find a route over to the S Rimo glacier on the E side of the massif, we hoped to reach 'Ibex Col' (c. 6200m), at the head of a cwm on the SW side of Rimo I.

The weather on 30 June was bleak, with wind, cloud and frequent snow showers, but not bad enough to stop Jim, Dave and me spending four hours climbing from a camp below the SW spur of Rimo I to Ibex Col and back. The climb was straightforward and from the col we could see an easy snow slope leading down on the far side towards the S Rimo glacier. The cliffs above the col looked particularly hostile in this dark cloudy weather, offering little promise for an ascent of Rimo.

The weather remained unsettled for another two days, while we remained in our tents, acclimatising passively at c. 5600m — a situation which delighted Dave, as it gave his finger, injured in a fall into a glacial stream, more time to recover. Food supplies were now running low, so we went down to Advance Base to re-stock. In a few days the glacier surface had changed radically, crevasses gaping where there had been smooth slopes, and the afternoon snow was horribly soft, making the descent a tedious, wet, bad-tempered business. Serenity was restored at Advance Base, where we enjoyed an enormous meal prepared by the Bhotias who had now settled on the upper glacier. Harish had now rejected the idea of a long circuitous approach to Rimo III which they had hoped to climb from the far side via Ibex Col. Instead, he planned a series of forays up some of the nearer side branches of the N Terong glacier.

The evening of 2 July was wonderful. Everyone was particularly cheerful; the clouds had just lifted, the pressure was rising and, later, the mountains looked surreally beautiful under the light of a full moon. Only much later did I realise

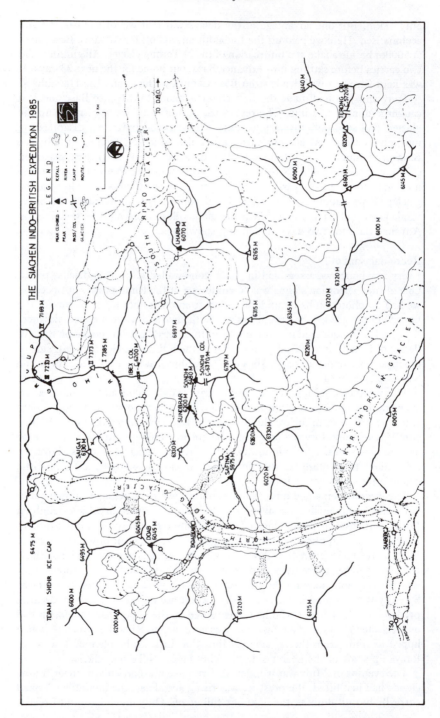

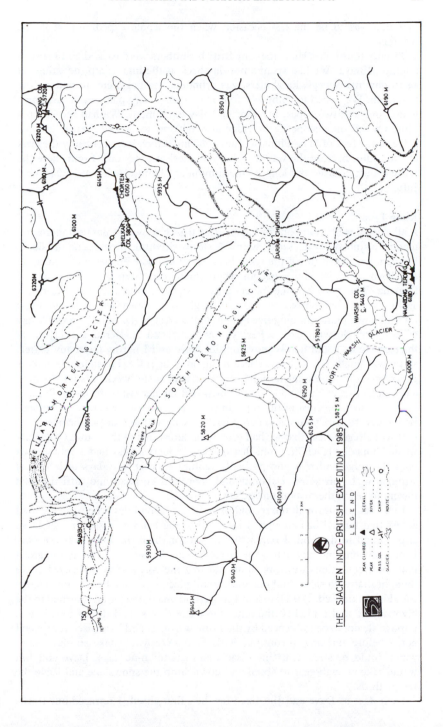

that this was to be the last occasion when the whole expedition would be together.

Twenty four hours later, the four British climbers were packed and ready to attempt Rimo I. We had spent a hot day back at the high camp, debating yet again how many pegs, karabiners, gas cylinders, tea bags, etc. to take on the mountain. We hoped to climb as a four man team — two pairs, each carrying a tent, stove and two ropes, but sharing belay equipment. We had settled on a route up the snow slope to the ridge at *c.* 6400m; we would then follow the ridge to the foot of 'The Pinnacles' at *c.* 6600m, which were probably the crux of the route, barring the way to 'The Shoulder' at *c.* 6580m. From there the route appeared easier but long, to the summit at 7385m. We left at 1.30am on 4 July.

Rimo I

It all started well; crampons biting on crisp frozen snow, luminous under a full moon. In spite of leaden sacks, we made steady rhythmic progress up the slope, but as it steepened to 50° the snow became softer and steps began to collapse. By dawn we were above 6000m where there had been little thawing and freezing. The snow became increasingly unstable and as the angle steepened again, rock slabs started to show through. We roped up to spend eight interminable hours climbing five pitches to the crest of the ridge — a whole day of hot struggle with ever softer, wetter snow and shattered rock. Jim, at thirteen stone, could hardly move uphill. Dave and I hardly fared any better, and it was finally left to Tony to lead us up onto the ridge. His lightness and his experience on unpleasant terrain, perfected over many weekends on the mud and chalk cliffs of England's S coast, provided the necessary delicacy of touch.

We reached the crest of the ridge in the late afternoon, exhausted, demoralised and with barely enough energy left to excavate the tent platforms.

It was already clear that we had grossly underestimated the route. Originally we had hoped to reach the pinnacles in a day. In fact one day had barely seen us onto the ridge and it would probably require another two days of laborious struggle with soft snow, elaborate and enormous cornices and difficult rock towers to reach the distant pinnacles.

I was halfway through the second pitch of the second day when Jim shouted across that he had had enough. I returned to the belay to discover that Dave also wanted to descend. I remonstrated but for them the route was not only hopelessly long and laborious — it was also plain dangerous. Tony and I agreed that snow conditions were appalling and that the cornices were dicey, but we thought that with slow climbing and careful placing of rock belays the dangers could be minimised. But Dave and Jim were adamant and we all returned to the bivouac site and repitched the tents for a day of rest and discussion. It was impossible not to be influenced by their dire warnings and I agonised for several hours before agreeing to continue with Tony. We would take six days food, which could be stretched if necessary, and gas for nine days. Dave and Jim would take enough gear to abseil and downclimb the snowslope and leave the rest with us.

Next day, as Dave and Jim fixed up their first abseil, I retraced our tracks

2   The Rimo group seen from Advance Base Camp on the N Terong glacier to their south. L to R: Saigat, Rimo III, Rimo II & I. Ibex Col is the notch to the extreme right. The SW ridge of Rimo I descends R to L into the centre of the picture.

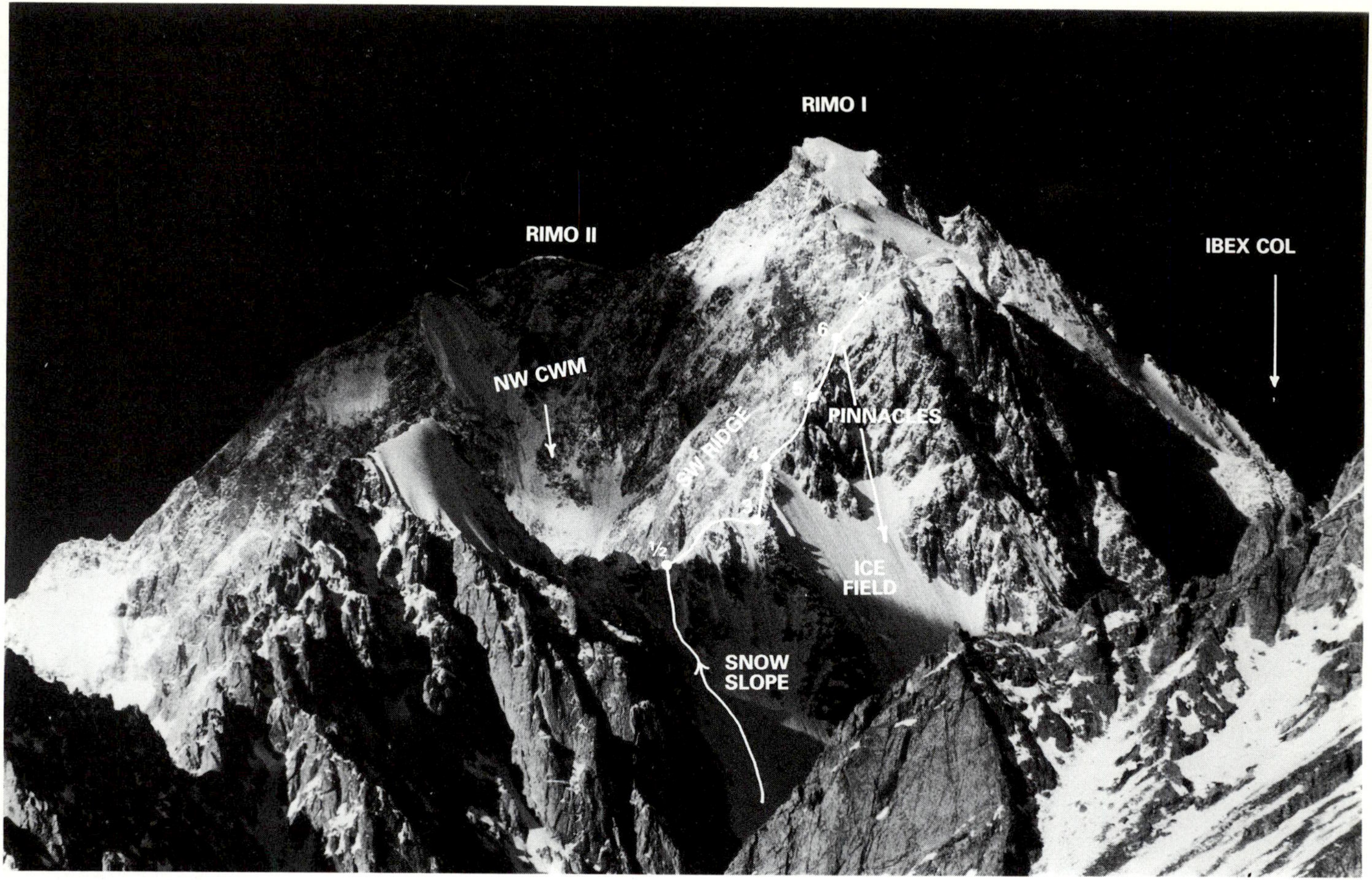

IBEX COL

RIMO I

RIMO II

NW CWM

PINNACLES

ICE FIELD

SW RIDGE

SNOW SLOPE

Photo: Stephen Venables

3 Telephoto view of Rimo I from ABC showing the route attempted.

4 *Telephoto view of Rimo III from ABC. The peak was climbed from the far side.*

Photo: Stephen Venables

5 Western branch of N Terong glacier from ABC with the 'Lake of Bones' in the foreground.

along the ridge. Tony broke new ground, traversing towards 'The Fortress' — a 50m high tower which barred the ridge. I continued towards it, scraping and shovelling my way across steep snow-covered slabs and worked up into a chimney which breached the rock walls. Tony's lead to the top of the fortress was a miracle of delicate climbing. Unknown to me, he was climbing a steep wall of atrociously loose granite 30m above my head. With supreme care he avoided dislodging all but one small rock, which only gave my shoulder a moment's pain. I led through to a ledge for a tea break. In the hot afternoon sun, we climbed two more pitches to a brèche between two towers. The snow was getting sticky and we were getting tired so we stopped to bivouac, pleased with our slow but steady progress and pleasantly surprised that we had actually enjoyed ourselves.

Day 4 was short. We climbed six pitches along the flank, avoiding huge cornices on the crest. Rock belays and the occasional ice screw provided security. At midday we reached the foot of the pinnacles. A snow shoulder, sheltered below a rock wall, provided a perfect campsite, where we spent a relaxing afternoon, drinking brew after brew and drying out boots and gloves.

Next morning, as Tony started up the first pitch of the day, the first glow of sunshine lit the summit of K2, 100km distant. While he worked, I had time to watch the Karakoram come to life; K2, the Gasherbrums, Mustagh Tower, Chogolisa and, much closer on the other side of the Siachen, those bulky giants, K12 and Saltoro Kangri. It was a wonderful start to a long day of hard climbing.

Hours had been spent at Advance Base staring through binoculars at the system of snowy chimneys and ramps which bypassed the pinnacles on their N side; now it was time to explore them. Once again there was no relenting of the difficulties and it took twelve hours to excavate our way up eight pitches.

In the afternoon, dark clouds which had been massing in the south swept towards us and snow began to fall as I started the seventh pitch. A tension traverse dropped me into a snow-choked chimney. The snow there offered no purchase and it was a case of scraping desperately with axes and crampons to find nicks in the rock underneath. The eighth pitch was worse — a prolonged, exhausting nightmare of loose snow on loose rock. Following on a tight rope, I never quite worked out how Tony had managed to climb it.

We had intended to reach the top of the pinnacles that day, but the last 50m looked very hard. It was late. It was snowing and I had had enough. We stopped to suspend the tent dramatically 10m below a belay upon a huge cornice.

The tent was battered by strong winds all night. We assumed that the weather was foul outside and it was only at 7am that we looked out to see a cloudless pale blue sky. After the usual slow breakfast and packing, we were away at 10.30. Three hours later we reached the top of the pinnacles. We had passed the crux of the route and, now that we were clear of the rocks, the snow began to improve slightly so that it was actually possible to kick steps and make steady progress round double cornices towards the big snow ramps leading up to the shoulder.

Late that afternoon, approaching the top of the ramps, I felt a deep contentment. At 6800m it was hard work and I was having to take four deep breaths to every step, but the snow at last had a uniform consistency and it was possible to establish a rhythm. It was a beautiful evening and as we gained height more of the arctic wastes of the upper Rimo glacier came into sight. If the weather held and if the gap beyond the foresummit held no insurmountable problem, we might be on the summit in two days.

It was time to stop for the night, so I halted on the crest of the snow to dig a platform, but first I wanted to get the heavy rucksack off my back. I rammed my ice-axe into the snow, took off the sack and clipped it into the wristloop of the axe. Before removing the axe-sling from my shoulder, I pulled in some rope to tie off the axe, just in case it should come out. A moment later I turned. The rucksack was sliding down the slope, unattached; apparently I had not clipped it into the wristloop!

I stared with incredulous horror as the sack gathered speed, sliding then somersaulting, bouncing and bursting as it disappeared to plunge 1000m into the NW cwm. Sleeping bag, duvet vest, food, tent poles and, most vital of all, the gas stove had gone. One tired, careless mistake had ruined everything and the only choice was to retreat.

Tony was a paragon of restraint. He uttered no murmur of complaint and was concerned only that I should snap out of my hysterical anger and misery and concentrate on the job of getting down alive. We reversed three pitches, dug a platform and suspended the pole-less tent as best we could from the belay. The temperature dropped to −30°C and the vicious N wind slapped at the loose fabric all night. Inside, sharing Tony's bivouac clothes, we shivered miserably and longed for hot brews of tea.

The morning of Day 7 was bitterly cold. It was also brilliantly clear and the perfect weather seemed a horrible mockery of my incompetence. Our only consolation was that the descent went like clockwork. In seven hours we descended 1200m to the camp in the cwm. Eight long abseils took us straight down onto the big icefield below the pinnacles. There, we were delighted to find good névé, which we could downclimb quickly. At the start of the abseils we had been struggling with numbed toes and fingers; seven hours later the cwm was a merciless heat trap. We stopped at the camp for our first drink in 28 hours. The enervating heat and the accumulated tiredness of six days hard work above 6000m suddenly took effect and three hours passed before we could persuade our lethargic bodies to repack the one rucksack and continue the descent to Advance Base.

At dusk, as Tony approached Advance Base he stumbled across an ancient Aschenbrenner ice-axe lying on the ice — a relic perhaps of Dr Visser's expedition in 1929. Closer inspection revealed two words written along the wooden shaft — Henry Osmaston. Against all odds Henry had charmed his way through to reach the Nubra valley and on up the Terong where he was now happily employed with his thermometers, ice drills and measuring rods amongst the ice pinnacles of the N Terong glacier.

After the bitter disappointment of the Rimo fiasco it was a delightful surprise to find him there. It was also good to catch up with the others' news. We discovered that the tiny dots we had seen three days earlier advancing up the cwm had been Meena and Boga on their way to cross the Ibex Col; now they were climbing 6070m Lharimo from the S Rimo glacier. Closer to camp, Arun and Muslim had climbed Safina and were about to go up with Harish and Dhiren to attempt more peaks in the cwm opposite, immediately to the east of Advance Base. Muslim had also been busy with Jim, finding a route from the head of the glacier up to the Teram Shehr ice plateau. Jim was about to leave with Dave to attempt Rimo from the far E side. They had just packed their bags ready to leave for the Ibex Col the following morning. Tony and I were already hoping for another try at our route on Rimo I — such a magnificent route deserved a conclusion. We now knew that we could cut out two days' hard work by climbing straight up the névé of the icefield to the foot of the pinnacles. But first we had to rest.

Rimo III   *Dave Wilkinson*

We had invested much time and money on this trip, so the decision to go down from Rimo I was not taken lightly. The poor conditions were reason enough for retreat but I had other good reasons too: my usual nagging high altitude cough was worse than I had ever known it and I was producing infected sputum. My finger was still quite painful and protracted hard climbing was a daunting prospect. A subsequent X-ray in England revealed a badly splintered fracture.

Back at Advance Base I spent a frustrating few days in good weather, the throat responding to antibiotics, the finger showing slower progress. Jim had a bare week before he had to go home to work. The weather was near perfect and we both felt the need for action.

From the N Terong glacier the two main mountains of the Rimo group looked equally impressive — Rimo I irregular but steep all round; Rimo III more symmetrical but also devoid of an easy line. My finger and Jim's time-shortage seemed to rule out any action here. We could opt for a smaller, easier mountain, but during my days of inactivity I had formed a more speculative notion. We had a photo, taken by the Indian Army the previous year, of the E face of Rimo I and its subsidiary summit Rimo II. It appeared to be a little easier than our side, but the photo was not a close-up and we were not sure. I made my proposal to Jim and he jumped at it with the alacrity of a man who had had similar ideas already. We would leave early next morning with a week's food and gas, and what little climbing equipment we could carry.

We had to cross the Ibex col at over 6000m, descend the far side and then do our climb which we had not seen yet. We had time for only a single, quick dash. I also had a 'B' plan in my mind, which I did not disclose yet. Harish's secret army map showed an easy ridge on the far side of Rimo III, not that we could be sure of the map's accuracy, but . . .

That evening, Steve and Tony came back from Rimo I, and told about the dropped sack and all. During my enforced idleness, I had scoured the mountain with binoculars, vainly trying to follow their progress and come to terms with my varied feelings towards them — 'What a fine effort! I hope they succeed.' Envy — 'Why am I not up there? Hope the mad fools fail!' Now this admiration and jealousy were overtaken by relief to see them safe and well. Curiously, their sudden return did not alter our plans at all. They could do no more without a good rest, and Steve was 'short of a few items' so there was no question of their joining us.

After the euphoric planning, the horrible reality returned with the night-time stumble up the glacier shouldering a monster load. 'Curse that Fotheringham, why is he so fit?' as I struggled to stay within earshot. 'Sorry, Jim, have to have 5 minutes.' First light saw us at the site of the camp below the Rimo I attempt. The weather remained clear, but a bitter cold wind brought out gloves and duvet jackets to comfort numb fingers and ears. A gruelling ascent to the Ibex col opened up a romantic vista to the east, like a traveller's tale from Tolkien.

The next white expanse of the S Rimo glacier stretched out before us. Beyond, as the big mountains ended, the hazy brown of the Depsang plains, with the shining silver ribbon of the Chip Chap river where goes the old trade route to the Karakoram pass over to Sinkiang.

The descent down our branch of the S Rimo glacier was easy but as fatigue took hold, my legs felt like mechanical appendages, carrying me on, but not totally in my control. We rounded the corner at the glacier junction, and immediately found a delightful camp site on a crystal gravel bank of moraine beneath Rimo I's E face.

As we brewed and ate the day to its close, we had ample time to look at our objective, but did not need long. A glacier face gave a zig-zag line between seracs to a prominent terrace at two-thirds' height. From here a choice of Andean finishes was available to the top of Rimo I: a steep fluted face, or narrow corniced ridges on either side. The adequacy of our food and time or my digital ability were of no consequence — one rope and a handful of ironware were clearly inadequate equipment!

The slightest glance towards Rimo III showed a gentle snowy NE shoulder. Whether Jim had also previously had this at the back of his mind, I do not know. In any case, he agreed to this change of plan with remarkable speed and flexibility.

Sacks were lightened by dumping some food for the return journey, and by leaving some of our already sparse hardware. This lightness seemed less evident next morning, as we crawled up the glacier branch between Rimo II and Rimo IV. The threats of serac fall from either side of this narrow way produced no startling turns of speed from us; but the threats were of some use, as they encouraged us not to stop for our next camp until the glacier widened a little, and our way went off right up another glacier branch between Rimo III and Rimo IV.

Next morning, we had our first view of the col between Rimo IV and our ridge on Rimo III. We had a route decision to make. The easy line to the col itself was abandoned, as some rock pinnacles appeared to complicate the first part of the ridge. We chose instead a bigger and steeper snow slope further left, which led to our ridge above all obvious difficulties. When we tried to climb this slope, it proved to consist of chest deep snow the texture of confetti, so it was abandoned for mixed ground just on its right. This gave 250m of alpine D to TD. The rock sections were very pleasant, but the snow had not consolidated much since our Rimo I attempt. Contrary to normal, the worst snow was found on the steeper ground, presumably because it was less exposed to the wind, or because it lay awkwardly on top of the rocks.

Above this section, we cut a vast camping platform into the easy ridge, and I made a vague effort to emulate Steve by dropping my Karrimat. This camp must have been at or over 6700m, so only 450m to 600m of easy ridge remained. We felt confident of success the next day.

We set off with really light sacks, but still managed no great rate of ascent. Altitude was making itself felt more and more, several panting breaths being required between each uphill step. Even so, steady progress was made, and it seemed that only the weather could stop us now, for dark clouds were gathering. However, these seemed to be of the slow-to-anger variety, and the main threat was to our summit views. A narrow corniced section of the ridge was mercifully short, some rock towers were easily passed, and only a Mont-Blanc type snow shoulder remained. The technical anticlimax of this ridge was countered by the fight for air, and the exhilaration of ever widening views coming and going between the gathering clouds.

At last we stood on the corniced top; but had to wait several minutes for the view to clear momentarily, first one way, then the other, to be sure we were actually there. One such clearing gave a dramatic glimpse of Rimo I and II close at hand, with a great banner cloud streaming in the wind.

Then I remembered something. In Bombay, Harish's son Sonam had given me a small flower in a tiny envelope asking me to place it 'on top of a mountain', some sort of Hindu tradition. I could not ignore such a simple and charming request, so placed it carefully in the highest snow, without knowing its exact significance. Later, we learnt that its purpose was to bring us good luck.

Reaching the top of a mountain is not, in the event, the great thrill which the layman might imagine. The main feelings are exhilaration, relief that it's over, and worry about the descent. As he sat on our highest ever summit, Jim summed up this anticlimax with a casual but telling remark: 'Shall we go now — there's nothing for us here?'

Shortage of pitons caused problems on the descent of the steep section, but adequate anchors for abseils appeared when most needed. We even descended off a rucksack's accessory strap and an ice screw driven into a rock crack. The weather deteriorated slowly. As we reached the Ibex col, snow fell gently. We returned to camp two and a half days after leaving our summit, and it snowed heavily that night. We had been on the go, glacier travel, reconnaissance, and climbing an unexplored mountain, for six days, well served by Sonam's little talisman.

Addendum   *Stephen Venables*

The most agonising aspect of our retreat from Rimo I was the continuing fine weather. Apart from a smattering of snowfall on Day 5, the weather had been fine for eight days. Any serious-looking clouds had stuck to K12 and Saltoro Kangri on the S side of the Siachen. After our descent, the sky remained a deep unbroken blue for another four days, while Tony and I stared helplessly at our summit ridge, wishing that we were still up there.

After a day's rest we had climbed up to the NW cwm to retrieve my rucksack and most of its scattered contents. That afternoon our liaison officer, Mahendra, returned to Advance Base from a near fatal attempt to cross the Terong river, reported that it was now dangerously flooded with meltwater. Four climbers were due to leave for home the moment they returned from their climbs and it seemed that the river had now cut off their retreat. Tony and I set off reluctantly to solve the problem.

Two days in the balmy warmth of the valley were actually very enjoyable and we spent several entertaining hours fixing 200m of rope across granite cliffs on the right bank of the river, securing an exit route which avoided the now unfordable river.

Ominous hazy cirrus clouds were now spreading from the southwest and all the signs pointed to an approaching storm. Finally on 16 July, the day Dave and Jim returned from Rimo III, snow started to fall bringing to an end 13 days of clear weather.

Tony was due back at work. He was prepared to risk the wrath of Lambeth Council by stretching his leave, if it would actually achieve anything; but it would now be several days before Rimo I might again be in good enough condition to consider starting another attempt. He packed his rucksack sadly and on the damp grey morning of 17 July, he set off down with Jim who was also due home. Arun, Boga and Henry had already left for Nubra.

It was a sad end to our hopes, but we did have the consolation that the expedition, overall, had been successful. Rimo III had been climbed and, during the same spell, Meena and Boga had climbed Lharimo (6070m) from the South Rimo Glacier. Arun and Dhiren had climbed Sondhi (6480m) and Sundbrar (6300m) from the glacier immediately opposite Advance Base, to the east. Muslim and Harsinh Senior had climbed Doab (6045m) just behind Advance Base. I still had the chance to do some climbing as I was one of the climbers staying for another ten days to investigate the other two glaciers of the Terong basin — the Shelkar Chorten and the S Terong.

For four days it rained and snowed and the rumble and clatter of rock avalanches outside drowned the music from the Walkman. Advance Base had been evacuated and eight of us — three Bombay mountaineers, two English and the three Bhotias — were waiting at Base Camp for a chance to explore the two remaining glaciers.

On 20 July the weather looked better so we departed on our parallel eastward journeys. I headed for the entrance to the Shelkar Chorten; the others for the South Terong.

We knew that Dr Wyss and Khan Sahib had climbed the N Terong to the lake at our Advance Base site, while Dr Visser and Franz Lochmatter had climbed 'over the appallingly broken glacier' of the Shelkar Chorten. The S Terong they had left untouched. Now, 56 years later, Harish and his team went to investigate.

The S Terong has retreated several kilometres up its valley so to reach it they had to cross a dusty plain and advance up a dangerous gorge which the river has cut through the terminal moraine. Then they struggled up the right bank of the glacier which squeezes hard against the valley wall, leaving no room for a proper lateral moraine. On the second day they escaped out on to the broad smooth surface of the glacier itself, which is striped with medial moraines. On the third day the party split up: Muslim and Harsinh Junior, accompanied part of the way by Dave, climbed a SW branch to the Warshi col (c. 5440m); Harish and Dhiren climbed the first of four branches which flow into the glacier from the NE, walking over a delightfully smooth surface to the broad Terong col (c. 5720m), which overlooks the S Rimo glacier. On the fifth day, 25 July, they all returned to Base Camp after a highly successful trip. They had made first ascents of two passes, which linked the Nubra valley to the S Rimo glacier. Provided that the gorge above Warshi is passable, it should be possible to cross the Warshi col and continue easily right across the S Terong glacier and up to the Terong Col, where Harish and Dhiren saw easy slopes leading down to the Rimo glacier. The Indian Army are investigating the Warshi gorge; if that proves feasible, we will have established a route from the Nubra valley to the Rimo glacier and Daulat Beg Olde, which could well be easier than the traditional Saser la route.

Meanwhile I had been doing battle with the Shelkar Chorten icefall. On the second day I continued up the wide glaring expanse of the upper snowfield to the head of the glacier, pitching the tent below 6075m Chorten Peak. I climbed the peak by a 300m snow and ice route the following morning, before crossing the Shelkar col to the S Terong system. By stopping for a midday snooze on a boulder I just missed bumping into Harish and Dhiren on their way up to the Terong Col. That afternoon I crossed the main glacier missing Dave's camp by a few hundred metres, and headed up into the next SW branch, towards Ngabong Terong (6185m) — The Double-Humped Camel of Terong. Because of atrocious snow conditions after mid morning, the climb of Ngabong Terong took three days. On the first a 50° snow/ice face led to a bergschrund at c. 5800m, where I camped. Next day, I continued up a delightful snow arête to the E summit and on across the connecting ridge to the slightly higher W hump. For a few minutes I savoured the last chance to gaze out over the hundreds of unclimbed summits of the E Karakoram, before descending to another longly vigil in the bergschrund. Finally, on 26 July, I spent ten interminable hours descending through drizzling rain to Base Camp, concluding a memorable six day outing.

Base Camp was desolate and deserted, so I had to wait until next morning for human company when I rejoined the others at the Terong river, where they were sorting out loads for the shuttle service across the rope traverse.

The close of the expedition was filled with memorable moments — wading side braids of the Terong river, awash with shin-battering icebergs — traversing backwards and forwards across the rope traverse on the cliff, doing eight load ferries — camping by a blazing fire of dead juniper beside the roaring river — Dave's close encounter with death on Mahendra's home-made aluminium bridge across the river (a bridge which pleased Mahendra no end, but which served no genuine purpose, for now that we had crossed the cliff and could walk out easily along the right bank and straight up on to the Siachen glacier) — the welcome arrival of ten Maharati Regiment jawans to help carry our loads down the Siachen snout on a last beautiful evening — dinner in the officers' mess — a special late night showing of *Silsila* at the camp cinema — the long drive back over the Kardung La, with an army convoy — and finally the return to Leh for an exhausting round of celebratory meals.

'Siachen Indo-British Expedition 85' made first ascents of eight peaks, including Rimo III. We came close to success on Rimo I on a route which Tony compared to the Eigerwand under winter conditions. We explored three large glaciers and reached five cols, crossing two of them. Perhaps most rewarding of all the expedition was an international success and we hope that the friendships we made will be the start of a continuing association between the Alpine Club and the Bombay Mountaineers.

At present the rules allow in three joint foreign-Indian expeditions a year to three areas — Saser Kangri, Mamastong Kangri/Rimo and the upper Siachen. However, in practice the army were unwilling this year to have civilian climbers visiting the Upper Siachen and, unless hostilities with Pakistan cease altogether, they seem unlikely to do so in the near future. On the SW side of the glacier, magnificent peaks like K12 and Saltoro Kangri and a host of fantastic spires and pinnacles lie on the line of control and for the moment are out of bounds. This axis continues SE down the right bank of the Nubra valley — a complex network of granite spires would keep generations of climbers happy, but so far no mention has been made of allowing climbers up these remote, little-explored valleys. In the meantime applications are pouring in to the IMF for the peaks on the NE side of the Siachen/Nubra valley.

This year, in August, an Indo-Japanese team made the first ascent of the magnificent Saser Kangri II (Shukpa) by the NW ridge. Sasers III and IV remain unclimbed; both are over 7000m. Mamastong Kangri was climbed in 1984 but nearby Mamastong II and Chong Kumdang remain unclimbed. These two 7000m peaks would provide interesting objectives, along with neighbouring 6000m peaks, accessible from the Saser La region. In the Terong basin there are still numerous unclimbed 6000m peaks, the finest of which, I think, lie along the SW side of the S Terong glacier, but 7385m Rimo I remains, at the time of writing, the most attractive prize. The route which Tony and I took may be the best, if one takes a direct line up the icefield to the foot of the pinnacles, thus limiting the really hard climbing to quite a short stretch. On the NW face a zig-zag ice couloir breaks through formidable rock walls to the top of Rimo II, a shoulder on the NNW ridge of Rimo I; it might prove the fastest route for a fit, acclimatised team, but the descent could pose problems. On the far side of the mountain, Dave and Jim spotted no immediately obvious route — the upper part of the E face consists of spectacularly steep snow flutings and the ridges, like so many Himalayan ridges, are long and intricately corniced.

Presumably Rimo I and the other virgin 7000m peaks will soon be climbed. The present rules encourage expeditions to concentrate on a specific objective in a specific area; but perhaps the rules will one day become more flexible and make it possible to retrace the steps of De Filippi and Dainelli and the Bullock-Workmans, making long ski traverses to link up the great snowfields of the Rimo, Teram Shehr and Siachen glaciers. For the time being, however, we must be grateful that we can visit the area at all. We certainly felt privileged to be the first foreigners and civilians since Independence to be allowed to travel to the snout of the Siachen glacier.

6 The Rimo group from 'Crystal Camp' on the S Rimo glacier. L to R: Rimo I & II, Rimo III, Rimo IV.

7 Diran IV (*route from Diran III*)

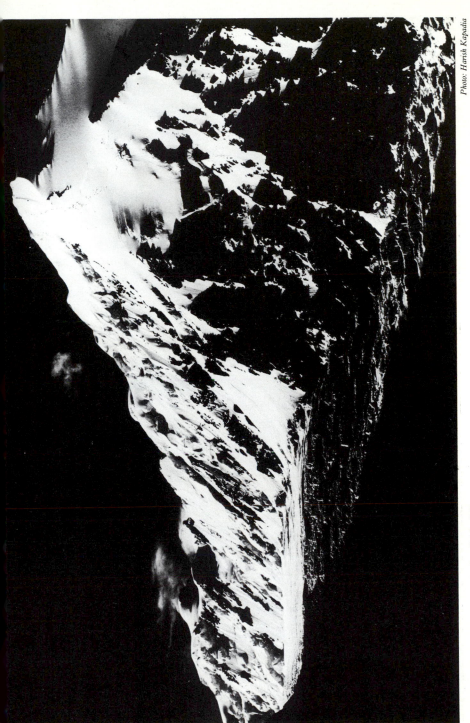

8 *Safina Peak (5975m) above the Sondhi icefall.*

Photo: Dhiren Toolsides

9   *East Karakoram panorama from the summit of Sondhi. L to R: K12, Pk 6330m (N Terong), Saltoro Kangri I & II, Ghent, Ghent NE.*

Photo: Stephen Venables

10   *Looking ESE from Chorten. Chong Kumdan I & II on horizon (L), Mamastong Kangri (centre).*

The Eastern Karakoram

Harish Kapadia
Plates 2–10

The early explorers knew no boundaries except those of mountain ranges but present day mountaineers and explorers have to respect political boundaries and territorial regulations. Only since 1984 have all the ranges of the E Karakoram been opened to climbers by the Indian Government. At first while planning for the Siachen Indo-British Expedition 1985 to the Terong valley, one felt that the area was not frequented, remote; that information was scarce and approach difficult. However, upon a little research it was found that more than 40 parties had visited the area. Information and various references were scattered over a large number of books and journals. The Karakoram has many opportunities for climbing and exploration and it is bound to receive many mountaineering parties in the future. In early days, caravans from Srinagar to the Siachen snout took nearly 50 days; now it would be but five!

The E Karakoram consists of the Siachen Muztagh, the Rimo Muztagh, and the Saser Muztagh as a sub-group of the Great Karakoram.[1] All these groups consist of various sub-groups and peaks as classified in the Karakoram Conference report of 1936. Out of these the Siachen Muztagh was explored thoroughly, while the Rimo Muztagh and Saser Muztagh received a few parties.

The Siachen Muztagh

The peaks surrounding the Siachen glacier form this group. In 1821, W Moorcroft passed near its snout and first acknowledged its existence.[2] In 1835 G T Vigne approached it from the west trying to reach the Bilafond la, but he never guessed the existence of such a large glacier across the divide.[3] In 1848 Henry Strachey was the first to discover the existence of the Siachen glacier and ascended it for two miles from the snout in the Nubra valley.[4] In the same year, Dr Thomas Thompson[5] also reached the glacier followed by F Drew in 1849–50.[6] E C Ryall of the Survey of India sketched the lower part in 1861. But he ascribed to it a length of only 16 miles. During his famous second Karakoram journey in 1889, Sir Francis Younghusband approached over the Urdok valley to reach the Turkestan la. Looking down to the Siachen from the north he felt that this was the main axis of the Karakoram.[7] This was finally confirmed by Dr T G Longstaff in 1909.[8] In fact, it was Dr Longstaff with Dr Arthur Neve and Lt Slingsby who were the first real explorers to traverse this great glacier. First, they came over the Bilafond la (or, Saltoro Pass, as Dr Longstaff would have preferred to call it) and named the opposite glacier as 'Teram' and peaks as Teram Kangri, after a Yarkandi legend: 'The learned men of Balti say that a large town was said to stand at the present site of the Teram Shehr. Yarkandis from this town often crossed to Baltistan to loot cattle and destroy villages. To protect them, Mullah Hazrat Amir gave the villagers a Tawiz (magic amulet) which was placed on the Bilafond la. Soon after, a great storm engulfed Teram Shehr destroying it and today not even grass and burtza would be found to mitigate the rocky desolation of Teram Shehr.'[9] After retreating to the Nubra valley, Dr Longstaff came up from the Siachen snout from the south and saw the same peaks as identified from the Bilafond la. In doing so he proved the length of Siachen glacier and the actual location of the Turkestan la. This was an important discovery as it now established the true boundaries of the Karakoram. He wrote:

'Younghusband was a true prophet. Col Burrard of the Survey had suspected the truth. The avalanche-swept pass, whose foot Younghusband had reached 20 years before, was on the main axis of the Karakoram range which thus lay miles farther north than had been believed. We had stolen some 500 sq miles from the Yarkand river system of Chinese Turkestan, and joined it to the waters of the Indus and the Kingdom of Kashmir.'[8]

The next most important explorers were the famous Workman expedition in 1911–12. They entered over the Bilafond la and camped on the glacier with a large entourage of porters and two Alpine guides. They visited and named Indira Col (after Goddess Laxmi — there is a misconception that this col, now the northernmost point of India, is named after India's late Prime Minister, Mrs Indira Gandhi). In a month long survey they climbed many peaks and visited almost all corners of the upper Siachen. Grant Peterkin was a surveyor attached to the expedition. He surveyed the glacier thoroughly and named a few peaks, particularly Apsarasas and Ghent.

In 1929 Dr Ph C Visser of the Netherlands was on his fourth trip to the Karakoram.[15] The advice of Dr Longstaff to them was: 'When it is desired to survey this unknown corner, will the party please proceed five miles up the Siachen glacier and take the first turning on the right.' This good advice was taken by the Vissers, they discovered the two Terong glaciers and the Shelkar Chorten glacier which were unknown till then. Dr Rudolf Wyss and surveyor Khan Sahib Afraz Gul stayed in the Terong valley and mapped the area. Thus they completed the survey of the lower part of this great glacier.

At the same time the Duke of Spoleto Expedition crossed the Karakoram by the Muztagh Pass and reached the Indira Col from the north. They descended from the Turkestan la after discovering Staghar and Singhi glaciers. In 1930 Professor Giotto Dainelli completed the survey and exploration of this area. Coming over from the south he established himself at the Teram Shehr junction in early June, '. . . thus reaching the Siachen tongue with all my baggage, a caravan of 70 coolies and six and a half tons of food for the men, carried by an additional caravan of ponies and supplementary coolies. On the 9th of June — exactly two months after my departure from Florence — I was heading for my first depot up the glacier. I hope my English colleagues will appreciate this rapidity of execution, which I consider a record!'[12] Compare this with the present timings. Technically one can be at the Siachen snout within three days from Delhi. Dainelli, with his only companion Miss Kalau, stayed at the Teram Shehr junction and carried out various geological surveys. Due to flooding of the Nubra, he could not return by the same route and hence crossed a 6000m pass to the Rimo glaciers in the east. He named this, 'Col Italia'.

With the Spoleto expedition, the survey and exploration of the Siachen was mostly over. It was now left to climbers to attempt the various high peaks in this area. These climbing activities are tabulated at the end of this article. Several expeditions arrived at the Siachen glacier from the west over the Bilafond la or the Sia la. In 1978–80 and 1981, Indian Army teams entered the glacier from the Nubra valley in the south and made excellent ascents. In 1984 a Japanese team approaching Rimo from the west over the Bilafond la was turned back. India had firmly taken control over the area stopping all access from the west and north. Since 1985 this area is selectively open for climbers approaching from Leh and Nubra.

The Rimo Muztagh
The Rimo glacier which is the main source of the Shyok has received very few visitors or climbers. Its end had been only roughly sketched by Johnson in 1864 and Robert Shaw in 1869. The Sir Filippo De Filippi Expedition of 1914 explored this great glacier and its feeders, thereby connecting with the Peterkin survey of 1912. Next came the Indian Army Engineers Expedition, after 70 years, in 1984 which climbed Rimo IV. The Siachen Indo-British Expedition of 1985 crossed over from the Terong valley to climb Rimo III. They narrowly failed on Rimo I. The Terong group (N and S Terong glaciers) and the Shelkar Chorten glacier were also thoroughly explored by this expedition. In all, seven peaks were climbed and various passes and cols reached linking the Siachen/Terong to Rimo/Shyok valleys. They approached from the Siachen glacier thus linking both Muztaghs.

Mamostong Kangri was first explored at close range by Dr A Neve and was surveyed by De Filippi's expedition. This peak was ascended by an Indo-Japanese expedition in 1984 approaching from the south over the Mamostong and Thangman glaciers.

The Saser Muztagh
The Saser Kangri area was first reconnoitered by Arthur Neve in 1899. In 1909 and 1922, the Longstaff and Visser expeditions reconnoitered it respectively. The main reconnaissance was carried out by J O M Roberts in 1946. He reconnoitered all the peaks of Saser and the surrounding area. In 1956 an Indian expedition led by N D Jayal, in 1969 led by C S Nogyal and in 1970 by H V Bahuguna failed to climb this peak reaching high on Cloud Peak. Both Roberts' and Jayal's teams climbed nearby Lookout Peak. The first ascent of Saser Kangri was made by an Indian team led by Joginder Singh in 1973 approaching from the Shyok valley in the east. An Indian Army team led by Col Jagjit Singh made the second ascent of this peak.

All the other groups in this Muztagh have not been visited and await exploration.

Nomenclature of Peaks in the Eastern Karakoram

Name	Meaning	Named by
Kharpo Gang	White glacier	Dr U Balestereri of
Staghar	Many coloured	Duke of Spoleto Italian
Singhi	Difficult	Expedition 1929

Name	Meaning	Named by
Apsarasas	Apsara = fairy sas = place (place for the fairies)	Grant Peterkin of Bullock Workman Expedition
Indira Col	Indira = Goddess Laxmi	1911–12
Tawiz	Magic amulet	
Hawk	Shaped like a hawk	
Siachen	Place of roses	
Sia Kangri	Rose Peak	
Ghent	Named after the Treaty of Ghent which terminated hostilities between Great Britain and United States in 1814	
Teram Shehr	Ruined town — as per the Yarkandi legend	Dr T G Longstaff in 1909
Teram Kangri	The peak of ruined town	
Bilafond	Butterfly	
Mamostong Kangri	Mountain of a thousand devils	Ladakhi/Yarkandi
Rimo	Striped mountain	Ladakhi/Yarkandi
Terong	Narrow gorge	Ladakhi/Tibetan
Saser Kangri	Yellow mountain	Ladakhi

Nomenclature in the Terong Valley: The Names Proposed by the Siachen Indo-British Expedition 1985.

'The nomenclature of a mountain region should not be forced: it should grow spontaneously, and we should never invent a name until its absence has become inconvenient.' So wrote Col Sir Sidney Burrard who, in 1906, was Superintendent of the Great Trigonometrical Survey of India (*HJ10*, p86). Climbing in an area with many unnamed peaks and valleys, it *was* inconvenient to refer to them just by numbers and heights and we have proposed the following names to the Survey of India. These are in line with the guidelines given by the Survey of India in 'Himalayan Nomenclature', *HJ31*, p334.

Name	Meaning
Sundbrar	A beautiful place.
Sondhi	A sudden beautiful appearance. There is a place by the name of Sundbrar in Baltistan. Kashmiri Brahmins and Hindus along with several thousand people used to gather at this place on a certain day in June. They would worship the Hindu Goddess Laxmi and wait for the rising of water praying for it to appear. At an appointed time a stream would fill the basin and the multitude would shout — 'Sondhi'. Above all, this phenomenon portrays the prevalence of the Hindu rituals deep inside the Muslim Baltistan (See *Gazetteer of Kashmir and Ladak, 1890*, p801).

Name	Meaning
Lharimo	Holy, painted mountain.
Doab	Meeting place of two waters.
Safina	Boat. In Balti philosophy this is a special boat which carries one to heaven.
Saigat	Leopard's leap. This peak particularly tilts (leaps) towards the giant Rimo peaks.
Chorten	The Buddhist symbol.
Ngabong Terong	Ngabong = Bactrian camel — the double-humped camel of Yarkand. A few are still seen in the Nubra valley.
Siab Chushku	Siab = meeting place of three waters (North and South Terong and Shelkar Chorten glaciers). Chushku = temporary camp.
Doab Chushku	Temporary camp at meeting place of two waters.

History of the Siachen Muztagh 1821–1985

Year	Expedition	Reference
1821	W Moorcroft passed near the snout and reported existence.	2
1835	G T Vigne approached it from W over Bilafond la but never guessed its existence.	3
1848	Henry Strachey discovered the existence of Siachen glacier and ascended it for two miles.	4
1848	Dr T Thompson visited the snout.	5
1849–50	F Drew approached the glacier.	6
1862	E C Ryall, Survey of India, sketched the lower part and ascribed it a length of only 16 miles.	
1889	Sir F Younghusband reached Turkestan la from the north and looked down on the glacier.	7
1907	Sir Sidney Burrard published a map on the Himalaya. It did not include Siachen though he mentioned possibility of a large glacier.	14
1908	Dr Arthur Neve and D G Oliver reached the snout and explored Mamostong Kangri.	10 35
1909	Dr Tom Longstaff, Dr Arthur Neve and Lt A M Slingsby, later joined by Capt D G Oliver first came over Bilafond la and later over the Siachen snout to establish the length of the Siachen glacier and exact location of various passes.	8
1911–12	The Workman Expedition coming from the west, named many peaks and passes and climbed a few peaks. Grant Peterkin surveyed the glacier thoroughly.	9
1911	V D B Collins and C S McInnes of Survey of India, surveyed Teram Kangri and other peaks.	10

Year	*Expedition*	*Reference*
1913–14	Sir Filippo De Filippi surveyed Rimo glacier system and published a map.	13
1929	Dr Ph C Visser, Netherland Expedition, surveyed Terong valleys and crossed the snout to Gyong la.	15
1929	Duke of Spoleto Expedition reached Indira Col from the north and discovered Staghar and Singhi glaciers.	11
1930	G Dainelli, Italian expedition, stayed two months at Teram Shehr junction and crossed Col Italia.	12
1934	G O Dyhrenfurth, International expedition, made first ascent of Sia Kangri.	18
1935	British Expedition led by J Waller with John Hunt attempted Saltoro Kangri.	19
1939	Lt Peter Young visited Gyong la on shikar.	16
1956	Austrian Expedition led by F Moravec climbed Sia Kangri W.	20
1957	Imperial College British Expedition led by Eric Shipton climbed Tawiz and visited passes.	21
1961	Austrian Expedition led by E Waschak made first ascent of Ghent.	22
1962	Japanese-Pakistan Expedition led by T Shidei made first ascent of Saltoro Kangri I.	23
1974	Japanese Expedition led by T Tanaka attempted Sherpi Kangri II via S ridge.	24
1974	Austrian Expedition led by W Stefan climbed Sia Kangri from SW.	24 25
1974	Japanese Expedition led by G Iwatsubo approached K12 from W. Two members reached the summit but died on the return without any trace.	24
1975	British expedition led by D Alcock attempted Sherpi Kangri.	
1975	Japanese expedition led by Y Yamamoto climbed K12 by the same route to search for the missing summitters. The search failed.	24
1975	Japanese expedition led by H Katayama made first ascents of Teram Kangri I and II coming over Bilafond la.	24
1975	Japanese expedition led by S Yamamoto attempted Saltoro Kangri I.	24
1976	Japanese expedition made first ascent by Sherpi Kangri led by H Hirai.	26
1976	Japanese expedition led by H Misawa made first ascent of Apsarasas I.	27
1976	Japanese expedition led by H Sato came over Bilafond la, crossed Turkestan la and made the first ascent of Singhi Kangri from N.	27

Year	Expedition	Reference
1976	An Austrian expedition led by Gunther Schutz came over Bilafond la and attempted Saltoro Kangri II.	27
1977	Austrian expedition climbed Ghent NE from Kondus glacier.	27
1978	Indian Army expedition led by Col N Kumar approached from Nubra and climbed Teram Kangri II.	28
1978	Japanese expedition led by H Kobayashi climbed Ghent NE from the Kondus glacier.	29
1979	Japanese expedition led by S Hanada came over Bilafond la and made first ascent of Teram Kangri III.	29
1979	Japanese expedition led by R Hayashibara climbed Sia Kangri from Conway Saddle, descended S face to Siachen glacier and trekked out via Bilafond la.	29
1980	Indian Army expedition led by Brig K N Thadani climbed Apsarasas I.	30
1980	West German team led by B Scherzer climbed Ghent.	31
1981	Dutch expedition attempted Saltoro Kangri II from W.	32
1981	Indian Army expedition led by Col Kumar coming via Nubra, climbed Saltoro Kangri II, Sia Kangri I, reached Indira Col, Sia la, Turkestan la and Pk36 glacier pass.	33
1983	Trekking parties over Bilafond la from W.	
1984	Indian Army expedition led by Col Prem Chand climbed K12 from Siachen glacier traversing from W.	34
1985	Indo-British expedition led by Harish Kapadia explored and climbed peaks in Terong group. They approached from Siachen, climbed Rimo III and attempted Rimo I.	

Bibliography

1. 'Karakoram Nomenclature' by Kenneth Mason, *HJ10*, 1938.
2. *Travels in Himalaya* by Moorcroft and Trebeck.
3. *Travels in Kashmir* by G T Vigne, Vol 2 p382.
4. *Geographic Journal 23* p53.
5. *Travels in Tibet* by Dr T Thompson.
6. *Jummoo and Kashmir Territories* by F Drew.
7. *Wonders of Himalaya* by F Younghusband.
8. *This my Voyage* by Tom Longstaff, pp160, 192.
9. *Two Summers in the Ice Wilds of Eastern Karakoram* by Fanny B Workman, pp161–162.
10. *Abode of Snow* by Kenneth Mason pp242, 141, 139, 177.
11. 'The Italian Expedition to Karakoram 1929'; *HJ3*, p102.
12. 'My Expedition in the Eastern Karakoram, 1930', by Prof G Dainelli, *HJ4*, p46.
13. *Himalaya, Karakoram and East Turkistan 1913–14* by Filippo De Filippi.

14. *A sketch of the Geography and Geology of Himalaya Mountains and Tibet 1907* by Sir Sidney Burrard.
15. 'The Netherlands Karakoram Expedition', 1929 by Jenny Visser-Hooft, *HJ3*, p13.
16. *Himalayan Holiday* by Peter Young.
17. 'First Ascent of Mamostong Kangri (7516m)' by Col Balwant S Sandhu, *HJ41*, p93.
18. *HJ7*, p142.
19. *HJ8*, p14.
20. *HJ20*, p27.
21. *HJ21*, p33.
22. *HJ23*, p4.
23. *HJ25*, p143.
24. *HCNL31*, pp4, 5, 16, 17.
25. *AAJ49*.
26. *HJ35*, p254.
27. *HCNL32*, pp19, 20, 34.
28. *HJ37*, p107.
29. *HCNL33*, pp7, 23, 24.
30. *HJ38*, p124.
31. *HCNL34*, p25.
32. *HCNL36*, p8.
33. *HJ39*, p109.
34. *HJ41*, p90.
35. *Geographical Journal 38*.

HJ   — *Himalayan Journal*
HCNL — *Himalayan Club News Letter*
AAJ   — *American Alpine Journal*

11 *Geoff Cohen, Paul Nunn and Clive Rowlands at Camp ½ with Gasherbrum I (Hidden Peak) beyond.*

12 *Gasherbrum III (L) and Gasherbrum II. The normal route on GII follows the snow ridge, traverses beneath the rock pyramid, and finishes up the skyline (R). The Polish 1975 route to GIII traverses below GII's summit pyramid to the saddle and the hidden valley. The ridge attempted by Rubens and party followed the rock ridge extreme L.*

Photo: Desmond Rubens

13   Gasherbrum IV on the evening after the 24-hour storm. The Italian 1958 route follows the ridge (R).

14   *Gasherbrum IV W face seen from Concordia. A porter can be seen crossing the moraine in the foreground.*

The Scottish Gasherbrum III Expedition

Desmond Rubens
Plates 11–14

The first obstacle to setting out on a Karakoram trip is to decide upon a suitable objective. Geoff Cohen and I spent many long hours in the SMC library, combing back numbers of journals. An 8000m peak? — attractive, undoubtedly, but in Pakistan as mobbed as the Buchaille at the Glasgow Fair. Under 8000? — definitely quieter and also cheaper. Indeed, our eventual choice, Gasherbrum III, at 7952m was probably the best value peak in terms of £/metre of mountain — and compare the crowds! 1985 saw eleven expeditions to Gasherbrum II and five to Gasherbrum I. In contrast, our expedition was only the second ever to Gasherbrum III.

Gasherbrum III is a retiring, rather ugly mountain, hidden from the Baltoro Glacier by Gasherbrum IV and placed well up the Gasherbrum cirque when viewed from the Abruzzi glacier. Its first ascent was made in 1975 by a Polish party which included Alison Chadwick and Wanda Rutkiewicz. Their route ascended much of Gasherbrum II, traversed beneath its summit pyramid to the snowy saddle between the two peaks and climbed a difficult summit gully.

During the 1958 Gasherbrum IV expedition, Cassin[1] made a brief solo excursion from a high camp which terminated at 7300m. We were uncertain where Cassin actually went but it seemed he retreated before getting to grips with the real difficulties which lie in the last 700–800m.

Thus, Gasherbrum III was virtually untouched, its secret faces and ridges well hidden from prying eyes. We were unable to obtain many useful photographs before we departed, though a picture from GIV in Moraini's book[1] showed a dolomitic-looking craggy aspect. Our plan was to go for the N ridge from a high col between Gasherbrum III and a 7300m peak on the coire rim. This would satisfy our exploratory urges and keep us well away from the crowds. Finally, we decided to go 'in good style'; lightweight, two-man, with no high altitude porters, fixed ropes *etc*.

The popular climbing term 'commitment' is best applied when the Pakistan Embassy cashes your royalty cheque. Only then are you truly 'committed'. The Pakistanis also required us to increase our two-man expedition to four. Paul Nunn and Clive Rowland made up the party. We arrived at Islamabad on 23 June and at Base Camp on the Abruzzi glacier (5100m) 18 days later.

Base Camp was a crowded 800m of medial moraine shared with the Gasherbrum I and II teams. Any lingering pretence of solitude was shattered by the helicopters supplying the army camp an hour further up the Abruzzi whence an occasional shell was lobbed over the Conway Saddle in the direction of the Siachen Glacier. Baltoro Kangri did its best to compete in the nuisance stakes but only its very loudest avalanches could compare to the human assaults on our aural senses. At least our visual stimulation was more rewarding. We had fine views of the whole Gasherbrum family, along with Sia Kangri, Baltoro Kangri and Chogolisa.

For the first week, we ferried loads up through the long, lower ice-fall of the S Gasherbrum glacier to Camp 2 at 6000m, initially using a halfway dump (Camp 1). The ice-fall was used by Gasherbrum I and II teams and so was well-marked. Ferrying loads was always very tedious and particularly so after a storm. It always surprised me to see a team coming up as we descended to BC, as the ice-fall became unpleasant as early as 8am. Certainly, as a small team, we always felt more mobile from Islamabad onwards and my only complaint at this stage was the injustice of Clive, a regular smoker who had not spent the preceding months training over the steep hills of Edinburgh, being constantly out in front.

On 21 July, Geoff and I began to push the route beyond Camp I, up the 800m ice-fall between Gasherbrums III and IV. This upper ice-fall was much steeper, heavily crevassed and had some enormous seracs. The upper coire was defended by a final 60m ice palisade which stretched the entire width of the coire. Shortly after beginning the exploration of this thoroughly unpleasant place, I contracted an infected tooth abscess and retired to BC with Geoff. Meanwhile, Clive and Paul explored the ice-fall as far as the ice palisade and dug a halfway snowcave at 6400m. While much of the ice-fall was dangerous, a vague ridge above half height increased the odds in our favour.

By 29 July we were reunited in Camp 1, ready to push on up to the upper coire. On the 30th, we found a way through on the left side of the ice-fall by climbing the steep but safe slopes under Gasherbrum IV to an exit gully between Gasherbrum IV and the ice palisade. By 2 August, we had a stocked ice-cave in the coire at 6900m under the SW ridge of Gasherbrum III. A little exploration also went on. Geoff had spent an afternoon visiting the col on the Italian route below Gasherbrum IV but his efforts were rewarded by fresh cloud. With Clive, he made another sortie far up to the back of the coire. Again, even from their furthermost point, it was impossible to tell if a feasible route existed up the N ridge of Gasherbrum III. The W flank of Gasherbrum III is very precipitous with one enormous vertical rock step below the summit. This step continues round to the north but how much further would require additional investigation. It certainly looked possible to reach the col below the N ridge, though not without difficulty.

I had been resting during these sorties, hoping that whatever ailment was affecting me would go away. I was beginning to discover that resting at 7000m was not a very effective cure. Now the weather, so far fairly benign bar one 24 hour storm, took a hand. On the morning of the 3rd, strong winds swept the coire and cloud blotted out the Gasherbrum basin as we made our way slowly over to the top of the ice-fall. Once in the ice-fall, we were sheltered but great care was required descending the steep slopes below Gasherbrum IV. By the following day we were back at BC, I for one particularly thankful to be back at a lower altitude. Our decision to descend was vindicated. Other parties were trapped on the hill (fortunately without serious consequences) while 1.5m of snow fell. Our main difficulty during the ensuing five days, apart from digging

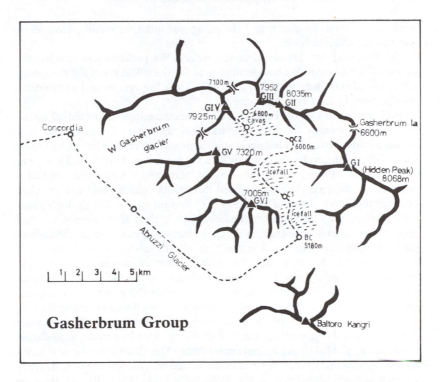

Gasherbrum Group

out our tents, was that our liaison officer chose this period to quarrel with us. Instead of the relaxation we keenly needed, the air filled with tension, only finally resolved when the LO departed towards Askole. The tension was gloriously dissipated by brandy supplied by the neighbouring French expedition in celebration of their success on Gasherbrum II. Clive then departed owing to business commitments and became quite ill on the walk-out.

On 11 August, Paul, Geoff and myself set off up the hill again. Our hope was that, with the snow cave at 6900m stocked, we could make a fairly rapid ascent. No snow had fallen for more than two days and we had had a good report on the snow conditions as far as Camp 2. This report turned out to be erroneous. Initially, we made good progress and by dawn had ascended most of the lower ice-fall. However, higher up, the snow had not consolidated and our slowness begat, as it always does, further slowness. The final mile across the plateau took four hours instead of the normal forty minutes and we arrived at Camp 2 exhausted after a 12 hour day. The dome tents were barely visible and we spent another hour digging them out and repitching them.

We took a rest day to recover and allow the snow another day to settle. Paul then decided to go down and Geoff and I went on alone. The following day we reached the ice-cave at 6400m. This had changed dramatically due to the collapsing seracs above but was still inhabitable. Next day, we returned to the coire ice-cave, Geoff leading one execrable pitch of waist deep snow on the way. However, once on the upper slopes, the snow improved and in the coire the wind had scoured the glacier and the going was more reasonable. Even so, it was still calf-deep at times.

The following day dawned clear but windy. We packed sacks and left the shelter of the ice-cave. We had decided to tackle the SW ridge of the mountain, a long mixed ridge seen in profile from BC. It was less remote and its problems were known, at least from the coire.

'Rather like a day on the Ben,' said Geoff, encouragingly, as he led off up the snow slopes towards the first gendarme on the ridge. I was quieter as I pondered this remark, but felt optimistic. This was, after all, what we had come for — lightweight, technical climbing on a big mountain. I just hoped it was not too technical. We gained height steadily, traversed a ramp and reached a prominent gendarme. The wind roared through the gap beyond and we could now see the upper slopes of Hidden Peak. Roping up, we led through about eight pitches. We kept mainly to the face, slightly right of the ridge which had appeared reasonable enough from the coire, but was certainly more difficult on more intimate acquaintance. The climbing was demanding — fairly steep and exposed, slabby, holdless and with enough snow to increase the difficulty. Any snow in quantity was in very poor condition, so that we stuck to the rock wherever possible. We had the satisfaction of seeing the great peaks come into view after an absence of many weeks — Masherbrum, Broad Peak and K2 now visible over the coire rim. As the afternoon wore on, we began to cast about for a decent ledge but the ridge, which had not appeared so unaccommodating from below, yielded us not a single decent site. The cloud was now well about us adding to our problems. We eventually settled on a narrow snow shelf, safely secured but uncomfortable in our mini-dome bivvy bags. By the time we brewed up it was dark. Still, we had made fair progress, judged by our position against Gasherbrum IV.

I woke to a fabulous dawn over Broad Peak and K2. We brewed, packed a few sweets, took a couple of ropes and some gear and left by 7am. The ridge was now more accommodating and we moved unroped. The wind was ferocious. Accidentally leaving my nose exposed yielded superficial frostbite within minutes. I pulled the hood of my down suit more tightly around my face and soon the skin became more pliable. Geoff (as usual) was out in front, but at least we were gaining height. The 7000m-plus peaks on the coire rim were now far below us. To the north, the brown lands north of the Shaksgam River contrasted with the great peaks of the Karakoram. Masherbrum looked straight at us, Hidden Peak reared its noble form clear of the rapidly moving cloud, Broad Peak savage indeed from its Chinese side, K2, monarch of them all.

We passed a tower on its leeward side gaining some respite from the wind. Then we followed steep ledges around the tower traversing back towards the ridge with the upper coire some 600m below our heels. No second chances here. Back on the ridge, we were on a narrow crest with a succession of small pinnacles. We gained some more height, then roped up, as the ground had become more difficult. Only two more pitches and we had run out of time. The cloud was now tearing through the gaps in the ridge and Gasherbrum IV had been blotted out for some time. Moreover, the way ahead was not at all obvious. Routefinding, rather than technical difficulty (though that was not lacking), was the problem. There was no question of descending this ground in the dark or of bivouacing without gear in this wind. I was certainly not sorry to go down as I now felt very tired. The weeks of being in the ice-fall had taken a mental as well as a physical toll. I estimated later that we had reached a point about 200m (vertical) below the summit. Even the most optimistic estimates would have required three to four hours to cover the remaining ground at that altitude.

We began to reverse the route. Back at the sheltered section I rested awhile. The sun came out and I tried to absorb some of the stark beauty of this, the wildest landscape I had ever seen. Reward enough, I thought, for the weeks of toil. We arrived back at the bivvi ledge at dusk, the bags flapping vertically into the air. We retied them and got in. Halfway through the night a knot came undone and I found myself suddenly four feet lower. I hauled myself back up hand over hand and retied the knot more carefully.

In the morning I knew my feet were frostbitten for sure. My hands had suffered slightly as well from taking sunrise photographs. With a tremendous struggle we got my feet back into my boots. Although it was still very cold, the weather was kinder but we were more tired. I recall applying first principles as I made a delicate traverse back onto the ridge during the descent. Three points of contact, one limb moving at a time, crampons searching for a foothold, slow deliberate change of weight, ignore the 1000m exposure down to the S Gasherbrum glacier. Images of home came to mind, encouraging my brain to keep in gear. From the ridge, we abseiled down. We reached the snow slope exhausted with the cave hundreds of metres below. Still, now we only had to move forward and we descended. Near the cave the ground sloped less steeply and it seemed like going uphill. I remember noting Geoff lying motionless in a heap. No point in stopping: twenty steps now to the cave, ten, five, one. I crawled in; filled the dixie; lit the stove; and collapsed into my bag. Geoff arrived and we began the recovery process.

A rest day, then slowly down the exposed slopes of the upper ice-fall for the last time. The following evening we reached Base Camp. I remember the last mile along the moraine in the dusk and wet snow falling. We were going at the slowest possible speed without actually being stationary. We arrived to find the tents wrecked by ice-melt, one ruined beyond repair: a very low point. Slowly we made two tents habitable and at last I got the stove primed with the wretched local fuel.

Next three days — holiday. We enjoyed the sun and peace of a deserted Base Camp. I was back in Britain by 3 September, Geoff a few days later. My feet eventually recovered though two toes have a more interesting shape than prior to the expedition.

Reference
1. Fosco Moraini *Karakoram — The Ascent of Gasherbrum IV*.

Excursions & Climbs from the Karakoram Highway

Doug Scott
Plates 15–17

We left Britain on 18 June 1985 for the Karakoram with the intention of climbing rock pinnacles in Hunza, Rakaposhi N face, and Nanga Parbat from the south. We failed on all of these but did climb Diran (7273m) and several minor summits.

Heat and disease severely weakened the party, a situation exacerbated by being constantly on the move establishing four different base camps and, to a lesser extent, by problems with porters.

For three days and nights we travelled from Karachi to Islamabad lying on the equipment between the steel sides of an ancient Bedford truck. Travelling from south to north with the sun at its zenith, stops were frequent to escape the heat of this mobile oven and to cool down in irrigation water and at Coca Cola stalls. Icelandic climber Helgi Benediktsson was our first casualty. He had to remain in Islamabad for 10 days in the care of the British Embassy staff whilst he recovered from severe vomiting and stomach pain.

After travelling up the Karakoram Highway we reached Karimabad on 30 June where the team split into two groups. One group (Michael Scott, Alastair Reid, Snaevar Guomundson (Iceland)) went up to the Passu Glacier area. The rest of us (Mark Miller, Sean Smith, Stephen Sustad (USA), Greg Child (Australia), Nazir Sabir (Pakistan & LO) and myself went up to camp 3 hours above Karimabad on a pasture at 2400m by the Ultar glacier. After waiting for fresh snow to clear, all but Nazir climbed (in two days) up a steep, dangerous couloir to a col beneath Bubli-Mo-Tin (6000m) a 1000m rock pinnacle SW of Bojohaghur Duan Asir. General lethargy prevailed, as everyone had diarrhoea and Greg was passing blood. Stephen and myself climbed a minor peak to the south of our col but with no enthusiasm. We retreated, dodging stonefall, down the couloir. Nazir, his fiancée, Fumi, from Japan and our cook Mohammed narrowly escaped a huge avalanche on a goat track above Base Camp. Many goats were not so lucky.

Back in Karimabad we took Greg to the local hospital — which was full of local children, also with intestinal infections. Temperatures at mid-day were over 40°C and remained high for several weeks — in the Hunza valley reaching 47°C. The Passu team returned also suffering from the heat and infection.

We moved our gear to Minapin and set off up to Diran. Clive and Sue Davies (Canada), two trekking friends, returned home as Sue was suffering from diarrhoea and severe dehydration. After 5 hours walking (spread over 2 days) we camped beneath the NE ridge of Rakaposhi in the ablation valley by the Minapin glacier at about 2400m. The 51 Nagar porters demanded £750 for this carry some of which we agreed to pay then and to discuss paying the rest with the local police chief on our return. An ugly incident ensued with them threatening us with sticks. Knowing that some German trekkers had been murdered by Nagars on a nearby glacier, we paid up. Later Nazir went down to fight a court case in Islamabad and *en route* reported the incident. Seven Nagars were put in jail. Periodically we were visited by the police and local leaders who informed us that the prisoners would be flogged and possibly jailed for six months. By this time Terry Mooney, QC, had arrived fresh from defending Irish terrorists in Belfast. He went down to plead for the Nagars on our behalf and succeeded in securing their release. Eventually this was settled on the basis that Minapin to Base Camp at the Minapin glacier, being an 8 hour carry, counted as one day only. Not long after Terry had to return home when an old knee injury put him out of action. Greg, Stephen and Snaevar also departed as their condition became worse.

Back at Base Camp, Mark made a fine solo ascent of Pt 5677 which lies due north of the N col of Diran, making this climb from the SE. Helgi was now in better health as were Mark, Michael, Alastair and myself. We moved up the Minapin glacier to camp at 4000m. From there we climbed up the original route of Diran in a two-day push to the summit. The same route was climbed the day before by Eddi Kobelmueler's Austrian Expedition. We descended to our bivouac some 600m down the WNW ridge. Helgi was unable to reach the summit with us so he went up next day with an Austrian climber whilst I waited just below the ridge for his return. Three days later Nazir returned from court to climb up with Sean to the summit plateau — bad weather prevented them reaching the actual summit. At last we were able to stretch ourselves with a few days climbing in the cold clear air. The weather was superb and from the WNW ridge we had fine views of the SE side of Rakaposhi and all the peaks between Diran and Nanga Parbat to the south — white above the heat and dust.

Meanwhile my wife, Jan with my two daughters, Martha (12) and Rosie (6), Helgi's wife, Anna and son Johnni (9), Sue Duff, Frankie Morton and David Marshall arrived at Base Camp to join the expedition for the next few weeks.

Four of the Austrian team climbed the unclimbed E summit (7010m) of Rakaposhi *via* the NNE ridge — we had planned to go to the main summit this way. Eddi Kobelmueler staggered into camp late at night telling us of this fine climb but also that right at the end of the difficulties one of his team had slipped and was now in Advanced Base Camp with serious head injuries. He asked us to go up with pain killers and do what we could to rescue him whilst the Austrians' LO went for a helicopter. Early next morning Mark, Michael and I arrived to find the injured man was dead.

We lost interest in this side of the mountain and in climbing in general, having just also heard of the deaths of our friends Roger Baxter-Jones and Don Whillans. Instead, we decided to explore the unclimbed S flank of Rakaposhi but poor weather and high porter rates changed our minds in favour of Nanga Parbat.

We arrived at Base Camp on the Rupal side of Nanga Parbat on 12 August after a harrowing tractor and jeep ride to the road-head followed by two days on foot and horseback. Our Base Camp was on lush grass surrounded by juniper trees by a clear stream gurgling out of the rocks at the foot of the S face. On 15

August Ali, Michael, David, Nazir, Martha and myself went up to the W side of Rupal Peak. After 3 bivouacs and some Grade-3 ice climbing we were established some 250m from the summit. All but Martha, who had bad stomach pains, and myself went to the summit via this new route.

Mark and Sean attempted a nearby un-named peak but retired, lethargic from a recurrence of intestinal problems. Mark left after realizing he was fighting a losing battle with ill-health. None of us were in very good shape so Michael, Ali, Nazir and myself decided to go for the SW ridge route on Nanga Parbat. We climbed appalling loose rock to camp at 6400m. Nebi and Mohammed, our two Hunza friends, helped us with load carrying part way and then descended. The next day we reached 7300m in a storm with hurricane-force winds. We backed down 150m and bivouaced, but Ali was very ill so we descended next day to Base Camp. A few days later our very much depleted party hired horses and galloped out to the road-head.

At home, before the Expedition, this grandiose plan had seemed quite feasible with relative ease of access provided by the Karakoram Highway and jeep roads up the side valleys. But in practice it had proved a disjointed expedition and one during which we were constantly contracting illness. The water supply in Karimabad was particularly suspect this year and it was exceptionally hot. The year before, most of us had walked the 14 days up to Makalu Base Camp (Nepal) and climbed six peaks including Baruntse, Chamlang and nearly Makalu. That had proved a far better experience as there had been a steady acclimatization on the walk-in, during which time we gained strength, and a rhythm of life developed more conducive to climbing than had been the case in 1985.

By early September we were all back home to lick our wounds, pay off our debts and to thank all the sponsors and friends who made it possible for us to visit Pakistan.

15   Bubli-mo-tin (6000m) S face which was first climbed by Patrick Cordier from the right via the coloir and the col.

16 *Nanga Parbat S face (Rupal).*

17 *Diran (7273m) NW face.*

18   *The central section of Hikmul's E ridge.*

19   *Ganchen seen from Hikmul E ridge.*

The Sosbun Glacier Region

Lindsay Griffin
Plates 18–19

The only disappointment on our trip to the Sumaiyer valley in 1984 lay in the discovery that the superb granite ridge on our only black and white photograph was, in the event, a heap of broken rubble. The sun shone, for over a month, from a deep azure sky; yet the excellent ice faces and snow ridges of the Silkiang peaks remained in an eminently climbable condition.

Those mouth-watering photographs of Karakoram granite give the impression that it outcrops everywhere. Alas it is confined to small and distinct areas, notably the lower Baltoro and Biafo peaks. Closer research led to photographs of the Sosbun glacier and eureka! — a vast array of unclimbed granite walls and pillars. But at the time, and further east, the unclimbed giants of the Siachen proved a far greater attraction. Only later when the dates of a proposed trip were confirmed unfortunately outside my holiday period, did I begin to investigate the Sosbun more fully. It was certainly off the beaten track — but what of its history?

Perhaps the first exploration of the area occurred in 1908 when an indefatigable husband and wife team, so dominant during that decade in the Karakoram, reached two cols at the head of the upper arms of the Sosbun and peered northwards onto the Sokha glacier. The Bullock-Workmans pronounced this a glacier with no outlet — one entirely surrounded by mountains — a scientific enigma? Of more importance was their identification and nomenclature of the two big peaks in the area, Ganchen (6462m) and its immediate neighbour Hikmul (untabulated but felt to be at least *c*.6300m).

Members of Shipton's 1939 survey expedition were next to examine these glacier basins. Tilman, after some deliberation and various 'tentatives' on a feasible approach to both Ganchen and Hikmul from the Basha valley, crossed the main divide north of the Hikmul la to gain the western branch of the Sosbun glacier. In order to clarify the somewhat confusing topography he ascended to the 'Workmans' Col' west of Sosbun Brakk before descending the Hoh Bluk to the Braldu valley.

Shortly afterwards, Mott surveyed the area from a rocky ridge just west of the main valley and above the terminal moraines. He then moved camp to below the 'Peninsula' ridge that splits the upper arms of the Sosbun and from atop this took yet more readings before descending to Nangma where he encountered Fountaine. The latter moved swiftly up the Tsiblu glacier, crossed the Hikmul la and descended steeply to the Basha valley. All parties seem to agree on almost continual disturbance due to avalanches down the faces of Hikmul and Ganchen.

Thirty seven years elapsed before the next expedition visited the valley. A 14 man German party under the overall leadership of Robert Wagner reached the Sosbun glacier in August after considerable delay due to bureaucratic and

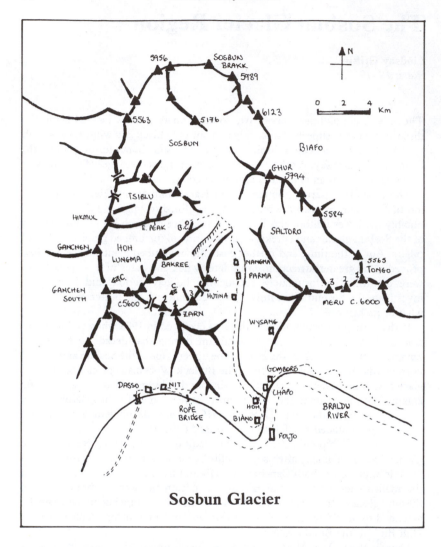

Sosbun Glacier

porterage problems. Splitting into two parties they reconnoitred Ganchen from the Hikmul la (this seems a very unlikely point of attack; were they perhaps confusing Hikmul with Ganchen?) and reached a height of about 5450m on Sosbun Brakk.

In 1978 an eight man Japanese team under Tohru Shibazaki made the first ascent of Ganchen from the Hoh Lungma glacier. From an advance base at 4850m they sieged the rock spur leading up to the Ganchen-Hikmul col. The ice slopes on either side are obviously too dangerous and although the spur looks of reasonable angle, the rock is decidedly rotten. Three weeks and 1000m of fixed rope were required before a camp was placed on the col at 5930m (29 July). Amazingly, three members climbed to the top the following day via the long N ridge and over four subsidiary summits. This rather suggests that the final section must be somewhat easier than it appears! This expedition also reconnoitred Sosbun Brakk and in 1981 another Japanese expedition from the Shigakukai Club, comprising ten climbers and led by Seichi Kawauchi, reached the summit via the S face on 4 July. Dangerous stone-fall was reported throughout the climb.

By late July 1985 we were sitting in the garden of the Dasso rest house, the roar of the Braldu river only occasionally drowned by the raucous whirring of helicopters carrying supplies to the troops fighting at the head of the Siachen glacier. Our five porters, organised by the resident Pakistani Intelligence Officer, were as friendly, honest and hospitable as one could imagine. Three mornings later we left the deserted grazing village of Nangma, a relaxed and happy team. Slopes of lush elephant grass led up towards the terminal moraine.

Chris Forrest and I had hoped originally to attempt the fine spires and rocky peaks that form the W Biafo wall. However, on reaching the lower reaches of the Sosbun glacier it became immediately obvious that, on this side of the range at least, the rock was universally appalling. Rather disheartened we transferred our base to the lateral moraine of the Hoh Lungma glacier whereupon it began to rain. At the time I was almost relieved as I felt one or two days acclimatization lying in the tent and eating would not go amiss. My only problem was how to deal with Chris's insuppressible urge to get on with the job. Unfortunately it rained most of the time and the only real fine spell developed on the outward march to Dasso! Chris is, by qualification, a chef and consequently we achieved, if nothing else, the highest standard of campsite cuisine!

An ascent of a nearby summit, Bakree Peak, was achieved in dubious weather and on awful snow, but the most compelling objective was the unclimbed Hikmul. Its E ridge looked long but objectively safe. Avalanches poured at very regular intervals from the flanks of Ganchen. First we needed some practice and a group of spiky alpine peaks around the head of the Chonga Hanmung glacier appeared to offer a suitable venue.

The ascent of this delightful valley and miserable moraine was memorable for the discovery of alarmingly huge 'Yeti' tracks in the mud — presumably belonging to a very large species of bear. An excellent pair of ibex or 'Bakree' horns protruding from the ice were dug up in order to export home — a decision quickly abandoned on account of their weight and stench. We pitched camp at about 4700m on the upper reaches of the glacier and after an initial sortie ended in a violent electrical storm, we spent four unpleasant days in sodden clothing and sleeping bags before a break in the weather allowed a retreat to base. Next day the bright sunshine leered at us and we retraced our steps to our high camp. Over the following days we climbed Zarn I, II and Hoh Lungma Peak, all giving relatively easy climbing although the ridge north from Zarn II gave entertaining mixed work.

The weather remained unsettled but time, as always, is a limited commodity. We loaded five days food and set off in diminishing drizzle on 14 August for Hikmul's E ridge, a fine route given the right conditions. In three days of climbing up, down and along cornices of every shape and size we were stopped about 500m short of the summit by a slope of bottomless, rotten snow. By now we had reverted to climbing at night due to the atrocious conditions encountered along the ridge, conditions that seemed to become more worrying the higher we rose. It was actually an hour before dawn and quite cold when the slope cracked and groaned — a crack which Chris both heard and felt.

'I'm not very happy!' I shouted down into the night but inwardly thought, 'You coward.'

'Do whatever you think best!' came the reply. Ironically our descent coincided with the most perfect of clear skies and we were consoled by splendid views of the Baltoro giants. It was somewhat gratifying to observe, two days later, the slopes below Point 5400m had avalanched — the fracture line neatly coinciding with our tracks.

Ever optimistic, we threw our last few days into an attempt on Ganchen South. A variation on the theme — we spent two depressing days camped above 5000m in a steady drizzle. Frostbite had been the least of our concerns during this mild month.

With sacks that were later found to weigh 38kg, largely composed of warm clothes we never wore and climbing gear we never used, we left the Hoh Lungma on 21 August, reaching Dasso via the intense furnace of the Braldu Gorge two days later.

Perhaps a little should be said of the other peaks in the area. The fine SW spur of Ghur rises from between two glacial basins at over 5000m, looks reasonably straightforward and leads directly to the summit. Access, unfortunately, is well guarded by steep ice-falls and narrow rotten rocky ridges. Perhaps when the peak is finally climbed it will be from the Biafo. The sharp spires flanking the upper arms of the Sosbun are composed entirely of very rotten rock and look rather unattractive. South of Ganchen a number of large snow peaks rise above the lower Basha valley and might be best attempted from that side, as the southern approach from Dasso is steep with complex ice-falls in the upper reaches. To gain the grassy lower section of the Saltoro valley would necessitate crossing the extensive and rugged moraine-covered confluence of the Sosbun and Hoh Lungma glaciers. A dry glacier appears to lead gently upwards to the enticing peaks of the 6000m Meru group. Were it not for these and the unclimbed Hikmul, both very worthwhile projects, one could not recommend the area to future parties.

Alpine Club Karakoram Meet August 1985

Brendan Murphy

The Karakoram Meet this summer was a unique event in the history of the Alpine Club. Never before has such a disparate group of innocents dared to venture into the very heart of such mountains. The Meet shared little of the meticulous preparation associated with more orthodox expeditions; indeed, detailed corporate planning was notably absent. The style of the Meet had more in common with a casual weekend in the Peak District than with a traditional expedition to the greater ranges.

The concept of the Meet was quite simple: Club members were invited to make their own way to the Chogolungma Glacier, there to spend their precious vacations scaling the mountains of the Karakoram. There was to be minimum overall planning and, to a large extent, everyone was to make their own arrangements. 'See you all on the Chogolungma, first ablation valley on the right . . . around 12 August, if not before', wrote Steve Town in his penultimate Meet Note. Steve worked hard to keep people informed of each other's ideas and to attempt to co-ordinate some kind of overall plan. His rôle, however, was more advisory than managerial.

There are two basic attractions in choosing the Karakoram for a casual trip of this nature. Firstly, in many areas there are no restrictions on 'trekking' up to 6000m; even technical climbing up to this altitude is officially classed as 'trekking'. Above 6000m, an expedition permit is required from the Pakistan government, and a peak fee of several hundred pounds is levied. In addition, a liaison officer is required, and the organization becomes prolonged and complicated. For us, all these irritating obstacles were avoided. Secondly, the Karakoram is in the rain-shadow of the monsoon so that, unlike Nepal, climbing is possible throughout the summer. Unfortunately, few of us were prepared for how hot and arid it was going to be . . .

The trip to Skardu turned out to be an experience in itself. Steve had chartered a forty-seater bus to take us and our gear the 500km to the roadhead. This impressively robust vehicle duly arrived, inevitably late, but lavishly decorated in true Pakistani style. But its ornate exterior cleverly disguised a lurking menace: throughout the journey we were to be tortured by the frenzied chanting of Urdu popular music. Do not think that 'noise pollution' is a peculiarly Western phenomenon.

The scenery the following morning amply compensated for our exhaustion, but the weather was poor and it was raining steadily. The monsoon had made an unscheduled, and unwelcomed, foray into the foothills. That evening, uncertainty about the state of the road ahead forced us to pay off our drivers and spend a night in Gilgit. There, Ted and Herbert decided that a couple of weeks in the Gilgit area would be preferable to another day on the road.

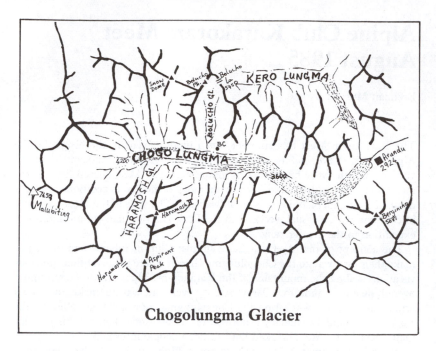

Chogolungma Glacier

Next day, we hired jeeps for our onward journey to Skardu but, before long, our progress was checked by a landslide. Exhaustive negotiations finally allowed us to continue by truck and, with some relief, we finally rolled into Skardu.

The walk-in from Skardu must compare favourably with many Himalayan approaches. For five days we were treated to the delights of Pakistan's mountains and the hospitality of its people. The Arandu Valley is particularly memorable: lush meadows, a colourful tapestry of terraced fields, lie below a backdrop of snowy peaks. The valley is abundantly rich in a variety of fruits and grains. It was tempting to spend each day lazing in the shade of this Garden of Eden.

Our relationship with the porters was generally excellent. They all won our admiration for the enormous loads that they carry, and for their characteristic cheerfulness. In return, Robin and Ronnie gained our porters' esteem for their respective skills in Gaelic dancing and flute playing. Indeed, Ronnie played a valuable role as the 'Pied Piper of Arandu', enticing porters away from their families to carry our gear. But on one occasion our porters went on strike. After a comparatively long carry above Arandu, they stopped at what they decided was a good campsite, and they refused to budge. It took some gentle encouragement by our sirdar and the promise of a slaughtered goat (for which we, in turn, were persuaded to pay), to coax them a little further up the glacier.

The following evening, they slaughtered the goat and afterwards they gathered around the communal campfire for a celebration sing-song. We joined in, contributing English folk songs in response to their Balti chants. We were promptly cajoled into some Balti dancing, which is really quite tiring at 4000m. These people certainly know how to enjoy themselves. It was a fabulous evening, and a fitting conclusion to our walk-in.

On the following day, we arrived at our base camp at the junction of the Balouche and the Chogolungma glaciers. The setting was superb, but the campsite turned out to be a rather bleak spot with very little grass, and no shade from the sun. The worst complaint was the ubiquitous sand which found its way into everything. Back in England I, naïvely, had expected to be camping on ice at this altitude and melting snow for drinking-water. As it turned out, 'Dust Camp' was more like a desert outpost, with temperatures reaching 50°C during the day. The climate was unexpectedly harsh and many of us suffered from the heat and sun. The whole area would be a desert, devoid of any vegetation were it not for glacial melt-waters.

The surroundings are equally extreme. The glaciers in this area are simply horrendous: huge expanses of tortured ice, covered in a blanket of nasty moraine, and cut up by huge crevasses. Walking on these glaciers was unpleasant work. The moraine is hard to walk on for long periods, especially when the sun loosens the surface boulders. The extensive crevasses require lengthy detours, and the ice-falls require great patience, and occasionally some quite technical ice climbing. On the mountains themselves, the rock seems to stay in place more through tradition than through any inherent soundness. Unlike Nepal, high altitude trekking in these parts would have little to offer the casual trekker even though the views from the passes are truly magnificent. The subtle changes in light and tone can be appreciated by the climber only, for photographs never can do justice to such ephemeral beauty.

The combination of difficult access, harsh environment, and widespread illness limited the extent of our climbing. The peaks turned out to be much more technically demanding than we expected. These were no simple snow domes up which to plod. Most of them require the planning and commitment of a small expedition.

Even so, several worthy ascents were made. Graham Elson made an enterprising solo ascent of Skari Lungma, followed a few days later by Ron Giddy and John Swift. Pete Payne, Robin Richards, Mike Gilbert, and Ian Haig made an attempt at a peak opposite the Balouche La. They climbed within 100m of the top before approaching darkness forced a retreat. They later made a successful ascent of a peak near Sencho, at the mouth of the Chogolungma. Pete and I made an enjoyable ascent of 'Aspirant Peak', right at the head of the Haramosh Glacier, giving superb dawn views over the Karakoram. This peak was so christened because of our youthful status within the club, and because we were aspiring to greater climbs soon after. Unfortunately, heavy snowfall put paid to these ambitions.

Everyone trekked extensively in the area, and we were all rewarded by spectacular and beautiful scenery. Mark and Penny Dravers stormed in across the Haramosh La, and then out over the Balouche La into the Kero Lungma. Ron Giddy and John Swift trekked out over the Balouche La, but at a more civilised pace. Pete and I trekked over to the Nushik La, where the magnificent view of the Hispar Wall made all the effort worthwhile. All of us experienced the unforgettable beauty of the Arandu Valley, and about half our number trekked over the Haramosh La and out through the enchanting Haramosh valley.

Of course, there are fundamental problems for a loosely co-ordinated meet such as this. Firstly, more comprehensive planning is required by individuals or small groups. Secondly, wasteful duplication of effort and equipment is almost inevitable and thirdly, the standard of living suffers, since communal equipment and services (such as big tents and a camp cook) are not available. For a fully co-ordinated approach to work, the meet must comprise a group of like-minded people, united by a common purpose and by similar objectives. If a meet is to cater for a wide cross-section of people, then it presents problems. Members on the Chogolungma Meet had different climbing objectives, different financial resources, and different levels of fitness. In such a situation communal planning would seem to compromise on everything and satisfy no one.

However, a casual meets such as this provides a very valuable opportunity for many more people to expand their horizons, and all at minimal cost. It opens up doors for those people who are outside the mainstream of Himalayan climbing, or for those who lack the time or money to mount their own expedition. In the right sort of area, it offers the opportunity of making Alpine-style ascents in a Himalayan setting.

I would guess that most people enjoyed their little adventure in the mountains of Pakistan. Indeed, another such meet is planned for next year. The walk-in alone was an experience that will linger long in the memories of many, as will the heat, the illness and the sheer grandeur of the place. On a more personal level, I made some very good friends and enjoyed myself immensely. The trip has whetted my appetite for further travel and inspired me to organize a lightweight expedition in a couple of years. Until then, I wait impatiently.

Those on the Meet, for all or part of its duration, were:

Tom Chatterley	Ian Haig	Robin Richards
Pam Chatterley	Ted Hanson	John Swift
Mark Dravers	Ted Hartley	Ian Thompson
Penny Dravers	Pete Herold	Steve Town
Graham Elson	Brendan Murphy	Fergus Ungoed-Thomas
John Finlay	Lyn Noble	Ronnie Wathen
Ron Giddy	Peter Payne	Ted Whalley
Mike Gilbert	Dave Pownall	

20 *Bhagarathi W ridge seen from Ganohim Bamak.*

21a & b   *Sunrise Pillar on Kedar Dome E flank. The route follows the crest of the ridge throughout.*

22　The initial diedre on the Sunrise Pillar.

23   Part of the E face of Kedar Dome, seen from the Sunrise Pillar.

Views on the Gangotri

Martin Moran
Plates 20–23

The Gangotri is only 300km from Delhi, an array of attractive snow peaks, and unlimited potential for Alpine-style ascents on granite prows and faces. This mountaineering dream-world was unveiled by the Indian authorities as recently as 1979, when the 'inner line' restrictions on the Tibetan border zone of the Garwhal were relaxed.

Access to foreign parties had hitherto been prevented for nearly 30 years, so that neither the Himalayan 'golden age' nor even the modern lightweight revolution had touched the region. The 1930s and '40s saw the initial explorations of the main Gangotri Glacier system, and the first ascents of the most accessible and easy summits.

Tilman and Shipton's 1934 Garhwal travels had reconnoitred the Chaturangi Bamak, the Gangotri's major subsidiary glacier, after crossing into the basin from Badrinath. In 1938 a German expedition penetrated and surveyed the full length of the Gangotri glacier itself, and in 1947 a Swiss party ascended Satopanth (7075m), which is the second highest of the surrounding mountains after Chaukhamba I at 7138m. Then, during the years of closure, Indian expeditions climbed several other summits including in 1974 the coveted prize of Shivling (6543m), the most beautiful and revered of them all, towering awesomely and so conveniently above the glacier snout and the Tapovan camp.

But when, in the wake of the Shivling E Pillar climb by Bettembourg, Child, Scott and White in 1981, *Mountain* blew a fanfare of publicity on the area, Gangotri was still an untapped goldmine to climbers of all ambitions. In the last four years of rapidly increasing popularity this situation has been gradually changed, yet so great is the potential that the many magnificent routes established have merely pointed out a wealth of intervening challenges for the future . . .

The Pilgrims' Trail
The district town of Uttarkashi is located deep in the tree-clothed Garhwal foothills, and the bus journey from there to Gangotri roadhead takes six hours if the road is clear of landslips, tortuously following the precipitous gorge of the Bhagirathi River to provide, in the opinion of many, the most frightening part of their expeditions. However, it gives the porters an easy ride for their first day's pay. Uttarkashi has several registered porter agencies as well as an excellent market and so forms the last major stocking point *en route* to the mountains.

Little is seen of the snow peaks during the trip nor even from Gangotri village, which is closely hemmed in by the valley's walls and offers no distant perspective save for the enticing sight of Sudarshan Parbat which fills the skyline above the final bend of the Bhagirathi. The village is excitingly sited at

Gangotri

the tumultuous confluence of the Kedar Ganga which drains the great cirque of Thelay Sagar (6904m) and crashes down to join the Bhagirathi in a roaring ravine of smooth bare granite. The shining white portals of its temple mark Gangotri's social and spiritual focus. Yet the place has a dishevelled and neglected atmosphere, especially in autumn when a piercing mountain wind blows down-valley raising the dust and wreaking havoc among the makeshift shacks of the bazaar and tea stalls as if to quicken the annual exodus of its populace to lower climes for the winter. The scheming entrepreneur would drool over the potential to convert Gangotri into one of the world's most delectable tourist resorts, but perhaps it is better left as it is — dirty but culturally intact.

The 16km walk to the Gangotri glacier is shared with a stream of pilgrims, for the Bhagirathi is worshipped as one of the sources of the Ganges. The glacier snout at Gaumukh, where the river emerges from a concave cavern of ice, is one of the four holy places in India to which the devout Hindu makes his lifetime quest. All castes and classes are seen on the well-made track, from the wealthy of Bombay, borne shoulder high in dandies, to frail and ravaged old men, clutching their cheap metal water pots, and shrinking inside thin white cloths at the chilling mountain vespers. Their ardour is rewarded by one of the most gentle and beautiful mountain rambles imaginable. It is therefore sad to hear rumours that a jeep track may be driven up the valley by 1990.

The trail is especially a revelation to the climber, whose gaze is upward and onward. Initially, sheer monoliths of orange granite rising over 300m frame the valley sides. Yet when Pat Littlejohn and John Mothersele climbed the striking dome on the south side of the river 3km upstream from Gangotri in October 1984 they were almost certainly making the first incursion in a rock-climbing paradise that could easily absorb a two month stay in itself. This 12 pitch route followed the NE edge of the dome, gave sustained HVS climbing with a crux corner of E3 6a, and was climbed from a snug bivouac in the woods beneath the face. With idyllic camping spots and the summer teashop at Chirbas close at hand, the joys of exploration on these sunlit walls could easily distract parties away from the high peaks, but they could also provide an ample consolation in event of failure or bad weather in the mountains.

However, as height is gained the brilliant snowcaps of Bhrigu Parbat and Manda are noticed peeping over the cliff tops and then, as the southerly bend of the river is turned, the Bhagirathis — II, III and finally I — are unfolded in a majestic tableau across the valley head. Their serried N and W ridges and faces were the preserve of British parties until 1984. B II presents a fine snow and ice face above Nandanban which was climbed in 1981 by the Irish team of Tommy Maguire, Ian Rea and Dawson Stelfox. Next in the ranks comes the rapier-edge spur of B III, a stunning line climbed in 'capsule' style by Bob Barton and Allen Fyffe in 1982, and etching a lofty skyline on the right, the snow arête of B I's W ridge which Charlie Heard, John Mothersele and myself did a year later. Since then a three-man Italian team has climbed the W ridge of B II, and most impressively the W face pillar of B III was ascended by four Spaniards in May 1984, a route already repeated twice and giving 20 pitches of perfect granite climbing, mainly on aid, topped by a 50°–60° ice face.

The ashram and rest house of Bhujbas is the final settlement in the valley, a place of well ordered peace as well as conviviality. The scene has opened and from here on Shivling's emergence captures all the attention, though a right-wards glance must be spared up the Panth Bamak, which reveals a shaded slice of white granite on Bhrigu Peak that defies all normal conceptions of scale, verticality and smoothness.

At Gaumukh, 4km further on, the pilgrims are left and the track forsaken for the rough and stony climb on to the Gangotri Glacier. There are two possible Base Camp sites, both on alluvial shelves which are shored up behind the lateral moraines, Tapovan on the W bank, and Nandanban further up on the E bank at the fork of the Chaturangi Bamak. Both provide grass, shelter, a wealth of alpine flowers in summer and fresh water, although Nandanban usually dries up in the post-monsoon period.

Arrival here at 4350m is immediate and exciting, but in the rapid approach lurks a big danger of altitude sickness. The transit from Uttarkashi at 1000m is typically pressured by porter requirements and economics, and usually takes just 2½ days. With no chance to adapt gradually to this height gain, base-camp oedema (and pneumonia) is a recurrent problem in the Gangotri, claiming the chances of one of our own team in 1984, and likewise a Polish expedition doctor in 1983 who had recently been to 8000m on Makalu.

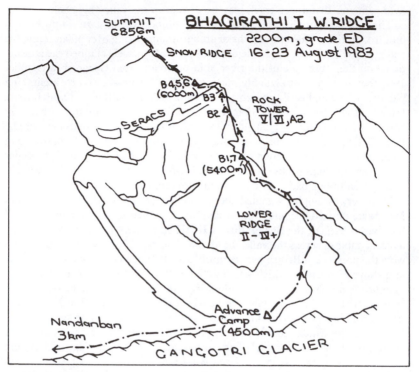

Above the Base Camp meadows, the glacier sweeps onward into a haze of distant peaks, and with a total length of nigh on 30km seems to have no end.

Bhagirathi I, West Ridge

For structural elegance and purity of line, the W ridge of Bhagirathi I touches the margins of perfection. A series of broken rock buttresses rises from the glacier moraines at 4500m joining and linking to support a smooth monolithic tower of granite at half height. With savage loose cliffs and hanging serac barriers on either side, the tower guards the only means of access to the upper ridge, a sculpted snow arête which after a brief pause sweeps up for 900m to the summit at 6856m. What great fortune and privilege to chance on such a route, in 1983 untried and untouched.

On 16 August the parallel was hard to draw as the three of us slogged up those lower ramparts in a cloying monsoon drizzle, weighed down by 15kg loads and double boots, and plagued by that aching altitude fatigue where the blood throbs relentlessly in the temples yet deserts the leaden legs. Two weeks earlier John and Charlie had romped up these slabs in shirt sleeves and training shoes on our first exploratory foray, and then a serious attempt had ground to a halt halfway up the tower in conditions not dissimilar to those we were now resigned to accept on this the crucial effort.

An overhung rock crevice 200m below the tower provided an ideal first bivouac, sheltered from the spongy mist, which overnight left a verglas shell that delayed our morning's departure until 10am when the sun poked its head over our ridge.

Its emergence provoked a surge of activity for we knew the clouds would be likely to regroup by mid-afternoon, and were compelled to complete the tower before a decent bivouac ledge could be expected. Therefore the grade V and VI flakes and grooves of the lower tower were reclimbed to our high point with barely a pause to appreciate their superb quality. In particular one improbable diedre into which Charlie had launched with an enormous aid climbing rack had yielded in 10 minutes to an athletic string of 4c and 5a laybacks and finger jams in hidden fissures.

Leads were alternated so as to share the joys of sackless pioneering and the agonies of load carrying. However, after I had surmounted another long flake diedre and Charlie had turned a prominent candle of rock by a ramp on its left, John was landed with the pleasures of an unprotected off-width chimney — its back choked with ice. Each intricate step of progress towards outwitting the tower brought an immense thrill, especially as every pitch had gone free so far, but now with 90 minutes of light remaining and ominous cloudmasses shrouding the ridge, a successful solution to its final wall and overhangs became grimly imperative.

After balancing up a tenuously protected series of wall flakes the fading light stopped me just 25m from the top, and we despondently accepted an open bivouac spread across the sloping ledges below. The darkness prevented any cooking, and soon after it began to snow thickly and heavily. The fall was later interrupted by an intense electric storm, which brought the continuous buzz of static, and cascades of burning charges down the rock candle just 15m to our left.

The dank and misty dawn found us unscathed but frightened, wet and buried under 15cm of fresh snow. The rocks were sheathed in a coat of slushy ice. Had we reached our limit? Every big Alpine route must have its crisis point, and this was ours. We elected to go on. A retreat from the top of the tower would hardly be more problematic than abandoning the cause one pitch lower.

I had to dig deep into unplumbed resources to go back up. Using aid from nuts and 'Friends' in cracks choked with melting snow the final roofs took four exhausting hours to lead, which only left us just sufficient time to seek a ledge on the banded shale slopes above for the night.

Being increasingly extended both physically and logistically, all our hopes resided in the weather, and a brighter morning spurred us up the 200m of loose mixed ground which debouched onto the slender snow crest that we had sought for so long. Yet hardly had we drawn breath at the sight of the summit crown of Bhagirathi and laid our sleeping bags out to dry, than the clouds closed ranks and here, at 6000m, a light snowfall commenced.

For 30 hours we were pinned down, squeezed into our two-man tent at the foot of the arête, with the great seracs on either side creaking and groaning, pondering with a tingle of excitement and a chill of fear the true meaning of Himalayan commitment. The sensation was appreciably enlivened when our gas stove exploded the following evening nearly incinerating both our tent and ourselves.

Our provisions now comprised only one breakfast, a family sized Yorkie, a freeze-dried stroganoff and two days of fuel for water, but on the morning of our expected retreat the skies cleared and the temperature plunged, enabling a 'now or never' summit bid to be hastily mounted. We set out lightly laden, carrying a stove and pan but no sleeping gear. The mass of new snow clinging to the arête was crusted and stratified, but after cautious initial soundings we pronounced the surface safe. Cornices were small or absent thanks to the lack of recent wind and often our steps straddled the knife-edged crest which rose in waves from 30° to 50° in angle.

Already racing against the encroaching clouds, John led us strongly and relentlessly to a rock step at three-quarters height, and promptly decided to quit. His feet were wet and already cold, and he could not afford to risk a bivouac. Passion, ego, rationality and prudence were hopelessly tangled, but with John's encouragement Charlie and I went on, awkwardly rounding the step and ploughing up the final 200m to emerge in a white-out on the top. We staggered and wallowed about in deep powder to fix the highest point and then fled.

At 4.30pm, night was only two hours away, and the weather deteriorating by the minute. Climbing solo for speed and rhythm, eight hours of upward effort were reversed in a non-stop sequence. We desperately strained our eyes to find our tracks, which were fast disappearing under new snow and which were our sole means of salvation. By the last glimmer of daylight we rejoined John back at the tent, utterly drained, perhaps more mentally than physically. We had not seen much of it, but what a great and unforgettable route.

Two days later John and I staggered down to our advance camp with a dreadful weariness and sadness. We had left our closest friend on the mountain, killed when an abseil anchor failed on the shale bands, the only dangerous piece of an otherwise sound and objectively safe route. Our own deliverance was only secured by the spare rope which we had left at the top of the tower. Never can we properly celebrate the Bhagirathi climb, but I hope that those who follow will revel in its magnificence, and value the sacrifice that Charlie made in bringing it into being.

A Sunshine Climb on Kedar Dome

Kedar Dome (6831m) has a gentle NW flank that provides perhaps the easiest and most frequented climb in the Gangotri area, but its E side is of an altogether different calibre, a precipice of some 1600m in vertical height, and forming a sweeping prow of granite that would be ranked as one of the world's most beautiful rock structures were it better known.

Gathering the temerity to dare to violate this great fortress, Dave Cuthbertson, Pat Littlejohn, John Mothersele and myself càme to the Gangotri in late September 1984, a post-monsoon of brilliantly clear weather but bitterly cold and dry winds.

The aura of the E face is enhanced by its remoteness, being tucked away in the side valley of the Ganohim Bamak 16km upstream from Tapovan. The way there is cruelly rough, for the Gangotri glacier is a convoluted mass of rubble-coated moraines seamed with meltwater channels, dammed lakes and fields of

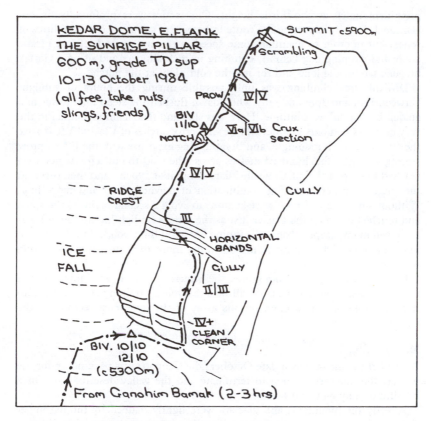

KEDAR DOME, E.FLANK
THE SUNRISE PILLAR
600 m, grade TD sup
10-13 October 1984
(all free, take nuts,
slings, friends)

SUMMIT c5900m
Scrambling
PROW IV/V
BIV 11/10
NOTCH
VIa/VIb Crux section
IV/V
RIDGE CREST
GULLY
III
HORIZONTAL BANDS
ICE FALL
GULLY
II/III
IV+ CLEAN CORNER
BIV. 10/10 12/10 (c5300m)
From Ganohim Bamak (2-3 hrs)

ice spillikins. Making the first trip to the site of an advance camp beneath the face, alone and with a 30kg load, gave one of the most gruelling yet inspiring days of my life. Ahead in the view Kharchakund (6612m) forms a graceful cornerstone to the Ganohim Bamak, never seeming to draw a mite closer whilst the Bhagirathis slowly file past on the left and behind, flies the 'butterfly' face on Shivling's S side.

The overpowering desolation and grandeur of the scene on my exhausted arrival below the E face was enough in itself to deter my ambitions, but more materially Cubby's serious illness, my wife Joy's own sickness, and a resultant lack of time and manpower prevented our even attempting the prow.

Eight days later I returned from the trials of valley reorganisation to the lonely Ganohim to find that John and Pat had just embarked on the W ridge of Kharchakund. Prowling about the glacier for a suitable solo objective I espied a clean rock spur plunging for 600m down from Kedar's E flank just to the right of the E face. The need for a partner was immediately solved by the chance arrival of the Kiwi hobo and climber, Don French at the advance camp.

On the following three days we enjoyed a happy and carefree climb, planned and timed with fortuitous perfection. From a bivouac on the edge of the ice-fall beneath the pillar we did 14 excellent pitches between grade III and V to a prominent notch at two-thirds height. Our tactics were profoundly unconventional. Rightly expecting the route to be bare of snow, we carried 6 litres of water, but in order to maintain some speed in the enterprise I left my plastic boots and sleeping bag behind, climbing in rock slippers and using a Gortex bivouac sac for the long and for me the cold night at the notch.

Difficult free climbing was only possible during the hours of sunlight between 8am and 3pm and only when dawn flushed the steep final tower to a golden brown did we continue. Here was slab and flake climbing equal to the very best on Chamonix granite, all free with crux pitches of VIa and VIb (to use the current French gradings), and breathtaking exposure with the E face prow rearing up just a few hundred metres across the void to our left. At noon we reached the top of the pillar, a subsidiary summit at 5900m, and then reversed the route by a nerve-racking combination of downclimbing and rappelling. Without any more water we were anxious to avoid a second night on the spur, and touched down on the glacier just as the stars were lighting up. Soon I was cocooned in my sleeping bag and supping hot tea at the bivouac, but the glow in my veins that night sprang from something more than the return of bodily warmth.

Overall deserving a *TD sup* grade, the Sunrise Pillar, as we dubbed it, is a route of classic dimensions, and will be a marvellous training climb for future parties before making a more serious assay of the innermost recesses of the Ganohim cirque.

No End in Sight

As we left the mountains in late October, the Gangotri was packing up for the winter, the bus service soon to terminate and the valley deserted save for a handful of holy men and hermits.

Already the mountains and glaciers were lightly daubed by the harbinger flurries of the coming snows, but recalling the view from the top of the Pillar, I dreamt of the array of unknown summits above the final arm of the Gangotri glacier and the oceans of smooth bare rock on the neighbouring peaks.

In two brief visits to the Gangotri I have been granted one of a host of great mountaineering routes, and made the slightest of scratches on the area's rock climbing potential — truly a rich personal reward. Yet I am glad and reassured that there is so much still left to the will of others.

4   *A gorge in the Zanskar range in Winter. This one is a tributary of the Chang Chu.*

25. *Views . . . the Tibetan wild ass . . . in bleak winter landscapes near Sangtha, Zanskar.*

26 *Near the top of the Kungi la in Ladakh, looking south.*

27. Ladakhis crossing the Gurla la in winter. They are taking loads of firewood to sell in Leh.

Photo: Simon Fraser

Mountains of the Snow Leopard

Simon Fraser
Plates 24–27

Very clearly, on the snow-covered ice of a frozen river, a set of pug marks led upstream into the high mountains which we had just crossed. I had lost count of the number of times we had seen similar tracks during our long journeys on foot and on ski. Almost wherever we went there were signs of this elusive and beautiful cat, the snow leopard, luring us further into the remotest corners of the Zanskar range. But now in March 1985, we were heading once more for Leh, tired and hungry after weeks of travel in search of snow leopards and the other large mammals such as bharal, ibex, argali and wolf, which roam the great mountain ranges of Central Asia and the Himalaya. We gazed at the tracks leading enticingly upwards, then turned and started the descent to the Indus valley. Another time maybe . . .

The 1981 Survey

My interest in snow leopards had been fired in 1977 when a Ladakhi friend and I heard two of the cats approaching our bivouac in the Chang Chu gorge on a cold November night. In January 1981 I arrived in Delhi with Ben Osborne, a wildlife biologist, to embark on a wildlife survey of Ladakh. Our purpose was to investigate the status and distribution of the mammal species of Ladakh and to look at conservation measures in this important region. We chose the winter season because there are several important advantages: the animals are easier to find because they descend to lower altitudes; snow cover provides more information from tracks and the animals are easier to spot; and some regions such as the Zanskar gorge can only be reached in winter conditions when the rivers freeze over. Information was collected from sightings, tracks, droppings, presence of dead animals, and from numerous interviews and conversations with local people. Until 1981, very little research had been done on wildlife in Ladakh, although there had been numerous visits by hunters during the era of British rule, which provided virtually the only documented information about the fauna. There was thus a conspicuous absence of up-to-date information about the wildlife in this huge area.

Since the introduction of civil flights to Leh in 1978, it is possible to fly there in winter when the Himalayan passes are closed to overland traffic. It is a spectacular flight which crosses the Himalaya in the vicinity of Kulu-Manali, with views eastwards to Kamet and Nanda Devi on the horizon and then over the bleak ranges of Rupshu with glimpses of endless ranges stretching into Tibet, giving a sense of vastness that no map can ever convey.

On arrival in Leh, we bought supplies and then visited the Markha valley. Although I had made several previous visits to the valley, it was a chance for Ben to get to know something of the environment and conditions in this part of Ladakh before venturing into other regions closer to the Himalaya. Markha is

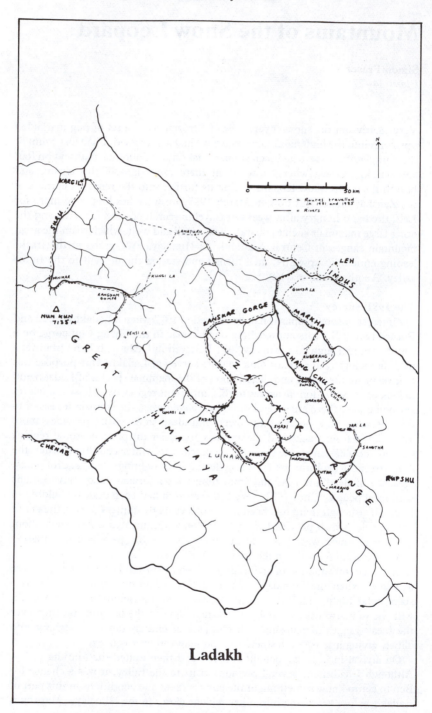

Ladakh

situated within the 3 hectares of the proposed Hemis High Altitude National Park and a survey by personnel of the Forest Department in Leh has counted over 1000 bharal in the area. There are several villages in the valley which has a population of approximately 300 people. Despite extensive grazing by domestic animals, there is a stable balance between human activity and the presence of wildlife which is not seriously threatened in this area. We wanted to cover as wide an area as possible in the survey and had divided Ladakh into a number of different sections. Each area would take months to survey thoroughly but we were confident that in the six months at our disposal we could pinpoint areas of serious risk to wildlife and identify prime areas for effective conservation management. Away from the main valleys are huge uninhabited regions which we were keen to see, as they might provide natural sanctuaries for animals. So far there was no reliable information to refute or confirm this, and it was essential to break new ground by covering regions not normally monitored by the Forest Department.

We were not rewarded by many direct sightings of animals in the Markha area on this occasion, but feeling fit and acclimatized we returned to Leh, resupplied, and in late February set off on what we expected to be a routine journey into Zanskar via the great gorge of the Zanskar river. News from higher up the gorge was bad. A party of six tough looking Zanskaris told us that the route was difficult due to unusually mild conditions. They laconically described the problem as 'chu mangpo' — a lot of water. As we continued, conditions indeed worsened and our two Zanskari companions were decidedly unhappy, saying that the route had changed beyond recognition in the last ten days.

In the gorge there are no known escape routes in a 50km section, and safety lies at either end. Dave Mallon, a biologist who spent four recent winters in Ladakh, has travelled the gorge several times in varying conditions, on one occasion being marooned in a bivouac cave for five days with vertical cliffs and open water ahead, and retreat cut off when the ice below broke up. From enquiries with the Zanskaris, we learnt that there have been no fatalities within living memory, mainly because there are always experienced people in any party. No doubt there have been numerous epics and narrow escapes.

We were forced to retreat to the Indus valley and decided to ski in from Kargil without further ado. In Sanku we met Guy Sheridan and his Norwegian friends who were commencing an impressive ski journey to Manali, (see *AJ87*). We travelled up the Suru valley on ski, which proved to be incredibly hard work in atrociously soft snow conditions. The weather was poor for several days with fresh snow and low cloud, but we spent this time at Panikar, gathering much information about wildlife from the local people, many of whom are keen hunters. Then we slogged on up the valley, putting our slow progress down to a combination of heavy loads, lack of previous experience on ski, and bad conditions. Months later I was relieved to read that Sheridan's party considered these snow conditions to be the worst they had ever encountered!

We reached the Buddhist monastery at Rangdum in a blizzard and stayed for a couple of days waiting for the surfaces to improve (to no avail) before pressing on towards Zanskar. The fresh snow meant slow progress and during another four day snowstorm on Pensi la, we ran short of food for the arduous push over the top. Ben had a deadline to leave India in order to take up a project on deer in Mongolia and could not risk being delayed. We watched ibex foraging for food on some highly dangerous looking avalanche slopes, then returned to Rangdum to resupply, suppressing our frustration at failing to reach Zanskar again.

Now we had to decide on which exit route to take. Neither of us wanted to return down the Suru valley. From Rangdum there were three passes that would bring us out on the Kargil-Leh road but two of them were reputedly very avalanche prone, and the Kungi la was the pass that we were advised to take. Well fed by the kind monks of Rangdum, we set off, determined to get through into new country. We ski'd up an easy valley for a day until we reached 'the third ravine on the left' where despite the heavy snow cover we could see traces of a summer path climbing steep ground just beside the entrance to the narrow gorge that led towards the pass.

We were still seeing ibex herds, and the usual wolf, fox and snow leopard tracks, but for the most part were more fully occupied with the business of travelling, eating and resting. In these mountains only a small fraction of the time is spent in actual research. Much of the time is taken up with getting there, getting back, surviving, waiting, or other activities that have to be done before one can get to grips with the fieldwork. As a biologist, Ben found this particularly frustrating, and at no time more so than now, when we were entering fascinating country with some exciting glimpses of animals but with a difficult pass and time limits taking priority.

The tributary gorge proved to be a tricky problem, with water and slush pouring over the ice as spring approached. To avoid it we climbed over a shoulder on unstable snow slopes that made a couple of frightening bangs but stayed put. Then we descended a steep gully to rejoin the gorge, which we followed upstream along a roller coaster of cones of avalanche debris, increasing in size as we climbed higher. This was worrying country to travel in. We had to take the skis off in one place to clamber up a massive wall of avalanche debris, 100m high, that filled the narrow V-shaped valley. But we eventually saw safer terrain ahead and found some rocks where we could rest and brew up. Anxious to cross the pass before the next spell of bad weather, we decided to head for the top that evening. To avoid disturbing the slope by zigzagging, we made a bee-line up steep snow to the pass, approaching the top gingerly, hearts in mouths as the slope felt so creaky, with an eggshell crust covering masses of powder. At the top (c.5170m) in the fading light, I caught a glimpse of huge cornices and steep cliffs dropping into the gloom on the N side.

We had no rope but our fears were unfounded for the morning revealed a convenient gap in the cornices and we descended a rocky spur on the left to reach a small, snow-covered glacier. The views of the Karakoram far away to the north were superb. The south-facing ridges ahead of us were brown and snow-free but this was misleading, for the valley floor and N sides of the ridges still held plenty of deep snow. However, we were definitely entering a much less snowy zone, in the rainshadow of the Himalaya, and we expected no further problems except for the ski descent. Neither of us had ever ski'd downhill before except for a few sessions on a dry slope at home. We were rather unbalanced by our heavy loads but it was an exhilarating and relatively effortless descent, with the occasional tumble. I will never forget the pleasure of sliding down after so many days labouring to go up or along.

We weaved our way down the upper slopes, down and down, until we reached a difficult section that tested our patience to the limit. It was a snow covered, frozen river in the process of thawing, with very steep and unstable scree slopes at the sides, which offered no passage. The rotten ice was covered in slush and water, in turn covered by about 60cm of 'depth hoar', a convenient term that we discovered later in a skiing book. Without skis one sank deeply into the slush. With skis, the fragile honeycombs of the depth hoar gave no support whatever, and we were reduced to a snail's pace, having to lift the skis high at every step and breaking a trail with ski sticks because the tips of the skis caught under the thin crust as we tried to move forward. There was nowhere to camp or even to sit and have a rest without getting drenched in freezing water and slush, but in the distance we could see a spit of gravel at a river confluence, so we slowly closed the distance and eventually camped there. The next day the crust was just strong enough to support us and we ski'd on until the snow finally ran out. Adding the skis to our packs, we plodded on down the immense Kungi gorges whilst bad weather swept over the pass behind us.

Ben then proceeded to Mongolia, whilst I teamed up with Ian Coward. We set off at the beginning of May to walk from Lamayuru to Padam, with a quick foray into the Shadi district and some very wild and formidable country further east in the heart of the Zanskar range. It was austere and forbidding terrain, totally uninhabited, harsh and bleak, but with a high density of prey and predator species in comparison with more populated regions of Ladakh. We had some excellent sightings of ibex and bharal, and there was abundant evidence from tracks of the presence of wolf and snow leopard. By now we were able to make comparisons between different areas; from the Suru valley where probably the pressure on wildlife is greatest; to the Markha valley where there are steps being taken to conserve and manage wildlife in an inhabited area which is very accessible to modern trekking tours and other developments; to the empty wilderness regions of the Zanskar range, where an estimated 3.5 hectares of undisturbed country provides a natural sanctuary for large mammal species[1].

In June we crossed the Umasi La (5295m) but by now the snow conditions were excellent and it was a thoroughly enjoyable trek in fine weather through some impressive glaciated country. We decended into luxurious, knee-deep grass and flowers and the forests of Kishtwar. We had planned to have a look at Barnaj II, but time was pressing, Ian lost his only pair of trousers during an awkward river crossing, and I was tired after five months in the mountains and fancied a rest in Kashmir, with some enjoyable climbing on an accessible peak. We camped for a couple of days in a forest glade below the lovely peak Agyasol (6200m) and I revelled in the greenery after months in the harsh, arid country beyond the Himalaya. Then on, down the huge Chenab valley to Kashmir where we ended our travels for this season by trekking across the range between Pahalgam and Baltal and ascending the S face of Kolahoi (5425m), where the views extended from Nanga Parbat to Nun Kun and Sickle Moon. Everything went as planned, travelling light, climbing two peaks and two passes and enjoying the magnificent alpine flowers, and hospitality from kindly herdsmen.

On our return to the UK, we got together with Dave Mallon, who had spent the winter surveying the Ladakh urial, and published our findings in Oryx[2] (see references). This paper stimulated considerable interest in the wildlife of Ladakh amongst other researchers and drew attention to the potential of Ladakh as a stronghold for various species, despite conservation problems typical of a fragile mountain ecosystem. We were keen to make further visits to the area to concentrate on wildlife photography and to penetrate some of the wilderness regions of the Zanskar range. Several popular routes are used by summer trekkers, but huge areas remain untouched, frequented only by snow leopard, wolf and the roaming herds of ibex and bharal.

The Wildlife of Ladakh
based on the 1981 survey[2], and work on the urial and snow leopard by Dave Mallon.

The whole area of Ladakh is mountainous and subject to a harsh continental climate, with scanty rainfall and cold winters. The landscape is generally arid and inhospitable, with oasis-like settlements mainly confined to the major river valleys of the Indus, Zanskar, Nubra and Suru, separated from each other by rugged mountains cut by deep gorges. The plants consist of alpine, steppe and semi-desert communities. Human influences on the environment include cultivation, animal grazing, fuel collecting and scrub clearance, hunting, and modern development projects such as new roads.

The snow leopard, *Panthera uncia*, is an endangered species and extremely difficult to study in the wild due to its shy nature and a low population density, distributed in high and remote mountains. A small, stable population exists in Ladakh, estimated[1] at 100–200. In most of its range across a large area of Central Asia, the snow leopard is threatened by hunting and from human population increases, which cause grazing competition between livestock and wild ungulates, which are the main prey of snow leopards and are also hunted. In Ladakh, snow leopards often attack livestock in winter and may be killed by villagers. Other cats in Ladakh include the lynx, *Felis lynx*, and Pallas's cat, *Felis manul*, both of which are very rare. There is a small population of brown bear, *Ursos arctos*, in the Suru valley and N Zanskar, the E limit of this species in Kashmir. Wolves, *Canis lupus*, are widespread and common in Ladakh, and prey on livestock all the year round, posing far more of a threat than snow leopard. Traditional wolf traps can be seen near many villages. Wild dog or dhole, *Cuon alpinus*, is now extremely rare in Ladakh. Foxes, *Vulpes vulpes*, are common, and there are several species of mustelid. The wild ass, *Equus hemionus kiang*, is fairly common on the plateaus of E Ladakh but is not seen in the main areas open to foreigners. Another E species is the argali, *Ovis ammon hodgsoni*, which lives mainly above 4500m on the plateaus. A rare species of wild sheep in Ladakh is the Ladakh urial, *Ovis orientalis vignei*, with a total population[3] of 1000–1500, a considerable reduction from the numbers reported by early visitors. It is found in the Indus valley and tributaries and is therefore the most accessible and vulnerable to hunters of the ungulates of Ladakh. Ladakh is a stronghold for bharal (blue sheep), *Pseudois nayaur*, which is common in the E half of Ladakh. The Siberian ibex, *Capra ibex sibirica*, is common in the W half and is regularly hunted, particularly in the Suru valley. Its territory overlaps with bharal in some places. Several other smaller species to be seen include marmots and hares.

The 1985 Survey

Dave continued his research each winter, but due to work commitments, Ben and I were unable to return to Ladakh until January 1985. The plan for this year was to travel quickly to Zanskar and to spend as much time as possible in the Shun-Shadi district which had proved so promising in 1981. The challenge of travelling there in winter, the relative abundance of wildlife, and the sheer remoteness, gave it an irresistible appeal. Our choice was not made without extensive discussion beforehand about the merits of going to a better known and more accessible region where the chances of photographing animals would be higher since we could afford proportionately more time sitting and watching and waiting, essential ingredients for successful wildlife photography.

Unfortunately I succumbed to a virus infection in Leh, followed by pleurisy, so we were delayed for about three weeks before starting up the Zanskar gorge with three Zanskari porters.

The journey to Padam was straightforward, though in places we had to climb rocks or wade through water flowing over the ice, an unpleasant experience in the sub-zero temperatures, with bare feet sticking to the rocks as soon as we emerged. The Zanskaris sang songs, lit fires to thaw out and rubbed mustard oil on their legs. The ice was fickle, ever changing. In some places, the deep blue water flowed silently, cold and malignant, with only a narrow pavement of ice attached to vertical cliffs, linking sections of more secure ice cover. Sometimes the water roared over rapids and disappeared under the ice again lower down. To fall in the river did not bear thinking about. The surface underfoot was infinitely variable, from hard polished ice where we tumbled like skittles, to sections of breakable crust where we crunched through tinkling shards like broken glass, or rotten honeycombs of ice and slush. The ideal was flat ice with a dusting of snow to give a better grip. More often the surface was irregular, bulging with slippery, polished domes over hidden boulders, or broken into crazy patterns as the ice cover had collapsed with a drop in water level. Occasionally, frozen waterfalls plunged from the cliffs like gleaming white pillars.

At night we bivouaced in caves and then travelled all day, the conditions becoming colder and snowier as we approached Zanskar, with 95% of the river frozen over, winding in frigid silence between the towering cliffs. Pools of open water gave off frost smoke in the brittle, cold air, and frequently a wind whistled down the gorge, adding a further chill to the intense cold. After six days we reached the first Zanskari settlement, blanketed in a white mantle of powder snow about 50–60cm in depth. In some winters, with 3m of snow, travel would become extremely difficult, and in the areas we were heading for, any movement would be virtually impossible due to the avalanche risk, let alone struggling huge distances in 3m of powder.

We reached Padam on the eighth day, rested two days and pressed on up the

Tsarap Lingti Chu through the Lunak (demons) region. Signs of wildlife increased dramatically, with numerous sightings of ibex and many tracks of fox, wolf and snow leopard. I had travelled through this area twice before and remembered it as a deep cleft cutting through the mountains. Compared to the Zanskar gorge, it now seemed like a gentle dale. It was striking to notice how much more vegetation there was in this area than in Ladakh, and the marked increase in the density of animals the environment could support. A day from Padam, the deep snow ended and we made faster progress with our heavy loads of supplies. At night we stayed in villages and were always given a warm welcome. After staying at the beautiful monastery of Phuktal, we pressed on into wilder country and spent several days at a cave in the Shadi region, just below the valley leading to Tso Tok Fu, a lovely lake hidden in the mountains. We spent some time exploring the area and watching bharal and ibex, and crossed the ice of Tso Tok Fu to visit the upper valley, inaccessible in summer because of cliffs around the lake. The valley beyond was lonely and beautiful, with jumbled old moraines leading up to meadows of yellow winter grasses beside a meandering river fed by springs. At 4200m were dense woods of gnarled willow trees, and empty valleys beyond, leading to unknown passes.

Just as we got back to camp that night, Sonam Jorpel told us excitedly how he had seen a big snow leopard emerge from the valley we were descending, a few minutes ahead of us. Sonam was fetching water from the river when the cat ambled past him on the other side. We raced off to track it but it was almost dark and we were too late to get a sighting. Next day we set up the cameras with a radio controlled shutter release but there was no more sign of the snow leopard and it could be weeks before he passed this way again.

The original plan had been to cross the pass behind Shadi with one month's food, to the area I had visited with Ian in 1981. My illness in Leh had delayed us so much that we were unable to attempt this, but with hindsight this plan could have been very problematic, with midwinter temperatures probably well below −30°C above 4300m, the difficulty of carrying sufficient food, and the serious risk of becoming completely cut off by a heavy snowfall.

With new visa regulations we had to leave India in April and had flights home booked in advance. We had to be sure of reaching Leh in good time, and as always, felt the pressure of time limits, and now a dilemma as to which route to take to Leh. If the passes were uncrossable so early in the year and the ice in the gorges broke up then we could be seriously delayed. We decided that we would have to attempt the first pass no later than 9 March, so that if we failed to cross it we would have enough time (we hoped) to take the long route back down the gorges if the ice was intact. Once over the pass we assumed it would be plain sailing, with time in hand to watch animals and explore new areas.

We headed up the great Shun gorges and in one long day reached the hamlet of Marshun. At the last settlement, Sutak, we hired two men as guides, because with the summer trails hidden by snow we could not risk wasting time losing the route to Marang la in the numerous tributary gorges below the pass. Beyond Sutuk the weather was bad and we lay up for a day whilst it snowed. The guides only had two days food and we had very little extra to feed them or wait for an improvement in the weather. Next day was no better but we pushed on up gloomy canyons obscured by mist and falling snow to a bivouac cave at 4650m. Luckily the weather cleared and we headed for the top on a fine day with a howling gale from the SW. The Marang la is unrelentingly steep for 1000m and we lost all rhythm as we struggled up loose scree, blown bare by the gales, or sank into deep snow drifts. We paid off the Sutuk men by the ragged prayer flags on the top at 5400m, broke through a small cornice on the far side and were soon up to our waists in snow. There followed the most arduous descent in snow that I have ever known, forcing a trail down through thinly crusted powder with more fresh snow on top of that. It was essential to reach shelter that night for we only had one small tent, and a little paraffin for the stove, as we were relying on wood and animal dung for fuel. We could not subject our Zanskari companions to a night out in such conditions.

After many hours of toil we reached a frozen river and the deep snow was behind us. Using some wood we had carried over the pass we had a much needed brew before carrying on to find a bivouac cave where the Zanskaris, expert pyromaniacs, lit a hillside of scrubby vegetation which made a blazing furnace outside the cave. But our troubles were by no means over yet. An error on the maps cost us a lot of time and energy looking for Sangtha, a Changpa nomad camp, where we resupplied just as the food ran out. The nomads were a cheerful and hardy bunch, dressed in rough sheepskins and living in yak-hair tents. Even in March it was bitterly cold and windy and I marvel at how Europeans such as Heinrich Harrer travelled across Tibet in winter with little food or equipment. Nothing would induce me to spend a winter with the Changpa.

From Sangtha, another exhausting slog in deep snow led to the Yar la (4930m), but on the way we were thrilled to see a group of kiang (wild ass) for the first time. From the pass, it was downhill to Karnak, the main autumn camp of the nomads, occupied now by three old men and a couple of young yak herders from down the valley. They seemed to be perfectly happy in their isolated home. Beyond Karnak we passed the place where I had first heard the snow leopards in 1977. A young Changpa with a herd of 214 yaks told us he had seen one the day before at Tantse Sumdo. We stayed there for two nights but there was no sign of any wildlife at all. The Zalung Kurpo La looked very snowy, so rather than a guaranteed slog, we preferred to push on down the Chang Chu and cross the Ruberang la which was still an unknown quantity. The Chang Chu was delightfully easy in its winter condition with only five wades rather than the 70 necessary in autumn. Chased by snowstorms which closed in behind us, we had an easy, snow-free crossing of Ruberang la (4970m), and reached the village of Markha where we received a very warm welcome from old friends and the customary large quantities of chang. The final pass was Gunda la (4970m), crossed on a superb sunny day, with a good sighting of the small, isolated herd of argali that live there. That evening, our last in the mountains, we saw fresh snow leopard tracks but we were not to be tempted from our goal of food and mail in Leh the next day. Upon reaching the Indus at 3250m, we basked in warm air at last, amidst the sounds of insects, birdsong and running water. Spring had arrived. There was no fuel, so with the ice axe we split up the willow staves which we had used for the last 500km and lit a fire for a final meal of tsampa and butter tea with our Zanskari friends before hitching a lift up the road. Leh now seemed to be a noisy and bustling metropolis.

Postscript

The journey was over and it was now a time for reflection. Searching for the elusive animals of the Himalaya had proved to be a time-consuming, arduous but satisfying task, and in winter conditions had provided some exciting travelling and memorable moments. One never forgets the first sighting of wild ass, or of ibex grazing on patches of vegetation clinging to huge crags, or of fresh snow leopard tracks leading tantalisingly up deep and awesome gorges. It seems inconceivable that these animals should ever disappear from the mountains. Yet that is what has happened and is happening in many areas of the Himalaya. The record of Ladakh is the exception rather than the rule, and urgent measures are needed to arrest the destruction of habitat and wildlife throughout many parts of Asia. In an article in *AJ89*, Rob Collister maintains that 'a taste for landscape, for natural beauty, for wildness . . . is not innate in human beings, it is an educated response'. How much more so of the response to conserve what George Schaller describes as 'the dying mountain world of the Himalaya'.

In his book *Stones of Silence*[5], Schaller drew attention to the plight of Himalayan wildlife and the degradation of the environment. After years of work in Pakistan and Nepal, he wrote 'Anyone who consciously observes the exponential destruction of wilderness becomes almost automatically an advocate for the natural world. To conserve a remnant of beauty becomes an ideal and this ideal possesses one until it becomes a faith: it takes a believer to understand sacrilege.' Effective sanctuaries for species such as snow leopard and its prey need to cover very large areas, and Ladakh is one of the few regions of the Karakoram-Himalaya where suitable conditions exist. In our journeys, we found that there are viable populations of large mammal species in Ladakh, and extensive areas of relatively undisturbed country. Despite the limitations of a harsh environment, the outlook is favourable.

It is our privilege to have the resources and freedom to visit the Himalaya for our own interest and recreation. We do not have to struggle all our lives to wrest a living from the land, to endure the hardship and poverty which is so widespread in Asia. Any struggles for survival in which we indulge on the mountains are contrived by us for our own satisfaction. As devotees of the mountain world, our 'springs of enchantment' should embrace not only personal adventure and achievement, but the continued well-being of the environment to which we are so compulsively drawn. That is to say, an environment where habitat destruction and the serious endangering of wild species, both plant and animal, becomes a thing of the past. We have the knowledge; surely it is not impossible to ensure that the knowledge is applied.

Schaller's poignant words set a challenge which we cannot ignore: 'the fact that a living being can vanish from this earth solely because of man's improvidence and neglect is appalling, and the utter finality of it touches the consciousness of far too few.'

References
1. Mallon, D P, 'The snow leopard in Ladakh'. *Int. Ped. Book of Snow Leopards. 4* pp23–37. 1984.
2. Osborne, B C, Mallon, D P, & Fraser, S J R: 'Ladakh, threatened stronghold of Himalayan wildlife'. *Oryx 17* pp182–189, 1983.
3. Mallon, D P, The status of Ladakh urial *Ovis orientalis vignei* in Ladakh, India. *Biol. Conserv. 27* pp373–381, 1983.
4. Schaller, G B, *Mountain monarchs: wild sheep and goats of the Himalaya.* Univ. Chicago Press, 1977.
5. Schaller, G B, *Stones of Silence.* Andre Deutsch. 1980.

A Dangerous Day

Mal Duff
Plate 28

We were numb. Not cold numb, although that was there at times, just battered numb: numb from eight weeks of strain; from scything wind cutting at the flesh; from swirling pirouetting columns of spindrift driving and dancing around us; from weighty effort and load carrying; from eating, drinking and living high on the NE ridge of Everest.

I plodded on lost in a world of spindrift, casually watching as Tony was again hurled to his knees, everything on automatic, both sides of my brain arguing, bullying and reasoning.

'I'm hurting.' — 'But who wouldn't. After all I am carrying an enormous load. At this sort of altitude I deserve to hurt. Anyway I'm managing 50 paces between rests even though the wind's blowing out Tony's tracks and the bastard snow is falling as it has been for weeks.' — 'I'm over 8000m and stunningly tired.' — 'It's bound to hurt. What a wimp, just ignore it and keep going.' — 'God this is hard.' — 'Yes, but the oxygen should help, that's what it's for and anyway 25kg is tiring at sea level so no wonder this is bad. And when you carried up here a few days ago it was tough and carrying at 8000m is so much harder than going for a summit unladen. We're higher than the South Col but on a longer and harder route and still miles from the summit, so we have to carry. So that's that! OK?' — 'Well I really am OK but my lungs are heaving and my thighs burning.' — 'What the hell, *THIS IS EVEREST* and life is tough.' — 'I wish my goggles wouldn't keep steaming up and freezing and I wish I felt better because I'm more tired than ever and why did I try oxygen to carry an extra load when I was doing great at 8000m without?'

Tony was crouched on a rock 40m away, a small spark of life where none should exist. The spindrift swirled and battered, battered without respite, skirling over the ridge, pluming 100m before hurling itself upon us intent on extermination. Reaching the lee of the rock, a haven in the storm, and contacting Tony, another human in this madness, because all important. Fifty steps, then 60, then 70 . . . A shattering pain suddenly erupted low in my chest. As usual in the mountains problems arise with devastating swiftness. A muscle rip in my diaphragm choked the ability to inflate lungs. A moment of panic subdued by years of training. 'No matter what, I must try: try to live, to descend, or even to die but I must try. Do something. Try, think, work and rationalize because this is the big one, the master problem, that perhaps you've been seeking for years unwittingly.' But I couldn't help thinking of Pete Thexton on Broad Peak with a collapsed diaphragm; of him going blind and dying. I buzzed with panic. Zipping strokes of worry contested. A mental battle fought — the first I knew of many before the day or I expired.

We needed the oxygen regulator and mask for those coming up so we spent what seemed like hours unscrewing it from a thread caked in ice. The hose and valve were totally frozen. Realization dawned that I had been dragging this load and not getting any oxygen. I had been sucking atmosphere through the mask so it was not surprising that I had suffered, and now I was miles from anywhere with lungs like wet sponges, no power, maybe going blind and definitely slowly dying.

We dumped our loads, marked the spot and turned downhill. Now on this ridge some of it is flat, some up, and the majority down, but it is still an effort. It was nearly 1000m before I could reach the top of the fixed ropes and slide. I could only manage two or three steps at a time. It all seemed too much. Tony went to Camp 4 to pack his gear and packed mine too. I did not think that I could get off the mountain in one day and having my sleeping bag seemed a good idea. So I put on my rucksack and kept descending and monitoring progress. No sign of going blind which would have been very worrying, but a definite fuzziness, which wasn't surprising, as I was probably only absorbing the same amount of oxygen as I would at 9000m — which isn't a lot. I could manage three steps downhill or one uphill, with massive rasping pants in between. It makes for slow progress over 3km with 2000m before the glacier.

At the nasty snowstep above the second buttress I was mighty pleased that Allen Fyffe had fixed a rope there the previous day. This place was hard and dangerous, and it was really nice to clip in and slide down a little. A few hundred metres further brought the mixed ground leading to the fixed line down the second buttress. Tony had clipped on and gone on into the spindrift. I was confused. I missed a wand and ended up too low, got extremely angry and scrambled up in a panic. This was easy stuff to fall from, my balance was all wrong and what a bloody awful waste of energy, energy that I'd been harbouring for lower down.

At 7600m between the two buttresses I met Rick coming up and going well and Jon sitting down and looking tired. Both looked at me sort of sideways and asked if I needed help getting down. But I was still upright and not yet falling, so I declined and they went on to the Pinnacles. Tony was waiting at the top of the first buttress. We had a chat and he went on ahead to Camp 3 to put on a brew.

Between Camp 3 and Camp 2 we met Bob and Chris on their way up to Camp 3. At Camp 2 we reached the end of the fixed ropes. Tony went first in an effort to break steps because the snow had filled all the tracks. I clipped onto the rope and stumbled and slid, triggering avalanches which thundered down the couloirs. I tried not to sag on to the ropes — just in case . . . Energy dredged from the flesh of my body, until finally I reached the four huge abseils down to the bergschrund. Below, tied to Tony, I staggered across the glacier resting endlessly, to reach Advanced Base Camp late in the evening.

I was over one stone lighter.

Paldor

H. G. Nicol
Plates 29–30

It was Tilman who put Paldor on the map in his book *Nepal Himalaya*. He did his best to take it off again by dismissing it as a modest 19,451ft peak (5929m), whose only claim to distinction was that it actually had a name. Tilman and Lloyd climbed Paldor during the course of an expedition in the Langtang Himalaya but they were only seriously interested in the views they might obtain from its summit of the higher Ganesh peaks to the north-west.

What happened after it was climbed by Tilman in 1949 is not certain. John Cleare climbed Paldor in 1974, and Sir George Bishop climbed Paldor West, but not the main summit, in 1980. There is no mention of Paldor in any editions of the *Alpine Journal* or of the *Himalayan Journal* in the last 35 years. Eventually it became one of Nepal's 'trekking peaks'. There are 18 of these and the name simply means that they can be climbed with a trekking permit and on payment of a modest fee. Its low altitude, (below 6000m) considerably reduces its interest for the serious expedition climber. Was it too difficult for the packaged tourist on a four weeks holiday from London? Had it been climbed more than twice?

Paldor stands out impressively from the larger Ganesh mountains behind it, and on a good day can be seen quite easily from Kathmandu airport. The SE ridge looks inviting and not too difficult. The distance to it from Kathmandu, as measured out on the inaccurate trekking maps of Langtang and Helambu is about 65km. It seemed a suitable objective for a party of middle-aged but experienced mountaineers.

The easiest way to approach a mountain in the Himalaya from the point of view of time, comfort, and convenience is to make all your own arrangements through a trekking company. It will obtain your air tickets to Kathmandu, book a comfortable hotel, arrange trekking permits, advise on Nepalese and Indian visas, and in many ways ease your passage to the kingdom. It will supply tents, sleeping bags, mattresses, porters to carry them, cooks, Sherpas to point out the way, food and all manner of unobtrusive expertise. It is difficult to see how else one could do it on a short holiday, and within the strict limitations imposed by a 20kg baggage allowance (economy class) on all international airways. Moreover it is not as easy now as it used to be in the 1960's to disperse ice axes, crampons and karabiners within one's clothing or in a day bag on an aeroplane. It costs a lot to travel in style but for us it was worth it.

Our party comprised Malcolm and Barbara Gate, Terry Leggett, Roger Salisbury, Alan and Janet Wedgwood, my wife, Mary and myself. We left London by jumbo jet on Saturday 20 October 1984 and arrived in Kathmandu via Delhi airport the next day, minus half our baggage which was lost in Delhi and came on a day later. Had it not been for determined action by Mary and Roger, it would have been much worse for, as in previous years, there were 500

trekkers fighting for 125 seats on the Kathmandu plane, all with OK reservations, but very few with names on the official passenger list. 'Sit down Madam,
I come to you' the little brown man kept saying as he shuffled his lists about
kneeling on the floor of the transit lounge and surrounded by furious tourists.
This was the way it was done in India and this was the way it had always been
done, but Madam refused to sit down and we got the last eight places on the
plane, ten minutes after it should have left on its flight to Kathmandu.

Our departure date had been carefully chosen to avoid the Dasain festival
which occupies the first three weeks of October in Nepal. During this time it is
difficult to hire porters because they are all celebrating. The monsoon rains
should all have finished by mid October and the only climatic problems would
be the cold at high altitude and the short days. It had seemed to me in England
that the best way to approach Paldor was from the east, if possible over a high
col which would give the party some much needed acclimatization. There were
three possibilities, the Ganga La 5120m, Tilman's col 5486m, or the Laurebina
La 4608m, near the Gosainkund lakes. The first two were dismissed by
Mountain Travel as too difficult and too high. Perhaps it is just as well that they
were, because our selected route along the Tiru Danda ridge to the Laurebina
La proved hard enough.

The trek began on Tuesday 23 October conveniently and comfortably from
Kathmandu by bus. This took two hours to cover the 24 bone-shaking
kilometres to Sundarijal. We then only had to walk for four hours over some
delightful ridges to reach a campsite at Chepu Banjang (2250m) by mid-
afternoon. Here our tents were already erected, sleeping bags laid out, and a
cup of tea brewed to welcome us on arrival. A party of four American girls were
encamped only 200m away and before long they had sent over an invitation to
visit them if possible after dinner. Their leader, when we arrived, rapidly
monopolised the conversation. 'Have that man washed and bring him to me!'
she cried taking a fancy to one of our better looking members. Shortly after this
the meeting broke up and we returned to our tents. Perhaps it was just as well.
The route followed the Tiru Danda for the next two days and by Thursday
night reached a very cold and inhospitable campsite at Tharepati, (3650m). The
Laurebina La lies considerably to the west of the Tiru Danda at this point, and
the path has to traverse a steep and awkward hillside to reach it. In nine hours
of walking on Friday we covered six crow-fly km but a large Dutch party had
bagged our intended campsite and we were obliged to press on to a campsite
only 300m below the col itself.

In his article on acute mountain sickness ($AJ90$, pp68-73) Jim Milledge says
that the most important single risk factor is too rapid ascent. Above 3000m
'each night should be spent not more than 300m above the last, with a rest day,
ie two nights, at the same altitude every two or three days.' Had we adhered to
this rule we would have taken nine days to cross the Laurebina La from our
start point in Kathmandu. In fact the journey took four and a half days and
everybody reported mild headaches, nausea and lack of appetite at the campsite
immediately below the col, and walking across it the next day. Terry and one of
the porters suffered severely from headache, lack of appetite, nausea, weakness, dizziness, cough and staggering. The porter was put to bed covered by a

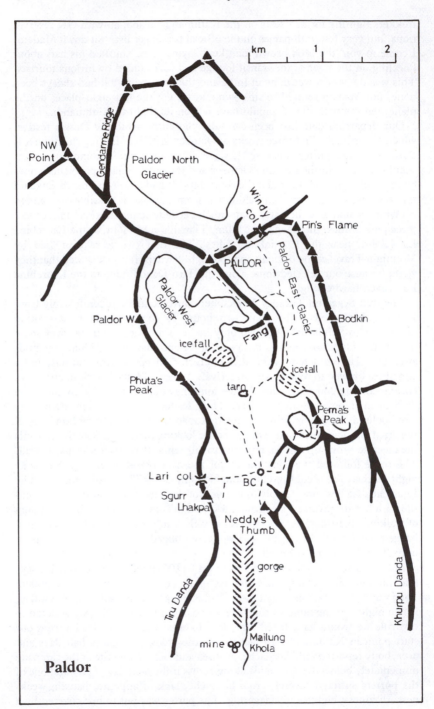

Paldor

Photo: Mal Duff

28   *Everest NE ridge in 1985.*

29 *Paldor seen from the E Paldor glacier.*

Photo: Hamish Nicol

30   The summit of Paldor seen from the Tilman ridge.

31   *The N side of Yuzhu* (*c*. 6400m) in the E Kun Lun.   Photo: Mike War

Photo: Mike War

32   *Yuzhu seen from the south.*

space blanket, but Terry was so reticent about his symptoms that nobody realized how ill he was. There were of course four medical doctors and two PhD's in the party!

Those not taking Diamox were the most seriously affected. Each member of the party had been asked to record their symptoms of altitude sickness every day on a special form which I had given them. Minor symptoms such as loss of appetite, weakness, irritability, counted one point each on the form, and more severe symptoms like severe headache, frothy sputum and the staggers counted three points. Over the first part of the trek, from 23-29 October the three people who were not on Diamox collected a total of 35 points, an average of 11.7 points per person. The remaining five were all on Diamox and scored an average of only 4.4 altitude sickness points per person. After 29 October everybody except Alan, who puts no faith in pills, was on Diamox, so no further comparisons could be made. During the first week of the trek there could be no doubt that Diamox, in a dose of 500mg per day, had proved its efficacy.

On 27 October, we left the campsite at 4100m at 6am and reached the top of the Laurebina La by 9am. For those who could appreciate it, the view was magnificent. In the foreground lay the Gosainkund lakes all sparkling in the sunshine, surrounded by easy rocky mountains going up to about 5000m. In the distance to the west, Himalchuli, Peak 29, Manaslu all the Ganesh peaks and eventually even Paldor itself could be seen clearly.

On the W side of the Laurebina La the descent to the Trisuli river is easy and delightful on carefully graded wide paths built for the thousands of Hindu pilgrims who visit the shrines of Gosainkund in August. In October we passed huge parties of trekkers toiling uphill under enormous sacks loaded with firewood. They were not enjoying themselves, for pleasure on mountains is inversely proportional to the weight of one's rucksack.

Syabru is a friendly little village perched in startling fashion on a ridge overlooking the Trisuli river. We walked steeply down to it from Sing Gompa, stopping frequently to inspect the magnificent peak of Langtang Lirung (7224m) on the N side of the Langtang valley, whilst nearby all sorts of strange birds twittered in the branches of the rhododendrons — the grosbeak, the white winged crested tit, the little pied flycatcher, each one identified carefully through the binoculars and then a second time in the pages of Fleming's *Birds of Nepal*. All this must have driven our patient sirdar Pemba Norbu to distraction, but he never showed it. Anyway it did not matter because Syabru was going to be an 'off' day well earned by our porters on the high col. Most of us could do with the rest, especially Terry, who was still not going well. A short walk down the village street and back up again made him look blue, ill, and short of breath. I listened to his chest with a stethoscope and to my astonishment heard lots of fine crackles at his lung bases. He had pulmonary oedema.

Luckily, the next few days of the trek would be even lower lying as the track crossed the Trisuli river at Syabru Bensi. So with the assistance of Frusemide tablets (a stronger diuretic used in cases of cardiac failure) he pressed on with us, and over the next four days made a steady recovery.

At Syabru Bensi the tourist parties abruptly ceased and for the next 21 days we were on our own and saw no trekkers, and very few local inhabitants. We camped at Thanjet, Gatlang, twice in the Mailung Khola, and on 2 November, 11 days out from Kathmandu, reached Paldor Base Camp.

Base Camp is at 4500m in a pleasant hollow surrounded by moraines and boulders below the confluence of the E and W Paldor glaciers. From our tents we had an excellent view of the S face of Paldor, and its SE ridge leading to the Fang stood out beautifully, especially in the setting sun.

It was obviously essential to climb Paldor as soon as possible but there was no point in rushing up it before the party was properly acclimatized. So on 3 November we climbed Phuta's Peak (5110m) while three of the Sherpas went off to reconnoitre the SE ridge of Paldor (the Cleare ridge). From our vantage point on the summit of Phuta's Peak we were astonished to see our three Sherpas already half way up the S face of Paldor on a new route! Tactfully they turned back without actually reaching the summit and made a very late arrival at Base Camp that night. They had shown that the Cleare ridge cannot be reached easily from the W Paldor glacier.

The plan was now to climb Paldor in two days from Base Camp, using a high camp on the Paldor E glacier at about 5200m. The six climbers set off at 8.30am next morning accompanied by all five climbing Sherpas and a number of porters. It was an easy walk up boulders and screes and then up the lower icy E Paldor glacier. The altitude of the Advanced Base Camp was 5170m and Ang Kami the cook and all five Sherpas were already there when we arrived. The porters had dumped their loads and were already on their way down. Within minutes tents were erected and sleeping bags unrolled. From the tents the NE ridge could be seen easily (Tilman's ridge). The route to Windy Col from the south was cut off by a steep bergschrund, so three of the Sherpas set off in the afternoon to fix ropes for our eventual descent of the Tilman ridge down this difficult slope. It had been decided that the whole party would climb the Cleare ridge and if possible descend the Tilman ridge, thus making a south to north traverse of the mountain. Roger and I meanwhile took a short walk up the glacier to reconnoitre the eastern approaches to the Cleare ridge.

The tents shook and flapped all night in the wind but with three in the two-man tents anchoring them down they did not blow away. Pemba got us up at 4.45am and we were off by 6.15am on 5 November. Fortunately the E Paldor glacier is gentle and uncrevassed and we made excellent progress. To my surprise, however, I found that the main party were heading straight for the fixed ropes on the Tilman ridge. Obviously Pemba had decided on a change of plan without consulting anybody.

Roger and I were very keen to climb the SE ridge so after a rapid shouted consultation we broke off from the others with Lhakpa. Alan and Janet, Terry and Malcolm with their Sherpas continued in the direction of the fixed ropes.

The Cleare ridge was as good as it looked. The snow was hard and perfect and our crampon points bit into it cleanly. It was never necessary to cut steps but Lhakpa found it steep enough to front point the last 150m to the summit. We moved continuously, slowly but without stopping. Base Camp could be seen 1200m down between our legs and there was not much in the way. Was it wise, I mused, for gentlemen in their fifties to risk their lives like this?

Fortunately Lhakpa, who was leading, quickly put a stop to such introspection with a quick pull on the rope. Quite suddenly he shouted, 'We're on top!' and shortly after 10.00am Roger, Lhakpa and I sat together on the summit. There was not much room and on the N side a prodigious overhanging cornice blocked the way for our friends, who were still little dots on the NE ridge 150m below. Lhakpa set to work on part of the cornice, hammered in an ice stake and suspended a fixed rope from it. By this time Pemba and Terry had arrived. Janet, Alan and Karsang quickly followed, and there were eight on the top. Malcolm with his two Sherpas was a short distance behind. Lhakpa, Roger and I now descended the Tilman ridge, whilst the others went down the Cleare ridge. All of us eventually traversed the mountain in both directions. It was a hard day.

Next day Advanced Base was dismantled and we returned to Base, spending a pleasant, lazy afternoon talking and taking photographs. Alan and Terry however, not content with the amount of exercise they had had already, climbed Neddy's Thumb by its S face in two hours from Base Camp. They found a pleasant route up it at about Difficult standard, almost certainly a new route.

Paldor is surrounded by many easier little mountains most of which look climbable. On 7 November Alan, Terry and I with Ang Danu climbed Pema's peak (5300m) on the E side of Base Camp. A cold wind blew across its summit chasing heavy cloud with some mares' tails. It looked as if the long spell of good weather was going to break. Next morning was colder and windier, a day better suited to reading than to climbing. However, after lunch Terry, Roger and I with Ang Dale and Lhakpa decided to explore a low peak on the Tiru Danda, which looked a bit like Sgurr Alasdair in the Isle of Skye. It looked fine on the western skyline from Base Camp but, instead of the fine gabbro of the Skye ridge, it was composed of rotting gneiss. Large pieces came away in our hands and from beneath our feet, and only Terry, Lhakpa and I, unwisely perhaps, completed the traverse. The summit was 4750m and on it we erected a tottering cairn, assuming I think with some justification, that a ridge so unpleasant would not have been visited before. We called it Sgurr Lhakpa: he said he did not mind.

On 9 November the bad weather turned to snow and it was time to leave. It was a very cold night, and face flannels froze inside the tents and so did water bottles. It would have been possible to reach Trisuli Bazaar in five days along the Tiru Danda and this had been our first plan. However by this time most of us had had enough of high altitudes and cold and were much attracted by an alternative proposal. This was to return via the Ankhu Khola, along the twisting and rarely visited valley to the west of the Tiru Danda. It took seven days to do this and to find a way back over the Tiru Danda to Trisuli Bazaar. The next day a chartered bus took us back to Kathmandu in four hours.

Near Kathmandu on a high ridge all the Ganesh peaks could be seen, Pabil, Lapsang Karbo, the Bat and Paldor too. Paldor was the smallest and the easiest but in such exalted company it was not disgraced: we were glad to have climbed it.

Across Tibet

Michael Ward
Plates 31–32

The Royal Society/Chinese Academy of Science Tibet Geotraverse, which crossed from Lhasa to Golmud in June and July 1985,[1] was the first large-scale, co-operative, scientific programme to be carried out in the central and northern part of the Tibetan plateau. Its purpose was to establish the geological events that are occurring as a result of the Indian plate moving northward and converging with the Asian plate forming the Himalaya and elevating the plateau of Tibet.

According to the very recently (1966-67) accepted Theory of Plate Tectonics, about 200 million years ago India, together with Australia, Antarctica and part of Madagascar were clustered around the South Pole. The combined European and Asian land mass was separated from this grouping by a sea — named Tethys after the greatest of the sea-deities and wife of Oceanus.

As the Indian plate moved north, the Tethys Sea contracted until finally a collision occurred about 40 to 50 million years ago between India and the southern part of the Eurasian land mass. As a result, it is thought that the earth's crust crumpled, throwing up the mountain ranges of the Himalaya and central Asia, the Tibetan plateau being formed by north–south shortening and vertical thickening. As the irresistible force of India's movement northward acts against the immovable mass of Asia (for the process is continuing at about between 2 to 3cm each year), earthquakes occur in the vicinity of the converging plates.

At present it is considered that the Kun Lun range is definitely part of the Eurasian plate whilst the Indian plate extends as far north as the suture line in which the Tsangpo and the Indus run.

The origin of the plateau in between is controversial, and by crossing from south to north it would be possible more fully to understand and date the geological events that have occurred. This is of fundamental importance in understanding how the earth works, particularly as the Tibetan plateau is the only part of the world where convergence is occurring between continental masses as opposed to an ocean and land mass as is the case on the W coast of North America.

In the last 20 years Chinese earth scientists have carried out a great deal of work in Tibet including the production of both a geological map and a topographical map (scale 1:100,000) in the course of multidisciplinary expeditions. Some of these have included mountaineering parties and Everest, Xixapangma and other peaks have been climbed. Each province and region of China has a Geological Survey Department — in the case of Xizang (Tibet) in Lhasa and for Qinghai in Xining.

For some years, Chinese co-operation with French geologists has been taking place in the southern part of the Tibetan plateau as far north as Amdo which is

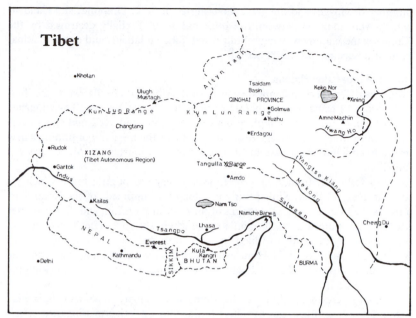

south of the Tangulla range — the boundary between the Autonomous Region of Tibet and the Chinese Province of Qinghai. So far Chinese geologists only have worked in Qinghai — the central and northern part of the Tibetan plateau and it was in this region that the main contribution of the combined Royal Society/Chinese Academy of Science party would take place. The Royal Society party consisted of geologists from Switzerland, America and Great Britain, and their specialities were matched in the Chinese group.

As far as the life sciences were concerned, by visiting and lecturing at the newly opened (Dec 1984) High Altitude Medical Research Institute at Xining, and by visiting the appropriate centres in Lhasa and Golmud, I would be able to fill in, at least partially, a very large gap — namely Chinese work carried out on the population that lived on the plateau.

Lhasa (*c.* 3650m)

The city is situated on a plain draining into the Kyi Chu, a tributary of the Tsangpo. It now has about 100,000 inhabitants and is dominated by the Potala, a unique building spreading over and seemingly growing out of a hill 120m high and 275m in length. It is the focus of the temporal and spiritual power of the Dalai Lama and externally was saved from the depredations of the Cultural Revolution. Many of the treasures inside were removed by the Chinese prior to this. The official residence of the Dalai Lama, at present in exile, it is, without him, a lifeless monument.

The main Buddhist temple in Lhasa is the Jokhang which is situated in the old town and is the centre of the purely religious life of Tibet. This also was looted and partially destroyed by the Chinese.

In the valleys of the surrounding hills (which rise to 4500-5000m) there are a number of villages and the great monasteries of Sera, Drepung, and Ganden, which were founded between AD 1409 and 1419. Partially destroyed by the Chinese, these are now being rebuilt using Tibetan labour, and open examination of novice monks has restarted.

Route Across the Plateau

The Jesuit Fathers Johannes Grüber and Albert d'Orville were the first Europeans to bring back authentic records of Tibet to Europe. Their journey from Peking to Lhasa took place between AD 1661 and 1662 and was undertaken not through missionary zeal but because of the necessity of finding a new route from China via Lhasa to Europe, as the sea journey by Macao was not possible.

They followed, from Xining to Lhasa, a very old pilgrim route which we used in reverse. From Xining this runs along the south side of the Koko Nor, crosses the numerous parallel ranges of the eastern Kun Lun and then traverses the Tibetan plateau to the Tangulla range where the route rises to 5000m and then gradually descends to Lhasa. After a short stay in Lhasa they continued south to Nepal crossing the Himalaya by the Thung La, and may have been the first Europeans to see Mount Everest. Eleven months after leaving Peking the party entered India.

It is an interesting fact that at this time China, Tibet, Nepal and India were open not only to European travellers but also to Christian missionaries. Their journey emphasised the connection between Peking and Lhasa rather than between Lhasa and India.

Nyenchen Tangla Range

This range runs between the Nam Tso or Tengri Nor and a wide flat valley north west of Lhasa. It forms one boundary of the Changtang — the very high, arid and sparsely populated plateau that occupies NW Tibet.

The two highest peaks are between 6700m and 7000m, and one appears to be at the NE part of the range. The other, a fine glaciated peak is in the SW section. Most of the other peaks were snow-covered in the bad weather of June and July which forbade good views being obtained. A number of the deeply incised valleys on the S side of the range were visited, as was the N side.

At Jangbajan, the wide valley on the SE side, there is a thermal station which supplies heat to Lhasa. A dirt road runs southwards crossing outlying spurs and then a pass, to descend to the Tsangpo valley and reach Shigatse.

The Tengri Nor on the NW side of the range is reached by a pass crossing the N part of the range. This is a beautiful salt lake ringed by vast pasture lands with immense herds of yak, sheep and goats. Small Tibetan encampments, usually tented, but some with mud buildings, are dotted about the green plain. The lake contains edible fish, and yellow poppies were found on the pass at about 4500m.

Tangulla Range

This forms the boundary between Qinghai, the province in which the N part of the Tibetan plateau lies, and Xizang (Tibet) to the south. The range runs east and west and contains numerous peaks around 5700-5800m. The highest peaks appear to be west of the Tangulla pass (c.5000m) with groups up to 6400m, whilst to the east a number of peaks about 6000m are found. The peaks are rounded with extensive snowfields and glaciers. The road across the pass climbs without zig-zags for many miles, and at its highest point is still a dirt road, though tarmac is being laid.

This pass is the highest point on the route between Xining and Lhasa and was probably that most used by travellers through the centuries, though there are a number of alternative routes crossing this range to east and west.

Some years ago a survey was carried out to pinpoint problems facing the construction of a railway between Golmud and Lhasa. The main one appears to have been permafrost.

In the course of this investigation it was pointed out to me by Dr Lu Tsung Chih of the Tibetan hospital in Golmud that in the Tangulla range Tibetans had worked continuously at altitudes of around 6000m for three to four months in summer for several years in succession, whilst living in tents at that height. They were probably mining high grade quartz crystals. They had not had to descend due to altitude sickness. By contrast South American miners working at Avconquilcha had found that working in the mine at 5800m brought on symptoms of mountain sickness. As a result a permanent village had been constructed at 5300m and not at the mine itself. Until now 5300m has always been considered the upper limit for permanent habitation even for those born and bred at altitude, but this figure will now have to be revised.[2]

On the northern side of the range hot springs are found.

East Kun Lun Range (Burhan Buddai)

The Kun Lun range runs for over 1600km delineating the N side of the Tibetan plateau in the same manner as the Himalaya delineates the S margin. The Kun Lun separates the plateau from the desert areas of the Tarim Basin (Takla Makan Desert) to the west and the Tsaidam to the east.

At its W extremity the Kun Lun abuts on to Pamir and is part of the melange of peaks through which the Karakoram Highway runs from Kashgar to the Indian sub-continent. The Kongur group of peaks are the highest in this region.

In the central Kun Lun, Ulugh Mustagh has been attempted unsuccessfully by a Chinese party. In the autumn of 1985 a Chinese-American party made the first ascent, with a team including Peter Molnar, Tom Hornbein and Bob Bates.

The E Kun Lun (Burhan Buddhai) has a striking feature. Part of it appears to be separated from the main Kun Lun by a gap several kilometres wide through which the Kun Lun Pass runs carrying the main road between Golmud and Lhasa. On the N side of this fragment is a flat valley, the Xidatan, 3-5km wide running east and west. In the floor of this valley runs a fault similar to the San Andreas fault in California which indicates that the Burhan Buddai range is moving eastwards at about 2 to 3cms each year, separating this part of the Kun Lun from the N part. In effect the N part of the plateau is being squeezed to the east, possibly due to the pressure exerted by India moving north.

Movements in the region of plate boundaries cause earthquakes. When two plates scrape along one another in opposite directions, as occurs in this instance, the rocks slowly bend and stress within, then builds up. Breaking point is reached and suddenly the rocks break and snap back to their new position. The focus of an earthquake is deep in the earth and movements occur in a series of jerks which produce waves going in all directions. The intensity of the shock depends on the size of the earthquake and is related to the total energy released. Measured on the Richter scale a reading of 8.6 is equivalent to 60,000 H-bombs.

The main peak of the Burhan Buddai, called Yu Zhu, is situated to the east of the Kun Lun Pass and is about 6400m.

Glaciers on the southern flank run on to the main plateau forming few if any glacial valleys, whilst those on the northern side carve out valleys, and the mountains themselves are much steeper. The peaks are not particularly steep, with rounded elevations, and having reached the main ridge it might be possible to ski along the rounded, broad crest.

On the N side of the valley, the mountains change dramatically — the peaks are jagged, but not glaciated, whilst the land becomes more arid. In some places rivers have sliced through both the surface sedimentary layer and the underlying rock, making narrow canyons 30m deep.

Further north the peaks become lower with snow lying only in the winter until finally they peter out altogether in the Tsaidam.

The road through the Kun Lun follows a series of east–west and north–south valleys; the gradient is always easy with no zig-zags, and it seems likely that this was the main centuries-old caravan route. An alternative more circuitous route through the mountains exists about 20km to the east of the main road and was followed from the plateau to the Tsaidam. This runs through a series of valleys to the north and south of the main east–west fault valley and is used by herdsmen with yak, camel, sheep, horses and goats. Small settlements of these semi-nomadic people are scattered up side valleys and, though narrower than the main route, lorries can follow this 'drovers' road. Skeletons of yaks and mountain sheep lying in the valleys have been picked clean by crows and give a surreal feel to the country. The herdsmen all carry rifles — however indiscriminate shooting is forbidden and numbers of kyiang, antelope and gazelle were seen.

Towards the Tsaidam the mountains become very arid with vegetation only in the beds of dried river courses. The peaks which rise to 5000m consist of rock and there are no glaciers — it is extremely hot during the day whilst temperatures fall precipitately at night.

The majority of the valleys on either side of the main highway were visited in the course of our stay in the Kun Lun, and the main 'fault' valley, the Xidatan, was traversed for much of its length. An attempt to distinguish a fossil series up the face of one rock peak failed after about 600m because of climbing difficulty. Artificial aids would have been necessary on a face that even here was remarkable for its friability and instability.

Koko Nor (3000m)
The Koko Nor, Tsinghai or Blue Lake is the largest expanse of fresh water in

China. The S side has grass-covered hills, with numerous herds of yak and sheep. By the lakeside are fields of corn and beehives. In summer, parties bathe though in the winter the lake is frozen over. At several points there are jetties with fishing vessels tied up — fish from the lake is a particular delicacy in the capital Xining. The N side has sand dunes extending to the water's edge. Several small islands serve as bird sanctuaries.

Xining, the capital of Qinghai, is a bustling town with a strong Moslem influence. The newly opened High-Altitude Medical Research Institute is situated in one of the two main hospitals and, with easy access to the Tibetan plateau, it is ideally placed. There is also a large hospital for traditional Tibetan medicine.

Kun Bun (Taer) monastery is south and west of Xining and was preserved during the Cultural Revolution by a direct order from the Federal Government. The present Dalai Lama's father worked in this monastery, which is an important centre of traditional Tibetan medicine.

Bibliography

Avedon J F; 1984. *In Exile From the Land of Snows* (Michael Joseph).

Chapman F S; 1938. *Lhasa. The Holy City* (Chatto & Windus).

Macgregor, John; 1970. *Tibet. A Chronicle of Exploration* (Routledge & Kegan Paul).

Mercier J L & Guangga L; 1984. *Mission Franco-Chinois au Tibet* (CNRS Paris).

Mathews B; 1954. *Limiting Factors at High Altitude* from a discussion on the physiology of man at high altitude (Proceedings of the Royal Society, B, Vol 143, pp1-42).

Pelliot P; 1924. *Huc and Gabet. Travels in Tartary, Thibet & China 1844-1848* (George Routledge & Sons Ltd).

Bishop, Sir George *et al.*; 1986. *Mountains of Central Asia* (Mount Everest Foundation & Royal Geographical Society).

1. Members of the Royal Society Party were: Prof R M Shackleton FRS, Leader, Prof J F Dewey FRS, Deputy Leader, Prof A Gansser, Prof P Molnar, Prof W Kidd, Prof M Coward, Dr A Smith, Dr J Pearce, Dr M Leeder, Dr N Harris, Dr D Watts, Dr M Ward.

2. A recent letter from Prof John West, leader of the American Medical Research expedition to Everest in 1981, tells of a Mr Copa who lives at almost 6000m (barometric pressure 373mm Hg). He has been there for two years and is one of the four caretakers of the mine at Avconquilcha. He spends six days of the week at the camp but comes down to a slightly lower altitude on Sundays to play football. Apparently there are no suitable pitches at 6000m.

The Lama and the Laser

Two Years in Bhutan

Nick Barrett

The tiny aeroplane began to twist and turn as it wound its way up the valley. A hamlet clung to the hillside and we banked so close to it that I felt I had only to reach out of the window to take a chilli from the rows that were drying on the roofs. A final bit of weaving and we landed at the little airstrip at Paro. I let out a sigh of relief. I had finally made it to Bhutan, my home for the next two years.

Bhutan is tucked away in the NE Himalaya. Chinese-occupied Tibet lies to the N and the Indian states of Assam and West Bengal to the S. It is roughly the same size as Switzerland and like that country has always sought to control its own destiny despite its large neighbours. Bhutanese history catalogues a seemingly endless succession of scuffles with Tibet and India, and no uninvited foreign cultures have been able to establish any influence within its borders. Bhutan, as recognizable today, was founded in the early 17th century as a theocratic state by a Tibetan monk called Shabdung Ngawang Namgyal. Since that time it has been bound together as a religious entity but it was not until the establishment of the hereditary monarchy in 1907 that the country became politically unified. Until then the different regions of the country were controlled by baronial figures known as Penlops, who cultivated a hearty dislike of one another and failed to agree on anything except when threatened from without. At such moments they would join forces, repel the invaders, then once more revert to squabbling amongst themselves. In due course the British Raj became irritated with some of the Penlops who were in the habit of marching down to the plains of British India and causing trouble for various beleaguered outposts on the North-East Frontier. A punitive expedition was contemplated, but discarded in favour of the idea of backing a single Penlop in an attempt to unify the country. The chosen Penlop might then be favourably disposed to the British and things could settle down peacefully.

In the event, one particular Penlop offered himself as a candidate for British sponsorship: Ugyen Wangchuk, the Tongsa Penlop, a shrewder politician than his rivals and an equally brave fighter. He gained favour with the British and accompanied Younghusband to Lhasa. The British perceived him to be reliable and clever, backed him, then sat back to see their man win through and defeat his rivals. In 1907 Ugyen Wangchuk was given a knighthood and, rather more importantly for him, became King of Bhutan. A treaty was concluded whereby Bhutan's internal policy should be her own affair, but foreign policy would be under the control of the British. In 1947, at Indian independence, the substance of this treaty was inherited by the new Indian government and it is still in operation today.

Following the establishment of the monarchy, Bhutan kept very much to itself. Cut off from the world by its mountains, it possessed sufficient spiritual and physical resources to sustain life, and unlike most other new nations, it never felt the need to proclaim its existence. But in the reign of the third King, Jigme Dorji Wangchuk, two things happened to force Bhutan out of its self-imposed isolation: Tibet was invaded by the Chinese and Sikkim was annexed by India. The rest of the world failed to react and since these events took place on Bhutan's back door-step King Jirme Dorji Wangchuk was forced to realize that in the 20th century there is no room for a country that wants to be left alone. In the 1960s Bhutan became a member of the UN and later of the non-aligned movement. The King turned to India for help with a development programme. Roads and schools were built, health, agriculture and forestry projects were initiated and tentative links with the outside world were established. By the time of his death in 1972 Jigme Dorji Wangchuk had justifiably earned the title of Father of modern Bhutan.

His son Jigme Singye Wangchuk (the world's youngest reigning monarch) is continuing the process begun by his father. There are Bhutanese embassies in Delhi, Dacca, Kathmandu and New York, and a trade mission in Kuwait. Bhutanese students have been sent abroad to study in places as far apart as Auckland and London, New Brunswick and Nairobi. With tact and courtesy Bhutan has tried to lessen its dependence on India, and today a number of non-governmental organizations from various western countries are involved in development activity. It was in this context that Voluntary Service Overseas were approached and asked to send a number of teachers. That was how I came to be climbing out of the country's only aeroplane at Paro.

Bhutan is beautiful. In the north the barren yak pastures lie beneath a spectacular array of unclimbed mountains. The Bhutanese sides of the larger mountains are steep and looked hard when I got up close to them. Kula Kangri, the biggest prize, has a W ridge that looks relatively straightforward but its principal challenge, the exquisite S ridge, would involve some very hard climbing. The largest mountains form the border with Tibet and there are considerable access problems, but there exist a host of shapely but lesser peaks that could be attempted from a sensibly located base camp.

This northern region is politically sensitive. The Chinese have built a road right up to the disputed NW border and the Indian Army maintains a heavy presence at all places where a crossing could be contemplated. The majority of the population lives in the central belt of the country in little villages scattered between a height of 1000 and 3000m. They pursue a wholly subsistence way of life. The valleys are arranged in a higgledy-piggledy fashion in a spectacular array of steep-sided hills dense with trees or jungle. These hills slowly subside into thickly jungled foothills and finally into a narrow belt of plain running along the southern border of the country. Bhutan is so small that a week of hard walking could see you moving from tiger infested foothills to the bleak yak and yeti territory of the freezing north. There are few roads. Those that exist tend to be of the twisting variety that allow one to drive for a couple of hours and end up but a short distance from one's starting point. Not surprisingly the poor communications network has encouraged the preservation of distinct ethnic groups. There are many mutually incomprehensible languages among tribes loosely bound together by centuries of common religious practice and custom.

The southern part of the country is inhabited by Nepalis who are not linked to the other Bhutanese by race or religion. The southern Bhutanese, as they are called, settled within the last 100 years and now comprise about 40% of the population. A trip to the south is like a journey to another country; suddenly climate, food, houses, people, language, religion, custom and dress are all different. One of the major preoccupations of the government is its national integration policy, and the outcome of this fledgling initiative might very well determine Bhutan's political stability over the coming years.

Shemgang Dzongkhag district, where I taught for two years, is situated more or less in the middle of the central zone and is reputed to be the most backward district of the 18 that comprise Bhutan. The Dzongkhag is mostly mountainous jungle, situated in the shadow of the Black Mountain range that divides western from eastern Bhutan. Shemgang village itself is a remote, small and very traditional dot on the landscape, situated on the shoulder of a 2400m mountain. The people were delightful and friendly with an impish sense of humour. At the slightest provocation they broke off from work for strenuous and exhausting celebrations. Many a late-night session drinking the local *ara* and dancing merrily in circles has taught me that there is a lot to be said for the Bhutanese approach to life. The people are handsome and the women especially beautiful in their colourfully patterned cloth. I remember particularly our *Tsechu*, a week-long religious festival when the lamas came out from the *dzong* or monastery-cum-fortress, and performed a series of religious dances for the enjoyment and education of the people. What a sight! Horns blowing and drums beating; lamas in saffron robes or colourful costumes; intricate and horrifying masks; amazing statues of Guru Rimpoche and Lord Buddha; much leaping and clashing of cymbals; the villagers dressed up in their best clothes, eating, drinking, watching and merry-making; perfect weather and beautiful views, and not a tourist in sight! This was by the people for the people.

The Bhutanese are deeply religious. Their faith is the cornerstone of their life in the villages. In particular they are guided by 'the law of *Dharma*' which at its simplest might be described as a creed that tells us 'to do as we would be done by'. Another guiding principle is *karma* or fate; it implies a very positive acceptance of whatever life happens to thrust in your direction. A short story illustrates this. Recently in E Bhutan the government opened a school for blind children, but it has had great difficulty in attracting pupils. This is not because of a shortage of blind people but rather that the parents of the children firmly believe that God has given them a special gift and responsibility and thus are loth to part with their handicapped children.

After two years, when I climbed back into the aeroplane at Paro (it was by this time one of two), my friend Tshering gripped me by the arm: 'Now you know a little about my country,' he said. 'If you are asked to write anything make sure you don't get carried away. We are a real people with real problems.'

For Bhutan, the Shangri-La image is a mixed blessing. On the one hand it enables the Bhutanese to charge tourists and climbers very highly for the privilege of entering the country. The former are herded around in buses and shown only a small part of the country, and only that part which the Bhutanese want them to see. Few manage to escape the tourist beat and then only at a price. Climbers are similarly constrained, and need very considerable finances; only well-funded expeditions need apply. The Director of Tourism was quoted to me as saying, 'for centuries our mountains have proved to be our safeguard and now they shall prove to be worth their weight in gold.' It looks as if it is going to be mainly Japanese gold.

The rationale of this policy seems to be to expose only a few Bhutanese to outside influences in order to obtain foreign exchange that can be used to improve the quality of life for the rest of the population. It is a policy which has left its mark on those people who have been so exposed. On a visit to the northern yak-herding settlement of Lunana I encountered more mercenary activity and sheer greed than I have ever experienced in Nepal or India.

But the Shangri-La image has created a phenomenal interest in the country which will not go away. Development agencies and the well-heeled from all over the world are tripping over themselves in the rush to be permitted entry to a country which is still remote, spectacularly beautiful, and where the people can be so charming. In the face of this interest the Royal Government has stood remarkably firm, but foreign influences are permeating through none-the-less. A short stay in the capital Thimphu would convince all but the least perceptive that many Bhutanese heads have already been turned. So many developing countries, when exposed to the West, tend to latch on to the worst aspects of our culture; so easily packaged and marketed, so corrosive of other cultures. His Majesty Jigme Singye Wangchuk has said that he wants his kingdom to be a place where gross national product is equal to gross national happiness, where his subjects can enjoy an improved standard of living but at the same time maintain their ancient customs and traditions; where they can develop, but not lose their souls. A country where a lama and a laser can co-exist in perfect harmony.

This is what makes Bhutan such a fascinating country. It has come late to the development process and has set itself the goal of picking out only the good from modern western society to blend with its own heritage in an attempt to produce the perfect society. In theory at least it should be possible to learn from the mistakes of others. And certainly, blessed with an obedient and respectful population the government is not under any internal pressure to speed the process along in a way that might result in irretrievable errors. That somewhere in the world a country is in a position to take our good and reject our bad is very exciting. That they should succeed would be wonderful. That they should fail might indicate something about the essential greed and corruptibility of mankind. It is impossible for the west to help without in some way destroying more than it creates.

When I left Bhutan I had the feeling that were I to return in ten years I would find either a country that was even more delightful than the one in which I had spent the last two years; or a people whose lives had been desolated. The balance is a fine one.

An October Trek in Bhutan
Over the Nyeri La to Lingshi

Edward Peck
Plates 33–36

When Alison my wife and I visited Gangtok in 1951 the Indian Political Officer of the day, the late Hareshwar Dayal, showed us a film of his official visit to Bhutan. This glimpse of the mediaeval Kingdom fired our imaginations and we cherished a long-term ambition that we might one day visit Paro and Thimphu and see the high Himalayan peaks on the Tibetan border. We read the sparse literature on Bhutan: Ludlow's and Sherriff's Diaries *A Quest of Flowers*, G. N. Mehra's *Bhutan*, Michael Ward's *In this short Span* and John Tyson's account in *AJ83*, pp183-190, but we saw little prospect of realising our ambition. Visitors to Bhutan seemed to be botanists or medical advisers invited personally by the King. Nonetheless the opening of Bhutan to tourism in 1978 gave us reason to think a trek might be possible; the growing popularity of Bhutan in the press and the approach of my 70th birthday convinced us that we must lose no time in making the effort.

We hoped to enlist some of the Alpine Club members with whom we had trekked round Annapurna in Oct/Nov. 1981 (*AJ87*, pp186-196) but only our good friends, Phil and Gill Weinberg were able to join us. Nevertheless, we made up a good and fit party of over 60's. We chose October as being the month with the best weather, but it was also the busiest time for the official Bhutan Tourism Organisation who, instead of accepting us as a private group, insisted on our booking through a travel agency. So it came about that our group of seven friends was augmented by a further seven recruited by Exodus Expeditions, under whose auspices we were to travel. The Bhutanese organisation is commendably efficient and they wisely restrict the number of tourists to avoid straining their limited physical and administrative resources. The Exodus members included a former Chief Conservator of Forests in Nepal, an enthusiastic professional dendrologist and the delightfully versatile veterinary surgeon who acted as medical adviser to the party, and was also an untiring amateur botanist, ornithologist and musician.

The Bhutan Tourism Organisation, following the tradition of hospitality to royal visitors, reckon to provide for their (paying) guests in all respects from the moment of their arrival in Bhutan (or even before, at Bagdogra) until departure. Accommodation, whether in the luxury hotels of Paro and Thimphu, or in tents or on a hard floor in the shelter at Lingshi, transport of baggage whether by bus, pony or yak, together with an emergency riding pony and the services of a Liaison Officer and camp staff are all included in the overall daily fee (which stood at $85-95 in 1985).

On 5 October 1985, the 14 of us, including David Burlinson of Exodus as our organiser, assembled at Heathrow for the long non-stop Thai Airways flight to

Delhi. We flew on from Delhi to Bagdogra where we were met by Tashi, the Bhutanese Liaison Officer who took charge of us throughout our stay and until our return to Bagdogra.

The hot drive through the thickly populated Indian Dooars was by a small bus, seating the 14 of us and taking 4 hours to Phuntsoling, just inside Bhutan, in the humid tropical hill forest. I quickly realised why the British Raj, after absorbing the flat parts of one-time Bhutan that are now the Indian Dooars, should have been daunted by the prospect of penetrating into these steep forested hills rising so abruptly from the plain. Had they attempted to do so, it would have been a long and difficult traverse of the hills before they reached the pleasant valleys at 1800-2500m where the main centres of Bhutanese population are situated. Even for ourselves in a comfortable bus, it took 8-9 hours to cover the 170km to Paro.

There followed a day of sightseeing in Paro; first the National Museum, housed in a fine round look-out tower above the imposing Para Dzong and displaying all aspects of Bhutan from snow leopard, by way of textiles and butterflies, to jewellery and a collection of ancient ceremonial vessels and an attractive array of modern postage stamps. Next we visited the Dzong itself, a fortress accommodating, as in mediaeval England, the civil administration and a monastery; and two small mediaeval *gompas* (monasteries) outside the town from one of which we were hurried out as the Abbot was about to receive the Queen Mother. The next day combined a training walk with a visit to the spectacular Taktseng shrine (Tiger's Nest) perched 1000m above the Paro valley on a vertically plunging cliff, where the Guru Rimpoche arrived in the 8th century on the back of a flying tiger. Although now included in the normal tourist round, the steep climb to 3100m and the vertiginous approach puts Taktseng beyond the reach of some. It is one of the extraordinary and unforgettable sights of the East. The collection of prayer flags on tall poles on the ridge 300m below the shrine, the weird moss forest, the mist swirling round the cliff-top and the narrow ledge by which the path crosses the waterfall to reach Taktseng, set the scene. One is deeply moved by the devotion of these mountaineering monks who over the centuries established this group of buildings on the cliff, including a tiny meditation cell clinging to the rock and reached by ladder. One must hope that Taktseng will preserve its remoteness and air of mystery and not suffer the fate of the Meteora monasteries in Greece.

On 10 October we were all set for the start of the trek to the E foot of Chomolhari three days and some 70km distant. We had a headstart by bus for the first 16km to the road-head at Drugyel Dzong, where the Bhutanese beat back the Tibetans in 1647. Burnt out in 1951, the Dzong reminded us of a 17th century Scots castle. Here we met our camp master, the good humoured and indefatigable Nam Gye, our cook and the two quiet well mannered boys who were to be with us throughout. Since Bhutan is so sparsely populated, there is no transport by porters, luggage being carried on ponies in the lower stages, changing about 3500-4000m to yaks, who do not take to the heat at any lower levels. The weather turned drizzly for our first 15km walk up through the rice fields and pastures of the Paro valley, to camp on a terrace at Shana, just beyond the army camp at Guni Chava. Here, at last, at 2800m we felt we were really approaching the Himalaya; the Paro Chu narrowed to a deep gorge, reminiscent of the Marsyangdi gorge in Nepal, but differing in the density of the untouched forest (which especially excited the admiration of the two professional foresters in our party) and the virtual absence of inhabitants. Indeed for the 27km from Shana to Seo there was but one single habitation and virtually no spot for a comfortable campsite for a group of any size. The sound of the rushing Paro Chu was continually in our ears. We had been warned that bears might be on the prowl in the thicker parts of the forest and as in Canada, were advised to go in pairs making a noise to scare them off. Just as Michael Ward described it in 1964, the track 'wriggled round trees, climbed cliffs and plunged into little side gorges. Roots, tree trunks, stones, boulders and bog made up its surface. It was never flat for more than a few yards.' The only point at which it seemed to show improvement was when a well-cobbled path led steeply up to the left (west) but we were strictly instructed not to follow that, for it led to Phari Dzong in Tibet, little more than 15km away over the Tremo La. Our track continued as before along the floor of the gorge, and shortly after crossing the first of the two bridges at Seyende Zam, but leaving the second on our right, we reached the camp site at Seo, 3660m.

We were now near the upper limit of the forest. Yaks were to be seen grazing in the brown autumn pastures, which were dotted with several varieties of autumn-flowering gentian. 12 October was an easier day, with a lunch stop at the hamlet of Jemphe — two houses and a crone dispensing illicit chang at 3 *ngultren* a can. This was followed (fortunately) by what John Tyson called a gentle afternoon stroll across the yak pastures, past a second 'thang', equivalent to a Swiss 'alp' or Austrian 'alm', identified as Dodebethang. This led us to the ruined Dzong standing boldly on its rock at the entrance to the short side glen leading to the moraine at the foot of the ESE face of Chomolhari (7315m). Bhutan's sacred mountain, virtually the only Bhutanese mountain known to the outside world, was first climbed from Phari in Tibet in 1937 by Spencer Chapman and Sherpa Pasang in the course of the Gould expedition to Lhasa. Although refraining from treading the sacred summit, the Indo-Bhutanese Army expedition of 1972 lost three of their members. Since then the Bhutanese Government have declared Chomolhari out of bounds to climbers. Mists veiled the face in the evening, but in the early morning the vast face glowed in the sun which moved rapidly down to raise the temperature at camp from below freezing to a more than comfortable heat in less than half an hour. The upper part — a dome split by yawning bergschrunds and seamed with avalanches — could provide a dangerous but technically not too arduous route to the summit, but the lower reaches, vertical cliffs alternating with hanging glaciers, looked forbidding indeed.

We were to spend a second night in this delightful spot at 4040m. Some of us went high on a spur overlooking the cwm between Chomolhari and its neighbour to the ENE, a long black bristling ridge, called Tseringmekhang, Tserimgang, or Gyu Kang (6532m). Others of us wandered a brief way up past Jangothang, the third and biggest hamlet (at least 4 houses) in the valley, to find revealed in all its splendour the glittering spire of Jitchu Drake (6793m), its S face rising 2600m above the moraine blocking the head of the valley. We

8 Chomolhari E face.

Photo: Alison Peck

35 *Jichu Drake S face.*

26. *Kangchehzi seen from the air*

picnicked among blue and mauve gentian, berberis in their flaming autumn colours and rocks draped with the red berries of cotoneaster as diaphanous wreaths of mist drifted about the fluted face and fearsomely corniched ridges of Jitchu Drake. Two Italians were killed on the S ridge in 1982 and it was climbed by the Japanese in 1984.

As John Tyson reported in 1978 it is difficult to disentangle the mountain names in this area. There can be no doubt about the great bulk of Chomolhari, though there is a lesser summit Chomolhari II somewhere about, possibly not visible from the E side. The range running NE from Chomolhari comprises three major summits which our Liaison Officer identified to us as Tsering-mekhang (but it has the alternative names given above), Jitchu Drake (also Jichu Dak Keth, Tseringegang, or Chumkang), and Kungphu (6526m), the conical peak due E of Lingshi, which also seems to be known as Takaphu (its NE face, curiously similar to the NE face of Jitchu Drake, is shown in Tyson's illustration 74, *AJ83*, p187). To confuse matters further, some writers transpose Kungphu and Takaphu, and Tseringkhang and Chumkhang. Further east the confusion and lack of names is even greater, showing how little the region has been visited by people interested in climbing the high mountains. The list given by Capt Kohli in his article in *AJ90*, p20 is a brave attempt to rationalise them but the alternative names in his list highlight the confusion. From the Lingshi area we had a distant glimpse of the peaks towards Lunana, but the one that stood out, probably at the headwaters of the Mo Chu, was a formidable mountain mass like a huge molar tooth crowned by several summits with a jagged isolated fang at its N end. This we judged to be Kangcheda (7000m) otherwise known as Kangchita, Gangkhen Tag, or even Jakiengephu!

But I anticipate, as we had to cross the Nyeri La before seeing the NE face of Jitchu Drake and catching our first glimpse of Kungphu and other peaks to the north. On 14 October, on another cloudless morning, we set out to cross this 4840m pass to Lingshi. Across the stream, the highest reach of the Paro Chu, at Jangothang, two obvious tracks zigzag up the E slope. It is tempting to cross the first bridge only to find oneself embarked on a track leading to two narrow lakes in a high valley looking back over to Chomolhari; there are some minor peaks to be scrambled up here. For the Nyeri La it is important to continue past the uppermost house of Jangothang to cross the second bridge, closer to Jitchu Drake, and take a well-trodden zigzag track up the far side of a steep ravine where a broad burn tumbles down from the upper yak pastures. After a steep pull-up of some 350m the route flattens out and it was sheer delight to wander through gentian-studded pastures, glancing back at the full span of the frontier ridge of Chomolhari, Tseringmekhang and Jitchu Drake. Hereabouts, we sighted large herds of shy *bharal* (or blue sheep) through binoculars. After speculating whether the Nyeri La was at the head of one of the broad side-valleys we found that the track twisted sharply upward to the left, wound round some scree and climbed steeply up to the summit prayer flags, invisible until close below them. The track we had followed was well-trodden, but it could be a problem in mist and snow to select the right pass from the south. Crossing north to south would present less of a route-finding problem, since the steep N side follows a narrow valley, albeit subject to avalanches.

From the top of the Nyeri La, a magnificent panorama opened up. To the NW the symmetrical cone of Kungphu towered over an intervening scree ridge, though Jitchu Drake remained hidden. Stretching away to the NE towards Laya and Lunana, was a succession of high, virtually unknown and certainly unclimbed peaks of which the formidable Kangcheda was one. Below us a deep valley led to Lingshi, with a pass opening towards Tibet to the NW, and to the E a series of passes which Ward in 1964 and Tyson in 1978 had followed from and to Laya. As we descended a short distance to lunch out of the wind, afternoon cloud began to obscure some of this splendid view. Over lunch we again saw herds of *bharal* grazing on steep scree slopes, but perhaps they were only snuffling out mineral salts. The rest of the descent to Lingshi is a pleasant walk, first steeply down to the stream crossing, where an older track led direct to the cluster of unremarkable buildings that characterise an army camp and signal station in most of the world. (We were later to be grateful for the existence of that station in this remote spot.) We followed a newly cut track on the level through varieties of gentian and profusions of rhododendron and spiraea. From the ridge at the end of this stretch, we looked steeply down on our blue tents already set up and saw beyond, on its hog-back ridge, the beautifully situated white square of the Lingshi Dzong illuminated by a shaft of sunlight. The tents were pitched on open level ground beside a rather draughty round house shelter with a central fireplace which we later came to know only too well.

Our plan was to spend two consecutive nights at this camp, move up the next day to the foot of the Yale La, 5000m, thus easing the crossing of the pass, and then follow the Thim Chu downwards for three days to Thimphu. This plan was fine for the first day — another lovely clear day. Some rested in camp; the more energetic climbed a high bump early in the day to catch an unclouded glimpse of Kangcheda and the Lunana peaks. I had my eye on an alp close under Kungphu, which led to what was to prove a delightful ablation valley — a grassy hollow squeezed between the cliffs of Kungphu and the crest of the moraine crumbling away into the lower section of the big glacier coming down between Jitchu Drake and Kungphu. I judged this would provide excellent close-up views of the fluted NE face of Jitchu Drake as well as an abundance of flowers. What I had not reckoned with was that the alp would turn out to be a couple of well-built stone chalets, their shingle roofs held down by large stones, which, had it not been for the prayer flags up the slope behind, might have been the subject of any print of 18th century Switzerland. The sole inhabitants were a courteous Bhutanese grandfather, suffering badly from eye trouble, and his small grandson. Calling off his mastiff, he waved me through as if Europeans were a daily occurrence. The next surprise, as I followed a track into the ablation valley, was to find a *chorten* on the edge of the moraine (difficult and dangerous to go round this one clockwise!) and a small *gompa* closely pressed against the cliff above. After this I found myself walking ankle-deep in edelweiss on a level meadow between the cliffs and the moraine, following the ablation trough onwards and upwards, and watching the seracs thunder down from the upper hanging glacier. I was amazed to see the narrow band of pasture winding on upwards past the big icefall. It put me in mind of Alpine tales of the 'forgotten alp' — pastures cut off by advancing ice. I had no time to follow it to the very end but it might provide access to the big cwm behind Kungphu. Our friend the vet, who had independently followed my suggestion of exploring this enchanted valley, was delighted with his day, seeing plants in bloom and collecting them in seed, being dive-bombed by a *lämmergeier*, sighting a flight of *grandala*, the blue Himalayan rock thrush and best of all, surprising a *bharal* a few yards away. We wandered contentedly back to camp, through a herd of peacefully grazing yaks, some immersed in a shallow pond for all the world like Ayrshire cattle. We felt ready for the approach march to the Yale La the following day.

But one of those sudden changes in Himalayan weather caught us by surprise as it did a number of better prepared expeditions that October throughout the Himalaya. In drizzle and low mist portending snow we started up the track, past the conspicuous *chorten* marking this approach to Lingshi, past a flattened area marked with stones spelling out 'Heli' and then southwards up the steep-sided upper valley of the S branch of the Mo Chu. A fair track wound in and out of the lateral burns and with the yellow-brown vegetation below, the scene closely resembled a roadless Scottish glen with the mist hanging close overhead. Sleet turning to snow decided us to camp on the valley floor rather than climb to the two lakes, from which we had hoped to make a short hop over the Yale La. Snow fell throughout the night and indeed for the next 36 hours; the men were up beating the snow off the tents, and two tents collapsed. Next morning (17 October) despite continuing snow, we decided to try to cross the pass that day, since there was no other way out, save the equally high Nyeri La, or the series of high passes eastwards to Laya. So, after waiting while the skittish yaks were loaded, we set off, first having to be ferried across the stream, flowing cold and fast, by the two so-called riding ponies, led by a solemn little boy of only twelve. The stalwart Nam went ahead to find the way in the expectation that the yaks would take over higher up and beat out a good track. When the yaks caught up, they had different ideas and, despite two efforts to head them back uphill, they (or the yak men) decided that they were not having any more. They spread out in a muddled herd, useless for track beating, and in the white-out the Yale La might have been anywhere over an arc of 120°. Even Nam returned exhausted saying the snow was over 1m deep.

So there was nothing for it but to retreat, not just to our camp of the previous night, but back to the round-house shelter at Lingshi. This decision was taken too late in the day, for the long march back took twice as long in the deep snow. Paddling through the shallow snow-covered lake beside which we had expected to camp, regardless of stream crossings in an interminable trek, it was after dark before we all arrived at Lingshi where we assembled round a fire fed by dry roof planks from the latrines! We spent the next grey and snowy day drying out. The friendly and efficient Deputy District Commissioner (*Dungpa*) Tsawang Rinzen came to inspect his unexpected foreign visitors some of whom were in poor condition. He considered that the Army might not be able to collect their supplies for up to 15 days. Our own food supplies were short, being geared only to a three to four day trek to Thimphu and thus were inadequate to stand a prolonged delay. So we decided to ask for rescue by helicopter through the Bhutanese Army radio station over the hill. Tashi made his way up the 300m of steep drifting snow to send messages to Thimphu. On return he said that he had virtually to 'swim' through the deep snow — skis would have been useful but seem to be unknown to the Bhutanese. Over the next two days messages, painfully transmitted in morse or by crackling voice, were relayed up and down his trail.

Fortunately, after three days there was another abrupt change back to hot sunny days. We were able to complete the drying out process and to make minor excursions. Slots of musk-deer were seen in the snow, as well as the unmistakable pug-marks of the elusive snow-leopard. We had solicitous visits from the business-like *Dungpa*, accompanied by his spiritual adviser, an owlish-looking monk who simply observed but did nothing. The *Dungpa* offered to lend us some of his exiguous stores and promised to replace the burnt latrine roof planks. Another visitor was the local Veterinary Compounder, English spoken after training in India, wearing a yak hair eyemask against snowblindness. I overheard our own vet giving advice (and development aid in the shape of a syringe and a bottle of dope) for a less painful method of castrating yaks.

Sunday, 20 October was another fine day and an Indian Air Force helicopter, an Alouette, flew in almost on the level to take us out. At 4100m this was almost at the limit of its altitude capacity, and it could only take two passengers at a time (three when the fuel load was reduced). Though the flight to Thimphu or Paro took some 40 minutes, the round trip was never less than 2½ hours so that only 3 flights were possible in daylight. Seven of us, the 4 ladies and the 3 older men, went out on the first day and the remainder followed next day. The Indian Air Force pilots did a superb job and evidently enjoyed the experience of operating in the high mountains. The flight was unforgettable. The helicopter gained what little height it could by flying some distance up the valley towards the Yale La, giving us a glimpse of the slopes deep in snow where we had retreated. Circling back we had stupendous views back to Kungphu and Jitchu Drake, while the ominous bulk of Kangcheda with its accompanying ugly fang filled the horizon at the head of the Mo Chu. Below us, the impenetrable forest, with roaring torrents and steep gorges confirmed how impossible it would have been to escape from Lingshi by the classic device of following the water downstream. Past Punakha, we flew low over the Dochu La and its twisting road and down to the helipad at Thimphu, at much the same time as if we had adhered to our trekking schedule.

A modest trek for the elderly one might say, given that the trek itself was cut short by the weather and we only crossed one 4850m pass on our feet. But we shall all remember our visit to Bhutan and how its courteous and independent mountain people welcomed us. Besides that, we were near the border with Tibet in remote, scarcely explored Bhutan Himalaya. In this troubled 20th century it is consoling to hope that the wise ruler of this beautiful country may succeed in preserving its forests, its traditions and its peace.

Sherpas and Skis

John A. Jackson

S-s-h-h-h — the soft sibilant sound of running skis and a swish-h-h- of snow spraying sideways on a smooth turn as white glistening crystals and flat glinting naphthalene-like plates of snow lost their pure smooth virginity in the early morning. A crisp cold wind freezes tissues, chills the cheekbones, nips the ear lobes and eyes water as air whips at the lids and loose surrounding skin. The heart beats strongly as blood courses through the body feeding oxygen to muscles and tendons now working smoothly, absorbing shocks, turning tips, releasing heels and biting edges. Nerve endings at feet, ankles, knees and eyes transmit messages to the brain at high speed, then back again to produce the perfect co-ordination of mind and muscle that is the essence of efficient downhill skiing in mountains. The slope steepens, sharpened metal crunches and bites into hard ice — a rock protrudes, edges release, and a swift side-slip avoids the danger as the skier speeds on at thirty to forty miles per hour. At last the angle eases, there is a chance to look up and see the hills, as legs, still working smoothly, continue to transmit their important messages to skis and brain.

This is how skiing is anywhere and it was skiing also for my wife Eileen and me on the virgin snows of the Chola Khola glacier in the Khumbu Himalaya. With Sirdar Dawa Tenzing, Lakpa Thondup and Ang Norbu we had set up our glacier ski camp at approximately 5500m on the glacier. From that camp for the next few days we extended the experience of our sherpas on ski, but our first full day was the best. We were up and away from ski camp early, reaching the Chug-yuma La just after dawn. The sun soon warmed us but at first the snow was crisp and as Eileen and I had a first run, we experienced those thrilling nuances of skiing that I have tried to describe. At the pass we looked down into the Nimagawa and across to mountains dividing the Ngojumba or Upper Dudh Kosi from the Bhote Kosi. In the clear morning air Kariolung, Numbur and other peaks of the Rolwaling seemed but a stone's throw away and over in the NW, Gaurisanka, and Menlungtse dominated among the serration of peaks etching the azure blue sky at the Tibetan border. Condensation snow crystals sparkled and glistened on the surface of the glacier around us as spreading webs of light dispersed by ice and snow on the high ridges expanded into our domain. Above and beyond the ridges and peaks that flanked the northern side of the valley plumes of ice particles curtained southwards from the summits of Everest, Nuptse and Lhotse. Amongst those majestic timeless hills it was not just the keen cold morning air that took our breath away.

Sherpas learn quickly from visual example which is essential teaching practice for skiing. Some verbal instructions, minimal and to the point were needed and this we managed with a mixture of basic English and a few words of Tibetan — the Sherpa language. Yawa (meaning right) Yumba (meaning left) were in constant use and a source of amusement to Eileen as she watched me make turn after turn over the snow closely followed by Lakpa or Norbu. As our figures dwindled in size and went almost out of sight across the glacier the sounds of yawa — yumba — yawa — yumba, constant as a metronome, floated back to her. Soon the snow softened, slowing the skis a little which was good for Lakpa and Norbu. For several hours they ski'd, making rapid progress with basic swings and wide stance basic parallels. Then soon, with real assurance, they ski'd away for a mile or more across the glacier until almost out of sight.

This was also the day that our old friend Dawa Tenzing, proud that sherpas were learning to ski, came up to watch — but not for long. Eventually he could not resist the temptation and asked if he could have a try, and he did! He sat down unintentionally a few times but persevered for an hour or more and was then content to let Lakpa use the skis again. Good old Dawa. We had to take off our hats to a man who at 74 years of age had just taken his first ski lesson at almost 5600m! He was well satisfied with his efforts and was content not to try again either in the Chola Khola or later in the Ngojumba. Always he would say 'I want the young sherpas to learn to ski,' and it was clear that he was looking ahead to the future of his people.

Lakpa Thondup, with his strong social conscience developed whilst a scholar at Hillary's Khumjung school, often enthused saying 'This is a good thing for sherpa society. I must show our children how to ski when the snow comes to Khumjung in November.' With his words in mind, we hoped we could leave skis and sticks with Lakpa when we left Sola Khumbu, and this we did.

Postscript

In 1976 we taught our sherpas to ski when we travelled in Khumbu for six and a half weeks. Lakpa Thondup is the son of Changup who carried to Camp V with Tom McKinnon and me on Kangchenjunga in 1955. That same year, Ang Norbu was our youngest sherpa on the mountain and carried to Camp VI at 8200m. Dawa Tenzing of course was our Sirdar in 1955 and 21 years later in 1976 we were delighted to pay him as Sirdar again, though in fact he came along with us on our Khumbu travels as a very dear friend. I am sure that at the age of 74 it was his last six weeks as a Sirdar in the mountains and I know he was immensely pleased. For us, and the younger sherpas, it was a privilege to have him with us. Amongst the many highlights of that time in Khumbu, I am sure that Dawa would mostly remember us taking greetings and 'chang' to Tony Streather's 'Soldiers' at their Everest Base Camp, the audience he arranged for us with the Incarnate Lama of Thyangboche (Dawa was a very religious man), our meeting with Gunther Sturm following an ascent of Goumouktse, and of course his experience with the sherpas on skis above the Chug-yuma La on the Chola Khola glacier.

A Winter Journey Through Eastern Nepal

Ian Haig
Plates 37–40

The twin Otter 'plane slipped over the last intervening ridge and began its descent to Lukla in the Dudh Kosi valley. The ground now seemed to be rushing up towards the plane as it rapidly lost height. Moments later, with the engines roaring, the plane hit the hard dirt runway with a terrific bump and came to a stop in 50m. Anu, the sirdar, and his team of Sherpas, who were to support me for the next five weeks of trekking and climbing through Eastern Nepal were there to meet me. I quickly located him and was soon introduced to Ang Nyima the second Sherpa, and Ang Pema, the cook.

I had travelled on my own with local men before, in Ladakh, and had found the experience much to my liking, so I had resolved to make a similar journey through Eastern Nepal. I had been told that the winter months in Nepal were the best, so here I was in Khumbu towards the end of November. The plan was quite vague to begin with; first, spend a little time in the Khumbu villages acclimatising, then go up the Bhot Kosi valley to the Tashi Lapcha to try the peak called Pharchamo, return to Khumbu; then cross into Hongu over the Mingbo La, march around to the Mera La, try Mera, back to Lukla and finally take the Tilman route from Lukla to Tumlingtar across Nepal. It all sounded very simple and it had the merit that, for the most part, it took me off the heavily frequented Everest Base Camp trek route.

On arrival at Anu's house in Khumjung, Pasang Phutar, Anu's wife, who was a leading Khumjung citizen and a member of the local *Panchayat* (Council), made me most welcome. Their two little boys Mingma Nurbu and Pemba Gyaltzen and their little girl, Mingma, just could not get over my being about the house. I was soon sitting by the fire in the upstairs room, cradling some hot chang to warm myself against the chill of the late November evening.

After a brief stay, we set off in brilliant cold sunlight from Khumjung for Tengboche. The smoke from the cooking fires of the Sherpa township formed a blue cloud in the still air. Cows and yaks with their tingling bells were being driven by small boys up the slopes of Khumbui Yal Lha above the village to graze on what they could find on the sparse hillside. Crows floated around uttering their harsh cries keeping watch for any scraps that might be thrown out. We stopped briefly at the Shrine in the centre of Khumjung for Anu to pray and for him to show me the Yeti scalp that is kept in a box there. This was the scalp taken around the world by a special Sherpa representative described by Desmond Doig in *High in the Thin Cold Air*.[1]

We had come to Tengboche Monastery or Gompa for Mane Rimdu, which is the major Sherpa festival in Khumbu; so had hundreds of others! In fact, the green meadows were a veritable forest of tents, trekkers, Sherpas and traders.

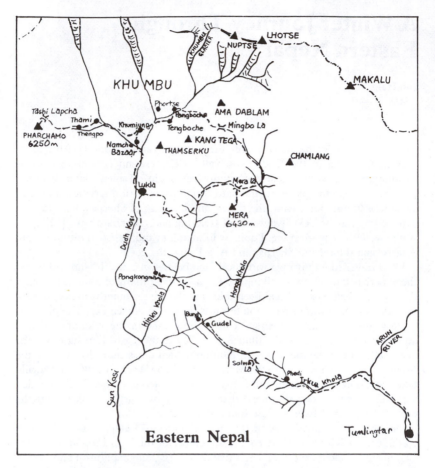

Eastern Nepal

The Gompa Hotel/Lodge did a roaring trade, selling, according to Anu, the most expensive chang he had ever come across. Still three glasses of chang at 3 rupees each compared rather well with a bottle of beer at 50 rupees. The Lamas certainly had an eye to turning the festival to good account. Mane Rimdu is a splendid mixture of religious fervour, dancing, drinking and merry-making and large numbers of Sherpas come from throughout Khumbu to join in the fun. The processions, prayers and wonderfully graceful dancing of the Lamas, magnificent in their brilliant silk costumes, are quite unforgettable. None of us had much sleep due to the incessant noise from crowds of friends merry-making all night and the intermittent groaning and parping of the huge alpenhorn-like trumpets of the Monastery.

After the partying, we headed for the more serious stuff up the Bhot Kosi to Thame on our way to the Tashi Lapcha and Pharchamo. But once again we had some calls to make. As Anu quaintly put it, we were to visit his wife's two fathers! One lived at Thame, the other at Thengpo. Naturally, I was intrigued by this interesting state of affairs. All was soon explained, the mother of Pasang

37   *The Drolambao glacier seen from Tashi Lapcha.*

Photo: Ian Haig

38 Mera (L) and Hinku (L centre) seen from the Zatra la path.

39   Ama Dablam seen through the Mingbo la from the ruined hut in the upper Hongu.

Photo: Ian Haig

40   The Rolwaling Himal seen from the Zatra la

Phutar, Anu's wife, had married two brothers. It was in fact a polyandrous marriage which, I learnt, was not very common in Khumbu these days. Both fathers were very prosperous, dignified elderly men who owned large numbers of yaks. Pasang Phutar's mother was a very hospitable and kindly woman who provided us with some really excellent chang when we called at her house.

That evening, three Tibetans from Tingri came in to talk and trade with Gyaltzen, Anu's brother-in-law. They had come over the Nangpa La, the traditional route between Tibet and Khumbu. The men were noticeably different in height and dress from the Sherpas. They were taller, somewhat dishevelled and dressed in strongly smelling sheepskins. Each man wore a necklace of semi-precious stones which the Sherpas tried to buy from them. They had brought rock salt which they showed me, to trade for food and other supplies. The next morning they were gone.

We made a leisurely start, our idea being to take it easy to Thengpo, only two hours away, and have lunch with the second father. He, too, was most hospitable. Our afternoon walk along heathery hillsides up the deep trench of the Tashi Lapcha valley, gave delightful views back to the Khumbu peaks and the Mingbo La over which I hoped to cross into Hongu a week later.

An undemanding stage brought us to a snow bowl where we camped just about 300m from the top of the pass and clear of stonefall from Tengi Ragi Tau. I spent a wretched night, not getting more than a couple of hours sleep before I was called at 4.30am. We were away by first light and as I had had little to eat I made sure that my pockets were crammed with Kendal mint cake.

We were soon on the easy ledges that led up on to the névé and there, seemingly very close, was the blue Vee in the sky of the Tashi Lapcha. The sun was now up and its warmth began to revive me so that I pressed forward more strongly towards the pass. There, we were met by an icy blast from the west wind. We put on everything we had, I crammed mint cake into my mouth and we turned towards the icy ridge of Pharchamo.

The ridge steepened so we roped up and started kicking steps. The conditions were superb, the front points of the crampons bit beautifully into the 50° ice slope. On the right far below, the Drolambao glacier stretched up into the heart of the Rolwaling Himal, with cold icy peaks standing sentinel on either side. On the left was our camp on the glacier and there, far beyond, all the mighty peaks of Eastern Khumbu. I went at the slope now with a will, exhilarated by my fine position, panting furiously after every 20 steps. The angle eased and we now found ourselves at a bergschrund, above which the ridge steepened again. It was a long awkward step up, which required a strong pull up on the ice axe, not the easiest thing to do at nearly 6000m. Another ice slope followed, also in superb condition. All this time, I was steadily munching my way through my Kendal mint cake to power me up the mountain. But my drive was now fading and I suggested that we stop for lunch. Unfortunately when the food was unpacked I discovered that Ang Pema had put in no potatoes, cheese or dried fruit for me but only food for the Sherpas. So swallowing my annoyance I nibbled some of the Sherpas' food and concentrated on filming the stupendous views of the Rolwaling and Khumbu Himalaya. I was beginning to feel fairly exhausted, after such a bad night and lack of acclimatisation. I estimated we were some 100m from the top, but that the ridge went on for some way yet. So, reluctantly, I decided to return.

The descent of the ice slopes went well and I did the long jump across the bergschrund without tumbling over down the ridge. When we reached the col, it was a pleasure to get out of the roaring wind into the relative calm of the lee of the mountain. On reaching camp Ang Pema produced a tin of mixed fruit half of which I gobbled down much too quickly and was promptly sick. Later by degrees I began to recover my strength through drinking a large quantity of sweet milky tea. The Sherpas were now anxious to be off. We decided to aim for Thengpo which we reached just before nightfall. We had been going with only two half-hour breaks for 14 hours.

Having said our good-byes in Thengpo the next day to Anu's second father-in-law and his little girl we set off down to Thame at a cracking pace. At the monastery just above Thame, we met Dr Gil Roberts, who had been on the successful 1963 American Everest West Ridge Expedition. After hearing where we had been, he told me of epic crossings he had made of the Tashi Lapcha.

Our journey back to Khumjung was enlivened by meeting quite a number of Sherpas staggering back to Thame in a cheerful mood having imbibed chang and rakshi rather generously at the Saturday market in Namche Bazaar.

After a rest in Khumjung, we set out for the Hongu valley. We crossed the Imja Khola and began the long trudge up the hillside to Llabarma. Pumori could now be seen, perfectly framed at the head of the valley running up to Everest. Anu told me it was one of the most beautiful peaks in the Himalaya, with which I concurred, and how much he wanted to climb it. He suggested that I should organise an expedition to it with himself as Sirdar, so he could climb it. I, of course, agreed! I later checked up on its availability and found that many others agreed with him on its attractiveness. It was booked for years ahead. I also learnt from Anu how much he wanted to climb Everest. He had been six times without oxygen to camps above the South Col and had lost count of how many times he had been to the Col itself. He could describe in minute detail the ordinary route up the mountain, excepting the icefall which changed all the time. I hoped, for his sake, that he would find an expedition that would give him the chance to fulfil his heart's desire.

We made camp at the end of the level grassy area above Mingbo, used by Hillary as an airstrip to supply his expedition in 1960-61. It was a delightful place with a fine prospect in the evening light of Taboche and Gyachung Kang. I fell asleep that night to the haunting songs of the Sherpas and Sherpanis sitting round the fire.

Despite the bitter cold we were off early. As always the view on the left was of Ama Dablam, brooding heavily over us. Anu pointed out two of the tents of a Korean expedition who were climbing the mountain by the ordinary route. Not surprisingly, he had a great deal of respect for Ama Dablam. As we rounded a corner, we caught sight of the Mingbo La, which we intended to cross on the morrow. It still looked a long way. We eventually reached the site of Hillary's green hut in the late afternoon after a lengthy tramp up the moraine. The cold mists came up again in the evening and blotted out the scene so I was glad to turn in soon after supper.

We made another very early start as we intended to cross the Mingbo La and the glacier in Hongu. The unnamed peaks at the head of this valley are an awesome sight of steep glittering fluted ice, and are mostly unclimbed. Very soon after starting, we entered a small icefall so our route looped backwards and forwards to avoid the crevasses. The snow conditions were excellent so the Sherpanis and Sherpas in their basketball boots negotiated the glacier with ease. Anu and Ang Nyima rushed ahead to set up the fixed ropes while Ang Pema and I brought up the rear. By the time I reached the bottom of the ice flutings, half the party were already up and the Sherpanis, climbing unroped, were doing splendidly in the steps cut for them by Anu. Much to my delight, I was able to record their feat on my cine, to the accompaniment of whistles and shouts from those at the top. At 5800m the Mingbo La gave superb views across the Hongu basin to Chamlang and Baruntse in the east and to the Rolwaling Himal in the west. There was a great deal of discussion amongst the Sherpas over the views as most of them had never been into Hongu. After half an hour on the pass, I took my last lingering look at Khumbu and trudged off down the glacier. It was now late afternoon and, in the lengthening shadows, the cold was bitter. I reached camp at about 4.30pm very cold and exhausted but very satisfied by our successful crossing of the pass.

The upper Hongu is a wild, desolate place with Lhotse and Everest looming at its head and Chamlang and unnamed peaks on opposite sides forming the Hongu into a deep trench. It can only be entered over very high passes and is not a place to fall ill, as evacuation would be difficult. As winter was now beginning all the lakes we passed on our long walk down the valley were frozen, so we amused ourselves as we passed, by sending stones skating across the ice.

We could now see Mera, our next objective. It looked very straightforward but was obviously a long way from the Mera La. Anu pointed out the rognon where we would make our high camp; I reflected that it looked like a windy place. Naulekh, Mera's sister peak, also looked a very inviting but straightforward prospect. I was interested to know if there was any pass by which one could cross the wall of the upper Hongu valley before Chamlang, so as to cross into the Arun river system. But an examination through my cine viewfinder did not show up any immediate obvious weakness.

As we ascended from the Mera La, the views to the north and west of Gyachung Kang, Everest, Makalu and Chamlang, expanded all the time. Our camp at the rognon on a large ledge above the Naulekh glacier had a superb view of Kangchenjunga 130km away through a gap in the eastern Hongu valley wall. We anchored our tents securely, but even so the strength of the wind caused us to sling another rope around each one. I still had one or two alarming moments during the night when I felt the tent billowing up under me and I thought I would find myself flying down to the glacier far below. Dawn was exquisite as the rising sun behind Kangchenjunga, turned the snow pink.

That next morning I had enormous trouble getting my boots and gaiters on, but after some fierce pushing and pulling I was ready to go. The snow was perfect and we crunched steadily uphill. We trended to the left as the way steepened but our crampons were biting crisply, so there was no difficulty.

Every now and then we stopped for me to film and take photographs. I was gradually slowing up due to the altitude. Higher up a bitter wind blew spindrift into our faces. We reached the E summit of Mera at 6400m, three and three-quarter hours after starting. It is a wonderful viewpoint standing back from the main line of the Himalaya and sufficiently high to overtop its nearest neighbours. From its summit you can see most of the Eastern Himalaya and no less than five, 8000m peaks: Cho Oyu, Everest, Lhotse, Makalu and Kangchenjunga. To the south we could see wave upon wave of blue hills descending, to the Indian plains and there, glittering in the sunshine some 60km away was the great Arun river. A little down the leeside we found a place we could crouch out of the wind to eat our lunch. We considered but rejected going on to the summit about 1km away and about 20m higher, but into the teeth of the wind. We made it back to the tents by the early afternoon and descended down to the Hinku valley to camp just before nightfall.

We now took it more easily down the Hinku and then climbed up over the Zatra La to return to the Dudh Kosi valley. Crossing the pass and seeing the familiar peaks of the Rolwaling Himal was like meeting old friends again. The descent down the other side was long, steep, and not a little awkward.

Ten days after leaving Pangboche, we reached Lukla. Perhaps a discreet veil should be drawn over our activities in Lukla, but suffice it to say that our very jolly celebration that evening at a Sherpa hotel drew down the wrath of the local police for keeping the township awake. We made a rather hurried and surreptitious exit early next morning for Chutok.

The last part of the trek, which would take me across Eastern Nepal to Tumlingtar on the Arun river, was to be a contrast to the rugged stuff we had been doing up till then. From Chutok the route took us pleasantly to Pangkongma, a village of friendly people and fine houses. That evening the atmosphere was idyllically still. Some smoke from forest fires formed a layer right across the valley so that the Rolwaling peaks seemed to float magically above the earth in the sunset.

Later as we climbed up through Gudel, crossing the grain of the middle hills, I understood the frustration Tilman[2] felt, which he put into his little verse:

'For dreadfulness, naught can excel,
The prospect of Bung from Gudel;
And words die away on the tongue,
When we look back on Gudel from Bung.'

The route then passed through some wild forest country and over the Salwa La, which formed the watershed between the Dudh Kosi and Arun river systems. The journey was enlivened by troops of wild grey and brown monkeys leaping about in the trees along the way. They were completely unimpressed by our whistles. Finally, on the tenth day after leaving Lukla, we turned a large spur, dividing the Irkua Khola from the Arun and there below us saw the mighty jade-green river that rises in Tibet and cuts its way right through the Himalaya range. All that now remained was the ferry crossing and a long trudge down the quiet reaches teeming with bird life to Tumlingtar, our journey's end.

1. Sir E. Hillary and D. Doig — *High in the Thin Cold Air.*
2. H. W. Tilman — *Nepal Himalaya.*

The Mountains of Wadi Rum

Tony Howard
Plates 41–47

Wadi Rum, if it means anything to anyone, probably conjures up visions of Lawrence of Arabia for it was from there, in that remote region of desert mountains, that he based his raids on the Turks and Aqaba. Since then little has changed. Old men, some of them old enough to recall riding with Lawrence, still travel the desert by camel and the mountains that wall the valleys described by Lawrence as 'Rum the Magnificent . . . vast, echoing and God-like . . . a processional way greater than imagination' stand aloof and unknown to all but the Bedouin.

We were fortunate to be the first climbers to be invited to the area by Jordan's Ministry of Tourism, to assess the region's potential for mountaineering and trekking. We spent five weeks there during the months of October and November in both 1984 and 1985. In 1984 the party comprised Di Taylor, Mick Shaw, Alan Baker and Tony Howard. They were joined by Wilfried Colonna from France in 1985.

Wadi Rum is a singularly impressive region of about 800 square kilometres of desert and mountains, with red, yellow and purple sandstone towers and walls rising steeply and windworn into arabesque loops and whorls, with tier upon tier of overlapping slabs melting into space. These walls start from the desert at *c.*900-1000m and are capped with huge domes of white smooth sandstone leading to summits of *c.*1500-1750m. The two highest face each other across Wadi Rum and are Jebel Rum 1754m, reputedly Jordan's highest mountain, and Jebel um 'Ishrin according to the map only 1m lower. Actually there is a higher mountain than Jebel Rum, this being Al Hamareyn, 1769m, which we located to the south, on the Saudi border, in 1985. It is however nothing more than a rubble heap and totally without interest for the mountaineer.

East of Jebel um 'Ishrin, and across the wadi of that name, are the pyramidal peaks of the Barrakh's and Abu Judaidah. To the south, dozens of smaller domes of white sandstone rise like petrified cumulus cloud: 200-300m from the sands, giving short enjoyable climbs. We originally named them 'The Pleasure Domes' but then opted for 'The Tots of Rum'. These cover the regions of Qabr Amra (Amra's Grave), and Abu Khsheiba. East of here, the area is bounded by the peak of Burdah which has a rock bridge high on its N ridge. Immediately south of Wadi Rum, the bulk of Jebel al Khush Khashah and Al Khaza'li squats over the desert, split by a giant ravine on its N side decorated with Thamudic rock drawings, and fronted by 300m of gently overhanging rock to its west.

Despite what at first appears to be very unstable and suspect rock, most of the major summits have been climbed by the Bedouin though we ourselves reached the top of one unclimbed peak, Jebel Kharazeh, actually overlooking the 'Beau Geste' style fort of the camel corps, the few houses and the black

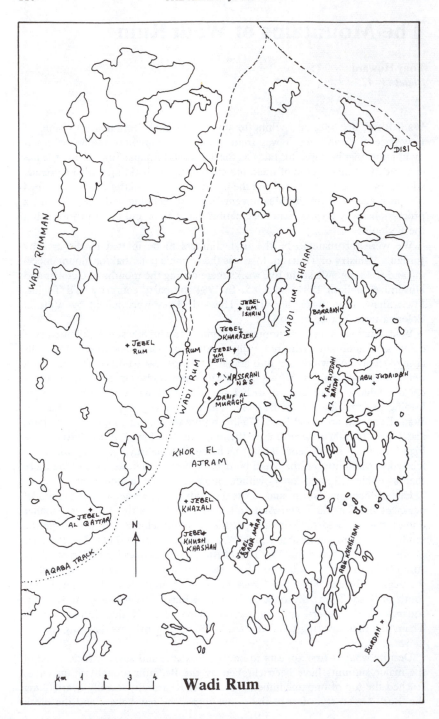

Wadi Rum

Bedouin tents of Wadi Rum village. The most notorious of the unclimbed peaks however is Nassrani, 1560m, a giant twin-topped dome with vertical walls of up to 600m on every side and most of them completely blank or crossed by row upon row of overhangs like bracket fungi. Our one probing route on these peaks, up a rather horrendous cleft which we called 'The Glass-Chimney' ended in a couloir with a few bushes, beyond which the rock became dangerously loose. We were amazed to find that the Bedouin go up to this point, barefoot and solo to collect these very shrubs for camel food!

We also followed a few other Bedouin hunters' routes up the peaks of Wadi Rum using information provided by Dayfallah Atieeq, a young man of the local Howeitat tribe. His knowledge was indispensible and his friendship was an instant introduction to the otherwise closed camps of the Bedouin. The difficulty, complexity and length of these routes was a constant surprise to us and we could but wonder at the Bedouin soloing 300-400m up, in bare feet on grade 4c rock, often with a gun and the spoils of their hunting slung over their shoulders.

Our first attempt at climbing in Wadi Rum was on one such route and ended with an impromptu bivouac on the descent with neither equipment nor water, the Bedouin having dismissed it as a 'walk'. Our arrival back at our camp the following day with parched throats caused much amusement!

Despite earlier scrambles, this was our first real experience of the complexity of these peaks, in particular Jebel Rum, the routes to the summit of which, though only 700-800m, can often be measured in kilometres as the peak is slashed by barrier walls and ravines or siqs running the full width of its summit plateau and often crossable at only one point which is rarely easy to find. One particular chasm, which we named 'The Great Siq', bisects the mountain just north of the summit and the only way across is supposedly by a log placed there by the Bedouin. This log bridge is allegedly so polished that a heap of Ibex bones lie in the chasm below! We failed to find it despite three searches so that our attempts at the summit from the north in 1984 were frustrated just below the top.

We did however spend two fascinating days on the north plateau that year, reaching many of its small domes, with their incredible views of the desert, and standing in awe on the edge of unknown canyons 300m deep, or on the lip of the Great Siq where it drops into 'The Pit', a hole in the heart of the mountain a hundred metres deep and wide, vanishing finally through a giant arch beneath which the early morning sun streams in. The route we had taken was another remarkable Bedouin climb known as *Al Thallamiyyah* which roughly translates as 'The Dark One'. The way appears obvious, starting up a giant ravine, but even this had its moments, as we repeatedly took wrong turnings up various minor branches out of the main couloir. Once the way is known, the climbing is really enjoyable, and the difficult sections are reduced to 4c by Bedouin cunning, in the form of rickety steps, branches rammed into cracks, and holds chiselled into the rock. No ethics for these people! (Having said that, they explicitly asked us not to fix any pegs or slings as aid points on any of their routes, as they have no wish for the routes to be made easier or for anyone to climb them who is not capable of doing so without additional help.)

Once out of the ravine on the crest of a superbly airy ridge, it appeared that the route finding problems were over, but with almost 2km to go to the summit they were only just beginning and we went 500m out of our way before realising our error. The route in fact takes a walking terrace under an overlap for 500m round the N and E sides of the mountain before breaking out onto the upper slabs. Another 500m of devious route finding followed, over domes and across crevasses until the way descends over an overlap, hanging from a Bedouin cut hold to drop onto a ledge below. Another short descent led to an area of desert previously concealed between the domes and criss-crossed with ibex tracks. It was at the southern edge of this desert that we came to an abrupt halt on the lip of the Great Siq. The summit standing on the N edge, we named 'Amen Dome'. In 1985, with greater knowledge of the mountain, we completed the route, abseiling into the *Siq*, thus making a long and fascinating route to the summit covering 2.5km of Alpine Grade *Difficile* climbing mostly at 4a/b with some 4c.

Our attempt to complete a *grande traverse* of Jebel Rum from north to south met with almost predictable failure when we ran out of time and water trying to find our way through the maze of ravines and barrier walls south of the summit. A large section of the mountain still remains inviolate as our earlier attempt to reach the summit from the Bedouin camp of Abu N'Khala to the south was foiled whilst still 1km from the summit, on 'Frustration Dome' with the dark recesses of the hitherto unknown 'Southern Siq' gaping at our feet. This canyon, like the Great Siq to the north, cleaves its way from one side of the mountain to the other and maybe there are others between here and the top. Hampton Court Maze has nothing on this place!

The Bedouin have explored the mountain over many generations and the 8km long E face of the mountain has three other masterpieces of Bedouin route-finding. Their route to the E Dome of Jebel Rum is a classic grade *D Sup* with well over 1000m of climbing up slabs and cracks, split halfway by a devious descent into and out of a narrow ravine. It emerges onto the summit domes through a unique cave where the slabs disappear beneath a 30m roof and the side walls converge from 30m to an exit cleft 1m high and wide. The view out from this point was incomparable in our experience of mountaineering, and we called the climb 'The Eye of Allah'. The route, however, does not connect with the main summit, and when we finally did reach this elusive spot in 1984, we followed yet another Bedouin route up from the SE edge of the Great Siq and wandered over the high domes and hidden little deserts, home of the ibex, to the final ridge. We bivouacked up on the plateau for the second time that year, enjoying its remote isolation. Sandy areas abound, albeit sometimes covered with snake tracks, and there is sweet smelling juniper wood in plenty for the fire. On both occasions, in late October and early November, whilst we sat beneath starlit desert skies, storms raged about 3km away on Jebel um 'Ishrin sending flash floods thundering down the walls and over the bivouac site we had used on our first ascent of Jebel Al Kharazah.

The route up Jebel Al Kharazah was long and complex and we needed two bivouacs to complete the ascent and descent of this 1000m *Très Difficile* route. The second one was unplanned and the Bedouin children in the valley below

41 *Peaks of the Barrakh group and the massif of Abu Judaidah (centre rear) seen from N Barrakh looking SE. All are possibly unclimbed.*

42 *View E from N Barrakh to Disi.*

43 The unclimbed E face of the E dome of Jebel Rum. 1: Reconnaissance of 'Direct'. 2: Reconnaissance o 'Sidewinder'.

Photo: Tony Howard

4 *Burdah E face (N section) with the rock-bridge ('R') clearly visible, the line of the route climbed, and its variation (broken line).*

Photo: Tony Howard

5 *Jebel Kharazeh ('K') and Jebel um Ejil ('E') seen from Wadi Rum. B: Bivouac. 1: Lower half of Vanishing Pillar. 2: Perverse Frog. 3: The Beauty. 4: The Beast.*

46   View SE from the desert track to Aqaba. 1. Jebel Khush Khasah. 2. N ravine with cave drawings. 3. Jebe
Khazali.

47   The W faces of N and S Nassrani seen from Wadi Rum.

cried and said we would never return! The climb was excellent, keeping a constant grade of 4b and 4c with some 5a jamming cracks thrown in for good measure. A choice of line high up on the route resulted in a wrong decision and 200m of climbing came to a stop at a blank wall just below the summit and had to be reversed.

The climb on Jebel Al Kharazah was our first major climb in the area and our doubts about rock quality and the feasibility of climbing here were well and truly dispelled. However we did learn not to place too much trust in abseil pegs. One fell out whilst in use and another, used during an earlier reconnaissance, was later removed by hand. As we became familiar with the rock, its idiosyncracies became more acceptable and we had an unforgettable five weeks spending almost every day in the mountains climbing, or exploring their canyons, some of which make amazing treks through the heart of the massifs, though to be trapped in a canyon by a flash-flood could be disastrous. The name of one of the mountains, Jebel um 'Ishrin, which means 'Mother of Twenty' is said to be derived from one such occasion when 20 Bedouin were caught by a flood and killed in one of the many ravines that split the massif. Floods and loose rock are not the only objective dangers. Occasionally we saw sand snakes, supposedly harmless, but once one of us almost stood on a Palestinian Viper. Another time, a scorpion scuttled, tail erect, from a handhold, whilst one night, Mick awoke during a desert bivouac to find a scorpion walking up his arm! Wildlife, in fact, is quite plentiful; even the shy ibex were spotted a couple of times whilst *lämmergeier* frequently circled overhead and other vultures and eagles were sighted daily. Lizards are plentiful as are rock hyrax and the tracks of nocturnal animals such as the jerbel are to be seen everywhere in the desert.

Our good friend Dayfallah showed us Thamudic cave drawings and Nabatean buildings and stairways hewn into the sides of canyon walls, some of which were apparently previously unknown to the authorities.

In 1985 we had similar success, not only in Wadi Rum where we put up a dozen more new climbs and reached two more unclimbed summits, but also in the mountains around Petra, the fabled 'rose-red city', 100km to the north on the King's Highway between Aqaba and Amman. Here, a range of peaks some 20km wide runs north to south for 100km between the Highway and the Rift Valley desert of Wadi Araba, south of the Dead Sea. These mountains are of a similar sandstone to those of Rum, but are more massive with none of the great isolated towers and massifs that make Rum so unique. However, a number of large canyons cut into the range descending from the 1500m plateau (along whose rim the King's Highway winds its way) to the hot sub sea level depths of Araba. The most northerly of these is Wadi El Hasa. Narrower and more dramatic is Wadi Dana with its old stone village perched on the rim. Lawrence rode past here in 1918 on a camel, alone, through waist deep winter snow carrying 6000 sovereigns, and the Israelis drove their tanks up to here in 1967. A short distance south of Wadi Dana is the ancient Crusader fort of Shaubak, and then that most famous of 'lost cities', Petra, accessible only (so the tourist leaflets tell you) through the great chasm of the kilometre-long *Siq*, a narrow canyon just a few metres wide with 100m rock walls on either side. South of

Petra two more huge steep sided canyons can be seen from the Highway through the heat haze. They too may offer both climbing and trekking opportunities for the adventurous. All around 100 to 300m rock walls of sandstone or igneous intrusions beckon the curious.

Climbing in the environs of Petra itself, whilst certainly possible, would seem to be somewhat sacrilegious and for that reason we left it alone. We were, however, attracted by the shadowy depths of the canyon of Wadi Dana, and the puzzle of the unknown exit of Petra's Siq canyon. The exploration of these two canyons was our first priority in 1985, and we were not disappointed. The day trek through Wadi Dana was superb. We bivouacked in its depths, somewhat perturbed by the numerous scorpions and the howling of wild dogs which were reputed to have killed someone recently. The following day, we continued down the valley, the greenery of the wadi bed contrasting with the stark bare heights of the surrounding peaks and the occasional intriguing rock walls. But Wadi Dana was completely outshone by the unexpected delights of Petra's secret canyon. The entrance to this is said to be jealously guarded by the Saidi-Yin Bedouin who, we were told, are likely to shoot passing strangers in the off-chance they might be Israeli (the border is only a few kilometres away). Nevertheless, we decided to take our chances, and were rewarded by a brilliant trip. The two day trek back out of Araba revealed hidden waterfalls and clear pools where we bathed and washed off the desert dust. When bamboo jungles filled the narrow ravine, we bypassed them by scrambling along the granite walls. An impasse in the ravine, formed by a giant boulder wedged between the walls, its base in a pool, forced a detour over a col in a 300m basalt wall and we finally reached Petra after a trip described by Wilfried as one of his best days in the mountains.

Once more in Rum we turned again to the more serious business of climbing. Here, Wilfried discovered a superb smooth-looking black wall of 200m actually in view of our camp. As the 'finder' of the face we awarded him the choice of route, the result being a superb TD climb at consistent 5a, 5b up a series of layback flakes. Alan very cleverly managed to latch on to Wilfried for this route, leaving Mick, Di and myself with its 'twin' up the other side of a huge finger of rock, the crux of which was an evil 5b off-width above an overhang. We met on the summit (previously unclimbed) and named the routes The Beauty and The Beast! To further rub salt into the wound, Wilfried had spotted another line up the wall left of The Beauty which he led a few days later. This was to be Jordan's first *TD Sup*, with continuous 5b and 5c pitches.

Jebel Rum continued to intrigue us. We discovered another Bedouin climb known as *Rijm Assaf* — The Steps of Assaf — a truly amazing route, mostly grade 3, with two harder sections where the Bedouin had built hair-raising rock 'steps' to bypass overhangs. With true Bedouin boldness and ingenuity, the climb winds its way up an impossible wall, dripping with overhangs. Once the right way has been found it is amazingly easy and we soloed up the curving interconnecting purple ramps of rock, roping up only for the frightening passage of the Bedouin steps at the final overhang. Beyond, we continued solo up a pleasantly angled ridge, the steep walls on either side adding spice to its airy isolation. It was the first climb on Jebel Rum to cause us no problems. We reached the summit in four hours to be greeted by a couple of ibex running across the slabs. Elsewhere we followed Bedouin hunters up the 1000m slabs of the Barrakhs and made our own ascent of other peaks up 300m *D Sup* and *TD Inf* routes such as 'Orange Sunshine', 'Purple Haze' and 'Black Magic', the names indicating the colourful and bizarre nature of the climbing.

The route of 'Orange Sunshine' on the E face of Burdah, the easiest of this trilogy, took us to what is probably the best summit for panoramic views in the whole area. To the south, the peaks of the Saudi border clustering around the high point of Al Hamereyn were only a few kilometres away. Eastwards the heat shimmered off the mud flats of Abu Suwwannah and the rubble peaks beyond. North and west all the peaks of Rum were spread out before us — the grey squat mass of Khush Khashah, the chasm riddled hulk of Jebel Rum, the provocative unclimbed domes of Nassranniyeh and the elusive possibly unclimbed top of Jebel um 'Ishrin. Nearer, the steel grey pyramids of the Barrakhs and Abu Judaidah reminded us of the days spent on camels exploring the hidden ravines and the relaxed company of our Bedouin friends.

In 1985 we witnessed one of the rare but notorious flash-floods that sweep through the many rock crevasses and ravines whenever there is heavy rainfall. A couple of days previously, Mick and I had been up on the E face of Jebel Rum's East Dome for the second time, trying to find the best line up. In 1984 we had reconnoitred the 'Direct' as far as bad rock at 200m. This time, together with Wilfried, we had explored a line up the right edge of the wall and had fixed a couple of ropes intending to return. However, an hour of torrential rain on the summit plateau produced countless waterfalls which cascaded 300 to 500m down the face, carrying with them rocks and sand from the ravines above. One such torrent roared its way down the line of our fixed ropes leaving us in grave doubt about their security.

By the end of the two expeditions we had hardly scratched the surface, discovering far more canyons, peaks and potential routes than we could ever hope to visit or climb. The opportunity for exploration of easy and middle grade routes is immense. High standard free and aid routes also exist and our ascents of a 1000m *TD* and a 300m *TD Sup* merely point the way. Our two reconnaissances of the 600m vertical E wall of Jebel Rum involving 5b free moves and aid climbing on nuts and pegs are but an indication of what may be possible for future expeditions. There is surely no other area so close to Europe with such a wealth of potential climbing.

The Bedouin themselves contributed greatly to the depth of our experiences. We were welcomed at their desert camps and invited to their feasts, one of which lasted three days involving the slaughtering of 15 sheep for maybe a 100 guests. There were impromptu camel races and in the dark of night the women, veiled completely in black, danced eerily under the stars to the sound of the men's spine chilling guttural chant. Virtually every day was spent climbing and exploring, with weekly excursions to Aqaba for extra provisions and to swim amongst the coral and tropical fish of the Gulf. For ten weeks Wadi Rum was indeed our home. Its mountains, deserts and people have much to offer. Go there and be prepared for a mountain experience the like of which you have never had before — you will not be disappointed.

Through the Ice Window to Nelion

Richard Allen

The thrill of poring over the maps and guidebooks, the endless lists of food, clothing and equipment has brightened up many a long winter's evening. Oliver Turnbull and I had made detailed plans in February 1982 to spend a fortnight climbing on Mount Kenya. A painful flight to America following a routine dental appointment and filling convinced me that my tooth required further attention. Even if I could cope with the altitude it was clear that my tooth would not. The offer of an evil looking dental tool three days before our departure, to remove the filling if necessary, convinced me that this was not the time to go. We consoled ourselves over whisky and haggis in Glen Brittle, climbing the Black Cuillin in snow.

A last minute decision by a British Minister in September 1984 to visit the new road being constructed between Thuchi and Nkubu to the east of the mountain gave me an excuse and opportunity I could not resist. Oliver was unable to join me at such short notice but through a colleague I contacted Peter Brettell who was prepared to climb with me although we had never met. Peter having lived in Nairobi for some years did not seem surprised when I phoned confirming I would only be able to spend four days on the mountain. His relaxed response, 'What route do you have in mind?' really puzzled me until he explained that he and Ian Howell frequently go up to the mountain for a weekend's climbing. Surely, this wasn't the same mountain? I decided that Peter was in another class and I hurriedly mentioned which Scottish winter climbs I had done, and without waiting for an answer mumbled that I had heard that the W ridge and the Ice Window are classic routes. Peter thought that the W ridge was too long and there was too much ice. The Ice Window had been climbed by Peter in 1978 and he remembered the crux being roughly equivalent to Scottish grade 3.

After a couple of phone calls, and an urgent request for ice pegs, I flew to Nairobi, landing early in the morning. I was introduced to Peter, swigged a cup of black coffee and we drove north to Nanuki. We registered at the National Park entrance and continued up the greasy mud road to a clearing in the forest at 3000m. That was as far as we could drive.

We took five hours to walk up through the forest over the high moor where the giant heathers grow, and along the Teleki valley past giant groundsel and lobelia to the Rescue Hut at 4100m. The sacks felt heavy even though we were not carrying ropes and some of the climbing gear. Peter and Ian usually approach the mountain by this track leaving equipment in the Rescue Hut. By the time we arrived at 4.00pm the temperature was already falling and it had been raining for three hours. Although this hut is small it is very well arranged and within no time Peter had brewed the first of many pints of tea we were to consume on the climb. Those devotees of winter reading will have noted the reference in the Kenya Guidebook (mountain medicine section) 'the lighter and the larger the volume, the better the hydration. "Clear and copious", should be the watchwords. . . . the correct fluid intake also seems to aid the acclimatization . . .' A good stew completed the meal, another brew and into our bags for the night.

We slept well. On Peter's advice we had a leisurely morning walking up the valley sides for a better view of the summit, which was clear and dusted with new snow almost down to the hut. Looking up at the Diamond Glacier, I began to wonder if we were not being too ambitious. Vivienne de Watteville, when she witnessed the second ascent of the mountain by Eric Shipton and Wyn Harris in 1929, referred to it as 'that wicked little Diamond Glacier, which seemed literally to hang between the two summits'.

At noon the clouds covered the peaks. We scrambled up to the small glacial lake at the base of Tyndall Glacier passing 'American Camp' and for the first time we carried full sacks. We continued to the bottom of Darwin Glacier, where we chipped open the door of the bivi shelter (a cave in the moraine), left the heavy gear, and traversed to Two Tarn Hut. This hut, though not as new or comfortable as the Rescue Hut, has attracted rock hyraxes, fearless little animals determined to survive on the rubbish left by the visitors. Another good meal with tea and into the bags before the cold penetrated too far. Peter suggested we sleep on the floor which has been covered with a layer of foam. A fine idea until awakened by the cold I was sure I could hear rustling close by. After anxious minutes of breathless contemplation I decided it had to be mice. I slept fitfully until the alarm roused us at 5.00am. Peter, a seasoned hut visitor, had slept through the invasion and found my breakfast silence puzzling.

A clear sky was encouraging. Using head-torches, we made good time across the rocks, following markers left by others. The first glow of the day appeared as we collected the climbing gear from the bivouac site. It was a beautiful sunny day and we were climbing for the first time, roped up and festooned with gear. Peter set off up the Darwin glacier, kicking steps in the surprisingly soft snow. We did not traverse diagonally into the right fork but approached the glacier on its right side and climbed straight up. It was strenuous work and I took over the lead up to the top of the lower Darwin. I belayed, determined to take a rest, while Peter led diagonally left across the upper glacier to the top left-hand corner where 'the old ropes' still hang down. Peter, being more experienced on rock, descended to the snow covered slab and climbed the ramp to a rock belay to the left. As I joined him he commented that he had expected these rocks to be clear of snow and dry.

I had been puzzled why this route was not climbed until 1973, whereas the much harder Diamond Couloir was being attempted by Ian Howell in 1971. It is not until this point on the Ice Window route when looking diagonally left that the hidden couloir becomes obvious. Peter's earlier description of the easy angled couloir which he had kicked steps up didn't fit the picture at all. What we were looking at wasn't generally too steep but consisted of a series of hard ice walls of various heights resembling a frozen waterfall. The weather was deteriorating rapidly and the narrow couloir was soon enveloped in cloud.

It was starting to snow when I traversed to the ice. I spent some time persuading an ice screw to bite into the hard material. I hadn't used an ice peg for many months but this was ridiculous. With a runner on I climbed the first couple of obstacles. Peter struggled just as I had done, which at least made me feel better. He led on while the snowfall got heavier. When leading time seems irrelevant, it is only at belays that reality is apparent. The snow, fine balls of dry powder, hissed off the ledges, pouring over both of us. Peter's lead took us to the point where the S face route departs to the right. Out of the confines of the narrow couloir we could hear voices, but shrouded in cloud and snow we could only guess that the other party was climbing Point John.

Thunder rolled around the mountain as we briefly discussed the options. We were both aware that the conditions were unusual. Ahead we could just see the '6m ice wall'. It didn't look too hard when compared with the previous pitches, but seemed longer than Peter remembered. However, it is only supposed to be one pitch and it was a long way to have come to take the easy option, so we decided to go on.

Peter kicked up to a good belay and having joined him I took off my sack. The crux didn't look as easy as it had from the previous stance. The pitch was stepped like those below. I got over the first wall with the moral support of a good runner, climbed up to the second and screwed in another peg before fighting that wall. I was tired and the sack hauling emphasised the altitude and my lack of acclimatization. Peter came up quickly, his natural ability shining through. He led the next pitch, which although not as sustained was as hard as the previous pitch. We had taken eight hours to get this far and we were not going to get to the top that day. One more steep wall on the third pitch and we could see the ice cave directly above. The couloir peters out and the right wall merges into the rock face which leads up and forms the right flank of the ice cave. The other wall drops away revealing the headwall of the Diamond Couloir which suddenly dominates the view to the left. We crossed under the rock face on deep loose snow and I asked Peter to lead the last pitch into the cave. The pitch was steep, a combination of poor ice and rock.

It was 4.30pm, we had been going for 11 hours and both of us were tired. The prospect of a further five or six hours' climbing to arrive at the top in the dark did not appeal and we decided to stay in the welcome sanctuary of the cave. The floor of the cave was flat, the back wall dry rock, and a curtain of icicles protected us from the elements. The stove was lit for a quick brew but before it boiled we were asleep in our bags. Three hours later we awoke, changed the cylinder and finally drank our hot tea. We obviously needed food but our tiredness, queasy feeling and slight headache deterred us from eating. I had unwisely failed to put my boots in my bag during our first unintentional rest. The weather improved after sunset and under a clear sky we settled down for the night, wearing our wet clothes. We drowsed fitfully through the night. Sleeping with 'two old boots' is no fun!

In the morning, still not relishing food, we had more hot sugared tea and were ready to leave. The exit, described in the quidebook as a window, is no longer in the roof but is now at floor level. There is a long knotted sling attached to an ice peg screwed into the floor adjacent to the hole. Peter climbed down about 2.5m to an ice shelf in a very exposed position above the Diamond Couloir. Traversing to the left, round a curtain of icicles, Peter was at the bottom of the Diamond Glacier. He climbed up the poor ice trying to make a suitable belay. Eventually in desperation he pushed his two axes and a deadman into the snow. Listening to the noises amplified in the ice cave I could not imagine what he was doing. A distant shout advised me to 'come on but do not fall off!' I removed our peg and slithered inelegantly out of the hole, down to the shelf, and cautiously climbed up to join Peter.

Sir Halford Mackinder climbed diagonally across this steep little glacier on the first ascent in 1899. On the second ascent Eric Shipton decided to climb the face of Nelion direct, later admitting to Miss V de Watteville that they would have tackled any kind of rock rather than go across the glacier. With modern crampons and two short axes we made steady progress straight up the centre of the glacier, leading through four long pitches. We front-pointed the last pitch on hard ice into the warming sun. The temperature changed instantly, the ice became soft snow and I was soon looking over the Gate of the Mists. It was a relief to have reached the ridge. I was reminded of the Brèche Zsigmondy on the Meije, a snowy gap between two rock summits with a spectacular view on the other side, perhaps more satisfying than actually reaching the summit. Peter had last crossed the Gate in PA's! Feeling more at home on rock Peter led off over the snow covered rocks, placing two good runners before moving onto a snow slope to regain the ridge. We were both more tired than we realised. Peter fell, sliding some distance but obviously thankful for his rock runner. After a brief rest he moved to better ground and we climbed to the summit, arriving at 11.40am. Throwing off all our gear we moved over to the hut.

Howell's hut is situated only a few feet from the top of Nelion. For Ian Howell to have carried all the pieces from the Lewis glacier seemed an incredible achievement. Sitting by the door of the hut we protected our stove from the wind and brewed up. Having proved the 'clear and copious' rule we set off down the ordinary route, as the clouds and predictable snow rolled in. Our ropes were wet and our abseiling slow. Fortunately Peter was on familiar ground and found all the stances. Five hours and ten long abseils later, having passed Bailey's Bivi which appeared wet and inhospitable and de Graff's variation, we reached the moraine. Another two hours took us to the Rescue hut by which time it was dark and even the mice did not disturb me that night.

I had been advised that Mount Kenya should not be under-estimated. The relative ease of access to altitudes in excess of 4500m often leads to acclimatization problems. I had been lucky only to have experienced mild headaches, nausea, numb toes and fingers and an occasional tendency to feel faint when the blood rushed to my cold extremities.

We had climbed a classic route in unusual conditions which had extended my experience far beyond that previously achieved in the Alps.

Yukon — A Winter Excursion

Guy Sheridan
Plates 48–50

On 22 March 1985 the dawn broke a little before 7am and the cold light of an Arctic sky grew in intensity from a steely blue through the range of red and orange until the valley below was bathed in sunlight. That morning I had woken up promptly at 6.30 and fumbled for my small torch in the pile of clothes that made up my pillow. The successful search had ruffled the slumberings of my two Norwegian companions, of whom the only visible sign of life was a misty column of breath issuing from the tightly drawn entrance of each of their sleeping bags. As I flicked the beam of light around, it revealed a generous coating of hoar frost around that tiny breathing space. Confirmation that it had been an extremely cold night was provided by a deluge of centimetre-long ice crystals which fell from the roof of the tent as I wriggled and struggled with the entrance zip. I silently cursed the manufacturers of our small home and asked myself why they always seem to make zip fasteners so small.

My efforts with the zip lasted what seemed to be an age and muffled curses in Norwegian from beneath the two slugs of down beside me induced an urgency into my numb fingers. It seemed to do the trick and the zip released with such startling speed that the tent got a good shaking and another heap of ice crystals came deluging down. Our cooker lay just outside the flap of the tent but before I gripped it and the fuel bottle beside, I glanced at the thermometer hanging from a loop in the fabric and it revealed what I thought. The mercury was riding at −40°C and with this cheery news I announced to my chums that I thought it was going to be another nice day. I don't think they heard me exactly under all those feathers but the acknowledged grunts indicated that further urgency was required to shut the door and get the stove alight.

An hour later, tea and breakfast had been consumed and the early light of the morning had long since penetrated the green fabric that surrounded us. It was Erik who was always first out of his feather slug. Tobben and I cherished that extra few minutes' warmth that we had been given so unselfishly every morning on this winter journey through the mountains of the Yukon.

The cloudless sky did indeed herald another good day, but the high pressure that we were experiencing did not seem to be abating and it was only cold comfort to know that we could expect a few more days of these depressing temperatures. The cold, like pain, was quickly forgotten as we gathered up that impetus, fired by at least 500 breakfast calories, that seemed to be a routine part of the three of us and which was so necessary to complete the journey that we had started ten days before.

As the sun rose, the shadow that was cast over the steep defile ahead of us by the bulk of Mt Christie narrowed and the sun's warmth slowly drove the mercury into the lower −30sC. A welcome difference it was too. To the west

48 Mount Wilson (2276m) in the Yukon and its spectacular 100m E face.

49 Peaks in the Tombstone range. Moonlit Peak (centre) was first climbed by Peter Steele and party in summer 1981

50   Tombstone Mountain (R) and the impressive interconnecting ridges and precipices of the range.

51 Unter Schüsselkarturm. The Schober route follows the centre cracks going direct to the summit.

rose the spectacular pyramid of Mt Wilson, 2276m, whose 1000m E face was now looking even more uncompromising under the revealing light. What a plum for someone, I thought, and it would have been there for our picking if we were only coming this far. My thoughts and dreams of first ascents were quickly shattered by the reality of our situation and the need to get on. We were two days and a good 60km from our first cache of food, and a steady ascent up to Christie Pass was the main task of the morning.

That night we relished the memory of passing close to the W flank of Mt Christie, the dominant peak of the upper S Nahannie river basin. It was a really startlingly beautiful place with peaks, faces and lots of small glaciers high up on them: yet so remote and so cold.

Two days later, with no respite from the temperature, we reached our depot. We were by calculation about 276km from the nearest human being and it was about now that the daunting nature of our journey first had its impact on me. I wondered secretly if my two Norwegian companions shared the same feeling and if we were mad! But then, commitment is exciting and if others are in the same boat the bonds of friendship and interdependence become those immeasurable things that drive you on.

Earlier we had caught a brief glimpse of the summit of Keele Peak which, at 2975m, is the loftiest summit in the MacKenzie range and we eagerly looked forward to passing around its E flank to enter the Selwyn valley. Ice-falls, blue and forbidding, tumbled down from every aspect of the summit and the serious nature of the peak was very evident. Alas, for us an ascent must remain for another occasion. But for those dauntless few with the time and resources to venture far into this unremitting wilderness, winter or summer, there will be unparalleled rewards.

We were never to enter the Selwyn valley and the upper reaches of Bonnet Plume nor pass close to the flanks of Keele Peak. Our disappointment was on account of a critical, potentially dangerous break up of our ski boots, and the nature of the problem was sufficiently alarming to convince us that further progress would be foolhardy. Our escape to Ross River, 260km away, is another tale, and although we may have missed the best part of our winter journey, our spirits did not remain low for long. Within two weeks we had found and bought some new boots, were back on course and were skiing towards the Tombstone mountains, some 100km north of Dawson City in Klondike country.

The Oberreintal

Ian Chrystal
Plate 51

Warming up on four climbs on the Tannheimer and Karwendel, we felt that something more classic was needed. The routes, all excellent around grade V+, should have satisfied us; however that vital touch of spice seemed lacking.

The Austrian-Bavarian border extends through mountain groups of Tannheimer, Wetterstein, Karwendel, and eastwards to the Kaisergebirge, all offering tremendous alpine rock climbing. Walter Pause's huge alpine rock book which I had humped from Scotland gave two classics in the Oberreintal, the Schober and Gonda, both great climbs of grade VI, which offer exciting, quality climbing.

Walking in from Partenkirchen, our four-hour walk led through the deep gorge of the Partnach Klamm. Organized as a tourist attraction it cost DM1 to enter. Hewn into the limestone walls, a narrow pathway threads its way above Partnach's fast flowing water — alarming tourists who have to squeeze past climbers and their overladen rucksacks. The ravine's close walls block out the light and tourist and climber collide in the path's black, linking tunnels. Beyond, a sunny forest track brings relief from this murky trench and the immense heat makes many watering stops necessary at the adjacent river.

The Oberreintal hut is reached via a lone gate blocking the track. 'Sigwenda' (that is the best I can pronounce her name) is the lady hut warden, a lively character, who encourages the climbers' pranks. Saying more would detract from a visitor's surprise. Busy, she organizes her hut well, preferring to do all the cooking, including the food carried up by us.

The hut, sited below a rock shelf, is overlooked by three grand features: the 2371m Oberreintaldom in front, and the 1940m Oberreintalturm behind. Between, like a mighty Cioch the perpendicular monolith Unterer Schüsselkarturm commands the high alpine corrie. Here the Schober route takes a direct line to its 2200m summit. The Herbst Teufel, a grade V companion route, runs parallel. Being easier, it was a preferable choice after the long, hot walk in.

My partner, Bob Kinnaird, was itching to start. As it was past noon, his agitation was well warranted, for we had 40 minutes of walking, and 250m of climbing on the Herbst Teufel.

Rid of the creature comforts which one takes to a hut, we raced below the shelf, passing a group of German army tents. This was the Bundeswehr alpine course in progress, or in their case at ease, training having been completed during the cooler part of the morning. 'Do as the natives do;' I pondered upon the saying as I began to break sweat again.

Up in the high corrie, the Unterer Schüsselkarturm towered above us, its cracks and water-carved features now easily distinguishable. The Schober line looked an exciting prospect for tomorrow. Impatient, we were sorely tempted, but the morning's effort and a continuing thirst restrained us.

Upon the N face a climber was negotiating the Schober's overhanging crack. It looked intimidating. Eagerly we surveyed the line; this was the key to its final defence. In silence we wondered if we had the ability.

A wooden board dangling from the Herbst Teufel indicated its start. Apprehensive and slightly overawed by the magnificent situation, we began climbing. Limestone cracks and runnels made side pulls an easy option, whilst adequate friction helped speedy movement. As pitch gave way easily to pitch we found our trepidation diminishing.

By now the sun had angled round and was scorching down the route, making us seek shady belays, thus losing time by interrupting our sequence and forcing us to select new points. The heat nagged at us, our spent energy on the walk-in now taking its toll. We were needing liquid and I cursed the folly of not carrying water. With long leads and parched throats it was simpler to resort to tugs on the rope than to call.

A lead took me to a dark recess without a belay. I squeezed in and scraped around in the gloom for a suitable anchor, the coolness of the dark limestone cleft a welcome relief from the hot sun. Bob glanced enviously at my cool arbour as he passed and I felt impishly pleased that the heat was also affecting him. After two more leads we reached easier ground where it was safe to unrope. In character with the area, with declining steepness we encountered loose rock. Dehydration was affecting our climbing so it was with slow and tedious caution that we finally reached the summit.

The view was marvellous but short-lived owing to our need to find water. A fine ridge ran back to the Oberer Schusselkarturm, a formidable obstacle which we would have to cross. With a combination of crawling and staggered moves we edged along the ridge, our patience strained by having to be abnormally careful. But we reached the scree descent eventually and comparative safety. Caution kicked into touch, we raced down, creating clouds of dust, until a water seepage point was discovered amongst the rubble. Our thirst was temporarily sated, and with improving water stops we descended to the hut. It had been a cracker of a climb, we had seen the Schober and would be fresher tomorrow.

As with Llanberis, the week-end attracts many climbers, and the hut was filling up. Young Germans, some accompanied by their girls, were arriving. The night was warm and many took to sleeping out.

The evening developed a jovial atmosphere. Roars of laughter echoed as an unfortunate hiker was caught by a hut joke, for here in the Oberreintal, climbers rule supreme.

With so many climbers about we needed to be up early for the Schober. I did not relish the thought of queueing whilst it became warm again. Morning found us tiptoeing through the mass of sleeping climbers and some already rousing. We had developed that curious route-bagger's syndrome, fearing that many would be heading for our chosen route.

Bob was already restless and did not need much to get him going. Sigwenda had given him the coffee, which he had ready outside on the grass. Away from the morning's gathering confusion we breakfasted while our plans for the day were finalized.

When we looked across to the upper corrie the weather did not look so good. A shroud of mist wreathed around the Unterer Schüsselkarturm. Rumour from the alpine guide camp led us to expect deteriorating weather. We became indecisive, since in poor visibility the route would be difficult to follow.

We retraced our steps of yesterday doubtful of the outcome. I recalled times when I had seen this type of cloud recede with the day's heat. Nearing the route two shadowy figures could be seen through the gloom. Someone had beaten us to it. Were we too late?

They were Germans, racking up for the Schober. They surprised us by offering to let us start first. Being diplomatic Brits we returned the gesture, shrewdly thinking it would save us route finding in the mist. This was declined with firm continental politeness. Hang it, this 'After you old chap' situation could not continue. We had the lead and were committed to route-find into the bargain.

Bob hurriedly consulted our climbing topograph — we had come a long way since our first translation from a German guidebook — and with some help he was becoming good at it. Short of paper we had once written the route description on toilet roll leaves. A near misadventure in meeting the requirements of nature caused us to use our improvized guide for its primary purpose, leaving us guideless on a climb.

Mountains tend to create their own magic, the Oberreintal being no exception. Like a magician removing his cloak, the cloud rolled back abruptly, revealing the Unterer Schüsselkarturm. Stifling an 'I told you so,' I craned back to see the route. Seeing the overhangs in their stark reality I half wished that it was an illusion. We were going up there?

The grade VI entry crack started our serious climbing. It was short and enjoyable and Bob led the pitch speedily. Moving through I came to the long pitch of VI. This was to be the most sustained. The rack full, and firing all guns I bridged up the crack. Placing runners easily I continued, beginning to feel a flow of confidence. That most illusive quality foundered when a handhold broke away from an overhang blocking the way into the next crack system.

Faltering beneath the difficulties I was aware that the Germans were nearing Bob. Pride increased the pressure on me and I struggled for inspiration. The move came as one strenuous pull and I gained the next crack. It continued to be steep but now the grade was easing as rope and runners ran out at the belay. Ammunition was indeed exhausted.

Bob passed, seemingly impressed with the pitch, and was on his way as the first German reached me. It transpired that he was a guide with his client, the guide doing all the leading. I noticed that he occasionally used chalk, his dabs being infrequent and economical. I have to admit to carrying chalk, but it was hardly needed, the limestone tending to have a degree of dust.

Helmets and body harnesses being the fashion, I found the chest attachment good for this type of belaying, giving a better rest on the steep walls.

Bob's pitch brought me to a descending traverse, where the route began to weave through the overhangs. The traverse was delicate, my heels in space above the overhang. A balance problem, I saw the walls sweeping down to the corrie floor. That delectable feeling of extreme exposure was sensational as I edged across. I was wondering where my prusiks were in case I slipped, when I found a place for a 'Friend'. The limestone provides good cracks for them. Soon a wire 'Rock' consolidated my security and I was able to move up on steady V terrain with the occasional peg runner. By British standards there seemed to be many pegs, but it would be foolish to rely on them, and on these long routes it is vital to climb ably between the pitons.

Bob had an awkward start into the overhanging crack. Here I could see the holds, but it still looked fearsome. Bob had done a good job on the pitch and when I followed I found that the awkward start gave way to excellent holds in the crack which continued with a mixture of steep, exposed bridging.

The major difficulties over, grade III and II climbing led us to easier ground where we speedily drew away from the guide and his client. Our condition when we reached the summit was fresh in comparison to yesterday. Having the afternoon left to descend, we lingered to savour the grandeur.

Relaxing beneath the large maple trees surrounding the hut is a pleasant way to while away an afternoon. Time to reflect on the climbs. The Oberreintal has many good routes. Similar to the Schober but not as fine was the Byrch, a grade VI on the Oberreintalturm. On the Oberreintaldom the Gelber U, a grade V+, looks spectacular when seen from the hut but only provides a few reasonable pitches. More equal to the Schober is the Gonda, a grade VI. This seems an exciting challenge for a return visit.

Of Schober himself, it was 1938 when he pioneered his route. It was the breakthrough of that period. With a handful of pitons he forced his way through the overhanging sections on the Unterer Schüsselkarturm taking a nearly direct line to its fine summit. Schober was not to survive the following war, or he would surely have found greater acclaim. They say that where you find a Schober route it is one of quality. If others compare with his route on the Unterer Schüsselkarturm, I would agree.

Margherita Guinea Pig

Miriam Baldwin

Last summer we traversed Monte Rosa via the Dufourspitze and visited the
Margherita Hut. Situated on the summit of the Signalkuppe, at 4554m it is the
highest hut in the Alps. I did not know at the time that it is both a climbing hut
and an observatory for scientific studies.

We retired to bed shortly after our arrival for a quick snooze. I was somewhat
surprised to be roused from my afternoon slumbers by a young man in a T-shirt
and jeans, waving a questionnaire. He was conducting a survey on Women at
Altitude. My climbing companions had apparently volunteered me. They were
nowhere to be seen — melting snow outside the hut, it later transpired. The
young man indicated that I should follow him upstairs to a table in a corridor. I
was eager to participate, feeling flattered to be asked. I felt in excellent shape,
in spite of a gruelling day during which I had lugged a heavy pack.

The questions were easily answered in spite of my complete lack of German.
The questioner spoke some English — 'When had I last been at altitude?' 'Had
I experienced any adverse effects then,' etc, etc? Then the young man put me
through my paces. He listened to my breathing — felt my pulse and took my
blood pressure. 'Good. Now shut your eyes and hold out your hands in front of
you — good. Now walk in a straight line down the corridor placing one foot in
front of the other — good. Now I am going to shine a light into your eyes.' He
did so; the light was horribly bright and I struggled to keep my bloodshot,
sensitive eyes open for him. I assumed that he was a PhD student — he
probably was; I still have no idea! So far I continued to feel good. Whatever the
game was, I was winning.

I was then taken through a door into the inner sanctum. 'Now we will take
some blood,' said the young man. I laughed. 'I need all my blood for tomorrow
— I want to traverse Lyskamm and Castor. How much blood do you need?'
'Only a little cupful,' he replied in deadly earnest. By now I had taken in my
surroundings. I was led to a comfortable bunk, made up with inviting pillows.
At the back of the room stood five other people, one a woman. They smiled at
me encouragingly. They were quite right, I was beginning to feel anxious. It
was virtually impossible to retreat. My pride would not allow it. I had given
blood before . . . This time it appeared that the reward would be a tumbler of
wine, rather than tea and biscuits . . . It might be worth it. I lay down and
thought of England. After all, I was a Woman at Altitude, and there weren't
many of us in evidence at the Margherita Hut. Perhaps they knew more about it
than I did. A different young man approached with a syringe. He smiled, but
he meant business. I had resigned myself to losing a little blood to these friendly
youths. When they took the second syringeful of my precious blood supply, I
felt that matters were getting out of hand. Still I lay there, inert and acquies-
cent. My courage would be rewarded soon. Instead, a third gentleman
approached. He was very smooth and charming, and his English was perfect.

He was somewhat older than the others but also attired in T-shirt and casual trousers. He began to chat to me in what I now realise was a professional bedside manner. He talked to me of Doug Scott and of Messner, both of whom had helped him with his surveys. I talked to him of the Alpine Club, and the Meet I was on, and of my aspirations for the morrow. He had lulled me into a false sense of security. 'Please remove your breeches,' he said, 'I wish to take blood from this region.' He put his hand on my groin. Once again I found it impossible to object. I wanted to say 'Why?' and 'Who are you?' but felt too amazed to ask. All I could croak was 'I'm afraid it will affect my climbing tomorrow!' Messner's doctor — or whoever he was — calmed me once again. 'A girl who has traversed the Dufourspitze will have no problem traversing Lyskamm — don't worry!' 'But what about my blood?' I wanted to shout — but didn't.

He had a little trouble getting the great long needle into the right bit of my groin to withdraw the blood. It took three attempts and although he was obviously competent and confident, it hurt. I was no longer doing well and I felt truly shaken. After it was all over, bar the giant sample bottle given for my continued co-operation, this mysterious man did explain that he had needed arterial blood — hence the strange letting point. Friends have told me since that I was foolish to allow anyone to attempt to take arterial blood without seeing their credentials. And I had not even asked what the man was doing!

The cup of wine was *minute* — not nearly enough to compensate my blood loss or my wounded pride. I needed a bottle at least. I was ushered out to drink the thimbleful elsewhere. I realised then, of course, that I was only a guinea pig. I will probably never know the results! Did they like my blood?

I awoke the next day feeling queasy, weak, dizzy and sore. We delayed setting out so that I could recover. I will never know whether I would have felt like that anyway! People are supposed to in that hut. Anyway, we set off at 7.30am to 'do' Lyskamm — the conditions were perfect and we romped along, enjoying the frozen, delicate ridge, the superb views and bright blue skies. Already my sufferings in the name of Science were forgotten.

Winter Climbing on Beinn an Dothaidh

Ken Crocket

'Never perhaps within the experience of the climbers had the Scottish mountains borne an aspect so truly Alpine. Immense quantities of snow filled all the corries, especially to the north. The summit ridges were crowned with huge cornices, overhanging in many places by ten feet or more the grand unbroken slopes below, upon the surface of which were frequently seen the evidences of recent avalanches.'

So began the report on the SMC Easter Meet of 1894, held at Inveroran Inn near Bridge of Orchy (*SMCJ3*, pp76–80). This meet is perhaps better known for the activities of three of its participants, Dr Norman Collie and his two guests Solly and Collier. The small inn was bursting at the seams and Collie and his friends moved on. First they went to Glencoe, where they recorded the first rock climb on the Buachaille with their ascent of Collie's Route, then to Ben Nevis, where they made the first ascent and first winter ascent, of Tower Ridge.

That autumn the West Highland Railway opened and Collie, flushed with his success on Tower Ridge, persuaded his fellow members to switch the 1895 Easter Meet to Fort William. But other deeds were done from Inveroran Inn in March 1894. Apart from Collie's group, participants included names no less well known — Professor Ramsay and his son William, Willie Naismith, Gilbert Thomson, Rennie and Douglas, Maclay and Willie Brown to name some. From this meet at the west end of Loch Tulla several parties began the exploration of the winter routes on Beinn an Dothaidh, so starting a process that, with a gap of many decades, was to continue for over 90 years.

On the Sunday of the meet, the two Ramsays, Campbell, and Moss left the shore of Loch Tulla, and crossing the NW spur of Beinn an Dothaidh entered the small coire under the NE face. Traversing leftwards they 'came to a big gully [and] . . . cut up this and came out just west of, and perhaps one hundred feet below the summit.'

This first ascent, of the grade I West Gully, had been led by the Ramsays, taking two hours of step-cutting. Ramsay Jnr, however, had noticed other gullies waiting to be climbed, and the next day, Monday 27 March, he persuaded Boyd, Douglas, Thomson, and Naismith to accompany him on another foray into the NE coire of Beinn an Dothaidh. In 1894 Inveroran was on the main route north to Glencoe, there being no road continuing up past the E shore of Loch Tulla and over the Blackmount, as there is today. Consequently, to save a long trudge via Bridge of Orchy the party arranged for a boat.

'The sheet of glassy water, with its fringe of woodland, formed a beautiful foreground for the white tops around, and the rich glowing morning suggested June rather than March.'

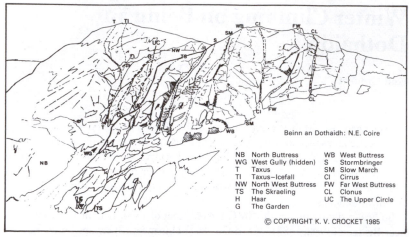

Beinn an Dothaidh: N.E. Coire

NB	North Buttress	WB	West Buttress
WG	West Gully (hidden)	S	Stormbringer
T	Taxus	SM	Slow March
TI	Taxus–Icefall	CI	Cirrus
NW	North West Buttress	FW	Far West Buttress
TS	The Skraeling	CL	Clonus
H	Haar	UC	The Upper Circle
G	The Garden		

© COPYRIGHT K. V. CROCKET 1985

The party was indeed suffering from overheating by the time they entered the coire, pausing to examine the possible routes in front. The fine gully/chimney lines on what was later to be named the West Buttress (see diagram) were not described by the party. From their angle of view they may not have been obvious lines of weakness, and in any case would have been immediately classed as being too severe. Instead attention was at first concentrated on the gully which was the left-hand branch of West Gully, the easy snow gully climbed the previous day.

'A long consultation was held as to the propriety of attacking the left-hand branch of the double gully, which led almost directly to the summit . . . A nearer inspection confirmed what was previously suspected, that the gully, filled as it was with ice, would probably be too severe a tax upon our time; and a traverse was made below the buttress to the smaller corrie.'

William Ramsay's party was obliged to rope up and begin step-cutting, the five climbers splitting into two ropes. The first consisted of Douglas and Naismith. The small cornice which topped the coire to the left of North Buttress had appealed to Douglas and they climbed this snow slope to give Central Gully, grade I. Though of an easy nature, the slope below the cornice was measured as being at an angle of 59 degrees, which is steeper than the top section of Zero Gully on Nevis.

Ramsay, Boyd, and Thomson meanwhile traversed further left, to climb a zigzag gully consisting of snow, short ice steps, and a few moves on rock. Their route was also grade I, affording them practice at step-cutting. They arrived on the ridge in time to drop a rope down to Douglas and Naismith. The latter pair could have safely climbed the 3m cornice, which was vertical at the point of ascent, but this would have given them a tedious time and they accepted a pull on the top-rope quite happily.

Following this meet of 1894 Beinn an Dothaidh was abandoned for bigger things further north, though East Gully, grade I, and lying to the left of the zigzag gully climbed by Ramsay, Boyd, and Thomson must have been climbed at some later date.

The Southern Highlands suffered an unjust neglect by the SMC guidebook writers, as it was not until 1949 that John Wilson's District Guide was published. This contained a mention of the above snow routes, as well as two v.diff. rock climbs which had been found on the mossy rocks of the West Buttress. As Wilson's guide had enjoyed a large print run it was not until 1972 that the second edition, by Donald Bennet, was published. One winter route had been added by then, the left-hand branch of West Gully. The new route, a 180m grade III gully, rises steeply out of West Gully, about one-third of the way up the latter, to gain broken ground just below the summit. It was recorded by a party from Edinburgh, Arthur Ewing and A J Trees, on 8 March 1969. A possible earlier ascent was not recorded.

Ewing and Trees named their Grade III gully Taxus, obviously having read the account by Thomson of the 1894 examination. The second edition of the District Guide suggested that two hard winter routes might be found on the section of buttress right of West Gully, an accurate prediction, as the next route recorded was Haar (III), by the Edinburgh University party of M H Moar and C Walmsley on 12 March, 1972. As there had been no diagrams or photographs published to this date there was a mistaken ascent of the same line three years later by the Greenockian party of 'Big' Bill Skidmore and 'Black' Jim Crawford. A route of 140m, Haar has its difficulties at the start, a short ice pitch leading to the crux ice wall, with easier climbing above.

From now on exploratory climbing in the area became more intense as interest in the cliff's potential grew. First ascents were to be dominated by two groups of climbers; the 'Greenock Boys', and a Glaswegian element.

The route after Haar was Cirrus (III/IV), by Crawford, John Gillespie and Skidmore. This fine 140m route lies on the right side of the West Buttress and was climbed on 24 March 1974. There were no first ascents in 1975, but rumours of lines were beginning to percolate through. On 25 January 1976 the Greenockian team of Crawford, Skidmore, Dave Dawson and John Madden straightened out the finish of Taxus by climbing the Icefall Finish (III/IV). At a length of about 90m it provides an excellent, steep and sustained finish to Taxus, landing one right below the summit. A few weeks later it received its second ascent by Ian Fulton and Ken Crocket. Finishing a III/IV first ascent in another coire these two walked over the summit to examine the NE coire. A traverse under the cliffs led to the start of Taxus and despite the late hour an ascent by the Icefall Finish was made, ending at sunset with an eery purple light suffusing through a band of summit mist. The race was now on to climb available lines.

Crawford, Dawson, and Skidmore climbed the very fine line of West Buttress (III), a 120m mountaineering buttress route on 1 February 1976. Fulton returned later that month with John Hutchinson to climb The Skraeling (IV). Its 245m length includes an easier-angled lower tier which can be avoided. Above this, the steep section of the North-West Buttress was followed up a corner, gained by a difficult right traverse.

Boxing Day 1976 was successful for Skidmore and Hodgson, working off their Christmas calories with an ascent of Clonus (III/IV). This route follows the incut 120m slot to the right of Cirrus. Three buttress routes now remained to be climbed on the West Buttress. The first fell to Colin Stead and Colin Grant two days after the ascent of Clonus. Their line, Slow March, took a tortuous route up the buttress left of Cirrus, and at 200m and Grade IV its length includes some traversing. The scent of competition was still in the air when two ascents were made on the same day, 3 January 1977. Stead and Grant climbed the 140m Far West Buttress (III), while the relaxed partnership of Fulton and Crocket, starting just right of Haar, succeeded on the imposing start of Stormbringer (150m, III). Later that day a thaw set in, but the major lines on both the North-West and West Buttresses had been completed.

This interesting period of exploration over two years had seen seven routes of Grade III and above. All of these, when in condition, are worth climbing and several are indeed well recommended. As a postscript, several pairs of eyes from amongst the climbers mentioned above had been fixed on the buttress between West Gully and Taxus. Other crags and other mountains were to draw these climbers away for several years however, and it was left to S Kennedy, N Morrison and A Nisbet to climb The Upper Circle (205m, III), and The Garden (210m, II/III), both on 10 January 1981. The Upper Circle looks to be the most interesting, following a ramp above West Gully.

It would be a fool who would claim that Beinn an Dothaidh is worked out, though it is evident that the obvious lines have been climbed. The routes are not in condition as often as those on higher mountains, though the extra vegetation on the buttresses require only a freeze and a dusting of snow to provide good sport. Climbing there has gone a long way since the visit by Professor Ramsay in 1894.

Torrone – Orriental + Central.

Climb High Down Under

A. S. Hunt
Plates 52–53

Chris Baxter is the editor of the excellent *Wild* magazine, a sort of Australian *Climber and Rambler*, and it was his lecture at the BMC's Buxton Conference in 1982 that gave me a foretaste of what to expect on the 'Oz' rock scene. He also gave me a warning of the particular humour to be expected 'down under' when he described one of the then current car window stickers that advised 'Grow your own dope, plant a Pom!'

In 1983–84 I had the good fortune to spend some time in the Australian State of Victoria and was able to taste some of the very best outdoor experiences that part of the world can offer, not least a visit to the New Zealand Alps — the mecca for 'Oz' ice climbing experience and an important testing ground for those who are involved in the increasing number of Australian Himalayan probes.

Rumours and talk of Australian daring do have been around and growing for some time now and many of you will have heard of Kim Carrigan, their answer to Ron Fawcett, and Arapiles, 'the best crag in the world' according to Henry Barber! The advance of standards in the Southern Alps of New Zealand has reached levels that, despite lacking the protagonists and publicity of their European counterparts, stand up well in terms of boldness and skill. A major loss to the mountaineering strength of this part of the world occurred with the recent tragic deaths of Mark Moorhead, Craig Nottle and Fred From, all Australians, and New Zealander Bill Denz; all died in Himalayan accidents on Makalu and Everest. Denz was the perpetrator of several new, difficult and committing ice routes and Moorhead was the fearless originator of many of Arapiles' high standard modern rock climbs.

Next time you hear about gear being pinched in South America, border disputes in Pakistan, increased peak fees throughout the Himalaya, the alarming cost per head of a Chinese/Tibet trip, bad weather in Alaska, bears in Yosemite, no camping at Boux, rain in Wales or a thaw on the Ben, think of a trip 'down under'. No language problems, well not really! Guaranteed good cragging in 'Oz', equally guaranteed grip in New Zealand, no queueing for routes although a fine couple of days at peak season may mean a tight squeeze in the more popular New Zealand Alpine huts, and a bank holiday weekend at Arapiles may see an increase in the chalk content of the local atmosphere.

Getting there is not that expensive through one of the many 'Visit your Relations' clubs or via the local 'bucket shop', and living, once you have arrived, is a bargain. Most 'Oz' crag-access campsites are free and very pleasant places to be, with the delights of 'billy tea' or nourishing cask red wine at give away prices, and of course the friendly sociable locals for company. Watch out for the 'sandbagging' though (stoking you up a route that is likely to frighten, by understating its problems!). You could pay for your trip by selling off your modern gear and the surplus you had the foresight to take with you.

Arapiles is the crag to go for without a doubt, over a thousand routes of all grades of difficulty, an excellent guidebook, an unfamiliar yet appropriate grading system from one to thirty, and a bunch of regulars to show you around. Other Victorian crags offer longer quality routes, for example Mt Rosea or Mt Buffalo, and are well worth a visit, and up in New South Wales there are crags of all sizes with routes of quality to suit everyone. Further north just over the border into Queensland is Frog Buttress, a small crag by some standards but it has something about it that attracts folk from all over, not easy routes though! This is the crag for hand and finger jambing or desperate face climbing and best visited in the Australian version of winter (July/August) when the crags further south may be a wee bit damp from time to time. Up at Frog it will be warm and balmy with shorts 'all the go', but beware the 'crawlies', the spiders or snakes. The sloughed off snake skins on the belay ledges at Frog testify to the 'true' story of the climber who had just struggled up the 'Oz' equivalent of a HVS crack and reached the finishing jugs only to come face to face with a malevolent brown snake: he flung himself off into space preferring to take his chance in flight rather than risk a deadly bite! If all this should prove too much go and explore the Dividing Range Mountains, their 'High Country', or get down to the surf if it's 'pumping'.

New Zealand is that bit further and as in any high mountain area, the weather can affect the experience. The mountains seem much bigger than they really are, without telepheriques to help access, although flying in and out by ski-plane is now commonplace and not too expensive. The New Zealand Alpine Club and the National Park services have an excellent system of open huts equipped with all facilities and often a two-way radio to help with weather bulletins or safety checks.

The Mount Cook National Park area is the best known with a good valley and mountain hut system and reciprocal rights arrangements should you be a member of a UK club. There are a tremendous range of routes here to suit all levels of ability and experience. Classic pass traverses such as the Copeland, one of a few to breach the main range; easily approached huts in wild surroundings, such as the Tasman Saddle hut; classic high summit traverses; or ice climbing at its most fearsome. Other areas such as Mt Aspiring, offer fine tramping and climbing in wilderness surroundings and the Darren range will satisfy anyone who has a taste for granite mountains in a remote and inaccessible setting. If the nor'wester stops you going out (the Kiwi version of an Atlantic depression) you can always go and look up those long lost relatives or that friend of a friend you used to know in the Lakes: they will be more than glad to see you. They may even take you down to the local pub at the weekend, an experience not to be missed if it turns out the same as when I went. There was the distinct air of the old West at times when the younger set started to get lively! Have a good trip.

1. *Classic Climbs of Australia* by Joe Friend, Second Back Row Press, 1983.
2. *Mt Arapiles — a rock-climber's handbook*, edited by Kim Carrigan for the Victorian Climbing Club.
3. *The Mount Cook Guidebook* by Hugh Logan, New Zealand Alpine Club, 1982.

Cordillera Apolobamba —
The First Ascent of Palomani Tranca

Jim Curran
Plates 54–56

The Cordillera Apolobamba is 130km NE of Lake Titicaca in SE Peru on the Bolivian border. It had been visited from Bolivia but seldom from Peru, and never by a British expedition. One summit, Palomani Tranca 5633m, remained unclimbed. This much information, gleaned by Geoff Tier after many fruitless hours in the RGS and AC libraries, was more or less what I had expected, for Geoff has that enviable knack of Finding Things Out. Moreover, he then Does Something About Them. As I lack both these attributes almost entirely but compensate for the lack with a proven and long standing flair for being led astray it was inevitable that, around the beginning of July, I would find myself with Geoff once more at Heathrow's Terminal 3 in double boots, salopette and furry jacket, clumping aboard a DC10. With me was an unopened letter from my bank manager marked 'Urgent and Confidential'.

Generous support from the MEF and the BMC enabled us to fly to Lima where we met Andy Maskrey, an old friend of Geoff's, who had been working for five years in Peru running a disaster agency. His fluent Spanish was without doubt, the key factor in enabling us to get anywhere near our range for it must be said that once away from the main tourist circuit, some Spanish is essential. Andy's Peruvian girl-friend Chepi also spoke Quechua so that in many respects Geoff and I had a very easy time. We found out very quickly that in South America you are not a *sahib* but a *gringo* — a big difference.

Travelling by bus to Arequipa, train to Puno, taxi to Juliaca and thence by lorry we reached Ananea a small goldmining village, some 50km from Lake Suches at the foot of the mountain. There we pondered our next move and the means by which to make it. Occasionally fact is stranger than fiction and this occasion could have come straight from the *Ascent of Rum Doodle* for it consisted of a midnight walk with five very small children and a wheelbarrow. Only, I hasten to add, as far as another lorry at the far end of town, whose driver had been persuaded by Andy and Chepi to drive us to the lake. Next morning the lorry trundled over the high altiplano, following the vaguest of tracks over terrain as rough and featureless as the top of Bleaklow.

Under a canopy of luminous blue sky and in bitter cold, we breasted the crest of a rise and saw the snowy domes and ridges of the Apolobamba filling the horizon ahead — a moment of huge relief for all of us. They were obviously well worth coming all that way for. While our mountain scarcely qualified for any 'Last Great Problem' status, it was easy to see why it had not been climbed for it was separated from the rest of the range by a high glacier and had rocky ridges that its neighbours lacked. Nevertheless, it looked fairly straightforward.

In Lima it had been impossible to obtain a decent map from either the Army or the Instituto Peruano del Deporte so, despite perfect visibility, on our first reconnaissance of the approach, it was almost inevitable that we would get lost. This we did, by leaving the lakeside too early and gaining too much height, descending and re-ascending unseen valleys before arriving, tired and ill-tempered, at a beautiful high pasture immediately below the glacier which separates Palomani Grande from Palomani Tranca. We dropped our loads in relief and slogged back to Base Camp, arriving at nightfall. After a day of organizing food and gear we all moved up to occupy Advance Base Camp. The weather was bitterly cold but settled, and our optimism knew no bounds. We hoped to climb Palomani Tranca by ascending the innocuous glacier above us to a col, then climb the short N ridge of the mountain. Then who knew? A new route up Palomani Grande was beckoning, as were several very tempting traverses.

The following day brought us down to earth. After an early start and travelling very light, we still managed to pick an appalling way onto the glacier, and made slow progress on hideous slaty rock, unstable scree and vile debris-covered ice. At last we gained the upper glacial basin, already way behind schedule, and received a further unpleasant surprise. The basin was covered in bottomless powder snow partially or wholly concealing vast crevasses. Geoff's progress was abruptly halted by threats of mutiny. 'A wise mountaineering decision' was the order of the day but even so, it was almost dark before we returned to the tents. Chepi fed us endless Cuppa Soups and was proving to be an invaluable addition.

Next day Geoff decided to have a look at the way on to the long W ridge of the mountain while I ascended a big hill behind Advance Base Camp hoping to get a good view of the upper section of the ridge. Andy and Chepi nobly volunteered to return to Base Camp for more food and a bottle of contraband whisky.

Geoff ascended an immensely long pinnacled ridge of appalling rock that finally led onto the crest of the W ridge proper. From his high point it looked possible to move along the crest of the ridge but the snow seemed to be as awful as on the glacier. His view of the upper reaches of the mountain was confusing, as he could see two possible summits, one a long way off the W ridge. My view did little to help, for from the top of my hill I could see four! Unfortunately, I could not see how, or even if, they were connected and the topography of the final few hundred metres looked surprisingly complex. But I could see that Geoff's route on to the ridge could be substantially shortened by the ascent of a huge scree slope which appeared to cut through a rock buttress barring access to the ridge itself. That evening we decided to place a camp on the ridge, as it was around 3km long, and to take enough food for three days. While Geoff enjoyed a well-earned rest-day I ascended the hideous scree slope to find that after three hours, there was indeed an easy way through. I left the little climbing gear I had carried in a small cave and slithered down to pass on the good news.

We made a leisurely and late start the next day plodding in our own time up the scree, and then interminably up a long snow slope on to the ridge. As late afternoon turned with bewildering rapidity into night, we found a perfect

Photo: Frank Solari

52 *Mount Cook and the Tasman river flats.*

Photo: Alan Hunt

53 *Mount Tasman from Graham Saddle.*

Photo: Geoff Tier

54 *The highest peaks of the Cordilera Apolobamba — the Chupi Orco massif — 8km N of the Palomani massif. No routes have been climbed from this (Peruvian) side.*

Photo: Geoff Tier

55 *Ananea (5842m) (L) and Calijou (5827m).*

56 *The summit pinnacles of Palomani Tranca (5633m). The furthest summit is the highest. There are deep cols either side of the central pinnacle.*

57　*Collecting geological samples on Brabant Island.*

58　*Storm.*

camp-site in a snowy hollow, with bands of shattered orange rock protecting us on each side. In the red afterglow of sunset, we looked out over the Bolivian border towards the Cordillera Real.

After a restless night Geoff forced himself awake at 4am and resumed the never-ending battle with the stove. We were away before dawn and to our delight cramponed up an easy ice-slope on to the ridge, hoping fervently that it would last. It did not. We gained the ridge just as the first rays of sunlight lit its crest. It was a breathtaking position: superb views down to the grey sheen of Lake Suches still in the shadows; a range of jagged peaks beyond in Bolivia; mushroom clouds rearing behind them from the Amazon Basin. Doubts dispelled and confidence growing, we set off unroped along the ridge, finding out very quickly that its very crest had to be followed precisely — one step either side and powder snow made progress almost impossible.

The ridge undulated. We gained height and ground slowly. It was hard to gauge progress and harder still to see what was coming next, but after three hours progress was abruptly interrupted by a big serac wall topped by a huge cornice. Time to rope up. Geoff led a good ice pitch up and round to the very crest of the ridge where the cornice petered out to belay on a tottering pinnacle poised over a huge drop to the glacier on our left. Another rope length followed and the angle eased off. By now we hoped we were approaching the first of our potential summits and the moment of truth. Another 50m and all would be revealed.

It was and it was not. Some 200m ahead a big black fang poked up above an intervening snowy gendarme. It was undoubtedly higher than we were, but not much. The other contender for the top was definitely lower for we could now see over it, some 600m away. This was a relief for getting to it looked appalling. But getting to the real top was still an unknown quantity. Between us and it, was a knife-edged snow ridge that even from here, was partially concealed by the gendarme. It looked very uninviting. We decided to give it a try, leaving our rucksacks and spare gear on the summit of the ice crest.

At once we were into a different world: high exposure on either side, appalling snow and even worse rock. Geoff led, as he had done all day with enviable determination. I followed, and poor Andy floundered in the steps that I had reduced to a trench. Belays were strictly for form's sake and the pitch up the snowy gendarme was steep, hard and dangerous. At last we could see the final section, a steep descent to a snowy col then one or possibly two rope-lengths up the final summit pinnacle. It looked repulsive but only marginally worse than what had gone before. Half an hour of tension and the discovery of a real belay (the first and only one on the entire climb) and Geoff led the final few metres to the top.

For me this was a unique event. I had spent five previous expeditions nearer the bottom than the top of the mountains I had come to climb and was by nature very reluctant to assume that this trip would be any different. Suddenly perched on a tiny patch of trampled snow I had broken the habit of a lifetime. It was everything I had ever imagined: big grins all round, vigorous handshakes, beyond description.

The day was only half over. We had to down-climb the descent in its entirety, but it was uneventful though wearying. The memory of it remains vague.

Next day the weather began to break. We had been told that high winds would start by the end of July and this certainly seemed to be the case. Three days later amidst snow flurries and darkening skies, we left on the long haul back to civilization.

Several possibilities remain. The W ridge of Palomani Grande is the most obvious, but there are innumerable new routes and long traverses to be made in the area. Climbing earlier in the season, May or June, might give better snow conditions than we experienced. We were fortunate in achieving our main objective and learned a lot. Very small trips to remote areas, even if the objectives are not serious, do need some planning and a lot of luck. Geoff and Andy supplied the former and I suppose I was due for a break!

One day I'll open the letter from the bank.

Joint Services Expedition to Brabant Island, Antarctica

John Kimbrey
Plates 57–58

The Antarctica is remote and for most mountaineers, totally out of reach.

When an opportunity arose in summer 1982 I wanted and needed to go. I applied to Commander Chris Furse RN, the expedition's leader, and was interviewed along with many other hopefuls at the RGS in London, a very impressive establishment. I could almost feel the presence of those great men in the old building as I tip-toed carefully along the corridors so as not to disturb anyone. Seven days later I received a letter inviting me to join a meet in North Wales a few weeks later at the first official team gathering. I had made it into the Winter Team, one of only four people to do so at this stage.

Brabant Island is nearly 56km long and 24km wide and is the second largest island in the Palmer Archipelago. At one time it was one of the largest still to be explored in the world. It lies 400km south of the Antarctic convergence and east of Grahamland, sitting in a rather weather-beaten zone where winds are regularly above force 12. Temperatures drop to around $-40°C$ in winter and rise to about $+10°$ in summer. The island is largely covered by mountains, the highest, Mount Parry at 2522m. The island's neglect over the years is due mainly to the large ice-cliffs which almost completely protect its coastline from the sea. Brabant Island was named by Adrien De-Gerlache who led an expedition in 1898 and was first to land on the SE coast with Dr. F. Cook and Roald Amundsen.

Over the next 18 months we trained in the rough but tranquil area around Dundonnel in Western Ross, in Cornwall and in Norway, with a final wild two weeks in the Cairngorms in January 1984. The Summer Party had flown south in December to Chile where they had embarked on HMS Endurance, our transport to and from the island for the next 16 months. Change-over day was 24 March.

At last, nearly two years from my initial enquiry, I arrived. On our flight ashore we flew past the mountains and glaciers we had come to climb. It was a fantastic day; sun, mountains, snow and ice and something I was not so keen on, 10,000 penguins. Base Camp was right in the middle of a colony and the smell took some getting used to. We set about unpacking and organising our 15 tonnes of kit, and by late afternoon all changeovers had been completed. Farewells were brief and our 12 man team had started its big adventure.

The first few weeks flew by as we erected a small tri-wall hut for use as a laboratory and a meeting place, and carefully worked out the stores and food area. This had to be marked and carefully recorded for soon it would be buried in snow. With a ready stock of most small things in the hut annex, our stores system worked very well, and only occasionally did we all have to dig in to find a special item.

Eventually with Base organised, everyone started to venture out with their skis and pulks. We skied with lightly laden pulks, splitting the load between back and pulk. As slopes were encountered the more we would put in our sacks and so on. Each person in these early days worked out his own preference for loading, but as always the best laid plans often fail, and when the snow got sticky or deep powder covered the surface, life became hell. Often we referred to Robert Falcon Scott and how incredibly hard his trip to the South Pole must have been. My first trip out took me to an area about 10km south of Base to relocate some food and fuel which had been dropped short of a cache site by the Summer Party. The day was pleasant and the snow superb as we set off up the hill above Camp. With three to one pulk, pulling together took a while to master but we persisted and after half an hour or so things were going well. The corrie to the east stretched for about 16km as it swept south then west back towards the sea. The tops were clear and sharp against the blue of the sky. The crevasse areas were immense and detours were often necessary. As we neared the cache the marker cane loomed out of the gloom, as now the weather had clamped right in. We pitched our dome tent and settled down to a night on the hill, our first of many. Avalanches roared during the night a couple of kilometres or so to the east. I slept badly: always there is that feeling of insecurity when a slide occurs, no matter how far away you are and no matter how secure the site. Morning dawned to brilliant sunshine and we ski'd around the ridge before heading back a different way to Base.

Those first trips were important in many ways, not only to test kit, but for some, apart from our training this was the first time in the mountains proper. We had a nucleus of four experienced mountaineers, and the leader, Chris, who spends half his life living with the birds, plus two or three people who had been around the hills for many years and knew enough to be regarded as seconds. As it happened, when our first big incident did occur there were two of the more experienced men in the party to organise the safe return of personnel and equipment from the grasp of a 30m crevasse.

As winter approached and the snow fell we started to cache stores around the NE to help us in spring when we pushed south. We had read of the transglobe expedition and their use of skidoos (in fact we bought two from them) and had spoken to Ollie Shepherd and Sir Ron Fiennes on the matter. We hoped the skidoos would perform well even on the island's difficult terrain. This, however, was not to be, as we found out through May on a three week trip which taught us all an incredible amount during a very eventful month.

We had set off in fine conditions hoping to make our progress by a series of ferries as the skidoos would not pull heavy sledges on their own. We therefore pulled one medium-loaded sledge with three skidoos, but this was so expensive on fuel that more trips were needed than we expected. There were minor mechanical problems, and the inevitable bad patches of weather, and in the first five days we managed to shift 2 tonnes of fuel, food and equipment only a short distance from Base Camp, although we did manage to set one cache at Rontgen Peak on the E side. In fine conditions, with good snow, driving was a pleasure, and at last we could see how a skidoo could operate. Alas the terrain and snow only allowed good loads for one or two days a month. So we had to ferry light loads and repeat the trips several times in order to operate at all. We made a second cache at Lister glacier — another 360kg dropped — and moved up the glacier to try to put a route in to Astrolabe Point. We hoped to make one more drop further south. We used a system of three drivers and three ski-orring and then used the skiers to 'recce' ahead when needed. Moving up to 700m we encountered thick fog and snow which was to stay with us for six days. One and a half metres of snow fell with only brief periods of respite. We moved on to two-thirds rations as food started to become short. On the seventh day we decided to move on skis, but as we vacated the igloos an avalanche swept past, barely missing us. Shocked by the incident, we headed back down to Lister Cache, food and safety. We had been away from Base nearly three weeks, with only a slim chance of finding a route without eating all our caches. I felt a return to base was our best choice, especially as we had no radio and I presumed the leader was becoming anxious.

We retrieved the 'skids' and headed off the following morning, reversing the outward journey except for a few variations where obvious lines had been seen from below the plateau. Conditions were difficult but we pushed on carefully and dropped back into reasonable visibility on the N side of the island. In retrospect, this was where we should have camped, but Base fever had us all as we pushed on along the north of the island. Claire's Finger, our friendly cache and starting point, loomed ahead and home seemed about 1 hour away. Suddenly the skidoo train stopped. Something was down. A large crevasse had opened and the 12ft sledge was suspended, tail down, 10m below. I skied over to assess the situation while the drivers busily placed Dead Giants to take the weight. Within 20 minutes the sledge was secure and the two front skidoos had moved on. More bridges were collapsing around us and the rumblings beneath my feet were a nightmare. Darkness was now nearly upon us and we were still in the middle of a crevasse field. With one skidoo and three skiers on the tail, we moved down and crossed on a bridge some 15m from the hole. The rumblings continued as we joined the others. I was impressed with everyone's quick thinking and ability in our first skidoo incident. The system was performed without a mass of direction; it just happened as if by instinct. We were now less than 1km from snow holes we had left 12 days previously so we headed for them, but the skidoos bogged in (our major problem with the machines) and we were forced to bivouac. Next morning, unbelievably happy, we returned to Base Camp to a welcome we had not expected, a few bottles, and story time as we talked over our first major trip and the lessons learnt.

June turned foul and we sat out in appalling weather on two occasions of four days and five days before heading back to Base each time dejected having failed to recover the sledge. Mid-Winter's Day cheered everybody up and our day was crammed with activities and feasting. The long night was helped along with performances by everyone and some refreshments which were made up from the 'hard stuff' and fruit juice: an excellent 24 hours!

Towards the end of the month the weather improved and we set out once again to bring the sledge to the surface. The marker canes were still visible, for most of the snow seemed to blow forever onwards and did not settle around our crevasse. We set a Dead Giant and skidoo belay, and I went down to inspect the problem. Amazingly the huge gap of the crevasse had amassed hundreds of tonnes of snow, and the top of the sledge was only just visible. For two days we dug around the buried sledge, removing equipment from its back as it became clear of snow. We attached a wire strop to the top shackle as a back-up, which was tensioned off by a winch on the surface. At one stage I had to cut the tow rope, and the crack that followed seemed to shake the whole mass of ice and snow. What made things worse, I was standing on the sledge at the time.

On the second day, with weather still bright, we had uncovered all of the sledge, but a pulk which was riding it at the time of the incident was stuck 15m down and under the vast snow bridge. The ice above the pulk created a problem we didn't need, and so with great difficulty we hacked and gouged enough to pull the pulk clear. We were now in some considerable danger, though we did not realize it at the time. The hole we had dug was across the width of the crevasse, but sloping downwards at about 40° deep into a bridge. After an hour or so the pulk was sufficiently loose to heave it out, but the rear attachment rope was stuck fast in the ice beneath the rear of the pulk. There was now a tunnel about 2m long with a loaded pulk slap in the middle. Our only option was for someone to lie head first down it armed with a knife and try to cut the offending rope whilst someone held his feet protruding out of the hole. John Beattie and I took turns to cut the line, eventually managing it to our great relief. Some 20 minutes later, with the Turfer Winch being cranked, the sledge slowly but surely climbed vertically out of the hole until it dropped heavily on to the snow surface. A spontaneous cheer rose from us all and we expressed our joy with handshakes and the promise of a few drams that evening when we returned to Base.

By July daylight had extended to seven or eight hours, and we were able to start organising and preparing for our move south in late August. We had at this time been exploring the north and carrying out a variety of science projects which involved the whole team. Mike Ringe was very busy. His speciality was geology, and he was amassing a large pile of carefully recorded rocks from all over the north. Our doctor, Howard Oakley, was still head deep in paper as he collated all the physiological results that we had supplied. This involved recording fluid balance, having thermisters taped to various parts of the body over a 24 hour period, plus the added indignity of a 15cm thermometer strategically placed for accurate inner core temperature measurements. We all performed this deed once a month and looked forward heartily to its completion. With samples and records on seals, fish, bugs, botany and birds we were all kept busy during our days in Base Camp.

July swept into August and plans were made solid for our move south. We hoped to leave Base for four months travelling in three groups using caches placed in autumn as we progressed, backed up by the skidoo team who would ferry several tons of food, fuel and equipment around to Harvey Heights. We would then move south to supplies dropped the previous summer, hoping to ascend Mount Parry en route.

Whilst ferrying stores from Base, John Spottiswood, Mike and I took the chance to climb a marvellous ridge which connected the lower plateau with the Mount Hunter range; 600m of fine Alpine style climbing gave us immense satisfaction. Some of the cornices were as large as I have ever seen and the exposure was greatly increased by the deep corries that fell away on both sides. The ascent took four hours, in a wind which increased to a steady blow. A marvellous view greeted us at the top: Grahamland far away to the west, and to the south Anvers Island, the largest in the Archipelago, with Mount Francais standing proud of the ridge along the island's NE side.

Due to unsettled weather it was not until September that we finally set off to the S end of the island. I left with three others, first to check the autumn's caches and dig out the supplies at Astrolobe Point — a journey of about 50km. We were hoping to arrive five or six days hence and then contact the skidoo team by radio, but we were in for a frustrating time due to a mixture of bad travelling conditions and appalling weather. The tents were constantly blown out and at one point we were held up for 12 days as the storms raged. We sat and repaired our kit, dropping down to half rations for the duration. We finally reached Astrolobe Point 29 days after leaving Base Camp, a little skinny and hungry but none the worse for the trip.

Our work had only just begun for the marker wands which were strapped to the food and fuel were not visible through the deep snow. We knew their approximate position and before long had found the top of one. A huge crater was dug to retrieve the stores which included the second radio. Over the next five days we tried to locate the second dump. We systematically cleared an area of 30m by 25m digging to a depth of 1.5m and found nothing. The cache had been placed next to a large boulder some 40m beyond high water mark, and behind the natural harbour wall which surrounded the Point, but it was evident that the sea had a far greater reach than we thought possible. We called off the search after seven days. Next day the remainder of the group arrived out of the mist. Eight weeks now remained before HMS Endurance was due at Metchnikoff Point to pick us up.

Mount Parry became our main objective. Four men would move south afterwards, whilst the remainder covered the centre of Brabant for geology, botany and mountaineering. During the next 12 days we ferried food and fuel up to Harvey Heights at 2100m for the attempt on Parry and to provide a central cache for journeys south and east. The weather, for a change, was good, although once through the ice-fall it snowed all through our rest day.

Next morning was very still, the mountain hidden in cloud that hung thickly on the N slopes. I had made sure the route upward had been well marked thus allowing forward movement to continue, so by 28 October we were camped at 1900m with plenty of food and reserves located at our lower camps for our return journey. Everyone had done really well and the weather was excellent. The following morning, 0400 saw 'cooks up' and by 0500 we were on our way up to the summit ridge. The morning was fine and clear, with light winds, the sun burning hot as we steadily progressed up to a point 5km from the summit. There, we pitched tents, brewed up and gazed at Mount Parry with Anvers Island, a superb backdrop, 100km beyond. At just after mid-day we set off on skis along a wide ridge south until it was necessary to don crampons and leave the skis behind. The ridge now was splendid, twisting and rising in a glistening array of ice platforms and seracs. A fantastic drop fell to a sea of cloud that masked the coastline 2400m below. At 16.20 our efforts were rewarded and we stood firmly on the summit on our small part of Antarctica, the first men ever to do so. We had been rewarded and were filled with satisfaction as we set off back to our tents, three hours to the north.

A few days later we once again split into groups. Chris Furse, Ted Atkins, Jim Lumbsen and François de Gerlache moved south with enough reserves to allow them to return north if the food dump there had also been lost. During a fine four-day spell they ascended 12 peaks and tackled some of the best ice-climbing on the island. The remaining five of us were to explore the central area around Hill Bay. John Beattie was an ardent Munroe bagger and we climbed most of the tops, at one point finding the highest plant life on the island at 300m. We had some marvellous days of mountaineering.

The weather turned towards the middle of November. We had hoped to ski along to Rokitansky summit but we were forced to spend four days in a tent constantly digging out and eventually moving sites completely. The storm threw 2m of snow down upon us from every direction. On the fifth day the wind abated and we managed to find our way back down through an ice-fall, topping up with fuel at a previous camp half way down.   We all moved a short distance to our main skidoo cache site and waited for the weather to clear. Eight days later, on 30 November, we decided to head back to Metchnikoff. It had been an eerie week. There was no wind, and fine flakes of snow drifted endlessly down burying us completely.

The remaining days at Base Camp passed uneventfully as we packed ready for our return, Jed Corbett, our photographer, taking special care over all the film he had shot. The wildlife had returned and we watched, fascinated, as the penguin chicks hatched and began their short lives. It was indeed a day of mixed feelings when HMS Endurance arrived on 29 December to take us back to civilisation . . . whether we wanted to or not!

The Children's Corner in the Alpine Club Library

Charles Warren

What makes the Alpine Club's library unique is that it is so wide ranging. Not the least delightful sections of it are the slightly unexpected ones: its Children's Corner for example. Not that juveniles are ever likely to trespass there without being 'put in the corner' alas! No, it is only those of our membership who have never quite grown up who can enjoy the books there. And there are certainly some of us who do so.

There are two classes of literature in which only a very few authors can hit the mark, and they are the humorous and the juvenile. Amongst the former one thinks of Edward Lear, Jerome K. Jerome, Hillaire Belloc and, now almost forgotten, Stephen Leacock — almost the greatest humorist of them all. Amongst the latter there were more who could bring it off, starting in the eighteenth century and going right up to the present time of our own delectable Beatrix Potter and Princes Charles with his altogether charming book, *The Old Man of Lochnagar*, written, we are told, for the amusement of the younger members of his family but sure to delight us all.

Most of the books written for children in the eighteenth and early nineteenth centuries had for their purpose either school-room instruction or moral uplift; in the latter, no bad thing perhaps. After all, there is something reassuring for a child when right triumphs over wrong as it so often does in these early tales.

One of the nice things about early children's books is that so often they come in pretty bindings and in miniature format. Furthermore, they are often illustrated. So let me draw attention to two or three of the more attractive items in the AC Library.

There is *Angelo* or The Pine Forest in the Alps, by Geraldine Jewsbury (1812-1888), a friend of the Carlyles. This contains four hand coloured engravings of drawings by John Absolon. In a charming contemporary cloth binding.

William Tell, The Patriot of Switzerland, by Jean Pierre Claris de Florian; translated. It has a very attractive engraved and hand coloured title page, and is illustrated with engravings in the text.

Claudine, or Humility the Basis of all the Virtues, A Swiss Tale, by Maria E. Budden (1780?-1892). She wrote *Hofer the Tyrolese* (in the library) and several children's books. Illustrated with engraved plates.

But we see also *Three Months Under the Snow*, by J. J. Porchat, in its pretty bindings and *Rollo in Switzerland*, by Jacob Abbott.

I have drawn attention to these items in the juvenile section of the library in the hope that those who are still young at heart will occasionally go and 'stand themselves in the corner'; the children's corner I mean!

Climb an Eponymous Mountain

Edward Pyatt

In some parts of the world colonized by Europeans where the native names for mountains either did not exist or were only with difficulty communicable, the first explorers allocated names for peaks in a fashion often arbitrary and uninspiring. The patrons of expeditions, great men of the moment, national heroes, rulers and so forth had their names spread all over the map by enthusiastic but unimaginative travellers. The principal area to suffer was North America, though the practice spread also to New Zealand, Australia, South America and the Polar regions. The highest mountain in the world carries, of course, a personal name — that of Sir George Everest, at one time in charge of the Survey of India; his name was bestowed on the newly measured Peak XV by his successor. It is the only eponymous mountain in the Himalaya, though K2 nearly became Godwin-Austen (or, as Keay tells us, it might have been Waugh, Albert or Montgomerie).

Taking into account the speed with which the colonization of the United States of America took place and the comparative lack of contact with the indigenous population, it is not surprising to find the mountains of the eastern States widely tagged with personal names. Presidents and statesmen have their peaks — Washington, Adams, Jefferson, Clay, Monroe, Madison and others. Mount Mitchell in the Blue Ridge mountains, the highest point in the eastern States, is named for Elisha Mitchell, professor of mathematics at the University of North Carolina, who was the first to climb it. He is buried on the summit and there is a commemorative pillar. Mount Marcy in the Adirondack Mountains is named for William L. Marcy, senator and statesman; Mount Oglethorpe for a hero of the War of Independence, who was founder of the State of Georgia.

As explorers moved westwards, they created personally named peaks all along the trail — the prominent Long's Peak and Pike's Peak took their names from expedition leaders; there followed others in wild profusion — Lincoln, Evans, Sherman, Elbert, Powell . . . presidents, governors, explorers, soldiers. It has to be admitted that they also came up with some local names and some highly imaginative new ones — Uncompahgre, Eolus, Redcloud, Lizard Head, Maroon Bell, Snowmass, etc. A large number of these inventions had to be made and the overall pattern is not too repellent. The process continued on westward with Gannet, Fremont, Whitney, Hood, Baker, Rainier, Adams and many others, again leavened with imaginative names in most cases more appropriate to their subjects.

Canada presents a similar picture, but here the exploration of the Rocky Mountains fell more to mountaineers and resulted in a rash of naming peaks for members of the fraternity; thankfully no one actually named a mountain for himself. Enshrined there for all time are mountaineers Forbes, Bryce, Woolley, Freshfield, Mummery, Ball, Bonney, Stutfield. Then come world figures like Roosevelt, Churchill, Stalin (the only Mount Stalin left in the world and there used to be several — the others were all changed after his death and rapid fall from grace), Lloyd George, Eisenhower. Finally we find mountains named for purely local heroes like the collection in the Cariboo Mountains — Sir Wilfrid Laurier, Sir John Abbot, Sir Mackenzie Boswell, Sir John Thomas. Both Canada and the USA have Matterhorns, all undistinguished in comparison with their eponymous Swiss original.

Alaska and the Yukon continue the theme. The highest, Mount McKinley, is named for the US President in office in the year of its firm location. Its local name, Denali, is increasingly coming back into use, but has not yet superseded the other. La Perouse, Dagelet, Malaspina, Vancouver, were in exploring parties, Tatum and Carpé are named for mountaineers. There are two mountains named for John F. Kennedy, one formerly the east peak of Mount Hubbard, the other the east peak of Mount Blackburn.

New Zealand presents a similar mixture of the not quite sublime and the some way towards ridiculous — Mannering, Harper, Teichelmann, Haast after local mountaineers; Cook, La Perouse, Torres, Tasman, Dampier after early explorers and a whole host of others of obscure origins, but no doubt with some relevance to the local scene. Some native names have been retained; for the highest, Mount Cook, the local name Aorangi is well known and may perhaps one day take over.

The highest peak in Australia is Mount Kosciusko, named for a great Polish/American patriot by Count Strzelecki who claimed the first ascent in 1840. This was disputed by Dr. Lhotsky, who claimed to have reached the summit even earlier (1834) and wished to call it Mount King William IV. The Count seems to have won the contest, though many Australians must wonder at the choice of the name.

In older established communities these oddities of nomenclature seem never to have arisen, except in a few isolated cases. There was no question of exploration by outsiders and the mapping authorities went to great pains to find agreed local names for their eminences to embellish their work. Errors did creep in from time to time, as in the case of the hill on Dartmoor originally 'Cosdon'. In the local accent this would sound like "Kaaz'n", which to the surveyor seemed to call for a spelling 'Cawsand', and this is how it appears on the map even today.

Lesser mountain features have attracted many a personal name usually in commemoration of the first ascender. In the first big expansion phase of British rock climbing just before the turn of the century that famous rock climber, our member Owen Glynne Jones, had his name appended to some half a dozen routes in the mountains of the Lake District. The practice came to be frowned upon and later generations of leaders missed having everlasting memorials on our rock faces.

Similarly in more recent times it has become customary for the names of mountaineers to be tagged on to routes in the Alps — double barrelled in the case of a party of two, eg Cecchinel-Nominé, Bonatti-Zapelli, Boivin-Gabarrou, and so on. Larger parties occasionally produce a real mouthful, eg Boivin-Diaffra-Vionnet-Fausset. Even so, these are undoubtedly to be preferred to the names of politicians and others in power in their home countries at the time of the climb.

Among this galaxy of topographical personalities there is only one instance of an individual making the first ascent of a mountain already named for him. The opportunity for so doing is not often presented, since personal names are usually only allocated posthumously. The man in question was the Conservative politician and statesman, Leopold S. Amery, a prominent mountaineer and one-time President of the Alpine Club. Early in 1928, the Canadian Department of the Interior decided to name a 3222m mountain situated at the junction of the Alexander and North Saskatchewan rivers in Alberta, Mount Amery in honour of the Secretary of State for the Dominions. On 20 August 1929 Amery made the first ascent of his mountain with Bryn Meredith and Eduard Feuz:

'We breakfasted and discussed whether we should go back and bring up bivouac kit for an attempt next day, or start at once in spite of the fact that it was snowing hard above and the weather looking anything but pleasant. We came to no decision, but began drifting up the long slope of guarding screes. An hour later we roped where our ridge and the one next to the north of it almost touched, making a cleft which opened into an amphitheatre which further up opened out into another even more impressive one. We traversed by shale bands into this lower amphitheatre and then back again to our ridge and so, by short steps of abrupt rock and zigzagging on shale ledges, made good progress till, about 12.30pm, we found ourselves up against the second and most formidable cliff band below the summit. On our own ridge the cliff cut us off abruptly. There seemed no feasible way out to the right, while to the left the cliff extended in a semicircle round the amphitheatre, black and forbidding, festooned with immense drip icicles and coated with vast sheets of glaze. Happily, just in the angle where our ridge joined, enough snow had lodged on the drip ice to make a feasible chimney of 70–80ft, which proved the key to the whole situation. More shale and another steep ice chimney with a traverse out to the left by good rock brought us to a broad shale slope forming the summit ridge (about 10,000ft). A raging blizzard hid everything from view and more than once nearly blew us off our feet. But there was no point in turning back, so we turned left up to where the shale joined the snow, and so on to the sharply defined but easy rock ridge leading to the final summit (about 2.45pm). On a fine day Mount Amery must offer a magnificent panorama of the main ridge which, from Forbes to Athabasca, curves round it. But a few hundred yards in occasional glimpses through driving snow was all we got, and five minutes at the top to build our cairn was more than enough.'

Years before (1902) Amery had been involved in the first ascent of a small peak on the Drakensberg and much later (though still long before his death) this was named Mount Amery for him.

In 1965 Robert Kennedy joined in the first ascent of one of the mountains in the Yukon named for his brother, the President.

It seems appropriate that a mountaineer, particularly an English speaking one who has considerably greater opportunities, should seek to ascend his eponymous peak, if indeed he has one, wherever it may be. Climbers with names like Everest or McKinley have an almost impossible task in prospect; on the other hand Pary will find his mountain in Anglesey is a mere 137m. Names which are colours are easily fulfilled: White for example has Mont Blanc, the Aiguille Blanche de Peuterey, the Weisshorn, the White Mountains of New Hampshire and Maine; Green has the Aiguille Verte, the Gross Grünhorn, the Green Mountains of Vermont; Red has many mountains but seldom serves as a surname; Black has the Aiguille Noire de Peuterey, various Schwarzhorns, the Black Mountains of Wales, the Black Hills of South Dakota and so on.

Mountaineers to whom this may appeal as an objective should look themselves up in a big gazetteer like the Columbia-Lippincott, for a selection of possibilities. Maybe their peaks will be half the world away and thus inaccessible even if not presenting a particularly arduous mountaineering problem. Translation of one's name into other languages is permissible, for example, Steel could consider a right to Mount Stalin, of which there were at one time plenty of examples, but now only one.

Taking a few names at random from the AC Members List we can see how the process works out. Messrs Adams, Anderson, Baker, Fisher, Gilbert, Grant, Hamilton, Hunter, Jackson, Morgan, Russell, Thompson, Ward, Warren, Wilson and Wood will find their eponymous peak in the USA, while Messrs Gilbert, Hunter and Russell find a second in Alaska, Hamilton a second in New Zealand and Gilbert even a third in Canada. Messrs Cook, Jackson and Ward will find theirs in New Zealand, Cook another in Alaska. This is merely an exercise fleetingly carried out; the potential when armed with a big gazetteer would seem to be enormous.

As another example, I seem to remember hearing that a member of this Club, correspondingly named, motored to Skye and made an ascent of Sgurr Alasdair on his birthday.

A small degree of deviation from exact spelling may also have to be accepted as will be seen from what follows. My own name in its present spelling will never be found on map or gazetteer. There are no famous, nor I hope infamous, holders of the name, though I do recollect a minor commander on the field diagram of one of the battles of the American Civil War. If spelling variations can be accepted, such as 'Piat' or 'Piet', the scope might possibly be enlarged, though again on the face of it there would not seem much cause for optimism. 'Piet' looks a bit like Afrikaans and there could be a minor hill in South Africa thus named. I had more or less given up hope, when a casual perusal of Ball's *Central Alps* revealed that there was in fact a Piz Piot at the head of the Averstal in the Grisons.

It is very minor as Alpine summits go, a mere 3053m, but on the main watershed with streams on one side flowing to the Adriatic and on the other to the Rhine. The name is derived from the Romansch 'piatt', which means flat, not an exciting name for a mountain. The text of *Bündner-Alpen* Vol 3 and the *Carte Nationale de la Suisse* do not indicate any insuperable difficulties, so that the ascent will, I hope, be reported in due course in these pages, if not by the writer, at least by the next generation of the family.

(Ted died shortly after writing this article. He never did climb his eponymous mountain. *Editor*)

In Commemoration of the Bi-Centenary of the First Successful Ascent of Mont Blanc, 8th August 1786

Enid M. Slatter
Plates 59–66

The first ascent of Mont Blanc was achieved on 8 August 1786 — two hundred years ago. In this attainment, the sport and science of mountaineering had its beginning. Until that time, the imposing chain of mountains, *les Rochers Blanches*, crowned by the highest peak in Europe, held little interest to anyone except local chamois-hunters and collectors of rock-crystals. For the hundreds of *Grand Tourists* who had been travelling across Europe since the late 17th century, the Alps constituted an annoying barrier on their way to Italy, whither they were bound in search of culture — not scenery, scientific study or exercise.

The mountain known locally as *le Mont Maudit* did not acquire its now famous name until Pierre Martel, an engineer of Geneva, who was making a survey of the district, wrote in a letter, dated 1742 and published in 1744, that the 'Point of *Mont Blanc*' was the highest 'perhaps of all the *Alps*'. He said it could be seen in France from as far away as Dijon (216km) and Langres (264km) to the NW. He also stated that the top was entirely covered by ice, blunt, but quite steep on the NE side at an angle of 25°–30°. In all of these points, he has been proved substantially correct. The name, 'le Mont Maudit', is now applied to a peak NE of the summit.

The first ascent came about through the enthusiasm and scientific curiosity of Horace-Bénédict de Saussure, also of Geneva. He had been fascinated by the mountains since his youth and was frequently 'upon the ice'. He may be said to be the first Alpinist for his studies of rock, ice and altitude during a period of thirty years. He longed to perform scientific experiments on the summit of Mont Blanc and as early as 1760, when he was only 20 years old, offered a prize to anyone finding a route to the top. However, fear, superstition and ignorance seem to have deterred the local people from making the attempt. They thought that the mountains were inhabited by evil spirits. Also, as the upper regions were bare of living things, it followed that human life could not be supported at such heights. Moreover, those who had clambered up to any appreciable altitude had noticed an uncanny darkness of the sky and believed that the Almighty was frowning with displeasure at their audacity in venturing so far heavenwards.

In the early 1780s, several climbers had narrowly failed in their attempts, but on 8 August 1786 the summit was finally reached by two Chamoniards, Dr Michel-Gabriel Paccard and Jacques Balmat, the latter, thereafter, dubbed *Mont Blanc*. Saussure immediately tried himself, but bad weather robbed him of success. However, the next season, on 3 August 1787, he at last achieved his ambition — at the age of 47 — and was able to carry out some of his experiments on the summit. A week later, on 9 August, a third successful ascent was made by the astronomer, Mark Beaufoy, who correctly established the latitude of Mont Blanc as 45° 50′ N. He was the first Englishman — but by no means the last — to make the ascent. In fact, it was the English, who put Chamonix, then known as Le Prieuré, 'on the map' and caused the establishment of the Hotel de Londres (as long ago as 1743), followed by the Hotel de l'Angleterre, to make them feel at home. Many other hotels were built later when, during the 19th century, hundreds of tourists flocked there and the ascent of Mont Blanc had become almost a national English pastime.

Both Dr Paccard (aged 70) and Col Beaufoy (aged 63) died in 1827, but that year saw two more successful ascents by Englishmen — Charles Fellows with his friend William Hawes in July and, two weeks later, in August, John Auldjo. These were the 13th and 14th and brought up the number of Britons (Auldjo's certificate cites him as Scottish) to 9 out of 16 tourists to reach the summit. The other successful climbers had been of various nationalities — Russian, Swiss, German, Polish and American. Apart from these, in 1808 (some say 1809), there had been a party of 17 Chamoniards, led by Balmat-*MontBlanc*, which also included the first woman to make the ascent. She was Marie Paradis, aged 22 (some say 25 or even 30), who became known as Marie *de Mont Blanc*. It was not until 1834 that the first Frenchman achieved the goal. He was Henri, Comte de Tilly, a royalist living in exile in Venice, who proudly placed the white flag of the Bourbons on the summit. He, however, suffered very badly from so late an ascent — 9 October, the latest ever tried — his feet becoming so frost-bitten, that he feared he would lose his legs through ensuing gangrene. In August 1840, the Marchese di Sant' Angelo was the first successful Italian. He was the fourth titled person to have got to the top; others had failed in their attempts. M de Saussure and Mlle d'Angeville were also of noble families. The enterprise was very expensive and clearly only the well-to-do could hope to meet the costs of the guides, porters and provisions necessary. In 1827, the ascent had cost Fellows (the son of a wealthy banker) and Hawes £22:15:3 each; for Atkins with two others in 1837, it had cost £23 each; Erasmus Galton on his own in 1850 spent £34:6:0. But in 1855 a party of 2 (with guides and porters) had spent only £4 and Hudson's party of 6 (without guides) reckoned on spending a mere £2 each.

In 1838, Mlle Henriette d'Angeville was the first woman tourist to succeed and, at the age of 44, was also much the oldest climber (except for Saussure). However, in 1875, the Marquis de Turenne arrived at the summit with a large retinue at the advanced age of 72. Another French achievement of note was the unparalleled feat of climbing to the summit twice within the space of 5 days. This was realised in 1843 by a physician of Besançon, Dr E Ordinaire — surely Dr E[xtra] Ordinaire! His ascents were the 25th and 26th successful (out of 37) in 57 years. There was another ascent that year, then, in the next 20 years, there were as many as 44 more successes.

While listing famous successes, it is worth recalling the most famous of failures, the persistent Marc-Théodore Bourrit, a journalist and artist of

Geneva. He had made attempts on the summit nearly every year from 1766 until 1812, but, although getting to within a few hundred metres of his goal on five occasions, he never once achieved his life-long ambition. He died in 1819, aged 80. Apart from the dates of Paccard's and Saussure's climbs, the other most famous date in Mont Blanc history is certainly 1820, the year of the first fatal accident. Dr Joseph von Hamel, whose intention was to make some scientific experiments on the summit for the Russian court, set out with 15 other persons, including two young Oxford students. They got to within some 150m of the summit, when suddenly the whole party was engulfed in an avalanche and swept some distance down the mountain. When they extricated themselves from the snow, it was found that three guides had fallen irretrievably into a crevasse. On all subsequent ascents, the spot where these unfortunates fell was pointed out in hushed tones. Parts of their bodies, clothing and equipment finally emerged some 40 years later at the bottom of the Glacier des Bossons, about 7km away, as had been predicted by the scientist Professor James David Forbes. He had spent much time on the ice in the 1840s, mapping the glaciers and calculating their movement. Glaciers descend at the rate of about 30 to 40cm a day, or 1 to 1.5km in ten years. Like a flowing river, the centre moves faster than the sides. Forbes recorded finding pieces of a ladder and wood from a cabin set up in 1788 by Saussure, who had also propounded a theory of glacier movement. Forbes's own ice-axe was found years later farther down the glacier on which it had been lost.

In spite of the increasing numbers of persons making the ascent each year, accidents on Mont Blanc were fortunately few — though frost-bite and snow-blindness were all too common, due to insufficient clothing and neglect of precautions against the glare and the wind. In the first hundred years of the ascent, there were only 24 deaths — seven tourists and 17 guides and porters. Of these, five persons were killed in 1866 and 13 (eleven in one disaster) in the fatal year of 1870. In August 1866, Sir George Young and his two brothers made the ascent, unaccompanied by guides. In an unlucky fall soon after commencing their descent, the youngest brother broke his neck. Very late the same season, on the inauspicious date of 13 October, Captain Henry Arkwright and party of three were swept away by an avalanche very near the 'fatal spot'. Their bodies were recovered 31 years later, in August 1897. At about the same place, on 2 August, 1870, a lady, left in the charge of a porter while her husband made the assault on the summit, walked into a crevasse — the 'Hamel' crevasse again? In the September of that year, three Americans with eight guides, after reaching the summit, were marooned in a storm that lasted 12 days and perished, starved and frozen to death.

The route pioneered by Paccard and Balmat was the only way to the summit until 1827. It passed to the west of the last peaks, les Rochers Rouges, near which Hamel's party suffered their dreadful accident. Fellows, Hawes and party found a way, which diverged to the east — a passage called the *Corridor*, followed by a long, acute slope, about 100m high, called the *Mur de la Côte*. This, though more fatiguing since it necessitated the cutting of hundreds of steps, nevertheless, avoided the *Ancien Passage* of fatal memory, where an ever-open crevasse seemed to be waiting for its next victims. Although both Fellows

From The Illustrated London News, *22 September 1855.*

59   *The ascent of Mont Blanc by Saussure, 1787. The first guide carries the ladder and the porter (last but one),*
the bottles. Saussure (centre L) wears a tail-coat and wig with queue.

From: The Illustrated London News, *9 August 1862.*

60   *A guide showing Tyndall the fatal 'Hamel' crevasse.*

From: The Forms of Water, etc., by John Tyndall, 1872.

61   Hudson and party, 1855; from a photograph by G. E. Joad.

From: Travels Through the Alps, by James D. Forbes, 1843

62   Ascent of Mont Blanc from 'les Grands Mulets'; from a photograph by Bisson, 1861.

63　*Mlle d'Angeville using a ladder to cross a crevasse, 1838. Tinted Lithograph.*

From: Narrative of an Ascent to the Summit of Mont Blanc on the eighth and ninth of August, 1827.

64　*J. Auldjo's party, 1827.*

65   *Lying on the ledge at 'les Grands Mulets'.*

From: The Illustrated London News, *8 February 1851.*

From: Ascent of Mont Blanc with description, *by J. Macgregor, 1855.*

66   *The summit! Two tourists celebrating; one guide resting, the other just arriving.*

and Hawes published accounts, it was in fact John Auldjo, who followed their route a fortnight later, to whom the advertising of this new and safer way was due. Auldjo was to settle in Geneva, becoming British Consul from 1870 until his death in 1886. Although Sir Charles Fellows, as he was to become in recognition of his part in bringing the Xanthian Marbles to the British Museum in the 1840s, is better known for his archaeological journeys in Turkey, he never forgot his first great adventure and 30 years later would still warn of the dangers of the undertaking.

The new route continued to be used for the next 30 years, until the Rev Charles Hudson and some friends pioneered yet another route to the top in July 1859. This way, via les Bosses du Dromadaire, passed farther to the west of the *Ancien Passage*. It had in fact probably been discovered many years earlier by the redoubtable Chamonix guide, Marie Couttet, nick-named *le Chamois* or *le Moutelet* (the Weasel). In 1844 he had waylayed a French scientific party and offered to take them to the summit by a new route, but their guides refused and they continued by the old way. Couttet, the son of Saussure's guide, had spent his whole life on the ice and was acknowledged as a man of 'extraordinary intelligence', the best Mont Blanc guide. He had already been five times to the summit when he joined Dr Hamel's ill-fated party and he identified the remains years later; the ascents of Fellows and Hawes followed by Auldjo's were his 7th and 8th successes. He took Mlle d'Angeville to the summit, kissed her and even lifted her up, so that she could be the highest person in Europe ever! Although he suffered several severe injuries during the course of a life-time on the mountain, Couttet nevertheless continued to be obsessed by Mont Blanc into his old age, tagging along uninvited and becoming an embarrassment to organized parties. His last official climb was in 1850. He died, aged 80, in 1872. Jacques Balmat-*Mont Blanc* had also been unable to keep away from the mountain and was lost — perhaps murdered for the gold he was seeking — on its slopes in 1835, aged at least 70.

Hudson, one of the first real mountaineers to be interested in Mont Blanc, had already made several attempts on the summit by differing routes and twice achieved the objective in 1853 and again in 1855, on his second attempt. This was the first time a party had reached the summit without either ladder or guides. Hudson and his party had planned their route from the Italian side, in order to avoid the obligation of using Chamonix guides, who were, for them, both an unnecessary expense and a nuisance. They had the help of Forbes' maps of the glaciers and their own considerable experience instead. On the way up they bivouacked on the Col du Géant within the walls of Saussure's cabin, still standing after nearly 70 years. This was the 98th success — 62 of the climbers had been British, only 10 French. With Hudson, who was killed in the famous Matterhorn accident of July 1865, were Edward S Kennedy, who became the second President of the Alpine Club, and George Joad, a young photographer. He climbed to nearly 4000m before descending, leaving Hudson, Kennedy and three other friends to go on to the top. Joad's photo of the group at their camp (*c.* 3000m) was used as frontispiece to the book describing the 1855 ascents. The first photographs from the summit were taken some years later by Auguste Bisson, a French photographer. It needed 25 porters to carry the heavy, clumsy apparatus and chemicals. On 25 July 1861 Bisson took three large plates — and fixed them — on the summit. They were processed in his Paris studio and exhibited at the 1862 International Exhibition in London.

The ladder played an essential part in the early ascents of Mont Blanc. Under a useful rock, the *Pierre de l'Echelle*, at a height of about 2300m, was a ladder — Mont Blanc climbers, for the use of. It was employed, as today, not so much to scale rock faces, as to cross crevasses, by simply laying it over the gap. On returning, the ladder was carefully left again at the *Pierre* for the next party. As the numbers of ascents per year increased so several ladders were left at this spot. By the 1850s there was quite a collection of them. The climbers were not Alpinists in the modern sense, no *pitons* or tackle were used and the walk or ramble to the top was made by plodding slowly upwards with crampons of double-headed nails tied on to their shoes, or screwed into the soles. Both climbers and guides carried *batons* — poles about 2m long with an iron spike at the end — to test the snow and support themselves. When held between two guides, they became hand-rails. The guides were also very skilful in using them to control a descent by *glissade*, the tourist sitting behind a guide to slide rapidly down the slope, feet first. Ropes, 3–5m long, were used in dangerous areas, the tourist attached between two guides, the other guides roped together in threes.

Other necessities for the excursion consisted of blankets and straw for bedding; wood and a spirit stove for heating food and snow; an axe to cut steps in the ice; a long, cumbersome mountain-barometer (which usually got broken); altitude thermometers (likewise) and other scientific instruments; a telescope; a pistol to fire off on the summit; writing and drawing materials; a National flag. Saussure added a parasol and a tent to work in on the summit. He also took his personal servant with him, as indeed did Beaufoy. As well as all these items, vast quantities of food and drink were carried, at least as far as *les Grand Mulets* quite a lot even the whole way, in spite of the knowledge that, at high altitudes, most people lost their appetites, felt nausea even at the sight of food, and that wine and strong drink did not quench the raging thirst they all suffered. Nevertheless, Auldjo, for example, with eight guides, took 23 bottles of wine and strong drink, but only 2½ bottles of vinegar and *sirop* to refresh their parched throats. He also took 38 pieces of meat and fowls, not forgetting several 3lb loaves and a 'large quantity of cheese'. In the end, raisins sucked with snow were found the best against thirst and fatigue. The strong drink and wine were favoured by the guides at the overnight stop; champagne was, of course, essential for the toasts on the summit. The guides insisted on the provisions for fear of being caught by bad weather without adequate supplies, as actually happened in the 1870 disaster.

The ordinary 'travelling dress' of the period was worn, but extra socks, shirts, trousers and waistcoats were put on for the night and the day of the assault on the summit. Broad-brimmed hats were worn against the powerful rays of the sun, beneath which they kept on their night-caps, or used scarves, Balaclava style, to protect their ears and chin. Green veils or masks were worn to guard the face and green or blue spectacles for the eyes. Coarse cloth gaiters, like those worn by the villagers, were wrapped round the legs. Mlle d'Angeville affected a coyness at wearing full-waisted trousers under her skirt (both made of

Scotch cloth in a loud check), but she retained her femininity with a boa about her shoulders. She also took a mirror to make sure her bonnet was on straight. She tried unsuccessfully to preserve her face by the use of cucumber pomade, suffering, as many did, on her return to Chamonix with the skin burnt and blistered and her eyes very inflamed and painful. One lady is reported to have taken a live pigeon with her to keep her hands warm.

Pigeons were several times carried up Mont Blanc to test their powers of flight at high altitudes. Choughs and yellow-billed crows were known to fly near, if not over, the summit, but for pigeons it was a different matter. Dr Hamel took up a carrier-pigeon, but the unfortunate bird perished with the guide who was carrying the cage on his back. Its wing was eventually found in 1861, together with a leg of mutton — quite fresh — when the glacier gave up remains from the accident. Another poor bird, taken by Mlle d'Angeville, flew off the summit, but could not find its way home (N) and finished up as dinner for the *curé* of the village of Contamines (W). One pigeon in 1861 took 2 days to fly home to Chamonix, only 10 or 11km as the crow — or rather the pigeon — flies. Others, more sensibly, refused to fly at all.

More courageous have been the various dogs, both male and female, which have climbed to the summit. The first belonged to Henry Atkins' guide in 1837. At that time, Atkins, not yet 19 years old, was the youngest tourist to make a successful ascent. He later joined the Army, but died prematurely in 1842. The 'little dog', a rough-coated Griffon, wisely sat on his master's feet at every pause and on his lap on the summit. A Griffon bitch, *Diane*, who accompanied Mlle d'Angeville's party in 1838, slept for several days following her exploit, and in 1861 Professor Wilhelm Pitschner's dog lost its bark. Another dog is alleged to have been twice to the summit and one guide's bitch, *Finette*, formed the habit of ascending as far as les Grands Mulets on every occasion, going there 20–30 times over. But the canine mountaineer *par excellence* was the intrepid bitch, *Tschingel* (1865–79), which ascended Mont Blanc on 24 July 1875 and also ascended 10 other notable peaks, including the Wetterhorn, the Eiger, the Jungfrau and Monte Rosa (*c.* 4600m). The hospice of St Bernard with its famous dogs is at only a little over 2400m.

Perhaps the most intriguing little animal on Mont Blanc is the Alpine mouse or vole, the 'Campagnol des neiges', *Microtus [Arvicola] nivalis*. These animals live well above the tree-line, at altitudes between 2000m and 4000m. They do not change their coats and do not hibernate. They have even been seen in mid-winter. They are found at several locations in the Alps. They had been known to guides on Mont Blanc from the early 1800s, but scarcely believed in. A 'weasel' was reported in 1819 and 'mice' in 1834. In 1825 Clarke and Sherwill spent some time looking for one at les Grands Mulets as their guide said that on previous occasions, much to his surprise, he had found articles left there eaten, as if by mice! He described the little animals correctly as 'something like a weasel . . . larger than a rat, of a reddish colour . . . with a long tail . . . and whiskers'. Since no trace of them could be found, Clarke concluded they were chance visitors and had become extinct. Not so; they were finally described by the French scientist, Charles Martins, who had seen them on the Faulhorn in 1841.

Although the motives for making the ascent to the summit of Mont Blanc have varied from scientific and medical research to 'a love of hardy enterprise' (Jackson), 'the desire to witness some of the most stupendous of nature's works' (Fellows), pure curiosity and foolish vanity, the manner of achieving the objective followed a standard pattern. For each tourist, there were 5 or 6 guides taken from the same half-dozen Chamonix families, and as many porters as deemed necessary. They would start from the village at dawn, the tourists generally having the luxury of a mule ride as far as the tree-line, where a stop was made for breakfast. Then the hard work began, as fairly soon they had to cross the Glacier des Bossons, which was always hard going. After that it was a steady pull up to the overnight resting place, les Grand Mulets, the half-way point. Here the porters were sent back. The party would arrive in the afternoon, change their clothes, putting out the wet shoes and socks to dry in the sun, which at that height is very strong. Hot food was prepared by the guides; the tourists admired the view, took rock samples and did a little botanizing. They watched the sunset, truly splendid at this situation, but as soon as darkness fell, they all lay down to rest. They used a ledge, protected from the avalanches, 30m up the rocks. It was only some 3.6m long by 1.2m wide, so they were exceedingly cramped, some guides needing to seek a place elsewhere. *Batons* were put sloping against the rock-face and sheeting was laid over them to give some protection from the intense cold and wind. Although the writer of each account never seemed to close an eye, his companions always slept well enough, in spite of the precarious position and the thunder of falling rocks and ice.

The assault on the summit began before dawn, with the guides carrying torches. At about 4000m many began to feel the effects of altitude — nausea, headache, difficulty in breathing, faintness — and it became necessary to rest with increasing frequency, every 15, 10, 5 paces. Some lay down for a minute, but the danger of frost-bite meant the stamping of feet even at these times. The *Grand Plateau*, which is in fact a series of plains, was a very laborious undertaking to cross and, at about 4500m, many experienced a sort of mental apathy, when, with the summit clearly in sight and seeming only yards away, they were overtaken by a strong desire to give up, feeling that the conquest of Mont Blanc was, after all, of no consequence whatever. Perhaps this was the fundamental reason for all Bourrit's failures. Here the experienced guides would give encouragement and often physical support up the last slopes and on to the summit, which was accomplished in a kind of dream-state. Suddenly they found the ground 'no longer rising', in fact nothing at all around them. They had made it! A brief pause was all that was required to regain control and then contemplate the panorama.

The summit itself was usually described as being like an ass's back, with more or less of a ridge along it, steeper on the NE side, off which the wind blows fiercely. After a quick look around, the party would generally retire a few feet into the lee of the crest to feel the warmth of the sun and carry out some well-tried experiments, such as noting the feebleness of the report of a pistol; seeing the champagne cork fly off with great speed but little sound; finding the boiling-point of water; calculating the height of the mountain. Mont Blanc is nearly 3 miles high but, as the top is an ice-cap, the height varies from season to season and has been reported at anything between 4480m to nearly 4800m. A rock just below the summit, La Tourette, at about 4740m must be the highest actual peak in Europe — Monte Rosa is given as 4634m. On the summit, the sky was usually observed to be dark indigo in colour and the sun smaller than normal. As he approached up the final slopes, the Comte de Tilly saw the sun surrounded by 7 rainbows; Martins, who remained 'till evening, was awed by the vast triangle of shadow cast over Piedmont by the sun setting behind the cone of the summit of Mont Blanc'. Some of the guides claimed to have seen the stars in daylight and some — obstinately — to have seen the Mediterranean Sea near Genoa, a geographical impossibility. The Comte de Tilly and young Atkins both believed they could just make out Venice, 430km to the east.

Except for the scientists, who remained several hours on the summit — Saussure, 4½ hours; Martins, Bravais and Lepileur, who repeated his experiments in 1844, 5 hours — and those apparently competing in a race to beat the fastest time, who, therefore, only stayed a few minutes — Jackson, 36½ hours in 1823; Galton, 32½ hours in 1850; Morshead, who climbed alone without a guide, only 16 hours in 1864 — most tourists remained about 20–30 minutes, just long enough to check off the Alpine peaks; note the Lake of Geneva and Chamonix below them; perhaps make a few notes or write home, and then it was time to start back down the ice and snow to *terra firma* again. For them, to have achieved their ambition and experienced some spiritual satisfaction was sufficient in itself. Some believed they felt a certain lightness of body, as if floating just off the ground. More likely, it was a lightness in the head through altitude, fatigue and emotion. If lucky, they saw, but could not hear, the cannon fired off at Chamonix, whence their progress had been monitored by villagers, family and friends through telescopes — a spectator sport almost as thrilling as the climb itself. Two bizarre French ladies once organized a quadrille on the summit with their 16 guides, which must have been well worth watching! But that was in 1865, when 'Mont Blanc mania' was at its height.

The descent was quicker, but at times more fatiguing and hazardous, than the ascent, but the climbers enjoyed the exhilaration of the *glissade*. A pause was made at les Grands Mulets to collect their belongings and engrave their names on the rocks — Balmat had set a precedent in 1786! Some passed a second night there before struggling back across the Glacier des Bossons to the Cascade des Pèlerins, where Marie *de Mont Blanc* was wont to meet them with a picnic *sur l'herbe* of fresh bread, cream and goat's milk spread upon a white table-cloth. She died in 1838. The boulder, which caused the beautiful cascade, was swept away in 1853. Mules waited to take the tourists in triumph to the village and it became the custom to welcome them with cannon-fire, music, flag-bedecked houses and a banquet that night. The climbers themselves were not, however, always so pleased with this effusion, preferring to nurse their swollen, unsightly faces, frost-bitten feet and almost blind eyes. The villagers and summer visitors to the inns, though, enjoyed it all and the hotel-keepers did good business. The whole trip was calculated by Auldjo to be 54 miles; John Barrow, in 1861, made it only 35 to 40 miles, but the distance would depend on the route taken and the conditions of the ice and snow.

During the 1840s, increasing numbers of people made successful ascents, following the prescribed route and by 1850, fifty-two people (about half of them English) had got to the summit, with many more going as far as les Grands Mulets. A hut for their convenience was built late in 1852 following the ascent of Albert Smith, who, more than anyone should have been called *Mr Mont Blanc*. Smith was 35 years old when he realized his long-cherished wish to climb to the top. In August 1851, he had joined a party of three students with 16 guides, but he was out of condition and had to be pushed and pulled the last hundred metres or so, arriving in a state of hallucination. However, he soon recovered and the mountain-top rang to cheers and the popping of champagne corks. Smith revelled in their heroes' progress through the village on their return. They had also thoroughly enjoyed themselves at les Grand Mulets the previous afternoon. Here the hut was built, so that, in future, many more tourists, afraid of sleeping exposed on the ledge, could stay overnight to experience the wonderful sunsets and sunrises, or even continue on to the summit. It was, however, only about 4m long by 2m wide and soon became flea-ridden, as well as suffocating, since the guides, fearful of the cold, stopped up every cranny, so that the air was soon laden with wood and tobacco smoke. In September 1853 nearly 50 people endeavoured to pass the night in it, sitting in rows like negro slaves. They joked and smoked the night away and wrote their names on the walls before they left next day. In 1861 a guest-book was installed and, since ladies were going this far in ever greater numbers, in 1866–67 the hut was enlarged to 16m by 6m by the addition of three more rooms — one for the guides, one for the ladies and another for the gentlemen — the main room serving as a dining-room and for drying clothes near the fire. A real hotel now stands near this spot.

Smith's trip to Mont Blanc had followed the closure of his successful show in London, in which he had described his travels to the East against a background of dioramas. On his return, he put on an even more exciting entertainment at the Egyptian Hall, Piccadilly, relating his adventurous ascent, enhanced by dioramas, songs and humorous stories. For the first performance in March 1852 the stage was decorated with alpine plants, and a framed certificate — given to all successful climbers attesting the validity of their achievement and signed by the *Syndic* — had a prominent place. The spectacle was an immediate success and became all the rage. Smith was a natural showman and every season he brought new ideas into the performance. He made the stage into a Swiss chalet; added more songs; brought over guides from Chamonix and girls dressed in National (Swiss) costume; sold cow-bells and other Alpine novelties. Even Hamel and Auldjo took part, vying with several St Bernard dogs and some chamois as curiosities. In 1854 he took the show to Osborne House, the first of two royal command performances. Smith closed after the 1857/58 season, having given over 2000 performances.

In 1857, the Prince of Wales, aged 16, intrigued by Smith's Mont Blanc spectacular, arrived at Chamonix and was taken by Smith himself across the Glacier des Bossons to a height of about 3000m. 1857 also marked the foundation of the Alpine Club. By then, many other peaks had been climbed and mountaineering in the modern sense, as opposed to walking and scrambling up the mountains, had come into being. After Smith's success Chamonix became a popular resort. A through-service from Boulogne to Geneva made the journey quick and easy; Cook's Tours started in 1863. Tourists, especially the English, flocked there every summer. Soon as many as 50, 60 or more successful ascents were made each season and by the end of the century, nearly fifteen hundred had been made. Although 200 years have now passed since the first conquest of the mountain, for tourists, scientists and mountaineers alike, Mont Blanc still retains its fascination, continuing to be a powerful inspiration and a challenge.

Meconopsis

John A. Jackson
Plate 67

Stem: strong, leafy, 30 to 60cm, covered with short scattered prickles.
Leaves: alternate, irregularly pinnatifid, scattered prickles.
Flowers: 5 to 8cm in diameter; colour variable from greyish steel blue to purple blue.
Petals: four; Stamens, many; Ovary, one celled and style distinct.

There are several species of this 'alpine' perennial growing at high elevations throughout the Himalaya. The two species of which I have seen the most are *Meconopsis aculeata* (Kashmir to Kumaom) and *Meconopsis grandis* — the large Himalayan blue poppy (Nepal to Tibet). I have never seen them growing in great profusion but usually in small clusters or as a single plant. The generic name *Meconopsis* signifies in Greek that the flower bears a resemblance to a poppy and the plant is of the poppy family, it being of the natural order Papaveraceae.

To the north and east of the village of Gund in the Sind Valley of Kashmir lies a group of limestone peaks rising to almost 5000m. You can cross these mountains via the Yem Har — the Pass of the Goddess Yem, at the foot of which the semi-nomadic traders of Central Asia have for countless centuries stopped and made a brew of tea in thanksgiving for a safe crossing. A tiny lake or sar, the Yem Sar, lies at the foot of the pass supplying cool clean water to the many streams that irrigate the surrounding richly coloured and delicately scented alpine meadowland. There, among the angular glaciated boulders and in the damper areas of ground surrounding the Yem Sar you can find the blue poppy. It was there following a lone trek from the resthouse at Lidderwatt that I found my first *Meconopsis* — just a single isolated plant, its colouring enhanced by a black backcloth of shade provided by two arching rocks. It was sturdy with many blooms and the green of the leaves was the green of emeralds with a texture of velvet. Overall there spread a delicate glinting mass of golden prickles. Sunlight was shining directly onto the almost transparent flowers. Centrally, a five lobed style stood proud of the single green ovary surrounded by an orange ring of stamens, and this bright centrepiece was set against the blue background of the four overlapping petals. They were not a primary blue but a delicate pale blue faintly tinged in parts with an even more delicate barely hinted at royal Purple. I had often heard it said that the blue was the blue of the sky in early morning but I felt this description to be too simple. For me at that moment by the Yem Sar, the only similar delicacy of colouring, almost indescribable, was that of the blue-purple haze rising from distant Himalayan valleys at dawn. A peregrine falcon, wings ripping through the air as it dived, distracted my attention. My eyes returned from sight of bird, glare of sun and dark hue of lake and once again I was impressed by the breathtaking beauty and strength of the flower. Like the Central Asian traders, I brewed tea in thanksgiving for a safe crossing of the pass but remembered also to include thanks for my first find of the Himalayan Blue Poppy.

67   *Meconopsis, the Himalayan blue poppy.*

68 'Grüli' (Rütli, Lucerne) — John Ruskin (Private Collection).

69 'Messieurs les voyageurs on their return from Italy (par la diligence) in a snow drift upon Mount Tarate — 22nd January 1829' — J. M. W. Turner, 1775–1851; watercolour (British Museum).

70 *'Glacier of Montanvert' — John 'Warwick' Smith, 1749–1831; watercolour, 1802 (British Museum).*

71 *'Mer de Glace, Chamonix' — J. M. W. Turner, 1775–1851; watercolour, 1802 (British Museum).*

Homage to J. M. W. Turner

Charles Warren and Peter Bicknell
Plates 68–78

Read before a joint meeting of the Alpine Club and the Turner Society at the Alpine Club on 29 October 1985.

Introduction   *Charles Warren*
It is, perhaps, not inappropriate that a meeting of the Turner Society and the Alpine Club should be held in our club rooms here because, after all, Turner's famous champion John Ruskin was a member of the AC from 1869 until 1882 when, alas, illness then overcame him and shut him away from the outer world.

There are two ways of qualifying for membership of the Alpine Club: a mountaineering one; and an artistic, literary and scientific one. John Ruskin was elected to membership in 1869 in recognition of his literary, artistic and scientific contributions towards our greater appreciation of the alpine scene on the publication of Volume 4 of *Modern Painters* (sub-titled: 'Of Mountain Beauty'). But as has been pointed out by A L Mumm, his pedestrian activities in the Alps with his guide Joseph Marie Coutet at that date would almost have given him a mountaineering qualification too. Although no very serious rock climber, Ruskin tells us about his 'ridgework'. And he did, after all, climb the Riffelhorn above Zermatt. And he mastered the use of the alpenstock, he assures us, and advises other tourists to do so too. We know that he made some notable minor ascents around Chamonix, including a traverse of the Buet. Chamonix remained, throughout his active life, his favourite venue. He was there in 1851 when that flamboyant entrepreneur, but amusing character, Albert Smith climbed Mont Blanc and returned to the village and its tourists in triumph to the firing of cannon; and to Ruskin's righteous disgust. It was probably this episode which occasioned his famous diatribe against the mountaineers in *Sesame and Lilies*; but let me quote:

'You have despised nature; that is to say, all the deep and sacred sensations of natural scenery. The French revolutionists made stables of the cathedrals of France; you have made racecourses of the cathedrals of the earth. Your *one* conception of pleasure is to drive in railroad carriages round their aisles, and eat off their altars. You have put a railroad bridge over the falls of Schaffhausen. You have tunnelled the cliffs of Lucerne by Tell's chapel; you have destroyed the Clarens shore of the Lake of Geneva; there is not a quiet valley in England that you have not filled with bellowing fire; there is no particle left of English land which you have not trampled coal ashes into — nor any foreign city in which the spread of your presence is not marked among its fair old streets and happy gardens by a consuming white leprosy of new hotels and perfumers' shops: the Alps themselves, which your own poets used to love so reverently, you look upon as soaped poles in a bear-garden, which you set yourselves to climb, and slide down again, with "shrieks of delight". When you are past shrieking, having no human articulate voice to say you are glad with, you fill the quietude of their valleys with gunpowder blasts, and rush home, red with cutaneous eruption of conceit, and voluble with convulsive hiccough of self-satisfaction. I think nearly the two sorrowfullest spectacles I have ever seen in humanity, taking the deep inner significance of them, are the English mobs in the valley of Chamouni, amusing themselves with firing rusty howitzers; and the Swiss vintagers of Zurich expressing their Christian thanks for the gift of the vine, by assembling in knots in the "towers of the vineyards", and slowly loading and firing horse-pistols from morning till evening. It is pitiful, to have dim conceptions of duty; more pitiful, it seems to me, to have conceptions like these, of mirth.'

Despite all this, which was fair comment at the time, and a warning to us to get back to a proper appreciation of the alpine scene, he remained in the club and enjoyed the company of some of his friends there.

Others have lectured us here on our Philistinism, but not in quite the same way as in that rather marvellous Ruskinian diatribe *Sesame and Lilies*.

Look at this picture inscribed Grütli (Rütli on the map) (*Plate 68*) and you can see what he was getting at. We are to have a reverence for certain places of historical interest as well as an appreciation of natural beauty. Sir Walter Scott, in his only novel with an Alpine setting, *Anne of Geierstein*, refers to the 'immortal field of Rütli . . . where our illustrious ancestors, the Fathers of Swiss independence met' (William Tell and the leaders of the three Forest Cantons). And here it is, as seen by Ruskin. The 'immortal field', beneath the Seelisberg, on Lake Lucerne.

But now, had the Alpine Club been founded in Turner's day, he too would undoubtedly have been elected to membership not only because, as an artist, he was by far and away the greatest who had ever depicted the alpine scene, but also on his qualifications as an intrepid traveller for many years throughout the Alps.

Just look at this picture (*Plate 69*), which once belonged to our member R W Lloyd and is now in the British Museum, and hear what he had to say about it. In a letter to Eastlake, Turner describes the events upon which this watercolour is based '. . . the snow began to fall at Foligno, tho' more of ice than snow, so that the coach from its weight slid about in all directions . . . till the diligence zized into a ditch, and required six oxen to drag it out . . . bivouacks in the snow with fires lighted for three hours on Mount Tarate while diligence was righted and dug out.'

Another episode like this, *The passage of the Mont Cenis, 15th Jany. 1820*, was painted, after his return that year, for Mr Fawkes of Farnely Hall.

Turner once had himself lashed to the mast of a ship during a storm so that he could see and record the grand spectacle. About his picture *Snow Storm* he said: 'I got the sailors to lash me to the mast'.

What a man! Had the Alpine Club been founded in his day, he would certainly have been elected, probably to Honorary Membership, not only as an Alpine traveller but as the greatest watercolour artist of Switzerland there has ever been.

What a marvellous time it was when our artists and poets suddenly 'discovered' the romance of Switzerland in the late eighteenth and early nineteenth centuries. Think of Turner; and then of Byron and Shelley on the shores of Lac Leman in that wonderful year of 1816, the turning point in Byron's career as a poet. And then, later on, think of Ruskin who, above all others, taught us how to appreciate the alpine scene in the right kind of way. The alpinists not on their 'soaped poles'; the scientists not on their 'dead rocks'. But the aesthetes who simply loved the glories of the Alps like he did.

Turner and his Predecessors in the Mountains   *Peter Bicknell*
When in 1802 Turner, at the age of 27 first went to the Alps, some aspects of the mountain scene were familiar to British artists. The 'discovery' of the mountainous districts of these islands, which had been begun by a select band of artists and writers in the 1780s, had by the end of the century become so complete that tours of the mountains and lakes in search of the Picturesque were the height of fashion. Sketchers, both amateur and professional, flocked to Loch Lomond, Llanberis and Lodore. The cult of mountain scenery had become a subject for satire. Rowlandson and Combe, parodying the late Doctor Gilpin, sent Doctor Syntax on a *Tour in Search of the Picturesque*, the climax of which was when the doctor reached Keswick and was able to sketch the lake. Doctor Plumptre, himself a confirmed 'Laker', wrote a comic opera, *The Lakers*, making fun of the affectations of the picturesque tourists. And when it was proposed that Jane Austen's heroine Elizabeth Bennet should make a tour of the Lakes, she cried ecstatically, 'What are men to rocks and mountains?'

The 'discovery' which preceded Turner's response to mountains has in recent years been amply recorded in a series of exhibitions with well illustrated catalogues[1]; and was summarized in a talk which I gave to the Alpine Club in May 1980[2].

Richard Wilson's painting *Llyn-y-Cau, Cader Idris* (*Plate 72*) is a landmark in mountain art. When Wilson returned from Italy in 1757, he painted his native Wales in the manner of the landscape artists working in Italy in the seventeenth century. His well-known view of *Snowdon from Llyn Nantlle*[3] is arranged like a vision of Arcadia by Claude Lorrain. There are the conventional three planes — framing trees and figures in classical poses in the foreground, a well lit castle-like rock placed centrally in the middle distance, and azure mountains closing the distant view. *Llyn-y-Cau*, probably painted about 1766/7, a year or two after *Snowdon*, breaks with this tradition. Though the mellow glow of the golden age is still there, the picture seems to convey the direct impact of the mountain and its surroundings on a sensitive artist who had actually climbed to this lofty viewpoint. It was pictures like this that led Ruskin to say, 'with the name of Richard Wilson the history of sincere landscape art founded on the meditative love of nature begins in England.'

It is interesting to compare Wilson's view of Snowdon with exactly the same view by Philip James de Loutherbourg (*plate 73*). Here the elements are the same; there are the three receding planes, the framing trees, the figures and the feature of interest in the middle distance. But the tranquillity of Arcadia has been blown away by a wild gust of the Sublime. The clouds and the trees are racked by a wind that threatens to blow the hats from the rugged peasants and scatters the far from pastoral goats. In the second half of the eighteenth century, the artists who visited the mountains viewed them either as a prospect of Arcadia seen through the eyes of Claude Lorrain, or as a glimpse of the Sublime seen through the eyes of Salvator Rosa. The poet, Thomas Gray, visiting the Lakes in 1769, spent five days at Keswick 'lap'd in Elysium' and found Grasmere 'a little unsuspected paradise' — a paradise which is beautifully illustrated by Julius Caesar Ibbetson's painting of *Grasmere* (*Plate 74*). Though topographically accurate, it shows the scene as one of pastoral serenity, more suited to paradise than to Cumbria. De Loutherbourg, on the other hand squeezed all the sublimity he could out of the Lake District scene. He was closely associated with the theatre in London, and painted in a style which has aptly been called 'Drury Lane Picturesque'. A highly theatrical and essentially Salvatorian scene of a shipwreck is somewhat surprisingly of Windermere[4]. It records an actual event which had occurred in the previous century. It is one of two splendid pictures painted for the Curwens, and still to be seen in their highly Arcadian circular temple-like house on Belle Isle in Windermere.

Towards the end of the century visits to the mountain districts had become almost obligatory for landscape painters. Even Gainsborough, who is not usually associated with mountains, paid one visit to the Lakes, in 1783. The sketches he made on his visit with the exception of one drawing he made of the Langdale Pikes[5], are not topographical but are ideal arrangements made of elements which he found in the landscape. However, for the rest of his life rugged mountains appeared in his pictures, which owe more to Salvator than to Claude. Gainsborough was in the Lakes at the same time as his friend, de Loutherbourg; they may have been together. Certainly in Gainsborough's mountainous scenes there is a strong whiff of 'Drury Lane Picturesque'. Unlike Gainsborough most of the men that visited the mountains were primarily topographical draughtsmen. Men such as Paul Sandby, Thomas Hearne, Joseph Farington and Edward Dayes, working generally in line and wash, recorded the Highlands, North Wales and the Lakes in conventional views, arranged according to picturesque principles suitable for reproduction as prints. Turner along with his exact contemporary Tom Girtin learnt much from Edward Dayes. Their early topographical work in blue-grey monochrome is often very like the work of Dayes. His watercolour of Lodore and the head of Derwentwater[6] (like several other drawings of Dayes) was at one time attributed to Turner.

Before Turner first went to the Alps he had made three visits to Wales, one to the Lake District and one to Scotland. So mountain scenery had already played an important part as a source of inspiration. As well as having absorbed the topographical tradition of Dayes and Farington, Turner was profoundly influenced by both the Arcadian and the Sublime. He first visited the Lakes in 1797, as part of an extensive tour through the NE counties to Berwick, up the Tweed to Melrose, across the borders to Carlisle, through the Lakes from north to south, out over the sands and back by York, Beverley and Lincolnshire. The sketchbook which he carried with him is full of hasty and simple pencil records, mostly of castles, churches and abbeys. But in the Lake District, where antiquities are few and far between, they are of the lakes and the mountains, often partially or fully tinted with watercolour. Perhaps the finest of these is a completed watercolour drawing of Crummock and the head of Buttermere[7]. It is a true portrait of the view, but is suffused with a luminosity of atmosphere which transcends normal topography. Turner used this subject for an ambitious oil painting[8] which was exhibited at the Royal Academy in 1798. Although the outline of the hills remains the same and it is still a fairly accurate record of the natural scene, a rainbow has been added which transfers us from a world of natural appearances to the romantic world of 'my heart leaps up when I behold'. 1798 was the first year when poems could be appended to the descriptions of pictures in the catalogue of the Academy exhibition. Turner took the opportunity to quote five lines from Thomson's *Seasons*:

'Till in the western sky the downward sun
Looks out effulgent — the rapid radiance instantaneous strikes
The illumined mountains — in a yellow mist
Bestriding earth — the grand ethereal bow
Shoots up immense, and every hue unfolds.'

In the same exhibition he showed another Lake District painting, *Morning amongst the Coniston Fells, Cumberland*[9]. This was based on a pencil outline drawing in the sketchbook and a subsequent watercolour[10], and again its romanticism was enforced by a poetical quotation from *The Morning Hymn of Adam and Eve* in Milton's *Paradise Lost* (Turner altered 'steaming' to 'streaming'):

'Ye mists and exhalations that now rise
From hill or streaming lake dusky or grey,
Till the sun paint your fleecy skirts with gold
In honour to the world's great author rise.'

Wordsworth at just the same time, working on the drafts for *The Prelude*, was struggling with the same passage from Milton.

On 12 February 1802 (the year in which he was to go to the Alps), Turner was admitted to the Royal Academy as a full academician. He deposited as his Diploma Work *Dolbadarn Castle*[11], and it is significant that this picture which Turner must have considered important was a mountainous scene, deriving from sketches made on the spot. It had been exhibited already at the Academy in 1800, with a poem by Turner himself emphasizing the historical romanticism of the subject:

'How awful is the silence of the waste,
Where nature lifts her mountains to the sky.
Majestic solitude, behold the tower
Where hopeless OWEN, long imprison'd, pin'd,
And wrung his hands for liberty, in vain.'

Owen Glendower the captive champion of liberty, is closely related to Thomas Gray's *Bard*[12], another symbol of freedom and victim of a tyrant English king. Turner's many and varied images of Dolbadarn Castle tell us much about the versatility of his art. We can, for instance, see Dolbadarn as an element in the view of Llyn Peris and the mountains of Snowdonia, faithfully portrayed in the controlled watercolour of the topographer; Dolbadarn engulfed in a shimmering flood of light in inspired impressionistic washes; and Dolbadarn as a bastion of mediaeval romance in solemn and dramatic oils. Thus Turner went to Switzerland as an established academician, equipped with dazzling versatility and virtuosity.

He had been preceded in the Alps by four important English landscape painters, Pars, Smith, Towne and Cozens, each of whom had made his own personal discovery of the alpine scene. At the same time a flourishing school of Swiss topographers were revealing the beauties of their own mountains to a receptive public. Foremost amongst these was Caspar Wolff (1735–1798). He prepared a series of 150 paintings and watercolours for the illustration of a book, the first part of which appeared in 1776 as *Vues Remarquables des Montagnes de la Suisse avec leur Description*[13], containing 15 splendid coloured etchings of the Bernese Oberland. Wolff did not make ascents of the peaks, but he penetrated deep into them on the glaciers, and had a keen eye for the remarkable. In 1785 *Vues Remarquables* was republished with coloured aquatints after Wolff and others. The frontispiece was inscribed with the subtitle of the book *Theatre des Alpes et Glaciers. Dédié aux Amateurs des Merveilles de la Nature*. The marvels of nature are presented as a theatre for amateurs, at least three of whom are using the scene arranged for them by Wolff as a subject for their art. A pupil of Wolff was Gabriel Ludwig Lorry (1763–1840) who, with his son Gabriel Mathias Lorry (1784–1846), carried on the tradition of the *Vues Remarquables* with wonderful coloured plates of the Alps — a tradition which was continued by others well into the nineteenth century. These Swiss prints are familiar to many members of the Alpine Club through the collection of R W Lloyd which, along with his remarkable collection of works by Turner, is now enshrined in the British Museum.

When in 1770 William Pars (1742–1782), toured the Alps with the young Lord Palmerston, he had already travelled in Greece and Turkey, making drawings of antiquities for the Dilettanti Society. Pars and Palmerston were for much of their time in Switzerland in the experienced hands of the Mont Blanc pioneer, Horace Benedict de Saussure. From Geneva they went to Chamonix, already a Mecca for tourists; they crossed the Col des Montets to Trient and Martigny; up the Rhône valley and over the Grimsel to Meiringen; then over the Grosse Scheidegg to Grindelwald and down by the Staubach to Interlaken. Fortunately there are several of Pars' best watercolours in the British Museum and excellent reproductions are available in John Russel and Andrew Wilton's *William Pars in the Alps, 1770*. They are large freshly coloured watercolour drawings. He shows a particular interest in the glaciers, at a time when they came down much further into the valleys than they do today. His views of the glaciers of Chamonix, the Rhône and Grindelwald convey the same feeling of wonder that is conveyed by his companion, Lord Palmerston, who described 'the immense Waves, Pyramids and Clefts, which compose the Surface of the Frozen Sea'. The most remarkable of the views is one looking down the Mer de Glace (*Plate 75*) where the sea of ice seems entirely to fill the Chamonix valley. His mountains are usually carefully observed and shown without picturesque distortion, but here fantasy seems to have taken over from observation and the

Aiguilles are presented as repetitive piles of surrealist pinnacles. Eight of Pars' Alpine views were exhibited at the Royal Academy in 1771, and seem to have caused considerable interest. Five of them were engraved by the fashionable Woolett and published by Pars as prints in 1773 and 1774. They sold well enough to be taken over by the great impresario of prints, John Boydell, who republished them in 1783. So Pars' views of the Alps must have been known to a fairly large circle of cognoscenti in the metropolis.

In 1776 John Robert Cozens (1752–1797), six years after Pars, travelled through Switzerland on his way to Italy, returning in 1779. There is little precise information about his itinerary other than the evidence of dated sketches. In 1776 he was travelling with Richard Payne Knight, the notable connoisseur, collector and writer on the Picturesque. They were in Chamonix for a few days in August, and about a month later visited Lauterbrunnen, Grindelwald and the Reichenbach falls. From his sketches Cozens produced a large number of watercolours of the Alps, often repeating the same subject several times. At least eight patrons ordered copies of a view of the Rhône valley, *Pays de Valais*. His Alpine views were far better known than those of Pars from which they differ completely. Cozens is never recording the actual scene, but in muted blue-grey tones is creating a dream world of his own imagination, where the Aiguille de Dru and the Aiguille Verte are translated into strange pinnacles of rock perched unnaturally on mounds of snow. One can understand why Constable said that Cozens was 'all poetry'. The drawing of Cozens which most nearly shows us mountains as we know them is a view in Elba; and it is ironic that this most evocative image is of a scene which Cozens never actually saw, as he never went to Elba. Turner became familiar with many of these drawings, when as a young man he, with Girtin, was copying them in the studio of Dr Monro. In the words of Girtin's descendant, another Tom Girtin, the drawings 'contributed greatly towards opening the minds of English artists to the impressiveness of mountain scenery'[14].

Cozens was followed in 1781 by Smith and Towne, who accompanied each other on their way back from Rome. John 'Warwick' Smith (1749–1831), born at Irthington, close to the Lakes, became a prolific topographical draughtsman who was to tour North Wales and the Lake District and record mountain scenery on many occasions. His Alpine watercolours are similar to those of Pars. He attempted nothing poetic and made no extravagant concessions to picturesque arrangement of the subject. However, his view of the Mer de Glace, that most painted of subjects *The Source of the Arveiron*, (*Plate 78*) vividly recalls the days when the glacier like an open mouthed dragon had crept deep into the valley. Smith was responsible for the aquatint plates in the illustrated edition of William Coxe's *Travels in Switzerland*[15], though he did not accompany the author on his tour. These prints must have brought the Alps to a wider public than the drawings alone.

Francis Towne (1740–1816), neglected for over a hundred years, is now greatly admired and his works are well represented in most British public galleries. In his watercolour drawings of North Wales, which he visited in 1777 before he went to Rome, and of the Lake District, where he was in 1786, five years after his alpine experience, he shows no variation in technique. He draws the mountains in delicate brown ink line, sensitively observing and responding to their anatomy; the masses are then washed in with cool translucent watercolour, producing subtle patterns of contrasting light and shade. Most of his Alpine views are in this individual and consistent manner, often finished in monochrome. His panoramic version of the classical view up the Mer de Glace from the Montanvers (*Plate 76*) is an outstanding example of alpine topography, by an artist who appreciates and understands the form of the mountains. But occasionally their grandeur overpowered him. In his two versions of *The Source of the Arveiron*[16] he abandoned his habitual manner to produce, with broad sombre washes, patterns of contrasting areas almost abstract in character, and unique in eighteenth century art.

Turner we know had studied and copied the mountain views of Cozens. He was probably acquainted with those of Pars and Smith but, until 13 of Towne's Swiss views were shown in a one-man-show in London in 1805, he would not have seen any of these. Fortunately for those interested in Turner in the Alps, the subject has been magnificently covered by the publication of *Turner in Switzerland*, produced by a team of Turner experts. John Russel contributed an informative introduction; comprehensive survey notes and a check-list of finished watercolours are written by Andrew Wilton; it is generously illustrated with plenty of colour; and under the skilled editorship of our Honorary Member, the distinguished mountaineer, Walter Amstutz. I have little to add to what can be found in this book. The excellent maps of Turner's six Swiss tours show us that the first in 1802 was for mountaineers the most interesting, and for Turner it was the most formative. As part of an extensive European tour, made possible by the Peace of Amiens, he made his way to Geneva. Hence he went, like all the others, to Chamonix and Argentière, where he probably got as high as the Couvercle. He then did the western half of the Tour of Mont Blanc crossing the Col du Bonhomme and Col de la Seigne. From Aosta he crossed the Saint Bernard to Martigny; then from Vevey over the passes to Thun, Interlaken and Grindelwald, and by the Grosse Scheidegg and the Reichenbach falls to Meiringen and Lucerne. From Andermatt he crossed the Saint Gotthard to Faido and returned by the same route to Schwyz, then on to Zürich and the north. The conditions of travel were severe, the distances great, the physical achievement remarkable, he was constantly tired out, but never too exhausted to fill his sketchbooks with more than 400 drawings. These are mostly rapid pencil sketches, similar to those he had made in the Lake District. Like them they are often strengthened with watercolour, and sometimes they are finished watercolours. They furnished him with a fruitful source of subjects for the rest of his life. Subjects which seem particularly to have fascinated him were the dramatically sublime scenery of the Saint Gotthard and the Devil's Bridge, the Reichenbach falls, and the frozen chaos of the glaciers. A series of watercolour sketches of the Mer de Glace[17] are wonderfully evocative to those of us who have climbed the Aiguilles that flank the glacier. One of these, looking down the Mer de Glace to the Aiguilles Rouges, shows, high on the left, Blair's Hut, the predecessor of the Montanvers Hotel, which was built by the Englishman, Charles Blair, in 1779.

Turner's *Liber Studiorum* which was to have been a series of original

2 'The Summit of Cader-Idris Mountain (Llyn-y-Cau)' — Engraving by E. & M. Rooker after the painting by Richard Wilson, 1714–1782.

3 'Snowdon (from Llyn Nantlle)' — Aquatint by W. Pickett after P. J. de Loutherbourg, 1740–1812; 1805.

74 'View of Grasmere' — *Julius Caesar Ibbetson 1759–1817; oil, 1802 (Private Collection)*

75 'Mer de Glace, Chamonix' — *William Pars 1742–1782; watercolour, 1770 (British Museum)*.

76 *'Glaciere taken from Montanvert looking towards Mont Blanc, Sepr 16th 1781'* — Francis Towne
1740–1816; pen, ink and watercolour (Private Collection).

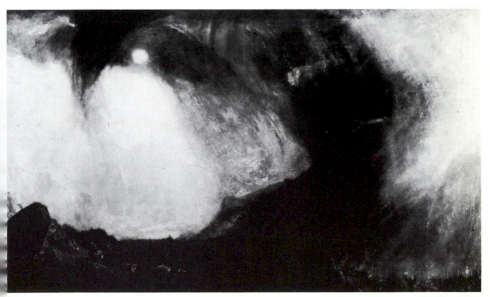

77 *'Snowstorm: Hannibal and his army crossing the Alps'* — J. M. W. Turner; oil, RA 1812 (Tate Gallery).

78 *Six mezzotints from Turner's Liber Studiorum.*
a: Mt St Gothard — Engraved by Charles Turner, 20 February 1808. b: 'Lake of Thun' — Engraved by Charles Turner, 10 June 1808. c: 'Little Devil's Bridge over the Russ above Altdorf' — Engraved by Charles Turner, 29 March 1809. d: 'Mer de Glace' — Engraved by J. M. W. Turner, 23 May 1812. e: 'The Source of the Arveron' — Engraved by J. M. W. Turner, 1 January 1816. f: 'Ben Arthur. Scotland' — Engraved by T. Lupton, 1 January 1819.

engravings to demonstrate the artist's powers of invention and design, was divided into categories one of which was 'Mountainous'. Of the 13 plates in this category eight derive from sketches made in the Alps in 1802, which include a view of the source of the Arveiron and a particularly dramatic one, looking up the Mer de Glace, showing the Petit Dru and the Flammes de Pierre des Drus on the left, the Aiguille des Grands Charmoz and the Aiguille de la République on the right, and the Grandes Jorasses in the distance (*Plate 78*).

In these brief notes on Turner in the Alps in 1802, I have been looking at his work from a very limited topographical point of view, seeing how far he visited places dear to mountaineers and how far his visions evoke our own experience. But if we look at one of Turner's masterpieces, inspired by the Alps in 1802, we can see that his experience invoked something much more profound than topographical images, *Snow Storm: Hannibal and his Army crossing the Alps* (*Plate 77*) is not only a remarkable vortex-like composition of tonal areas created in light and shadow, but, like the Diploma *Dolbadarn Castle* moving from topography to romantic history, it also shows a serious preoccupation with philosophical problems. The artist draws us into the misery of the army's struggle with the elements. The picture was painted in 1812, the year of the retreat from Moscow, and Turner saw parallels between Hannibal and Napoleon. The theme of the picture is 'The Fallacy of Hope', and it was accompanied in the Academy catalogue by eleven lines from Turner's poem of that name — Despite 'craft, treachery and fraud' still the chief advanced . . . with hope. 'In vain . . . each pass ensanguined deep with dead or rocky fragments, wide destruction roll'd'.

Notes

The talk which accompanied the 70 slides shown at the meeting has been adapted for this article for which the illustrations are strictly limited. The notes, as far as possible, indicate where the pictures mentioned can be seen.

1. See: *The View Finders*, Abbot Hall Art Gallery, Kendal, 1980; *Beauty, Horror and Immensity — Picturesque Landscape in Britain — 1750–1850*, Fitzwilliam Museum, Cambridge, 1981; *The Discovery of the Lake District 1750–1810*, Grasmere and Wordsworth Museum, 1982; *The Discovery of the Lake District*, Victoria and Albert Museum, 1984.
2. *AJ85* pp33–43.
3. *Snowdon from Llyn Nantlle*, Walker Art Gallery, Liverpool, and *Llyn-y-Cau*, Tate Gallery, both oil paintings, have frequently been reproduced. There is more than one version of each picture.
4. There is no published reproduction of this picture, but it can be seen in the house on Belle Isle which is open to the public.
5. *The Langdale Pikes from Elterwater*, 1783, pencil and wash, Private Collection, frequently exhibited and reproduced, previously exhibited at the Alpine Club. See: catalogues (note 1) 1981, 1982, 1984.
6. *Keswick Lake and entrance to Borrowdale* c.1791. Watercolour, Private Collection, exhibited Grasmere 1982 and AC 1981, 1982, not reproduced.

7. *Buttermere Lake*, 1797, watercolour, Tweed and Lakes sketchbook, British Museum, illustrated in colour, Gerald Wilkinson, *Turner's Early Sketchbooks*, 1972, p48/9.

8. *Buttermere Lake, with part of Cromack-water, Cumberland, a Shower*, 1798, Oil, Tate Gallery, illustrated in colour cat, V & A 1984, p51; Butlin & Joll, *the Paintings of J M W Turner*, 1984, no. 7.

9. *Morning amongst the Coniston Fells*, 1798, oil, Tate Gallery, illustrated in colour cat V & A 1984, p56, Butlin & Joll, no. 8.

10. *A Mountain Stream, Coniston*, 1797, watercolour, Private Collection, illustrated cat. Grasmere 1982.

11. *Dolbadarn Castle, North Wales*, 1800, oil, Royal Academy of Arts, illustrated Butlin & Joll, no. 8.

12. The Welsh Bard, the central figure in Thomas Gray's *Ode, The Bard*, was a popular subject for romantic painters such as Martin and De Loutherbourg.

13. *Vues Remarquables* included a preface by Albrecht von Haller, the author of the influential poem *Die Alpen*, and *Description d'un Voyage fait en 1776 dans une Partie du Canton du Berne* by J S Wyttenbach. There are fine copies of these books in the AC Library. See cat. *Treasures of the Alpine Club*, 1982, c31–33.

14. C F Bell and Thomas Girtin, 'The drawings and sketches of John Robert Cozens', *Walpole Society*, 1934–35. The drawings referred to are illustrated: nos. 8, 12, 433, plates 1, 2, 33.

15. William Coxe, *Travels in Switzerland, and in the Country of the Grisons: in a series of letters to William Melmoth Esq*. Third edition, 1794.

16. Towne's two watercolours of the source of the Arveiron have both been widely exhibited and reproduced. See Adrian Bury *Francis Towne — Lone Star of Water-colour Painting*. That in the V & A, see *AJ85*, p39; the other in a private collection reproduced in colour, Bury, *ibid*, p97.

17. Two of the views of the Mer de Glace, referred to here were reproduced in colour in an article by Walter Amstutz, 'Turner — Promethean of Alpine Painting', *AJ84*, pp31–35.

Does the Lung Pump Oxygen?
A short history of a classical controversy.

J. S. Milledge

In the summer of 1984 we mounted the first British physiological expedition to Pikes Peak in Colorado since the 1911 expedition led by the great Oxford physiologist J S Haldane. Our team included Edward Williams and Michael Ward of the Alpine Club and five other 'Gentlemen Physiologists'. We could find no evidence of the Haldane expedition and the Summit House where he and his team worked has been replaced by a grander tourist shop and cafe. Since returning I have been re-reading his original papers in which he sets out his evidence, gathered on this expedition, for the idea that the lung can pump oxygen into the body when man becomes acclimatized to high altitude.

All readers of the *Alpine Journal* are aware of the way high altitude reduces physical performance. Accounts of climbing on Everest and other very high peaks always emphasize the desperately slow rate of climbing, a few slow steps then a pause for gasps of air. The problem for the body stems, of course, from the lack of oxygen, or strictly from the low pressure of oxygen in the air.

However, while the low oxygen pressure is the same for everyone, people seem to vary a lot in their ability to cope with the problem; also the same individual improves with time spent at altitude due to the process of acclimatization. It was these considerations amongst others that led Haldane to support the theory that the lung was able, if necessary, to pump or secrete oxygen from the air into the blood against a pressure gradient. This ability, like most human (or animal) abilities, would be expected to vary from person to person accounting for the differences in response to high altitude. Also, like athletic training, this ability could develop over time accounting, in part, for the process of acclimatization.

The alternative theory was that oxygen passed from the air in the lungs to the blood by simple diffusion down a pressure gradient. The main protagonist for this 'diffusion only' theory was the equally famous physiologist from Cambridge, Joseph Barcroft. But neither of these men claimed originality for their theories. They represented the last and most colourful antagonists in a controversy which had lasted for at least 40 years before their time.

Up until the mid-nineteenth century if the transport of chemicals across living membranes was considered at all it was assumed to be by passive diffusion. Then it came to be appreciated that in some organs, for instance the kidney and bowel, membranes could pump certain chemicals across against a concentration gradient. In the kidney urea is pumped out in to the urine to a higher concentration than it is in the blood. Various glands were shown to secrete substances out of or into the blood uphill against concentration gradients. Could the lung be considered as an oxygen gland?

Continental Physiologists

Ludwig, a German physiologist in Leipzig seems to have been the first to suggest gas secretion by the lung in the mid-nineteenth century. He and his school published work suggesting that the lung secreted carbon dioxide out of the lung and probably oxygen inwards. This led his rival Pfluger in Bonn with his pupils to carry out experiments to disprove this notion and to their satisfaction they showed in 1871 that simple diffusion was adequate to account for oxygen transport.

However, this work was done with instruments which were far too crude to measure the partial pressure of gases in the blood to the accuracy needed to prove or disprove the rival theories.

Next on the scene in 1890 was the great Danish physiologist Christian Bohr, one of Pfluger's pupils. He improved the instrumentation and with his students carried out more exact experiments and came to the conclusion that under certain conditions carbon dioxide and oxygen were secreted. But in 1894 Fredericq, in Liege, claimed diffusion was adequate. Then in 1897 Haldane and Lorain-Smith published their first studies on the subject claiming the demonstration of oxygen secretion. So about the turn of the century the controversy was nicely balanced.

The Kroghs

August Krogh, a young pupil of Bohr and also a Dane, set out to prove his chief and the secretion theory to be correct. He improved the instrument for measuring blood gases, the aerotonometer, so that he could be certain about the relative values of lung and blood oxygen and carbon dioxide partial pressures. This was the crucial evidence for either theory. To his surprise he found that the blood (arterial) oxygen was always less than the lung oxygen even when the animal breathed a low oxygen mixture. His chief had been wrong.

Before publishing these findings Krogh did a lot more work on the different aspects of the problem. In some of this he was very ably helped by his physician wife Marie. In particular she devised a solution to the problem of estimating the capacity of the lung to diffuse oxygen across into the blood.

One of the arguments in favour of the secretion theory was that it was thought inconceivable that simple diffusion could account for the transfer of as much as five or even six litres of oxygen per minute which is required by a top athlete when running flat out. In order to refute this argument the Kroghs wanted to measure the diffusing capacity of the lung for oxygen, as did other physiologists of the day. To do this they needed to know the amount of oxygen taken in per minute, which was a standard measurement, and the driving pressure for oxygen. To measure this pressure they needed to know not only the pressure of oxygen in the lung, which was not too difficult, but also the mean pressure in the blood capillary. This last was impossible to be certain about. Marie's solution was to bypass this difficulty by using a trace concentration of carbon monoxide in the gas breathed and measuring the diffusing capacity of the lung for this gas. Carbon monoxide is a look-alike to oxygen in that it is taken up by haemoglobin in the blood in the same way as oxygen only more so. The advantage was that one started with no carbon monoxide in the body and so the driving pressure was simply the pressure in the lung of carbon monoxide. This could be measured. The value of diffusing capacity for carbon monoxide could be converted to that of oxygen from the known physical properties of the gases. The upshot was that the lung was shown to be a very good diffuser of oxygen. This is partly because it has an enormous surface area for gas exchange and partly because haemoglobin is so good at taking up oxygen. They showed that given the diffusing capacity they had measured, simple diffusion alone was adequate to transfer oxygen, even on exercise or when breathing low oxygen mixtures. And so another plank in the oxygen secretion theory was removed.

It is interesting and rather sobering to realize that Marie's work lay ignored by physicians for the next 35 years until it was rediscovered on the other side of the Atlantic in 1950 by Kety working with Comroe. They were interested in tests of lung function for use in patients with various forms of lung disease. What more crucial test of lung function than its ability to transfer oxygen? So Marie's measurement of diffusing capacity for carbon monoxide gradually became a routine clinical test and the total capacity divided by the lung volume is often known now as the 'Krogh factor'.

After August and Marie had amassed all their data on the subject they published their work in 1910 in a series of seven short papers which they afterwards referred to as 'The seven little devils'. August wrote in the introductory paragraph to the first devil; 'The results were contrary to our expectations and the publication has been put off till now in order that the problem might be approached in some other ways and conclusions reached representing, if possible, some sort of finality in the protracted discussion of this most complicated subject.' Wishful thinking on Krogh's part because the controversy in Britain was only just getting started.

J S Haldane

John Scott Haldane was born in 1860 of a distinguished Scottish family. His brother became Secretary of State for War during the First World War. After studying medicine at Edinburgh he worked first at Dundee then moved to Oxford where his uncle was professor of physiology. Haldane had become interested in air and what made it 'foul' under various conditions. He invented an apparatus for the accurate measurement of carbon dioxide and oxygen in air that is still used, in modified form, as the reference method in this field. With this he showed that in stuffy rooms the carbon dioxide level rises (slightly) and oxygen falls. This work led to work on the chemical control of breathing. He showed that carbon dioxide was the main stimulus, oxygen lack being a less sensitive drive (at sea level) as an earlier German physiologist (Mischer Rush) put it. 'Carbon dioxide spreads its wings over the oxygen needs of the body.' Haldane was, of course, fully aware of the importance of oxygen lack, anoxia as it was then called, and wrote, 'Anoxia not only stops the machine, it wrecks the machinery.'

Foul air was a particularly serious problem in the mines and Haldane was soon investigating the different forms of it. 'Black damp' he showed was 87% nitrogen and 13% carbon dioxide. 'After damp', found after an explosion, he found to have a high percentage of carbon monoxide. He reported after one mine explosion that of 57 bodies recovered only four had died of the violence of the explosion, the rest of carbon monoxide poisoning. He investigated the time course of carbon monoxide poisoning in mice and men; mainly on himself as subject. He showed that in small animals or birds the time course was much faster. He therefore advocated the use of a canary as a test for carbon monoxide.

His work on carbon monoxide poisoning led him to devise a method for using it to calculate the partial pressure of oxygen in the blood. The method was rather indirect compared with Krogh's aerotonometer and until I started this article I thought it had not been used by anyone else. The measurement of carbon monoxide in the blood involved a titration step in which the colour of one tube was matched to that of a standard tube while adding a solution drop by drop. The result is calculated from the amount of solution necessary to achieve a colour match. It is all too easy in such a situation, consciously or unconsciously, to add a drop or two too much or too little according to the result desired.

So using this method he published, first in 1897, his finding that sometimes the arterial oxygen was higher than lung oxygen indicating that oxygen secretion takes place. He later withdrew these results because he had used factors for the oxygen/carbon monoxide relationships in blood derived from ox blood. But in 1912 he published again using values from each subject's own blood. In this study he found that while breathing a low oxygen mixture, especially if some exercise was performed, there was evidence of secretion.

Pikes Peak Expedition 1911
In 1911 Haldane with Douglas, his young colleague from Oxford, joined two American scientists, Henderson and Schneider, for a physiological expedition to Pikes Peak. This is a 4300m peak in the front range of the Rockies in Colorado. Even in those days the summit could be reached by a rack railway in about 3 hours from the town of Colorado Springs. There was a Summit House at the rail terminus on the flat top of the mountain. In this stone building the team lived and improvised their laboratory.

The views from the top were breathtaking. To the east one looked out over the checkerboard of Colorado Springs and over the Great Plains to a straight sea-like horizon. In all other directions were the peaks of the Rockies.

In his hundred page paper on the expedition in the Philosophical Transactions of the Royal Society, Haldane was allowed to expand on all aspects of the expedition in a way that is the envy of present day scientists. He described the symptoms of mountain sickness in his own party and the sufferings of tourists arriving after he had acclimatized. 'The walkers struggled in looking blue, cold, exhausted and miserable often hurrying out again to vomit.' A reporter became blue and faint and had to be revived with oxygen. It is strange how this contrasts with our experience in 1984. Amongst the tourists who only spent an hour or two on the summit we did not see any of these alarming symptoms. But to return to 1911, the physiologists made observations on themselves and one visitor. They noted the progressive decrease in lung carbon dioxide and increase in lung oxygen level from an initial reduced value, with acclimatization. They recorded the rise in red cell number and haemoglobin concentration in the blood. They observed the extraordinary periodic breathing during sleep and obtained good records of the breathing pattern showing periods of cessation of breathing for up to 20 seconds. There are photographs of team members puffing up the steep incline of the railway with large rubberised canvas bags on their backs. These were the famous 'Douglas' bags for the collection of expired air.

But the finding which most excited Haldane was the evidence of secretion of oxygen. They carried out fifteen experiments on five subjects. Of these, in four oxygen was added to the inspired air and nitrogen in one. In the remaining nine experiments air was breathed. In all experiments the arterial oxygen was higher than the lung oxygen by an average of 36mm Hg indicating a significant secretion of oxygen by the lungs. Later Haldane was to insist on the importance of acclimatization in order to achieve oxygen secretion but his actual data show a 36mm Hg difference in the first experiment carried out on Pikes Peak. This was on Douglas seven days after arrival on the summit. Subsequent experiments on this subject showed no further 'improvement' with acclimatization. Oxygen breathing reduced but did not abolish oxygen secretion.

Thus by 1914 when the First World War halted much conventional physiology the question of oxygen secretion was very open, with the Copenhagen school maintaining that there was no such thing and the Oxford school insisting that the mechanism was available when oxygen was in short supply as at high altitude.

After the war the last great protagonist in the controversy arrived on the scene, Joseph Barcroft.

Joseph Barcroft

Barcroft was 12 years younger than Haldane. He was from an old Irish family with a country seat at Newry in County Down. He was sent to school in England and then to Cambridge where he read physiology. Though he went back to Ireland for holidays, Cambridge became his home for almost all his long, productive working life. He was soon involved in research and like Haldane did a lot of work on the way haemoglobin carries oxygen in the blood.

His first altitude expedition was in 1910 to Tenerife where at 3300m he studied the effect of altitude on blood/oxygen interactions. The following year while Haldane was on Pikes Peak, Barcroft was on Monte Rosa working from the salubrious hut on the Col d'Olen (3000m) and the far from salubrious hut on the Punta Gnifetti, the Cabana Regina Margherita (4572m). Again the objective was the study of the oxygen/haemoglobin complex in men at these altitudes and the changes in blood acidity.

During the 1914–18 War Barcroft was asked to investigate the problem of soldiers gassed by the Germans (as was Haldane). He realised that the men were dying due to lack of oxygen. The gas irritated the lungs producing excess fluid which hampered the free passage of oxygen. He therefore advised that they be treated in an atmosphere enriched with oxygen. To achieve this an oxygen tent was devised and certainly some lives were saved by these means. He also suggested that the same treatment would be helpful in treating pneumonia as indeed it is, though we now, of course, use a small face mask rather than a tent enclosing the whole bed.

After the war, perhaps partly as a result of these experiences, he had a 'glass box' constructed in the laboratory at Cambridge in which a man could live and the atmosphere be controlled. Carbon dioxide could be scrubbed out and the oxygen percentage adjusted as desired.

In 1920 Barcroft carried out a six day experiment in this box with himself as the one subject. The objective was to test the oxygen secretion theory. In 1913 he and Cooke had been the first to get blood direct from an artery in a human subject for gas analysis. Using this technique he hoped to provide direct evidence for or against the theory. It was an heroic experiment. He lived for six days in the box while the oxygen percentage was gradually reduced until on the final day it was down to 10%, equivalent to over 5500m. He took exercise on a stationary bicycle and each day withdrew blood from a metal cannula tied into his artery at the wrist. After the experiment the artery had to be tied off. Most people can manage without this artery and fortunately Barcroft was one of these. His programme was full with observations on his pulse, breathing, exercising, collection of expired air, etc. He kept this up for the planned six days although on the last day he felt quite ill, presumably from mountain sickness.

The experiment showed that the pressure of the arterial blood oxygen was always lower than the lung oxygen even on exercise at the highest altitude equivalent. So there was no need to postulate any other mechanism than diffusion. Haldane objected that under laboratory conditions acclimatization might not have occurred and, though Haldane did not make the criticism, there was only one subject who might have been atypical in this respect.

So the next year Barcroft led an international expedition to Peru, one of whose objectives was to test the secretion theory again, this time on more subjects and at real altitude in the field.

The Cerro de Pasco Expedition 1921–22
This expedition was quite an ambitious one with eight scientists, five from the USA and three, including Barcroft, from Britain. The British contingent sailed across the Atlantic, through the Panama and south to Lima. There they met their American colleagues who had gone ahead and made preliminary arrangements.

Their destination was the mining township of Cerro de Pasco situated at 4300m on the Alto Plano over the spine of the Andes from Lima. It is not a pretty place, a high altitude slum, mostly, and even the Andes are not very dramatic at this point. But the drive up from Lima, and even more the rail trip is one of the most spectacular in the world. The great advantage of Cerro for a physiologist is its accessibility from sea level and a large resident population (about 25,000). Barcroft was fortunate in having the full backing of the Railway Company who gave him the use of a couple of box cars which were fitted out as laboratory and living accommodation. In this laboratory they made observations on themselves at Lima and later at Cerro.

There were numerous projects on the various ways in which the body adapts to the low oxygen pressure. Amongst these were the measurement of arterial and lung oxygen using an improved method of arterial sampling with syringe and needle much as we do today, rather than the tied-in cannula used in the 'glass box' experiments. These measurements again showed in all subjects and under all conditions that the pressure of the arterial oxygen was always lower than the lung oxygen. Barcroft did not make a big issue of this fact in his reports of the expedition. He seemed now to have considered the matter settled in favour of the 'diffusion only' theory.

Barcroft became the authority on altitude physiology and his book *Lessons from High Altitude* became a minor classic. He seems to have been a most likeable man and though famous beyond physiological circles was always ready to listen to ideas and even criticism from younger workers. In the Second World War he did much work on nutrition and before that on neonatal physiology. But we remember him mainly for his altitude work. When asked about the cause of mountain sickness he is reputed to have replied, 'It would betray my nationality if I were to tell you that mountain sickness is caused by the oxygen which isn't there!'

In December 1922 the Royal Society arranged a public discussion in which, besides Barcroft and Haldane, T H Somervell and T G Longstaff took part, the latter two having recently returned from the 1922 Everest Expedition. Haldane maintained that, 'Mr Barcroft's results had not shaken the evidence furnished by the Pikes Peak expedition that increased oxygen secretory activity of the lung epithelium was the main factor in acclimatization', and he maintained that the fact that Somervell with Mallory and Norton had reached the astonishing height of 8200m without supplementary oxygen must mean that oxygen was being secreted by these well-acclimatized men. As late as 1936 the new edition of his book *Respiration* included a chapter on oxygen secretion by the lung. However, by the mid twenties the consensus view of physiologists was against him.

One pleasant aspect of this controversy was the courteous and magnanimous way in which it was conducted at least on the part of Krogh, Haldane and Barcroft. Krogh in the introduction to his 'Seven little devils' paid tribute to his teacher, Bohr, whose views he was about to rebut. Just after the Royal Society meeting mentioned above, Barcroft wrote in a review of Haldane's new book, 'No one who turns over the pages can but be impressed with the enormous advance which has been made in the physiology of respiration within the last thirty years, and the degree to which that advance has been due to Dr Haldane's work and to the stimulating influence which he has wielded over the minds of others.'

Where did Haldane, a brilliant and careful worker, go wrong and why did he persist in clinging to the secretion theory for so long? I have no quick and certain answer to these questions. I have hinted that there may have been bias, probably unconscious, in the rather subjective analysis used in the carbon monoxide method.

However, another possible explanation comes from the work of Ester Killick. She was a student of Haldane and worked as a physiologist in the Mining Department of Birmingham University. In 1938, using herself as subject, she examined the effect of repeated exposure to carbon monoxide on the relationship between lung and blood levels of carbon monoxide. She used the same method for estimating carbon monoxide as had Haldane. She claimed that with these repeated exposures there developed a gradient of pressure between lung and blood for either carbon monoxide or oxygen! Her analyses were checked independently so there was unlikely to be an error there. An alternative explanation for her results could be that the relationship between carbon monoxide and oxygen affinity for haemoglobin becomes different in the body as compared to the test tube with repeated exposure. Whatever the explanation, Haldane's Pikes Peak results might have been due to this odd effect of repeated exposure to carbon monoxide in himself and his subjects.

But I am sure that Haldane was committed to the secretion theory and the results on Pikes Peak only confirmed his already strongly held view. This goes some way towards answering the second question. Why did he persist in holding to the secretion theory for so long? It was as if oxygen secretion had become an article of faith for him.

In his later years he wrote and lectured extensively about his philosophy of science and of life. Part of this was an abhorrence of what he believed to have been a wrong turning taken by physiology in embracing a highly mechanistic view of the body. A strange view in one who by using a most rigorous experimental approach himself had made so many important advances. However, there is no denying that there was this mystical side to Haldane, at least in his middle and later life when he sought to emphasise the wonder of nature and life. It was therefore more attractive to think of the delicate living membrane that separates air from blood in the lungs as having a secretory function, facilitating the transport of life-giving oxygen into the body, than that it functioned merely as an inert membrane allowing diffusion like an artificial sausage skin.

Haldane died in 1936 and Barcroft in 1947. The oxygen secretion controversy is part of the rich history of science along with the Phlogiston Theory and the Theory of Humours. Like them it was a good idea and though false was valuable in stimulating scientists to devise and carry out experiments to prove or disprove it. In the course of such work techniques were perfected, ideas were refined and science was advanced.

An Introduction to Mountains

Jack Gibson

Some years ago a number of letters preserved by my mother were found in an old trunk, among them a dozen or so written by me from Switzerland between 1929 and 1932. From Cambridge I had joined the staff of Chillon College, then, until the great depression, a flourishing school between Territet and Ville-neuve, overlooking Lac Leman.

As I sit, 55 years later, in a chalet beside Lac Champex while it pours with rain, I transcribe some of these, wondering whether they may be of some interest for the light they throw on the differences between the ways we ski'd and climbed then and now.

Apart from a summer holiday walking and scrambling in the Cairngorms, I had done no climbing other than as a schoolboy getting stuck on the Cromer cliffs and rescued by coastguards — an experience that taught me that it is often easier to climb up than down; and I had spent, while at Cambridge, two winter fortnights skating and skiing in the Valais at Morgins where all ascents were then made on skins.

At Chillon College, I joined the Montreux section of the Club Alpin Suisse and with a guide reached the summits of the Dent de Morcles and the Dent Jaune of the Dents du Midi. No account of these climbs survives, but there follow extracts from letters found in the trunk:

29.4.30. On Good Friday I went off with the Swiss Alpine Club for the most marvellous four days. The train left at 4.40am and I had borrowed an alarm clock that failed to go off. I woke at 4.30 and ran the whole way to the station with my skis and pack, but missed the train by 4 minutes. I had to chase it in a taxi and caught it at Martigny where I joined the four Swiss who made up the rest of the party. We took the mountain train to Sembrancher, and from there a car to Châble. Then we had to carry our skis and packs with four days food and clothing to the snow. I thought I would die, but we reached the snow by lunch and rested for an hour. We then set out with another party of three to cross the col in the Alpe de Vatseret to get to the Cabane de Mont Fort which was to be our base. A frightful fog came down and although we climbed for five hours to a height well above that of the col we could not find it and had to ski back over our tracks: it was awful. The snow was very deep and as heavy as lead, and I was tired out. We had to turn all the time so as not to lose the climbing tracks and I fell at almost every turn. When we finally got down to the village of Verbier, just above the snow line, I was done in and went off to bed. However, hot chocolate and red wine — sounds a frightful mixture but did excellently — put me right. The next day it cleared for about four hours in the morning and we got to the cabane. The other party of three had slept the night in a cattle shelter and were there to meet us, but we couldn't ski because of more fog. All day long more and more people arrived from the other side of the col where there was a well marked track. That night we slept 38 in the tiny cabane, but it was all most amusing and we had a spendid omelette. The Alpine

Club huts are wonderful, very compact and well fitted out with excellent stoves.

The next day was absolutely marvellous. We were first up at 5am and started off up the Rosablanche, 100m higher than the Dents du Midi. We got to the top to find a very cold wind blowing over the ridge, but had the best descent I've ever made. We crossed two glaciers — the Grand Desert and the Glacier de la Chaux — the snow was perfect powder after the frost of the night before, and I've never enjoyed anything more. We got back at one, just as the snow was softening, and I went off to sleep till 5pm. Then, as the snow was getting into good condition again three of us started down into the valley on the other side of the col from which we had come up. As bad luck would have it, when we got about 750m below the cabane one of the others twisted his knee and couldn't go on any more. It was no good trying to go back so we sent a message by two others climbing to the cabane, and helped him down to a little village called Sarreyer where we arranged to pick him up the next day. The only bed we could find for him was that of the state *sage-femme* and we didn't start back till after 8pm. Though we were both very tired we had a marvellous climb up following our tracks down in the starlight, the mountains looking wonderful. We got back at about midnight to hot drinks, raw eggs and bed, and a most amusing night as someone would snore and the whole cabane failed to stop him. The next day we had a wonderful descent, picked up the injured man, drank a lot of Fendant and got back to Villeneuve yodelling and singing at 5 o'clock.

I had promised to take one of the prefects who had had to stay for the holidays on a walking tour for the last three days, so on Tuesday we were up at six and walked to Roche where we had a huge breakfast to extracts from Carmen and famous waltzes on a pianola. From there by goods train to Bex and on to Vernayaz on foot. We explored the Gorge de Trient, about 75m deep and only 2 to 6m across with a terrific waterfall above, of which my photo only shows half as it was too long to get in. The country is very lovely, meadows covered with kingcups and cowslips and hills lit up by the light green of larch just coming out. We had a very good supper in Vernayaz and decided to try to get up the Grand St Bernard the next day. Wednesday, walked to Martigny for breakfast, then up the valley to Orsières for lunch. After a bit of sleep we set off for Bourg St Pierre reaching it through the most ripping country about 7pm. We slept in the room said to have been used by Napoleon. Thursday was dull and cold with snowstorms higher up and we were advised not to go on. However, having got as far as we had and with nothing better to do, we decided to have a go and to turn back if we found it impossible. We soon reached the snow but were able to follow the telegraph poles to within the last 300m or so. Here the poles went over the rocks and we were afraid of starting a snow-slip if we tried to follow them. However, in spite of the snowstorm there was a terrific wind which kept the snow moving so that we could just follow the ruts of old ski tracks in the hard snow beneath. We had to take off the skis we had borrowed at Bourg and I had to carry both pairs as Johnson was getting a bit too tired. We walked up the last slope in a straight line so as not to start a snow-slip and when we got to the top we saw the monastery looming through the snow. It was 2 o'clock and they took us in, absolutely plastered with snow, gave us a magnificent bedroom, lunch with marvellous hot soup, and lent us clothes. We slept most of the afternoon and then saw over the Hospice and saw the dogs, and slept again all night. We got up at 4 the next morning to see if we could get down, as school began that evening. There was still a terrific storm raging, so I went to hear Mass sung and by after breakfast it had stopped snowing. With only mist and blown snow to contend with, we decided to sally forth. We went very carefully and though the snowstorm came on again we had reached the telegraph poles which made it safe enough as we could follow them. One of us stood at a pole while the other went ahead till he could see the next one. We returned the borrowed skis and walked down to Liddes where we managed to cadge a lift in a car to Orsières. There we lunched and caught a train to the valley, and so back to Villeneuve by 5.30pm. You should have seen the Grand Combin as we got out of the storm and the mountains the other side of the valley appeared in the most wonderful soft blue sky.

However, that's not the end of my adventures. Saturday I spent getting straight and had some good tennis, and on Sunday Blundell, Markham, Ryley and I set out to explore further up the valley of the Trient while the flowers were still good. We had a splendid day but I got back feeling rather tired and with a sore throat from eating too much snow. I was just off to bed after supper when the news arrived that one of the new boys was lost on the Malatrait, the mountain behind the college. It's a tricky mountain and I've been stuck on it, so off we went to collect a search party and lantern in the village. We heard him about 8pm and shouted to him to keep still while we tried to get up to him. First we got too high and couldn't get down to him, and then we tried up a ravine full of avalanche snow and I fell into a crevasse, but without hurt. Then we could hear him plainly and thought all was well. He sounded as if he was just out of the ravine to the right, but our difficulty was to get out of the ravine ourselves. Two of the Swiss wouldn't come, so I and the other roped up and had a most exciting climb in the dark with loose rocks hurtling round us. We got out after about an hour, only to hear his voice the other side of the ravine which had been throwing the echo back. We stayed where we were and yelled encouragement to him and directions to the other two Swiss who eventually got to him. We all got back safely and Hunter's hot whisky cured my cold. The boy, a Bonham Carter, had gone up with three others and coming down they had left the path to try to find a quicker way. Unable to agree, they had split up and poor B C had spent 7 hours sitting on a rock.

1.5.31. Back to work, but I had a wonderful last week of the holidays. I had promised to take Kendzior to the Britannia Hut and sent him on a day ahead of me so that he could do the long climb of about 2700m from the rail-head at Stalden in two bits. I left on Sunday morning, lunched and picked up Kendzior and Imseng, our guide, at Saas Fee and got to the hut for a very good supper and night's rest in comfortable bunks. It was fun to be with Imseng again after beating him in the Swiss Romand championship and I didn't want to be solely responsible for Kendzior in an area I did not know. We had four days perfect climbing and skiing: the Strahlhorn, Allalinhorn and Alphubel over 4000m, and the Fluchthorn, 3800m. The summits of the first two were very steep and we had to wear crampons, but we got to the summit of the Fluchthorn and above the Alphubeljoch on ski. Kendzior was not strong enough for the last which I did with Imseng. We left the hut at 5am and got to the top at 10 coming down very steep and roped between great crevasses and having to turn all the way — 1000m in 15 minutes without a fall. Of course the snow was perfect, powder on crust, but Imseng was quite impressed with my skiing. However, pride had its fall that evening. On return to Saas Fee we had our heavy packs to carry and at about 2700m got into heavy crusty snow. I fell and broke a stick and spent much of the descent trying to do jump turns out of fearful heavy tracks, often falling.

Date missing, but I think February '32.   I had a wonderful weekend with the Swiss Alpine Club last Saturday and Sunday. I left directly after work on Saturday and motored to Lac Champex with one of the party, the rest having started in the morning. We got there at 4 o'clock and started for the Cabane Dupuis which we reached at 9pm, doing the last bit by lantern across the glacier. The rest of the party were already in bed. On Sunday we all started at 6am and climbed the Aiguilles Dorées, getting back to the hut at 2pm and down to Orsières by 6, whence to Martigny by car, supper, and by train back here by 9pm. This is one of the more difficult climbs so was a great experience for me, and quite an honour being asked to go on it. Only two of us got up the most difficult bit, the Aiguille Javelle with a vertical chimney 12m high. I had to haul myself up parts of this with the help of the rope as it was too difficult for me without; but I didn't do too badly and had all sorts of new experiences such as cutting steps in real ice rather than hard snow, and coming down awful looking places by rapelle de corde. We did a lot of unroped climbing where I found myself a bit nervous to start with, but I soon got used to it, and it is much quicker.

15.3.32.   Two Sundays ago I had a grand day with the SAC. We caught the 5.30am train from Montreux and got out at St Triphon, between Aigle and Bex. From there we *walked* carrying our skis via Monthey and Morgins to the Portes de Culet. From the Douane Hut we had a ripping descent to the bottom of the Tour de Don where we had breakfast and skinned up to climb the Don. The top was all ice, but quite amusing. Instead of the usual way down to Châtel we went along the ridge to the Col de Croix and down the other side to Révereulax: what must be far the best run round Morgins. The valley is shaped like a glacier valley, without trees — 1000m of open running. At Révereulax the snow ran out so we walked back to Vionnaz and across the valley to Aigle. The Rhône valley has never seemed so wide before. What a day! I'm going to the Britannia Hut again. The SAC is holding a Course de Haut Alpinisme there for a week with lessons in bivouacking, practice rescues, etc, food and all for 55 francs for the week.

19.4.32.   We had only two really decent fine days at the Britannia Hut and for the rest of the time the temperature was from 20 to 27 below zero centigrade. It was very bad luck striking such weather, but otherwise it was well worth it and both amusing and instructive. It gave me some idea of what happens if one is caught out really badly by the weather when climbing. On the other hand we all managed to enjoy ourselves. The Swiss sang beautifully, all taking parts, and every evening after supper there was singing, yodelling, vulgar stories and chess or cards.

Short of the Folding Stuff

Tom Price

I am not much given to looking back. My photographs, curled at the edges, and my diaries scribbled in pencil in weather-stained notebooks, are stowed away in shoe-boxes under beds and in attics. They come to light only when we move house. But when this summer I toiled up to a col in the Pyrenees, and scanned the new panorama, and saw the Pic du Midi d'Ossau standing there, dominating the sky-line, it set up a train of reminiscence which on and off I have been reflecting upon ever since. It is strange how a mountain, once you have been up it and, so to speak, spent yourself upon it becomes easily recognizable even when viewed from new angles. It is almost 40 years since I was last anywhere near the Pic du Midi d'Ossau yet it seemed almost uncannily familiar.

Not an enormously high mountain, the Pic du Midi. But there are more ways than one of calculating the height and remoteness of a summit. People now get to the Himalaya with less expenditure of time and effort than we put into that approach to the Pyrenees. It was not only that there were no motorways and fewer planes. It was a matter of money.

There is curiously little mention of money in mountain literature. Perhaps it is because the climber leaves the mundane world of work, money and home behind for loftier realms, which have their own realities and harsh imperatives but of a different order. And the early mountaineers seem to have been so well off that money was not a consideration. The question on arrival at a Swiss hotel was not whether there was anywhere cheaper to be had, but whether the entertainment was likely to be adequate to a gentleman's needs. Transport, guides and porters were all hired with an Olympian disregard for cost. Even Robert Louis Stevenson, a mere writer after all, scratching a living by the pen, when he spent a night sleeping out in the Cevennes, found nature's 'green caravanserai' so satisfactory that he left money on the turf, enough for his night's lodging. That has always seemed to me, anxiously meting out my cash to stay as long as possible in the hills, as something akin to blasphemy.

Mountaineers when they have climbed a mountain by the easiest route seek further challenges by imposing various handicaps upon themselves. They choose harder routes, or winter ascents, or solo ascents, or ascents without oxygen, or ascents, if one is to believe McHaffie of Borrowdale, in boxing gloves and roller-skates. Presumably these carry a richer reward in terms of achievement and personal fulfilment.

The same can be said, in a way, for penniless ascents.

Just after the war the most you could take out of the country was £25. To us, however, that was so generous a ceiling as to be beyond our reach. We took £20 each, and subsisted for five weeks in the Pyrenees upon it. This penury led us into some memorable experiences. We never once slept in hired accommodation and so we were not just in the mountains for so many hours a day; we were there day and night, like the other animals. There is nothing like living out in the hills for bringing one into an intimacy with them. Coming down to a hut or hotel is like going home early from a good party: restful, perhaps, and prudent, but not so much fun. The fact that much of one's time and energy is expended on merely keeping alive and consequently less is available for getting up the peaks is not so great a disadvantage as all that. I think it was Sir Martin Conway who observed that climbers were on the whole too much interested in summits to the neglect of the rest of the mountains. Making brief sorties from under a roof and returning daily to the world of chairs and tables is being *in* the mountains, but not *of* them.

Not that living out is one long delight. On the contrary one often plumbs the depths. But after all, the same can be said of mountaineering generally; for all its moments of splendour, it is largely a catalogue of discomforts, dangers, tribulations and minor ill-health. But living out, one explores new levels of tolerance to the vagaries of the weather and the inconsiderateness of the natural environment. The great outdoors is a draughty place and full of insects, but there is something about it that soothes the savage breast.

On setting out for the Pyrenees, as my diary reminds me, though I had forgotten, I was visited by the usual misgivings about venturing forth from the security of home. My two companions had already set off the day before, to hitch-hike to the Channel. I was to go by train since as the son of a railwayman I could travel for a quarter of the normal fare. So I had a day of fretful waiting before I began my journey. On a clear evening, under a green and blue sky which remained bright long after the twilight had invaded the Liverpool townscape, I lifted my rucksack on my back and set off, wishing I was bound only for Ogwen, or could just go to bed at home. It was my first holiday abroad, and late evening is a sad time for departure. With no jacket, and my warm clothing stowed away in my rucksack, I felt lightly equipped for a long journey, but on the train I was put in the shade by a fellow passenger clad only in shirt, pants and shoes. 'Are you a DBS?' he asks me. 'Not yet', I reply. He is, and drunk. En route from Curaçao to Montreal his only luggage is money and cigarettes. The latter he hands round and spills on the floor with great generosity. Always keen on travelling light I saw in him a new standard to aim for.

With half of one side of the compartment at my disposal I could lie down in the foetal position and so passed a tolerable night. Time was on my side. I drifted across central London and continued quietly, sleepily and sunnily to Newhaven. It was a beautiful fresh breezy summer's day, and before long my two companions appeared. They had been there since the night before and had slept on a hill overlooking the town. On the voyage across the Channel we had lunch in the saloon and made quite an occasion of it, as it was to be our only restaurant meal for weeks.

The long trail south continued, spells of boredom punctuated by bursts of activity. Taking our places in a train was no easy task as the corridors were barely as wide as our loads. Edging along crab-wise it was hard on the spur of the moment to think of the French for 'Kindly retreat, madam, into the compartment as I cannot squeeze myself past you.' We humped our loads across Paris to the Gare d'Austerlitz and boarded the night train for Pau. We sat up all night on the hard green seats, heads toppling forwards whenever we lapsed into sleep. While the train was hurtling and lurching across France, emitting that occasional demented long-drawn-out screaming sound that used to be such a feature of the SNCF rapides, one could drift into a state of complaisant torpor and pleasant waking dreams, soothed by a feeling of progress, but the stops were an agony of impatience and discomfort..

The night passed and at eight in the morning we alighted at Pau. Pau has a fine esplanade rather like a seaside promenade, but instead of the sea it looks out over a broad landscape backed by the Pyrenees. Prominent on the skyline we saw a splendid jagged peak, the Pic du Midi d'Ossau. It was the first we had heard of it. Our background reading for this trip had been an atlas and Hilaire Belloc's poem about the fleas that tease in the High Pyrenees and the wine that tasted of the tar. But we now recognized it as what we had come all this way for. In the town we found a mountain equipment shop and there bought a Guide Ledormeur to the Pyrenees. Its maps were sketch-maps without contours, ridges and spurs being indicated by thick black lines. We had no map and this book became our sole source of topographical information.

We had been led to believe that food rationing was in force in France, though what we did not know was that no-one took any notice of it. We went to great lengths to find the appropriate office for obtaining ration cards. The man immediately in front of us at the *guichet* was having a passionate row with the woman behind the counter. She flew into a violent temper, and when the interview came to an end and he went out giving the door a slam that brought bits of plaster down off the ceiling, she thumped the counter and hurled abuse after him. She would have scant patience with us, we thought, with our halting French. Yet she turned to us with the utmost charm and urbanity, pulse normal, blood pressure a placid 120/80. I made up my mind that I would learn how to do that.

On the way back to the station we bought several feet of French bread, two bottles of red wine and a bag of peaches so ripe that they soaked through the paper and stuck our fingers together. By the time we boarded the local train with wooden seats we were getting very tired, and hungry, and hot, but spirits revived when we tucked into the bread and peaches, and passed round one of the bottles; and they soared when the other bottle, falling over on the luggage rack, exploded like a bomb and sent down a purple rain over Ken's head and shoulders.

At Laruns the noonday sun smote us like a hammer. From the dusty station an avenue led up a hill for half a kilometre to the village square. There was a fountain in the middle of it and by the time we reached it we were ready to drink it dry. The village lay stunned and torpid in the heat but life stirred faintly behind the bar of the Hotel des Touristes, and we laid out some precious francs for a pot of tea.

The weight of our packs was now a matter of immediate and pressing concern in that, now it came to the crunch, we could not carry them any distance. It was not that they were full of climbing equipment, most of which had not yet been invented, nor were they full of camping gear, for our tent was from a cheap offer in a newspaper, suitable for a child in a back garden, and we had brought it not to sleep in but to house our belongings while we were up in the mountains. What they were full of was food, and particularly coffee beans. We had believed post-war France to be seriously short of coffee, having naïvely accepted what was said in the newspapers, and in the hope of making a killing we had gone to Cooper's, an upmarket grocer in Liverpool, and bought a huge quantity of the cheapest coffee beans available. So our rucksacks bulged with ex-army biscuits, dried bananas, compressed dates, oatmeal, sugar and the like, but above all, coffee beans. Many of these beans had burst their paper bags and were running loose throughout our equipment.

The faint suspicion with which we were at first received in the bar of the Hotel des Touristes turned gradually to a fascinated interest as we unloaded our rucksacks on the floor and tried to gather up our stock of coffee beans. The patron kindly provided new paper bags. By some sort of telepathic communication the entrepreneurs of the village homed in on us. There was a good deal of amiable discussion but the consensus was that *roasted* beans were what everyone wanted. Green beans got the thumbs down. The auction, consequently, was a social success rather than a financial one, but we came away with fifteen hundred francs profit and a tumbler or two of the patron's red wine. There is nothing like trade between the great nations of the world for promoting international understanding and co-operation. Not only had we lightened our loads but had also been promised a lift up the valley in a lorry at some unspecified time in the late afternoon, from a nearby road junction.

Waiting for that lorry I count as one of the most delightful experiences of my mountaineering life. It was a pleasant cross-roads, with deep grass full of wild flowers and humming with insects of the more benign sort, under a generous, baking sun. We had our doubts about whether the lorry would indeed arrive, but we did not greatly care. Two girls came by and lingered with us, as though they too had all the time in the world. We had no past and no future, and the present was limitless.

When the lorry did come it was all the more pleasant a surprise for we had given it up. It was loaded with roof-tiles packed in straw, and on top of the load sat three picturesque characters whom we took to be drunken brigands but who were in fact drunken Portuguese workmen returning from a day off and singing, not altogether tunelessly. The afternoon was turning into a golden evening. The road climbed through a narrow defile, crossing from side to side of the torrent, tunnelling through crags and traversing tree-clad precipices. We passed through Eaux Chaudes, a village crammed in the narrows, and finally came out into a strath from which we caught occasional glimpses of our mountain, a formidable volcanic plug with almost vertical sides, the sort of mountain a child might draw from imagination.

Our lift brought us to Gabas. We walked straight through the village and made camp on the first bit of level ground we could find. This was at the bottom of a very steep field, hemmed in by trees and crags, and poised about 10m above a river-bed accessible only by a difficult rock climb. Everywhere there was the sound of cowbells. It was getting dark. We made a good fire, and after a frugal meal of biscuits, dried bananas and tea, we crawled thankfully into our sleeping bags close to the blaze.

'Night is a dead, monotonous period under a roof, but in the open world it passes lightly, with its stars and dews and perfumes.' So said old Stevenson, and there is some truth in it. Certainly it was an improvement on the last two nights which I had spent in railway carriages. Dreams and reality mingled together. At first it was too hot to sleep, later too cold. My weary mind was visited by romantic Stevensonian impressions of fire-light, a large moon, bright stars. Later there was mist swirling among the trees and I groaned and buried my head in my bag.

In the morning Norman made a foray into the village and returned with a green bottle full of milk. He was proving very useful on the public relations front, what with his uninhibited French and his capacity for getting a favourable response, from girls particularly, to openings which, if I had made them, would have earned me a thick ear. Ken and I, if pressed, would have had to say that Norman did not have the same commitment to climbing as we had. He was known to have expressed the view, for example, that a holiday should include a certain amount of enjoyment and indulgence. Over the porridge he argued strongly for a visit to the village inn, for diplomatic reasons as well as to further his acquaintance with the landlord's daughter. A glass of wine he said was not much to pay in exchange for all kinds of local information and goodwill.

At the inn the patron talked readily about the Pic du Midi. We made a casual mention of a good route on the N face. 'La Face Nord' he exlaimed sonorously, and held us with a glittering eye. 'Sit down, monsieur,' says Norman, and we make room for him on the new red leather settee.

'It was on October the 12th, 1923,' he says. 'a young Englishman, a fine strong type, an experienced alpininist, you understand, who called himself Monsieur Pop . . .' and he tells a graphic tale of a confident solo climber attempting the N face and failing to re-appear; of the efforts to find him; of the arrival of his family from England; of the summoning of first class guides from Switzerland; and of what they found of him . . . 'A small piece, you understand, messieurs, as big as that,' says the inn-keeper, picking up a glass. No, we shall surely kill ourselves if we go on the N face *sans guide*.

It was only years later that I realised that Monsieur Pop was in fact that distinguished young climber and AC member Hugh Rose Pope.

Young climbers are not disposed to learn from the misfortunes of other people, and still less inclined to heed the advice of non-climbers, but one thing the innkeeper said stuck in our minds. There were some soldiers camping at Bious Artigues, and they knew the mountain well. We should go and talk to them.

After lunch — last of the army biscuits — we left our gear at the camp and walked up a steep side-valley through woods. Breasting a final slope we came out quite suddenly upon a broad high pasture ringed by wooded summits and dominated by the high rock towers of the Pic du Midi d'Ossau. Slightly right of centre of this delectable meadow stood three small marquees, with the Tricolour waving above them. It was a splendid and unforgettable sight, and it will never be seen again as the whole place now lies at the bottom of the artificial Lac de Bious Artigues.

The camp belonged to a small detachment of *Chasseurs Alpins*, most of whom were away on a parachuting exercise. We chatted about climbing to two slim bronzed youths stripped to the waist, and made mention of the N face. They took us to a practice rock in the woods nearby and we did various boulder problems and hand traverses. The corporal, Jean, said he knew the N face climb and would go with us if the lieutenant agreed. This excursion to the boulders had been to give us the once-over. On getting back to the tents we found the lieutenant had returned, a handsome and voluble Basque who received us formally but with great warmth and charm. We reclined in the sun on a large sheet of canvas, and smoked and talked. We seemed to have found our way into a delightful upland world where friendliness and liberality held sway. It was hardly with surprise that we heard the officer suggest that we go down to Gabas, return immediately with a few necessaries, spend the night in the camp, and climb the peak the next morning. 'Do not bring any blankets,' he says with a courteous sweep of the hand. 'We have enough. You are welcome to our simple soldier's fare of soup and potatoes. But bring utensils.' So we run downhill again in a state of great excitement, cram food and clothing for three into one rucksack, leave the other two at the inn, and hasten back to Bious Artigues.

It is Saturday and some week-end climbers have in the meantime joined the soldiers; two hard men, clanking with ironmongery, a middle-aged extrovert held in much respect by the others — '*très fort, très très fort*' we are assured in earnest asides by the soldiers — and a lively blonde in blue pants and scarlet anorak. We shake hands. The conversation flashes about our heads like a volley-ball which we manage only occasionally to intercept.

It is now quite late and the summer evenings are shorter in these latitudes than at home. The lieutenant explains that he has a mess table in the tent but thinks it more agreeable to have dinner round the camp fire. The fire, which has been smouldering all day, is now built up into a splendid blaze and blankets spread all round it. On these we take our places with some decorum, though the party very soon becomes informal and voluble. Darkness falls as the meal progresses, and the later 'courses' are mysterious and delicious, particularly a rich, creamy, ambrosial substance piled high on slices of iron-hard rye bread which we later learn is made from cheese 'au petit lait' mixed with a tin of Lyle's Golden Syrup which we have contributed. The whole is enriched by copious draughts of 'le bon pinard', army issue, from a huge aluminium flask; the absence of the main body of the troops has created a surplus. It is a meal fit for the gods, and the good company, the great fire, and the magnificent towering face of the Pic du Midi, lit by a moon which has not yet itself come into view, and Venus shining brightly to the right, make this an evening never to be forgotten. Norman is in great form, and the climbers and soldiers all appear to be wags. There is an abundance of conversation on several planes, climbing talk, comparisons of prices, views on religion and politics, leg-pulling and vulgarity. We have seen today for the first time a new kind of climbing boot with a rubber sole called Vibram. The French men laugh at our nails and say that they are only for old men with long grey beards. The evening goes on and on, and none of us would miss it for the world, but I do mention to the lieutenant our projected early start next day. 'Ah,' he says, 'but it is very "sympathique" by the fire,' and he is perfectly right. We finally turn in well after midnight, in a tent whose middle is a big shallow trough full of straw. The very strong mountaineer, M. Arruyeux, who has already climbed the Pic du Midi 41 times, is not ready for bed even now, and provides a largely unintelligible cabaret show with candles for footlights and a hand-generated torch for spotlight. Impossible to believe he intends to climb anything next day. Finally we quieten down, or rather move into the snoring mode, and I spend a very short night with long dreams. In the middle of it one of the hard men asks me the time, and he and his friend move stealthily about in the clammy comfortless dark. Some-one drops what sounds like a hundredweight of old iron and the blonde wakes up and says something with a tolerant laugh.

At daylight we drink a little cold earthy coffee, eat some bread and cheese, and set off with the corporal, our soldier guide, through steep dense woods. As the sun gets up the going becomes extremely hard. We arrive at the foot of the rocks at about 9am, 'a little late,' says the corporal. Anyone who feels he cannot do the climb, he adds, should say so now, for he is not prepared to descend from half way up. We all feel unfit but hold our peace.

We rope up on a short, stout Army rope. It is more an assertion of the principle 'One for all and all for one', than a protection, for it is much too short for proper rope technique. The climbing is continuous and open and a bit like climbing on Lliwedd. As last man I spend every moment when not actually climbing looking anxiously for something to belay on. It seems logical, and to some degree takes my mind off the stones that keep spinning down from above. After a few hundred metres we reach an airy ledge at the top of our buttress, and eat some dried bananas and sugar, then make an upward traverse right, over beautiful slabs giving very enjoyable climbing, into an amphitheatre. We stop at a snow patch and suck some of it avidly. The corporal wraps a big lump in a cloth for use later on. Ken and I take turns with the rucksack and find it makes us breathless.

Easy rocks lead to a gap between a pinnacle and the main face, which beetles above us alarmingly. From here we descend into an astonishing rock cwm whose back-wall is a huge vertical cliff of yellowed rock, and over whose lip is another precipice. Opposite, a great stone shoot, very deep and narrow, leads up to another gap. From the depths we suddenly hear the strains of 'Hi yi yippie yippie yi' and make out the two hard men of the night before, dwarfed to leprechaun size by their immense surroundings. 'She'll be coming round the mountain' was the song they liked best in our repertoire at the camp fire.

Our route still trends rightwards and eventually an easy but tremendously exposed edge is crossed with a great vertical drop on the right and we attain the Fourche, the gap between the Grand Pic and the Petit Pic. It is time for more sugar, helped down by the corporal's snow. There is still a long way to go, but apart from a rather confusing section where a large rock-fall has occurred it is easy climbing. Moving all together makes for greater breathlessness, and the rocks, now in full sun, radiate a noon-day heat. We reach the summit at three.

We bask for an hour among the sardine tins, rich men, our minds still trying to encompass the splendours of the N face, our bodies screaming quietly for water. There is a tin full of scraps of paper bearing the names of climbers. We add ours, giving the corporal his full title, Jean Miaille, *caporal 1° classe*, and about ten letters denoting his army status. It is his sixth ascent.

On descending the *voie normale* we are received with applause by the other climbers who are sitting by a spring. The water brings about a miraculous improvement to our health, the equivalent, say, of a good night's sleep, and we continue in company with the others through a long green valley, about an hour's walk, and back to the soldiers' camp. No sooner do we get into camp than the lieutenant orders Jean to put on a beret and assist with the simple ceremony of hauling down the colours. We stand to attention, feeling like ambassadors.

We wash and drink. The climbers depart. We have a frugal Army meal off a table of branches and pine-fronds. 'Perhaps you would like to sleep' suggests the lieutenant, 'or shall we sit a little at the fire?' But we are still on a high and sleep is far from our thoughts. We liven up the fire, and all hands join in the French custom of jumping through it. Straw is fetched and a high sheet of flame produced and we leap through that too. The fire attracts some other campers and they join us sitting on the circle of blankets, a woman with two daughters and two or three lads. We sing songs, have French ones sung back to us, 'le bon pinard' circulates in the bottomless gourd, the girls tear our heart-strings with their harmonising of 'Au clair de la lune', and one wonders if the dark one, dimly seen through the blaze, can really be as pretty as she looks. The corporal's only English is 'OK boy', and the lieutenant's is confined to the phrase 'the food of a mighty race' taken from the carton of *Scott's Porage Oats*, but conversation flourishes nonetheless. Finally, after the company has dispersed with farewells and handshakes, I am left by the dying fire with the lieutenant, hopelessly waiting for tea-water to boil, and replying in worse and worse French to his political and religious views. I turn in very weary.

So that was the beginning of our vagabondage in the Pyrenees with many a night *à la belle étoile* and several undignified flights for cover in thunderstorms. We were to subsist largely on vegetable stews enriched by a substance from the butcher's called *matiere grasse*, and as we grew more expert our cooking fires were to become smaller and smaller. We were to climb the Mur de la Cascade at Gavarnie, and the Mont Perdu, and seek shelter in the wretched hovel of the Refuge de Tuqueroye. We were to have the meal of a lifetime at Pierrefitte Nestalas, its sauce the accumulated hunger of a month out of doors. Norman was to end up between the starched linen sheets of a hospital bed, minus his appendix, tended by nurses much intrigued by his surname, Wildblood, while Ken and I slept under bridges, and on a heap of sand in a builder's yard, and the verandah of a little *estaminet* in a wood, waiting for visiting time. Our life had its squalid moments, but for the most part we were lifted above it by the beauty and sublimity of the mountains. The stony uplands were washed and sunbleached to an austere cleanliness. The alpine glades and meadows were full of purple irises, harebells, gentians, speedwell, vetches, cornflowers, clovers and orchids. We found bilberries and raspberries, and liquorice roots to chew. I suppose we saw comparatively few summit cairns but we had a thorough acquaintance with lizards, flies, beetles, moths, ants, grasshoppers, butterflies and dragonflies. And clear running water was our constant delight.

Some day I think I must make a trip to the Lac de Bious Artigues, and try and recall once again the drowned meadow with the tents and the Tricolour waving over them, and Lieutenant Jauretche, dreamer and thinker cast in the rôle of man of action; and Jean Miaille, corporal first class, neat, compact, tough, efficient; and Blanc, the cook, friendly and 'sympathique' without ever smiling; and Perasseux, rough and wild with a bucolic wit; and of course the admiral's daughters who sang so well in harmony.

How many such delectable places have been drowned by reservoirs, I wonder. Perhaps, after all, it would be a better idea not to go back.

One Hundred Years Ago
(with extracts from the *Alpine Journal*)

C. A. Russell

Plates 79–82

Although the clear skies and settled conditions experienced in the Alps during the opening weeks of 1886 provided a welcome change from the heavy snowfalls of the previous year the intense cold which affected many regions meant that, again, very little climbing was possible. The only expedition of note during the winter season was the ascent of the Signalkuppe, or Punta Gnifetti, in the Monte Rosa group on 18 January by Corradino and Gaudenzio Sella, with Jean Joseph Maquignaz and three other men. Arriving at the summit by way of the Colle d'Olen and the Lisjoch, the party enjoyed a very clear view before descending to Zermatt, where they were received by the parish priest.

After a late spring cold and unsettled weather persisted until the middle of July, when conditions began to improve. In the Pennine Alps first ascents included the E face of Mont Pleureur on 19 July by Adolphe Tschumi with Joseph Quinodoz and the SW buttress of the Hohberghorn by the guideless party of August Lorria and Oscar Eckenstein on 30 July. Other expeditions of note were the first recorded ascent of the Adlerhorn, on the SW ridge of the Strahlhorn, by Lorria and C C Branch on 26 July and, also on 30 July, the first recorded traverse of the Windjoch by W M Conway, George Scriven and H H West, with J J Trüffer, Aloys Zurbrücken and Joseph Knubel, the uncle of the famous guide of the same name. In the Bernese Oberland on 29 July H Dübi and L Liechti, with Christian and Hans Hari, climbed the Balmhorn by way of the SE ridge, the first time that the summit had been reached from this direction.

On 5 August a famous refuge, situated on rocks beside an equally famous route, was inaugurated by the Milan Section of the Italian Alpine Club. The Marinelli Hut was named in memory of Damiano Marinelli who had been killed five years earlier during an attempt to make the third ascent of the couloir which now bears his name. The day after the ceremony a route from the hut to the summit of the Jägerhorn, under the Nordend of Monte Rosa, by way of the Nordend glacier and the Jägerrücken rocks, was opened by Paolo Palestrino and Luigi Simondetti, with Antonio Castagneri.

The principal expedition of the season was completed in the Dolomites where on 12 August the guideless party of Georg Winkler and Alois Zott made the first ascent of the Cima della Madonna, the western and lower peak of the Sass Maor in the Primiero district. After climbing the higher peak, first ascended by C C Tucker and H A Beachcroft with François Dévouassoud and Battista della Santa 11 years earlier, they returned to the notch between the two peaks 'and at 5.45P.M. started to attack the hitherto virgin W pinnacle. This presented most formidable difficulties, owing to the smoothness of the rocks and the fact that

79 *Gestola (R) from the Bezingi glacier, 1886.*

80   *The Moming ridge (L) and the Zinalrothorn, Valais.*

81   *The Napes Needle, Great Gable; from a lantern slide by G. D. Abraham Photo, Keswick.*

Sass Maor and the Cima Della Madonna

they frequently overhang. The summit was, however, successfully vanquished, after great trouble, at 8P.M. The party was forced to spend the night there, enjoying wonderful moonlight views and a splendid sunrise. Starting again at 4.30A.M. on the 13th, they spent three hours in regaining by their former route the notch between the two pinnacles, and reached San Martino di Castrozza the same afternoon.'

Some weeks later, on 4 September, the second ascent of the Madonna was completed by Count Denys de Champeaux and Henri Brulle, with the guides M Bettega of San Martino and Barbaria of Cortina. In his account of the climb, which was printed in the *Alpine Journal*, Brulle wrote that after inspecting the Madonna from the higher peak the party returned to the gap, where they prepared for the final assault by an attack on their provisions. Then Bettega took off his shoes and 'swarmed up the first gully while we crouched under some overhanging rocks in order to shelter ourselves against the stones which he loosened. We could not see him, but after an interval which seemed to us very long we heard him give the shout that had been agreed on as a signal that he was up, and at the same instant the end of our 100-feet rope fell on our heads. Each of us in turn climbed up this way with divers adventures *en route*, having always a terrific precipice beneath his feet. The gully came to an end below the first shelf of rock; so we had to climb along the wall to the left over a boss of slippery rocks, a very delicate operation. I did not see a worse bit either on the Meije or on the Petit Dru. The man who goes first in such a place must be a climber of most exceptional powers.

The second gully was nearly as difficult as the first. At its upper end we gained the second shelf of rock, where a small cairn, built by our predecessors, showed us that we were on the right track. The climb now changes its character. The peak still rises nearly vertically above one's head, and to the left even overhangs; but on the right it is hollowed out and consists of several very steep ridges leading up to the summit, which is still invisible. We took to the first of these ridges, and after overcoming several difficulties, which elsewhere would have seemed to us very serious ones, we found that we had won the day and that the Cima della Madonna was ours.'

To reach the summit of the Madonna, an undulating ridge surrounded on every side by tremendous precipices, was a remarkable achievement for the period. It is interesting to note that Winkler wore special shoes of canvas with hempen soles during the first ascent.

Despite mixed weather throughout August and September, when very fine spells were followed by cold unsettled periods many new routes were completed. Summits in the Pennine Alps reached for the first time were those of the Pointe Sud de Moming, between the Zinalrothorn and the Schalihorn, on 16 August by H Seymour King, with Ambros Supersaxo and Aloys Anthamatten, and the Blanche de Perroc, the N peak of the Dents de Perroc, on 1 September by J A Vardy with Jean and Pierre Maître. Other first ascents in the region were the W face of the Nordend on 17 August by Lorria and F O Schuster, with Peter Trüffer and Joseph Gentinetta; the N ridge of La Sale, the peak to the north of Mont Pleureur, on 27 August by J Isler, with Joseph Gillioz; and the SE ridge of the Nadelhorn, a section of the classic traverse from the

Lenzspitze, by H W Topham, with Xavier Imseng and Aloys Supersaxo on 29 August.

Despite the variable weather many other new routes of increasing difficulty were completed. In the Graian Alps on 5 August F Vallino and L Barale, with A Castagneri, A Sibille and G Martinengo succeeded in traversing the Colle Baretti, the steep and serious pass between the Becca di Gay and the Roccia Viva, while in the Mont Blanc range the N face of the Tour Ronde was climbed for the first time by F Gonella with Alexis Berthod on 23 August. On 7 September a new and somewhat dangerous route was completed in the Bernina Alps when Ben Wainewright and E J Garwood, with Martin Schocher and Christian Schnitzler reached the summit of Piz Scerscen by way of the SE flank.

Outside the Alps the principal expedition of the year was that of C T Dent and W F Donkin to the Caucasus, accompanied by the Swiss guides Alexander Burgener and Basil Andenmatten. Dent and Donkin, the first British party to visit the range for 12 years, were unlucky with the weather but succeeded in making the first ascent of Gestola (4860m), one of the peaks above the Bezingi glacier.

Arriving at the village of Bezingi on the N side of the chain, the party were accommodated in a house which was severe in its simplicity. 'It comprised one room, which was situated, rather literally, on the ground-floor. The front was of stone plastered over with mud, the chinks stopped up with anything that came handy. The floor was such as nature provided. The roof, constructed by the art of man, was of wood, decorated with prodigious festoons of cobwebs, and covered externally with turf. A hole, some three feet square, boarded up at night, admitted at once into our apartment air, light and the perfume of an adjoining stable yard. The room was furnished with an uncompromising seat, an uncertain table, and the framework of a suspicious bed.'

After a meal taken under the gaze of a continuous procession of villagers a remarkable visitor called, without being announced. 'An unkempt man, so dirty that he even surprised us by his state, entered and took up a good position. We made no sign, and he made no sign. For some ten minutes he stared at us in silence; then he examined an ice-axe closely. Whether he was pleased or not we were unable to tell. His features, from various causes, did not allow of mobility or expression. He put the axe back, and then fell to staring at us again. This time he took a twenty minutes' spell at it. Not a sound was heard to proceed from his lips. He spake no word. He spat once on the floor, but not in a manner calculated to give offence. Then he went away. The interview was over.'

After many delays due to bad weather and the incompetence of their interpreter a camp was established beside the Bezingi glacier on 26 August. Starting soon after 3am the party crossed extensive snowfields and climbed the great snow wall ahead to reach the W ridge. Addressing the Alpine Club in the following year on 'The Ascent of Tetnuld Tau' Dent, who later agreed with D W Freshfield that the peak should correctly be known as Gestola, described how the party advanced anxiously up the ridge. 'We could hardly believe that any insuperable obstacle would now turn us back; yet all was new and uncertain, and the conditions of weather intensified the anxiety. The heavy stillness of the air seemed unnatural, and made the mind work quicker. The sensibility became so acute that if we ceased working and moving for a moment the silence around was unendurable and seemed to seize hold of us. A distant roll of thunder came almost as a relief. A step or two had to be cut, and the delay appeared interminable. Suddenly, a glimpse of a dark patch of rocks appeared above looming through the mist. The slope of the ridge became more gentle for a few yards. Our attention was all fixed above, and we ascended some distance without noticing the change. Another short rise, and we were walking quickly along the ridge. We stopped suddenly; the rocks we had seen so recently had sunk below us on our left, while in front the arête could be followed with the eye, sloping away gradually for a few yards and then plunging sharply down to a great depth. It was all over; through fair weather and through foul we had succeeded; and there was yet another peak to the credit of the Alpine Club.

It was not a time for words. Burgener turned to us and touched the snow with his hand, and we sat down in silence. Almost on the instant as we took our places a great burst of thunder rolled and echoed around — a grim salvo of Nature's artillery. The sudden sense of rest heightened the effect of the oppressive stillness that followed. Never have I felt the sense of isolation so complete. Gazing in front into the thin mists, the very presence of my companions seemed an unreality. The veil of wreathing vapour screened the huge panorama of the ice-world from our sight. The black thunder-clouds drifting sullenly shut out the world below. No man knew where we were; we had reached our furthest point in a strange land. We were alone with Nature, far from home, and far from all that we were familiar with. Strange emotions thrilled the frame and quickened the pulse. Weird thoughts crowded through the mind — it was not a time for words. Believe me, under such conditions a man will see further across the threshold of the unknown than all the book-reading or psychological speculation in the world will ever reveal to him.'

The party was then faced with a late and dangerous descent of the wall they had climbed without difficulty and it was nearly midnight before they reached the safety of their tent.

Two days later they attempted Dykh Tau from the south but although this and other plans were defeated by more bad weather Dent was delighted with the ascent of Gestola, which he always regarded as his greatest adventure. The expedition marked the beginning of a period of intense activity by British mountaineers in the Caucasus during which many of the great peaks were climbed.

The Hungarian explorer Maurice de Déchy also visited the Caucasus, on the third of his expeditions to the range. As in the previous year he was concerned principally with photography and topographical work, devoting much time to glacier measurement in the Adai Khokh and Elbruz groups.

In Britain three climbs during the year were of great importance. Addressing the Alpine Club in April W C Slingsby gave an account of an ascent of Deep Ghyll on Scafell which he had made on 28 March with Geoffrey Hastings and J Mason. After describing the route in detail he made a plea to his fellow members which was to be taken to heart. 'The old whisky-bottle which used to be on the Pillar rock has been taken by Mr Haskett Smith on to the Sca Fell Pinnacle, and so far it contains very few names. Do not let us be beaten on our own fells by outsiders, some of whom consider ice-axes and ropes to be "illegitimate". Let us not neglect the Lake District, Wales, and Scotland, whilst we are conquerors abroad.'

At the end of June W P Haskett Smith made his famous solo ascent of the Napes Needle, at the foot of the Needle Ridge on Great Gable. Haskett Smith later recalled that he commenced the ascent feeling as small as a mouse climbing a milestone and that after descending safely he was relieved to stand on firm ground and look up at the handkerchief he had left on the top fluttering in the breeze. The ascent of the Needle, which was not repeated for nearly three years, was a remarkable achievement and it was not long before illustrated articles began to appear on the subject.

On the Isle of Skye A H Stocker and A G Parker of Lliwedd fame succeeded, on 19 August, in climbing the shorter and steeper W ridge of the Inaccessible Pinnacle, the highest point of Sgurr Dearg. They then descended by the E ridge to complete the first traverse of the Pinnacle, another fine achievement for the period.

These climbs, in particular the first ascent of the Napes Needle and the publicity it received, gave a considerable impetus to the development of rock-climbing in Britain.

An important date during the year was 8 August, the centenary of the first ascent of Mont Blanc by Jacques Balmat and Dr Paccard. The details of this historic climb were recalled and in an analysis of the available statistics it was noted that fewer lives, comparatively, had been lost on Mont Blanc than in other parts of the Alps.

In conclusion, the present writer and his readers should perhaps note the following extract from an article entitled 'The Madness of Mountaineering' which appeared in September 1886. 'Zermatt and Chamonix are by this time nearly deserted. And of all the scores of climbers who have crossed the snow-line this year, or any year, it may be doubted if one in twenty could give any good reason for his exploits, while few of the reasons given would agree together. It is the strangest passion. A man, often of mature and more than mature years, posts straight out from his counting-house or his chambers to some Alpine centre. He quits the comfortable shelter of his hotel to sleep in some draughty hovel, some hay-loft, or some hole in the rocks. Night comes, and he rolls himself up in a dirty rug, the common property of every passing traveller, and tries to sleep. At some unearthly hour in the morning his guide bids him rise to a chill dark world. He starts from the "hut", often stumbling and jolting over rocks by lantern-light, and ere daybreak begins the work of his day. And hard work it is: such as few navvies would undertake without high pay. To swelter through deep snow under a burning sun; to have to choose between opthalmia and green goggles, which clothe nature in an unnatural bilious shroud; to scramble up rocks, barking his shins and bruising his fingers; to shiver on an ice-slope while the steps are cut; to be dragged, not at his own pace or pleasure, but according to the strength and speed of others, knotted in the bight of a rope which hampers and at the same time preserves him; to be permitted occasionally to sit down on the snow and devour bread and ham: these are the ordinary incidents of every mountain expedition. At last he reaches his hotel, very wet and aching with fatigue, the skin peeling off his face, and sometimes with the sight of his eyes impaired.

And all this is without considering the hazards of the sport. Climbers say it is not dangerous; that experience, foresight, and skill guard against every risk. It seems, however, that every year lengthens the tale of the victims of Alpine climbing. Experience has to be bought at its own price; indefinite risks will claim their due; and a fusillade of falling stones or crumbling ice-pinnacles, a storm, a deceptive snow-slope, deceive, encompass, or overwhelm the most skilful and weatherwise. But strike these out of the account — how can answer be given to the question "what is it all for?". Some tell you it is for the sake of the scenery; but the fact is that when the climber stops, he stops to eat and drink. He busies himself with his rations, not with the scenery; and when he is in motion he might as well walk in blinkers: he must perforce walk warily, and his boots and his guide's footprints are the most distant objects within his ken.

Men are driven to scaling mountains by the fierce strenuousness of their race. It is the English who have made the sport and give it vitality and keep it in credit; and it is for the sake of the national energy that we pursue it. We are all mad together; and if we were a saner we should be a punier race. But mountaineering is so far different from all our other freaks, that only those who have tried it, who have bitten the fruit, know the passion; and even they can give no reasonable account of it.'

Who better to speak on our behalf than Dent, one of the finest climbers of his day, who concluded his address by exhorting his listeners to visit the Caucasus. 'If you wish to be far from the madding crowd, far from the noise, bustle, and vulgarity of the buzzing, clustering swarms of tourists — go there. Nature will, as it were, take you gently by the hand and seem to say, "I am glad to welcome you; come, and you shall look upon sights that I don't choose to show to everybody. Yet more, I will make a present of them to you; and in after times you shall call up in memory recollections of me, as I can be when in the mood, and you shall hug these memories with delight and even dream on them with enthusiasm." To the end of your days you will remember it with pleasure.'

Competition Climbing

Dennis Gray

Mountaineering has always had a competitive element, man against mountain, man against man, but never until recent times has there been an attempt to develop organised competition. In the Eastern bloc there have been speed rock climbing competitions which have had little or no real impact on the sport, despite the fact that they were instituted and developed in the 1960s. However, developments in the past year on the continent of Europe, particularly in Italy and France threaten to make an impact which will bring about fundamental changes to mountaineering.

In July 1985 a major rock climbing competition was held at Bardonecchia in Italy. Some of the leading European 'stars' took part, and Stefan Glowacz of West Germany won the men's competition and Catherine Desteville of France the women's. Significantly this competition had the blessing of the Italian Alpine Club, was sponsored by Italy's leading mountaineering manufacturers and had a distinguished panel of judges headed by Ricardo Cassin. Before the competition reservations were expressed (and some still maintained these throughout) about the worth of such an exercise, but many persons who had previously publicly opposed such developments were won over by the Bardonecchia experience.

Thousands of spectators attended throughout the days of the competition and debates were held about possible future developments. Reports were that the whole affair was well organized, friendly and that the hospitality was superb. During 1985 many initiatives on competition developed in France. Pilot competitions and trials were organized but such was the strength of feeling that it has left bitter recriminations amongst the French climbing establishment. This has led to a possible split, and perhaps a separate Federation will organize competitions there in the future.

These events have so far had little or no real impact in Britain but it is inevitable that they will effect our climbing scene. A feature of the developing competition structure on the Continent has been the involvement of commercial interests and a quickening of interest by the media. The climbing world is now too international for developments in one major country not to affect others. Thousands of British climbers visit France each year and are aware of developments there. Already the style of climbing favoured on French limestone, with pre-placed bolt protection is finding favour on certain British cliffs.

Is competition eventually going to split British mountaineering, dividing the old tradition of amateur, club and group orientated climbers, from new, thrusting, youthful, but rule orientated participants? For, make no mistake about it, competition climbing will mean accepting some form of rules, written down, with sanctions against those who break them. Everything is still in a state of flux but it is likely that the rules accepted on the Continent will, unlike Soviet speed competitions emphasize style and difficulty.

I believe it is essential that we avoid any split in British climbing. We need to oppose organized competition climbing developing in Britain and try to use such influence as we have abroad to do the same. Our arguments must be logical and make sense or they will not carry the day and we must make sure our young climbers understand and agree with them. If they do not, if they cannot support them, then we must for the sake of all our futures in mountaineering re-consider our position.

Our first concern must be the protection of our sports environment and access to it. We have not the unclimbed cliffs where competitions could take place, and the obvious venues are all so popular that to increase the pressure on these areas does not make sense. To develop competitions in our mountains will mean denying access, for if we are to hold such events, then whilst they are in progress non-competitors will have to be debarred. If a kind of league of teams was developed, or an individual 'super-star' table, then there would have to be a lot of money to make the thing work, and this could only come from two sources (I do not think it would have big spectator appeal but I might be wrong); commercial sponsors and/or the media — television, films, newspapers. I realize that the arguments that I am putting forward can be shot through with holes, but big money *will* make climbing different, it *will* rob the sport of its most special appeal, and it *may* destroy its soul.

Other competitive sports have been beset by evils the like of which we have never had to face in climbing; bribery, corruption and drug abuse. Where big money appears they are likely to follow. In a sport which has remained unfettered by rules and regulations, the introduction of these elements must have a singular effect.

It could be that all competitions will have to take place indoors on the network of artificial climbing walls that have been developed throughout the country in the last two decades. For one thing that France and Italy definitely have not, is our unreliable weather. One can hardly imagine the Peak All Stars playing the South Audley Street Casuals at Cloggy last summer, it probably never dried out. No sponsor or media company would take a risk on that! Indoor climbing wall competitions might be more acceptable but how one would develop rules and regulations which were fair for all, is hard to understand for the locals would have such an advantage that they would almost certainly have to be handicapped.

The whole business takes on a degree of farce and one could easily pass it off as a seven day wonder, but I think not. Ever rising standards, particularly in rock climbing, has meant an ever keener group of dedicated core of young climbers, often unemployed, who are in the process of developing a training methodology in parallel with other developed competitive sports. To climb now at the top standards needs total dedication and it is almost impossible to follow a profession or gainful employment. Organized competition would appeal to many such climbers. It would give them a chance to earn a living and mean even for some of them perhaps stardom with all its rewards. No one is currently making any real money from the sport, so the blandishments would be there.

The thing that is missing at the moment is an entrepreneur, someone who could package the sport in a way that appealed to the media but which did not offend too much against the ethics and attitudes of mountaineering as they have developed over the last century, and which did not prostitute the sport to such a degree that it became too boring. It would for instance still need to remain a high risk activity, with potential for leader falls and injuries. But really serious or fatal accidents might need to be guarded against by bomb proof protection. Certainly you could not have deaths regularly on the box, or Aunty might get a bit too alarmed!

Bouldering has also developed a competitive event, the 'Great Californian Bouldering Competition', which is held each year in the USA. This is a fun event, but nevertheless some take it seriously and there was a feeling of pride when our own Ron Fawcett won the event at his first attempt. Points are awarded for each problem climbed with a time limit for each ascent. The largest number of points at the end of the competition wins. There is no doubt that there are many bouldering areas in Great Britain where you could stage such an event, particularly in Derbyshire and Yorkshire on the gritstone. But if it did not attract a sponsor or media interest it would have only limited appeal and limited effect on the sport.

Where do we go from here? It is any one's guess. The BMC has decided to oppose any attempt to develop competition climbing, but it has agreed to keep this policy under review. The worst thing that could happen would be a split, and the two schools of thought to be so opposed as to be irreconcilable. My own view, for what it is worth, is that organized competition is not needed in British climbing. The possible detrimental effects on our sport are such as to be not worth the risks. But young climbers might feel differently and if we estrange them with paternalistic well meaning, but from their point of view out-dated, out-moded viewpoints, then we will drive them into the very path we do not wish them to take. Competition will be a major issue in our sport from hereon. Each of us will have to decide how we feel about it and whether we wish to be involved or to opt out, but whatever happens I do hope we manage to preserve the unity of British climbing.

AREA NOTES

China 1985

Chris Bonington

There were 33 mountaineering expeditions to China in 1985 of which 12 were successful. Six of these expeditions were to Mount Everest, of which only one, the Catalan Expedition reached the top on 28 July. They used oxygen only for sleeping. The monsoon period certainly seems a good time to try Everest from the north, when there is comparatively little wind and warmer temperatures.

With the failure of Mal Duff's expedition on the NE ridge of Everest, this remains one of the major unclimbed problems of the Himalaya. Another British expedition led by Bronco Lane is going out in Autumn 1986 and the Chinese are attempting it in Spring 1988. The other Everest expeditions were a Basque expedition to the N ridge route in spring, a New Zealand expedition to the W ridge, a French expedition to the N ridge in the monsoon period and a Japanese expedition to the N face, post monsoon.

Everest remains a focus of attention with a large American expedition organized by Tom Holzel going to the original N ridge route in Autumn 1986 to look for the bodies of Mallory and Irvine, in an effort to discover whether or not they reached the summit of Everest.

In 1988 there will be a joint Japanese, Chinese, Nepalese expedition to the N ridge of Everest hoping to make the first complete traverse, up the N ridge and down the SE ridge into the Western Cwm. Arne Naess had hoped to do this in 1985 but was not given permission.

Xixabangma certainly seems a better bet for success than Everest — it might even be the softest touch 8000m peak. All three expeditions were successful. At least one of these was a commercially organized expedition, in which the clients were guided up the mountain, a growing trend in the Himalayas. Muztagh Ata, because of its relative ease, is another popular venue for such expeditions.

Kongur had another unsuccessful attempt by a Japanese expedition. The only successful ascent is still that of the British expedition in 1981.

A Chinese expedition made the first ascent of the N face of Cho Oyu from Tibet on 2 May, with nine reaching the summit. This was probably very close to the line of the original ascent, most of which had poached into China.

A 46-strong Chinese-Japanese expedition successfully climbed Naimona Nyi (7694m), in SW Tibet, putting 13 climbers on the summit. A 52-man Chinese-American expedition went into the Ulugh Mustagh group in October. Ulugh Mustagh was reputed to be one of the highest unclimbed peaks in the world as well as being the highest of the Kun Lung range at 7723m, but it has been demoted to 6973m. It is in a bleak uninhabited region on the S edge of the

Takla Makan desert. The approach was across the desert from Urumchi. Five Chinese reached the summit on 22 October.

The Chinese are undoubtedly opening up more mountains and mountain areas. There seems a trend to do this initially for joint expeditions but Li Fa, head of the Tibetan regional sports commission announced on 8 August that all mountains in Tibet would be open to foreign climbers. They hope to have the facilities to handle 10,000 climbers annually by 1990. They plan to host other activities such as motorcycle and automobile races on the high plateau and rowing races on the Yaluzangbu river. I view these ambitious plans with more than a little disquiet. It seems very important to preserve the character and traditions of Tibet in such a way that climbers and other visitors can contribute to the economy of this magnificent region without destroying the very quality that attracts them.

I am very grateful to the Chinese Mountaineering Association for their cooperation in providing the information contained in these notes.

Nepal 1985

Brian Hall

Winter 84/85   The harsh weather of the Himalayan winter came early to Nepal in 1984 and dashed the hopes of many of the winter expeditions. Only the very early expeditions or experienced, physically strong and determined climbers succeeded. Such is the competition to climb 8000m peaks, that nine of the expeditions attempted these mountains. Attempts on Annapurna I, Cho Oyu and Dhaulagiri I were successful and the only other successes were on Jannu and Pumori, both over 7000m. Compared with last year, there was a lack of interest and success on lower peaks.

On Annapurna I a S Korean expedition climbed the N face by the Dutch rib. They reached BC on 22 November, then rapidly placed ABC and four camps before Miss Kim and four Sherpas, Pasang Norbu, Keepa, Dorje and Ang Temba, made the ascent stopping probably two hours short of the summit. Nevertheless it was a fine, well-organized ascent. It ended in tragedy on the descent when Keepa and Pasang Norbu fell to their deaths.

Over on the E side of Nepal another S Korean expedition succeeded in making the first winter ascent of Jannu. Ki Heyg Kim and two Sherpas, Ang Dorje and Lhakpa Gelbu, climbed the French route with variations, using four camps, reaching the top on 9 December.

In my opinion Kukuczka ranks as one of the best mountaineers of the '80s. He enhanced his reputation by making two fine winter ascents of 8000m in one season. First he was part of a Polish team on Dhaulagiri I where he and Czok made the second winter ascent by the NE ridge reaching the summit on 21 January. Kukuczka then joined the Polish-Canadian expedition to the S pillar of Cho Oyu led by Andrej Zawada. Two Poles, Berbeka and Pawlikowski, reached the summit on 12 February, and on the 15th (the last day of the official winter season) Kukuczka and Heinrich also reached the summit. This first winter ascent of Cho Oyu was made without using oxygen.

The only other success of the winter was by Richard Pierce and Richard Wilson, both from the USA, on Pumori. On 13 December they both disappeared without trace on the summit day. It is believed that they reached the summit. They used two camps and three bivouacs on the SW ridge.

Unsuccessful attempts were made on Ama Dablam, Annapurna I (including an attempt on the S face, British route), Annapurna S, Dhaulagiri I, Everest, Gangapurna, Himlung, Kangchenjunga, Kang Guru, Khatang, and Tilicho. Five climbers were killed. Particularly tragic was Chris Chandler's death high on Kangchenjunga's N face despite heroic efforts by his wife and Mangal Singh Tamung who both were climbing with him.

Spring   In spring, at least 45 expeditions were expected but only 28 turned up. There was little work for the many businesses set up by the Sherpas to service expeditions and treks, and instead of expanding they suffered losses. A big increase in peak fees in Nepal and economic recession in the West may have contributed to this but in my experience, the costs of mounting an expedition have only increased over the last ten years by the rate of inflation. Nepal is still excellent value and flights to the East have never been cheaper, but for British expeditions, sponsorship is very scarce and the grants from the MEF and the BMC have not kept up with the rise in numbers of expeditions or with inflation. This is reflected by the total absence of British expeditions during the winter and spring seasons. The 'dole' may finance high-standard rock-climbing but it certainly does not pay for trips to Nepal, let alone Himalayan expeditions. The expeditions which did not arrive missed the best March and April weather for many years and 21 expeditions were successful.

Certainly the most rapid ascents of the season were by Reinhold Messner and Hans Kammerlander who climbed Annapurna I and Dhaulagiri I within 23 days. On Annapurna I they climbed a new route on the NW face, first fixing one camp, then climbing the route in a four-day push, reaching the summit on 24 April. They climbed Dhaulagiri I in a rapid Alpine-style ascent of two and a half days via the NE ridge reaching the summit on 15 May. This is Messner's 12th and Kammerlander's 5th 8000m summit.

On Manaslu, Studer (Austria) and Ang Kami Sherpa climbed the E ridge using three camps to 6500m and in a long day, reached the summit on 1 May. One of his team died in a second summit attempt.

The impressive N face of Yalungkang was climbed for the first time, by a Yugoslav expedition. Using four camps and the help of Sherpas, Bergant and Cesent reached the summit on 22 April. Bergant, who used no oxygen, was exhausted and fell to his death on the descent.

Few of the expeditions to Everest have been so successful as the Norwegian expedition. With four camps, oxygen and Sherpas, they climbed the South Col route and put 17 climbers on the summit including six Norwegians and four Sherpas. Sungdare was the first person to make four ascents. Bonington (GB) and Bass (USA), in the space of a few days, were each the oldest men to climb Everest.

On Cho Oyu, the Polish-American team was stopped by the same gully system which stopped the British in 1983. Richey and Wilcox then climbed Ngozumba Kang which was almost on their route. Garozielewski and Jezierski climbed the SW face route of Cho Oyu on 28 May, in six days alpine-style climbing. Six Spaniards also climbed this route without oxygen or Sherpas. On Makalu, high winds prevented Maurice and Liliane Barrard (France) from reaching the summit. On both 10 and 11 May they climbed to within 35m of the summit having climbed the NW route.

Naoe Sakashita led a group of seven Japanese climbers. Based in the Khumbu valley, they did a lot of climbing and succeeded on the S ridge of Cholatse, Taweche SE face, and Ama Dablam W face (first ascent) and SW ridge. One member died on Ama Dablam. A Japanese-Nepalese expedition climbed the NW face of Gurja Himal but, there too, one member died and plans for further climbing were abandoned.

A Swiss-Nepalese expedition made the first ascent of Ohmi Kangri, climbing the E peak (previously climbed by the Japanese in 1982) and going on to climb the higher W summit.

Other successes were; Ama Dablam N ridge (Italians), Annapurna III N face (Nepalese Army), Chobuje SW ridge (New Zealanders), Gurja Himal NW face (Japanese and Rumanians), Himalchuli SW ridge (Hungarians), Makalu II W face to S ridge (French), Pumori SE face (Spanish), Pumori SW ridge (Austrian) and Tukuche N ridge (Korean).

Expeditions to Annapurna S, Dhaulagiri (Pear), Everest (Lho la, W ridge), Gaurishankar, Kangchenjunga (N ridge), Lhotse Shar (SE ridge) and Nilgiri N (W ridge) were unsuccessful.

Autumn   The most notable feature of the season was the unusually appalling weather in October. There were 22 deaths in 49 expeditions, only 15 of which were successful. Only three 8000ers were climbed — Everest, Makalu and Cho Oyu.

Disaster struck the Indian Army on Everest. Just below the S summit one member died and four more died in a storm on the South Col. Later, the Japanese succeeded, with seven members reaching the summit on 30 October (Yamada without oxygen). Another Japanese expedition succeeded on Cho Oyu, three members reaching the summit on 3 October after a rapid climb of the W ridge (12 days from arrival at BC). On the NW ridge of Makalu, four Italians and one Spaniard reached the summit on 1 October.

A S Korean team climbed Himalchuli N on 27 October (Lee Jae Hong with Sherpas, Lhakpa Norbu, Pasang Dawa, Ang Pasang and Zangbu). Shortly afterwards, Poles climbed the SW ridge to the SW face and then around to the E ridge. On Saipal Spaniards made the second ascent (first ascent 1963) via the W ridge on 22 October. Two of them traversed the mountain, climbing the SW face and descending the W ridge on 24 October. On Thamserku, two climbers from a French expedition climbed a new route via the W ridge to the N ridge, reaching the summit on 30 October. An American team climbed a new route up the SE ridge of Ama Dablam (Aprin, Harrington, Zabaleta) with four bivouacs and Athans soloed the S ridge.

Two international groups succeeded on Ama Dablam and on Baruntse; a Japanese-Nepalese team climbed Dorje Lhakpa W ridge; Poles climbed the E ridge of Gangapurna; Japanese, the S face–SW ridge of Himalchuli E; Dutch, Makalu II normal route; and a S Korean team climbed the N ridge of Tukuche.

1985 was a mixed year, with no ascents that can be regarded as milestones in Himalayan mountaineering. Eastern European and Asian mountaineers now predominate and the total lack of success by even a single British team is an indication of the low level to which British expedition climbing has sunk.

Most expeditions are repeating routes, ignoring the challenges of the many unclimbed faces and ridges. In general, rises in standards are due to a few E European teams and the individual talents of climbers such as Messner and Kukuczka.

India 1985

Harish Kapadia
Plates 83–85

Even before the echoes of the Indian climbs of Everest in 1984 had died down the preparations for the 1985 Indian Army Everest Expedition were far advanced with climbs of Shivling and other peaks for selection. Just before departure, leader Col Prem Chand injured his wrist and was replaced by Brig Jagjit Singh. This was to have a profound effect on the outcome. An early October storm which dictated retreat for a large number of teams in Nepal did not stop the Indian Army but bad news soon followed: Maj K I Kumar slipped and fell to his death near the S summit. Within a few days they had the mortification of losing four experienced mountaineers, found dead in their tents at the South Col. One of them Maj Jai Bahuguna was the younger brother of Maj Harsh Bahuguna who had dangled to his death on Everest in 1971. All rescue efforts on 10 and 11 October proved futile though they are amongst the most draining rescue efforts that might have ever taken place on Everest. A lot of questions were raised in the press and there were conflicting reports. Were they adequately rested? Did they have enough food, fuel and oxygen? Why did their survival instincts fail? No answers were forthcoming even on their return.

The Army then declared war on Everest and Brig Jagjit Singh was replaced as the leader by Col Prem. Many did not agree with this determined attack and felt that the mountain and the deaths should have been respected. Ultimately Everest won the battle, but not the war. We are told that they plan to return next year. The statistics are daunting. They crossed the Khumbu icefall on average 26 times and a maximum of 48 times individually. Twenty members reached the South Col and beyond. The route was refixed literally 3 times and 5 members reached the S summit and the team reached 7900m on the SW face too. Courage was certainly not lacking but still the mountain won. The last two years of Indian flirtation with Everest has cost public money worth Rs.10 million. I would not hesitate to agree with Shipton who wanted to get on with the *real* game once Everest was climbed.

The game was being played elsewhere. Swargarohini II (6247m) and III (6209m) in Garhwal were prized climbs by a Bombay team. Having failed last year they returned to climb these difficult peaks, one of which was first climbed by Dr Charles Clarke. In a similar vein, Mana (7272m) received a spirited attempt via the N face, this failed due to the October storm. Mana's neighbours Kamet (7756m) and Abi Gamin (7355m) suddenly received a lot of attention. Various teams from Delhi, Bangalore and Assam climbed the peaks while one from Gujarat failed. The best route on Kamet was climbed by the Indo-French Army expedition by the W ridge. This route was attempted first by the Kumaon regiment expedition two years back reaching 7000m.

The Indo-French team originally intended to attempt Kangchenjunga by the E (Zemu) face but permission was ultimately denied. They had climbed Kabru Dome earlier as preparation. It is interesting to note that Kabru Dome is usually declared a 'holy' mountain and permission to climb it is denied to many enthusiastic parties. Now, conveniently, the status was changed.

One of the pioneering expeditions was from Delhi to the unknown Jadhganga valley. This young team brought back many tales of exploration of these remote unvisited valleys. Not much is heard of this valley since Harrer and Aufschneiter escaped to Tibet through here. The party also attempted Chirbas Parbat (6529m). Nearby in Gangotri the Japanese climbed the W ridge of Sudarshan Parbat, while Shivling was climbed (S face) by the British and (W face) by Germans. Gangotri II and Shyamvarn were other two notable ascents. Bhagirathi III, W pillar, attempted by Americans and the S face climbed by French, have now become regular features.

In Himachal and Kashmir, Japanese climbers made three fine ascents — KR2 (6187m), Yan (6230m) and Menthosa (6443m), the latter by ladies. Bombay students climbed Phawrarang in Kinnaur while Bengal climbers ascended Chau Chau Kang Nilda (6380m) and Shilla (6120m) in Spiti. Two Indians lifted their rucksacks and entered Barashigri to climb Lion peak — no fuss about porters, permits and grants. An enjoyable effort! On the larger scale Nun and Kun were repeatedly assaulted. One almost pities the mountain but not the locals who fleece the mountaineers. Robberies have also taken place.

Eastern Karakoram

The E Karakoram has now a big queue for bookings. Indian and Pakistani armies face each other and mountaineers are specifically permitted from India to show who is boss. Officially, India claims every climb as a first ascent not recognizing the history of ascents with approaches from Pakistan. Unfortunate editors have to turn into Sherlock Holmes to protect the history of the area. Into such an area was the Indo-British expedition. The expedition was sponsored jointly by The Alpine Club and The Indian Mountaineering Foundation and led by Harish Kapadia. It explored the N and S Terong glaciers and Shelkar Chorten glacier thoroughly. A number of peaks were climbed and cols crossed. The major effort was on Rimo I (7385m) by Saunders and Venables, reaching 6900m on the SW Spur. The major first ascent was by Wilkinson and Fotheringham, of Rimo III (7233m) which was climbed from the east. Among Indian climbs; Dhiren and Samant summitted on Sondhi (6480m) and Sundbrar (6300m). Others climbed three more peaks and crossed cols. The venture was rounded off by two solo ascents by Venables and exploring of the S Terong glacier. The return was a minor epic due to the flooding of Terong river. A creditable exploratory effort, 55 years after the only known entry by Vissers in 1929.

A little to the south, Saser Kangri II (7518m) West was also climbed for the first time by an Indo-Japanese team. This was a joint expedition of the Himalayan Association of Japan and the Indo Tibet Border Police and was led by Hukam Singh. They approached from the Nubra Valley and the Sakang glacier fixing 2.5km(!) of rope. They climbed the NW ridge. One Indian died and four Indians reached the summit on 7 September. The Japanese returned from 300m below. The rush is on and one is sure to read a lot about this area in spite of the $2000 royalty.

Karakoram 1985

Paul Nunn
Plate 86

The general emphasis among the expeditions of 1985 continued to be towards the highest peaks. The pursuit of 'huit mille metres' has eclipsed efforts on the multitude of lower mountains at least in terms of the numbers of climbers and expeditions. A result is overcrowding of popular mountains like Gasherbrums 2 and 1, Broad Peak and K2, especially as most climbers are not innovating in the sense of trying new or less well-known routes. This does not mean that great achievements have ceased, but they tend to be buried under the efforts of earnest and unimaginative peak baggers following the *voies normales*. Nor can solo or very fast ascents have as much meaning when they take place on routes 'bashed out' by others.

In this perspective the ascent of the W Face of Gasherbrum 4 by Voytek Kurtyka and Robert Schauer stands out. They appear to have followed the route begun by Mo Anthoine's 1978 expedition and attempted since then by a Japanese Party. They climbed alpine style on difficult and dangerous mixed ground, reaching the ridge after six bivouacs. Voytek was disappointed not to have the strength to continue to the main summit, and retreated by the NW ridge with further bivouacs. They reached the valley extremely tired and, in Voytek's case, admitting to hallucinatory fatigue.

In the 8000m league, Gasherbrums 1 & 2, K2 and Broad Peak hogged attention. About 12 expeditions set out to climb the two 8000m Gasherbrums. They were spread through the summer, but made the Base Camp a strange and insanitary place, especially as several were either large or had considerable numbers of trekker clients or visitors. Problems there, and presumably at Broad Peak and K2 Base, and at Concordia, are comparable to those at the Khumbu Base below Everest.

Early in the season a strong team of Italians led by Agostino da Polenza climbed the SE spur on Gasherbrum 2. They opened up the route up the S Gasherbrum glacier and did the climb in a single push from the 6000m level. Da Polenza himself took part in the second group which climbed Gasherbrum 1 by the NW face. Da Polenza and Camozzi reached the top, but their companions went down. Subsequently on 19 June Calgano and Vidoni, two of the three climbers who had succeeded earlier on Gasherbrum 2, did an ascent of Gasherbrum 1 by a new route. Thus the project 8000m, in which a core of Italian climbers intend to do all the 8000m peaks in five years, got off to a creditable start using relatively lightweight tactics, no high altitude porters, no bottled oxygen and no fixed ropes. Unlike later parties they had to open all their routes themselves.

Subsequent climbs were more involved with other expeditions more complicated and more difficult to evaluate. Eric Escoffier and Benoit Chamoux (French) made very fast ascents of Gasherbrums 1 & 2. Escoffier climbed

Photo: H. J. Himiyar

83 *Kamet with Mead's col (R). The route follows the gulley and the rocks marked 'A'.*

Photo: S. Kapur

84 *View south from a camp on the W col of Chirbas Parbat. (L–R) Manda I & II, Bhrigupanth and Jogin wall.*

85   *The unclimbed W face of Saser Kangri I above the Phuckpoche glacier.*

86 Latok II glacier from the NW ridge of Latok II with the Biafo glacier behind. All these small peaks are unclimbed.

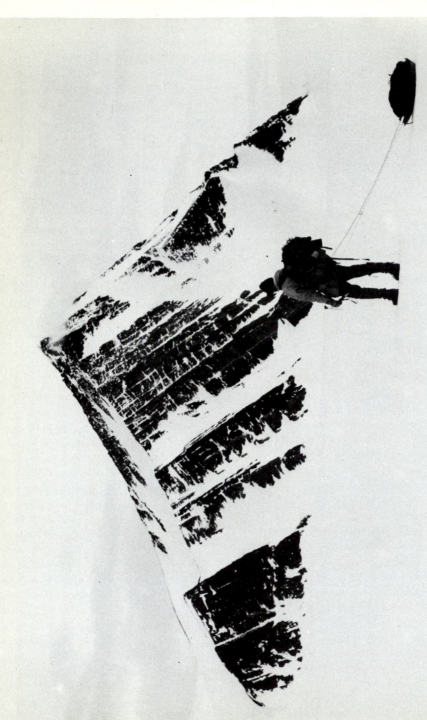

27. *Drangnæane. Peak near the head of Kajær Fjær Josef's Fjord, E. Greenland, at 0200hrs on 8 August 1985. The E. ridge is on the right.*

Photo: P. J. Sellar

Gasherbrum 1 in a day from 6000m, catching up with Chamoux who had set out the day before at 7500m and continuing soloing together to the top. He went on to climb K2 (below) and to make an attempt on Broad Peak. Unsupported by high altitude porters was Renato Casarotto's ascent of Gasherbrum 2 with his wife; the Swedish ascent including Tommy Sandberg (49) who has taken part in all previous Swedish Himalayan expeditions; the ascents by a Japanese party; and by two other French groups, one led by Louis Le Pivain and the other by Benoit Renard. A third French pair, Thierry Renard and Pierre Mure Ravaud, reached the top with the express intention of enabling Renard to make a ski descent. This he did, but instead of being solo it was joined by Michel Metzger of the Pivain group. The latter found skis belonging to an earlier 'spectacular' led by Jean Marc Boivin, and used them to good effect in skiing the S face with Thierry Renard. This caused some subsequent controversy as Renard's companion required support in coming down and Renard had billed his ski descent as a solo. Metzger poo-pooed the skiing difficulty, negated the solo and claimed that Renard had paid insufficient attention to the needs of his climbing companion.

This circus had been preceded by the even more elaborate French expeditions to enable Jean Marc Boivin to hang-glide from the top of Gasherbrum and Pierre Geveux to parachute down. Both were successful in mid-July. Unfortunately the Japanese film camera man, Tamoji Nakoro, died in an avalanche during the climb and a French climber also died, apparently of oedema. Boivin was beaten to the first descent from 8000m by the parachutist Pierre Geveux, who pipped him by four days on 14 July. Both were world records, but were surrounded by large scale expeditions including strong high altitude porters and hoo-ha of an extravagant nature summed up harshly by an unknown critic in Skardu — 'Boivin success — seulement deux morts'. Both involved strong climbing performances at altitude, but they, and much else, were obscured by the atmosphere of Chamonix-Karakoram. Later expeditions were not always so 'successful'. An Italian group did a new route on the left edge of the NW face of Gasherbrum 1, one member climbing it and continuing alone to the summit, then meeting his companions and descending with them in worsening weather. After a major storm in early August no more ascents were achieved, despite efforts by the Scottish Gasherbrum 1 expedition and an Italian group on Gasherbrum II. Geoff Cohen, Des Rubens, Clive Rowlands and Paul Nunn tried a new route on the NW face of Gasherbrum 3. They reached Base Camp on 11 July and at first followed the 'trade route' to Gasherbrum 2 (to Camp 1 at 6000m). They found the 'Cassin-Bonatti' 1958 route through the upper icefall of the S Gasherbrum glacier, and established Camp 3 at about 6900m in the upper coire of the glacier on 1 August. A severe storm drove them down, leaving ice caves at Camp 2 in the icefall and in the coire. Rowlands decided to go home. The others returned in better weather but bad snow conditions on 10 August to Camp 1. After another day of indifferent weather Cohen and Rubens pressed on to Camps 2 and 3, while Nunn went down. In several days of isolated and difficult climbing they climbed to about 7700m on the unclimbed NW ridge of the mountain, but were eventually forced down by windy conditions and difficult, complicated terrain. The mountain has been climbed once, by the Gasherbrum 2 standard route and S face, by the Polish-British (Alison Chadwick) party in 1975.

On K2 a large Japanese expedition was successful via the Abruzzi late in the summer. A Franco-Swiss party comprising Erhard Loretan, Nicole Niquille, Jean Troillet, Yves Morand, Eric Escoffier, Daniel Lacroix, Stephane Schaffter and Jean Francois Magnificat set off on the Abruzzi on 4 July. Climbing together solo they reached 6800m (Camp 2) that afternoon. Leaving at 4am next morning Loretan and Escoffier reached 7400m by 11.30am and the others joined them at 3pm. Magnificat decided to go down. Schaffter and Lacroix decided to rest until the next morning but Escoffier left with the four Swiss at 9pm. Nicole Niquille gave up because of leg pains, though she had spent two days above 8000m the previous week. At 8000m they failed to locate a tent left from an earlier sortie and had to press on. They took a traverse line under a serac on a slope of 50°, taking 3–4 hours to pass below it. From the shoulder the final 400m slope was climbed and they reached the top at 1.30pm, 15 hours after their departure.

They retreated meeting Schaffter and Lacroix at 8000m and reached 7400m by 7pm. Next day they descended to Base Camp. Schaffter and Lacroix also reached the top but became separated on the descent around 8200m. Lacroix failed to appear. Subsequent searches by Magnificat, who reached 8000m yielded no further information.

A Pakistani expedition from the Army School of Mountaineering was successful on Broad Peak. Led by Major Rayyaz Hussain they fixed three camps. On 30 July they left Camp 3 (7250m) at 2.30pm and moved to 7700m below the col. Next day they left at 7.30am and reached the top at 3.30pm. Three climbers, Major Rayyaz Hussain, Major Zahid Mahmood and Captain Jawad Pirzada, reached the top. Bad weather made the descent dangerous on this and other climbs at the beginning of August. Meanwhile Wanda Rutkiewicz, after climbing Nanga Parbat, was unsuccessful in her attempt on Broad Peak. One of her companions, Barbara Kozlowska, was drowned in a glacier stream on 20 August.

On Masherbrum the Japanese Kansai Karakoram expedition, led by Shin Kashu, did a new route on the NW face from the Yermanendu valley. They climbed expedition style with four camps and with fixed ropes. Leaving Camp 4 on 22 July, they bivouaced and reached the main summit (7821m) next day. The climbers were S Kashu, S Wada, M Yamamoto, Y Yabukawa, T Shigero, H Ito, T Terauchi, T Toyama, M Tatsuta and R Nishizutsumi. Near the summit they discovered the bodies of two Polish climbers, M Malatynski and P Nowacki, who died on the first ascent of Masherbrum SW (7806m) in 1981. They completed the first ascent of the N ridge and the upper part of the NW face. At the same time an Austrian party of six climbers led by Robert Renzler, climbed from the Mandu valley and ascended the left side of the 3500m NW face in 12 days. Three camps were set up at 5500m, 5900m and 6300m. There were dangers from seracs and ice avalanches. On 21 July they began their ascent with nights at camps 2 and 3 and a tent bivouac at 7200m. A rock-barrier was climbed at 7400m using ropes left by the Japanese. Three climbers, Andi Orgler, Robert Renzler and Michael Sarcber reached the summit ridge at

7800m and then the top before returning to their bivouac. In the night bad weather began and they descended in snow storms and avalanche conditions to the Yermanendu. Subsequently, they climbed the 1700m SE face of Urdukas Peak (5980m). In previous years Japanese and American parties had reached 5500m on Masherbrum N face. Mike Searle's British party tried the unclimbed, long E ridge without success. Masherbrum remains a formidable mountain. The main summit has been reached by four members of the American expedition of 1960 and in 1983 by two Japanese before this third (1985) ascent. Masherbrum SW remains unrepeated since the Polish three man ascent of 1983.

As usual there were a considerable number of expeditions on Nanga Parbat. The Polish all women's expedition set up four camps on the Kinshofer route on the Diamir face. Wanda Rutkiewitz, Anna Czerwinska and Krystyna Pal-mowska reached the top on 15 July. On 8 July two Japanese from Nagasaki reached the top, and the French, Bernard Muller and Laurence de la Ferriere likewise. On 11 July Michael Dacher and Peter Habeler were also successful. Laurence de la Ferriere was the second woman to succeed on Nanga Parbat, a success closely followed by the all women's Polish ascent. A Polish expedition also climbed the SE Pillar of the mountain. For the most part, they followed the route pioneered by Herrligkoffer's 1982 expedition. On 13 July Zygmunt Heinrich, Jerzy Kukuczka, Slawomir Lobodzinski and a Mexican, Carlos Carsolio, reached the summit. Piotr Kalmus from Krakow was killed in an avalanche between Camps 1 & 2. He was swept over 1000m on 10 July.

Doug Scott's expedition was successful on Diran, but did not manage Rakaposhi. Early efforts seem to have been distracted by the rescue of an Austrian climber and the expedition suffered porter and illness problems. Much depleted, they met bad weather which also prevented them climbing Nanga Parbat. An Austrian party climbed Diran and Lindsay Griffin and Chris Forest tried Hikmul (6300m), in the rarely frequented Sosbun glacier basin, without success.

Tragedy befell the South Wales Mountaineering Club party which set out to do the Biafo-Hispar Trek and to climb small peaks, and also to make recon-naissance for a possible future expedition of a more ambitious nature. A base camp was set up at Snow Lake in late July. Then Dave Parsons became altitude sick and departed with his wife down the Hispar. Bob Williams was injured in a crevasse fall and went back the same way with Don Hillman. The remaining pair, Mike Harber and Mike Morris, remained planning to try Lukpe La Brakk (6593m). When they did not return at the appointed time relatives and friends alerted the Pakistani authorities and the Foreign Office, and a major search ensued by helicopter and on the ground. The Snow Lake camp remained in existence, but there was no trace of Advanced Base, or of the climbers. The search discovered a body on the Hispar Glacier which remains unidentified. A Japanese expedition to Latok 2 NW ridge, led by Ikuo Sekikawa, discovered a body in the surface ice of the glacier and reburied it. Site and clothing confirmed that it was the body of Don Morrison, who fell into a crevasse close to the place where the remains came to the surface.

An Alpine Club visit to the Chomolungma area involved a large number of climbers, but the peaks, as so often in the Karakoram, were found to be harder than expected and few summits were reached. A Pinnacle Club party trekked into the Shimshal area. Most successful of UK efforts was the visit to the Siachen Glacier area of the East Karakoram. A party of six Indian and five British made major first ascents of rarely visited peaks near the Terong Valley. They explored 3 glaciers and crossed five cols. Leaving Leh on 12 June they started up the Siachen on the 14th. Dave Wilkinson and Jim Fotheringham were successful on Rimo 3 (7233m). They had set off for Rimo 1 by the Ibex Col but thought the proposed route too dangerous. Therefore they switched objectives and made the first ascent by a *TD inf* route. Other firsts were Sondhi (6480m) climbed by Samant and Dhiren on 13 July via the W ridge, and W icefall. Sundrar (6300m) was climbed by the same pair the previous day. On 12 July Boga and Agrawal did the S ridge of Lharimo (6070m. Doab (6045m) was climbed by Contractor and Harsinh on 15 July by the S ridge and Safina (5975m) on 6 July by Samant and Contractor via the W ridge. Rimo 1 was attempted by Tony Saunders and Steve Venables who reached 6900m on the SW spur. Saigat was tried by Kapadia and Pratapsinth who reached 5800m on the S face. Later in the expedition climbing was concentrated on the S Terong and Shelkar Chorten glaciers. Venables soloed Chorten (6050m) by the W ridge, on 22 July, Nagabong Terong (6180m) by the E ridge on the 24th. They had difficulty crossing the Terong Topko river during their return.

On smaller peaks near the Baltoro two Spaniards, Antonio Martinez and Joaquin Carril, climbed the NE face of Biarchedi (6759m). It proved to be a steep ice route of 2300m. The peak is in the Masherbrum Group and is reached by crossing the Yermanendu Glacier which descends from Masherbrum. Miri Ercolani, an Italian woman climber, reported a solo ascent of Gasherbrum 6 (7007m) from the Duke of Abruzzi Glacier. An Eiselin Sports group (Switzerland) led by Fredy Graf did Sia Kangri (7422m). Another Swiss party led by Anton Spiring climbed Kanjut Sar (6831m) and a Japanese party led by Yukiteshi Tanikawa climbed Bobisqhr Peak (6416m). Another succeeded on Passu Peak (7284m).

Arctic 1984–85

Derek Fordham
Plate 87

During the past few years there has been a great deal of expedition activity in the Arctic mountains but, in keeping with the trend elsewhere, much has been of small scale and has gone largely unreported.

The two most noteworthy expeditions of the past two years, of which details are available, were both British and both to East Greenland. The first, led by Derek Fordham, was the 1984 Mont Forel Expedition which made two unsuccessful attempts on the summit in May and was the subject of an article in *AJ90*. The second, the Kejser Franz Josef's Fjord Expedition, under the leadership of Iain Smart made a successful ascent of Petermann Peak, 2620m in the summer of 1985, just before the start of some bad weather. Zeyen and Todd climbed the NE ridge encountering much loose rock and a steeper section in the upper reaches that gave a couple of very difficult pitches. Slesser, Sellar and Smart climbed via the E ridge in six hours by a long steep scramble up disintegrating laminae of upended strata.

In the Staunings Alps an eight man expedition from Rome claimed ten first ascents in the Dansketinde/Norsketinde region although 'firsts' must be getting a trifle hard to find in such a well frequented area. The expedition also liberally applied confusing Italian names to local peaks; names which are unlikely to be acceptable to the Greenland authorities.

Further south, in July, an expedition of ten Italians, two Slovenes and two Greenlanders were helicoptered to the Kristians glacier area north of Angmagssalik. Despite bad weather they made a number of new routes on peaks in the Henri Dunant Bjerg/de Quervain Bjerg region. (A full list of the ascents claimed by both these Italian expeditions is in *The American Alpine Journal* 1985 pp220–222.)

In September Jaroslav Pavlicek and Miroslav Jakes from Czechoslovakia made a crossing of the Inland Ice from Angmagssalik to Sondre Stromfjord. As was to be expected so late in the season they encountered poor conditions and bad weather. The traverse of the icecap itself took 32 days, far longer than would normally be necessary.

Also in Greenland a Danish military team attempted to find previously undiscovered relics of the Mylius Erichsen 'Danmark' Expedition but were largely unsuccessful and hampered by a crevasse fall which necessitated a difficult helicopter evacuation of one member.

Elsewhere in 1984 a party led by Tony Billinghurst made an enterprising coast to coast traverse of W Spitsbergen from Ny Alesund to Mohnbukta, linking together explorations carried out in previous years.

In 1985 the Newcastle University SE Greenland Expedition carried out mainly scientific work in the area north of Angmagssalik and climbed some minor peaks in the Tasilaq area. They also met two Greenlander women who had wintered at Kangerdlugssuaq with Lawrence Wager and his wife some 50 years ago.

Further north in the Staunings Alps the I M Marsh College East Greenland Expedition established a base camp at the junction of the Bersaerkerbrae and Dunottar glaciers and made ascents of some 14 routes on peaks in the area. Ascents of Royal, D Eglin Spids (an un-named spire between Bersaerkertinde and Royal) and Dunottar SE face are believed to be the longest face routes in the Staunings.

Just south of the Staunings in Jameson Land the Gurreholm Bjerg Expedition under Geoffrey Shaw climbed a number of minor peaks whilst investigating the flora of the region.

The above are only a few of the many expeditions known to have been in the field and these notes can make no claim to be in any way comprehensive. Indeed, the Danish Ministry for Greenland announced to the press in 1984 that over 100 expeditions were planned for Greenland that year!

Canadian Arctic and Alaska — 1984

Ted Whalley

Mountains occur in the arctic of North America in two principal areas. The E arctic mountains of Canada extend from the Torngats of N Labrador in 58°N latitude to N Ellesmere in 83°N, a distance of about 2500km, and from about 60°W to 95°W longitude. They are said to have been formed, along with the W Greenland Mountains, when Greenland and North America split apart and formed Baffin Bay and Nares Strait about ɔ0 million years ago. The original peneplane was raised and split and weathered, principally by the Pleistocene glaciers. The Pleistocene glaciations seem to have started in our region, and the Barnes Icecap, in central Baffin, is a true remnant of the last glaciation. Its base is well below snowline, but its summit, at about 1000m, is well above, so it thrives at present, but would not reform if it were removed. The mountains are nowhere high, the highest being Barbeau Peak in the United States Range of N Ellesmere Island at 2670m. It is really a bulge in the ice cap, and snowmobiles have been driven to the summit. However, glaciers flow down to sea level, and in other parts the mountains are very rugged and require 1550m or more of climbing to ascend them.

The W arctic mountains extend from about 59°N latitude to near the N coast at about 70°N, but the principal glaciated mountains arc south of 64°N. In longitude they extend from about 134°W to 187°W at the end of the Aleutian Islands and merge into the related mountains of Kamchatka, the Kuril Islands, Japan, the Marianas, etc. They were formed principally by subduction of the oceanic crust under the continents, in processes resembling those that caused the Rocky Mountains.

Eastern Arctic of Canada

The eastern arctic mountains of Canada occupy N Labrador and Baffin, Devon, Ellesmere, and Axel Heiberg Islands. By all standards, they form one of the major mountain ranges in the world, but nevertheless they have no formally accepted name. They cover an area about three times the area of Great Britain. In eastern parts, the precambrian rocks are exposed, but they are covered with paleozoic sedimentary rocks in the west and north-west. Convection in the earth's upper mantle about fifty million years ago raised an ancient peneplane and split Greenland from the rest of the North American continent. Gently undulating highlands were formed on both parts, and the glaciations of the last several million years have attacked cracks in the rocks and formed the present-day landscape of mountains and fiords. Because of the rebound of the land after the ice melted, some of the fiords now have their entrances above sea-level.

A detailed history of climbing in these mountains would form a long article, but the pioneers deserve mentioning. The Inuit or Eskimo have lived in our area for perhaps 10,000 years. At the climatic optimum some hundreds of years ago they extended into the high arctic, north of the line between Lancaster Sound and McClure Strait, but abandoned it when the weather cooled. Recently, the Canadian Government has encouraged settlement in the village of Grise Fiord on the south coast of Ellesmere Island. So little is known in detail about the area that in 1976 we could find ancient Inuit camp sites on the shores of Makinson Inlet that were unknown to the anthropologists. The first Europeans to see our mountains were the Greenland Norsemen, who called Baffin Island, or perhaps Labrador, Markland, and they settled for two or three decades at l'Anse aux Meadows in NE Newfoundland. Martin Frobisher saw the foothills around Frobisher Bay in 1576 and John Davis saw the mountains when he penetrated Baffin Bay as far as Davis Strait in 1585 and named one of them Mount Raleigh. Robert Bylot, with William Baffin as navigator, sailed around Baffin Bay, and discovered Bylot, Devon, and Ellesmere Islands, but they were not believed (many false 'discoveries' in these parts had been reported by others) until their report was confirmed by John Ross in 1818. The last major discoveries were made by Otto Sverdrup on sledge trips around Axel Heiberg Island and along the W coast of Ellesmere Island and across it in 1899–1902.

Bylot Island is a mountainous island off the NE corner of Baffin Island and separated from it by Navy Board Inlet, Eclipse Sound, and Pond Inlet. It is a substantial size, its area being about half the area of Wales. Its exploration, however, is very recent. The interior was not seen by Europeans until Patrick Baird, who was part of the British Expedition to North Baffin Island 1938–39, spent the spring and summer of 1939 encircling the island and traversing it with a dog team. He found that it is not covered by an ice-cap, as the map then showed, but contains large valley glaciers separated by mountain ridges. He climbed an 1850m mountain. The Inuit of Pond Inlet have recently had a mountain and a glacier named with Baird's Inuit name of Inukssualuk.

The interior seems to have been reached only another three times. H W Tilman crossed from Cape Liverpool to the S coast in July–August 1962 thinking he was the first. Rob Kelly, Laurie Dexter, Greg Good, Jim Savage, and James Lamont crossed from Tay Bay on the NW coast to Button Point on the SE coast on skis in July–August 1977 and climbed 20 peaks including the highest, 2062m, and Baird's peak of 1939, all but two being first ascents. Another traverse from NW to SE on skis was made by Mike and Ulrike Schmidt, Dave Clay, Mike Wingham, and Fred Bushnell in May–June 1984 and many first ascents were made. Ferris and Ames in 1954 climbed Mt Thule, near the S coast, Van Cochran and seven companions in 1974 climbed a peak near the coast west of Narsarsuk Glacier, and Laurie Dexter has climbed another four.

The Chief Warden of Auyuittuq National Park on Baffin Island reports only two climbing expeditions to the Park in 1984. Yukio Tarashima, Teruji Yoivel, and Ivorio Hoshino made the first ascent of the W face of Mt Thor. Unfortunately, their base camp manager, Kazue Kumakura was swept into Pangnirtung Fiord while crossing a river and was drowned. Andre Filion, Louis Bareite, Guy Gilbert, and Jacques Trancia climbed secondary peaks of Asgard and Thor and a snow gully on the SE face of Freya.

Dave McAdam has continued his lone wanderings in Baffin Island and spent seven weeks in the S Cumberland Peninsula. Swollen rivers in Kangeetulujuk Valley prevented travel, but he climbed over 15 mountains up to 1820m in height.

The western Canadian Arctic and Alaska
In Kluane National Park, one group climbed Mts Wood, McCauley, and Steele, another climbed the S ridge of Steele, two climbed Mt Logan by the E ridge, and two by the King Trench. Jamie Moffat and Bill Maurer attempted the first winter ascent of Mt Logan and, in cloud, reached one of the several summits on the ridge NW of the W peak. The E ridge of Mt St Elias, Mt Alverstone, and Mt Kennedy were climbed by different parties. The 1 : 125,000 map of the Centennial Range, map no. MCR 7 (1967) marks the 1925 route up Mt Logan by the King Trench as going north of Queen Peak instead of south of it. This error still leads parties astray occasionally.

Mt McKinley was attempted by 695 climbers in 133 expeditions in 1984. The success rate was about 47% for both guided and unguided parties. Seventy-seven climbers had symptoms of acute mountain sickness, of whom three were hospitalized. Most climbers were on the standard W buttress route, but the Cassin and the S buttress were each climbed by seven persons, four succeeded on the NW buttress, and the Muldrow glacier, W rib, and S face had ascents. Frances Randall, who was also known as the Kahiltna Queen, has died of cancer. She had acted as the radio operator at the base camp at 2200m on the Kahiltna Glacier for nine summers. Her help and cheerful hospitality will be greatly missed. Naomi Uemura, who made the first summer solo ascent of the W buttress some years ago, died in a solo winter attempt, apparently after reaching the summit. The only other death in the mountains occurred when a Swiss guide skied unroped into a crevasse. The Park Service Rangers with volunteer medical doctors and mountaineers operated an emergency camp at 4410m on the W buttress which seems to have greatly helped to detect acute mountain sickness and coordinate rescues, and to encourage sanitation and removal of garbage. One party was given a citation for persistently leaving garbage and abandoning food caches. When six hundred climbers try one route on the mountain in the short summer season, waste and excreta must be properly disposed of.

A difficult new route on the S buttress — the Ridge of No Return — was soloed by Renato Casarotto; and Adam Blazej, Korl Frantisek, and Krizo Anton climbed a direct and difficult route on the south face exposed to severe ice falls. A well conditioned and acclimatized French Army team traversed the mountain from base camp to Wonder Lake in five days. New routes were climbed on the E face of Mt Foraker by Vachon, Decy, Gagnon, and Sanders, on the N buttress of Mt Hunter by Tedeschi and Grison, and on Mt Huntingdon and Rooster's Comb by Haberl and Rohn.

The first transit of the NW passage by a passenger ship — the Lindblad Explorer — marks a further stage in the opening of the arctic to travellers, and may eventually have some implications for climbers.

I am very grateful to Ray Breneman, Dave MacAdam, Lloyd Freese, Robert R Seibert, and Jamie Moffat for providing information.

South America 1985

Evelio Echevarría

Mountaineering activity in the entire Andes during 1985 continued on a smaller scale in comparison to the activity registered early this decade. Reasons for this reduction remain the same: the vogue acquired by the Himalaya and the changing weather patterns. Bad weather has now become a characteristic of the Andes. After a cycle of nine years of drought (late 1974 to mid 1983) which drastically changed Andean glaciers almost everywhere, unstable weather and unfavourable snow conditions seem to be now the rule. Curiously, rains and snowfall have been normal or below normal in the precipitation season, but abundant in the dry or climbing season of every area, which resulted in many unexpected failures. However, while it is true that Andean mountaineering is on the decrease, it has remained sufficiently active to be declared the most active high mountain activity in the world after Russia's. In Asia, much higher peaks are climbed every year, but this refers only to sporadic ascents. In the world of today, only the Russians can claim to routinely ascend peaks as high as those ascended every season in South America by both local and foreign parties.

Northern Andes

Foreign trekking parties have begun to scout the Andes north of the Equator so as to move away from the politically troubled areas to the south. The main ascents in the N Andes, however, have been accomplished by local climbers. In Venezuela, women have been particularly active. The first all-woman ascent of Pico Bolívar was an event of note, the more so considering the bad weather predominating in the Sierra Nevada de Mérida during early 1985. A party of five, led by Rosa Pabón, made the ascent of Pico Bolívar, highest in Venezuela (5002m), on 27 April, by the Bourgoin couloir. Another woman, Dora Ocanto, with José Betancourt, introduced a variant on the S face of Pico Abanico (4900m) on 20 May.

In Ecuador, the two main ascents by local climbers took place in 1984. On 1 January, O Morales, with the Frenchman G de Lataillade, climbed the 800m N face of El Obispo (5319m), highest peak in the Altar massif, a new route. In the last week of 1984, F Almeida, P Garcés, L Naranjo and M Reinoso, all with much experience in climbing in the same massif, opened a new route on Canónigo (5260m), which they climbed by its S face, with one bivouac. Finally, on 30–31 December 1984, L Griffin and M Woolridge of the Alpine Climbing Group, made a new route on the SSW face of Chimborazo (6267m), with a bivouac below the summit plateau.

Peru and Bolivia

The main events in Peruvian climbing belong to the Cordillera Blanca. The SW face of Nevado Alpamayo (5947m) attracted in 1984 several expeditions. It was ascended by a Frenchman, D Pivot (28 June), by Argentinians from San Juan led by G Raynié (12 July) and by Ecuadorians, who opened a variant of the Ferrari route. Also in 1984, Ramiro Navarrete and Marco Suárez, Ecuadorians, climbed the S wall of the imposing Nevado Santa Cruz (6241m), until they reached at about 6000m the SW ridge, which took them to the summit (4 August); they rappelled down the Jaeger route of 1978. Navarrete, a leading South American climber, returned to the Cordillera Blanca in 1985. An accident had deprived him of a companion and had to climb alone. He made, in three days from Huaraz and back, an ascent of the W buttress of Huascarán (6768m), declaring that this route is more difficult than the classic one, but also safer. Afterwards, he attempted the S ice wall of Chacraraju (6112m), but had to retreat due to the unsafe conditions of the ice. Still, he was able to climb the S face of Artesonraju (6025m), again in three days from Huaraz and back (18 July).

Elsewhere in Peru, a Polish expedition (K Ambrozy, E Chrobak, W Derda, M Kwasny) scaled the NW face of the fine Vilcanota peak of Colpa Anante (or Cayangate IV, 6110m). The Poles also attempted the N buttress of Ausangate (6372m), but bad weather forced them to abandon the attempt.

Political unrest kept expeditions away from several areas in Peru and Bolivia. In the latter country bad weather hit Andean areas throughout the climbing season (late April to September). Most of the repeat ascents registered during 1985 had to be done in deep snow.

For the first time since 1903, a mountain ascent in the Cordillera de Potosí has been reported. The first, and indeed the only mountaineer to climb in this unglaciated, rocky range located east of the famous colonial city was the German Alpine poet Henry Hoek (*AJ 23*, pp19–30). In May 1985 E Echevarría twice entered the range alone and made the first ascent of two rock peaks over 4900m and the second of three others over 5000m, all in the northern half of the range. Hoek had crossed over the Abra (pass) Illimani here in November 1903. In this new expedition it was discovered that members of the Instituto Geográfico Militar de Bolivia had surveyed the range in March 1956 and ascended several peaks, whose cairns and benchmarks were found on the summits.

Chile and Argentina

Northern Andes. Archaeology, not mountaineering, motivated the several expeditions that climbed in the *Puna*, or northern highland, of both countries, during 1985. After realizing several repeats over 6000m on the Chilean side, Johan Reinhard (American) and Louis Glauser (Swiss) drove into Argentina to meet two other Swiss. The first two climbers made the probable second ascent of Nevado de Pissis (6780m) (25 January), third highest elevation in the American continent. The group of four also ascended other peaks to inspect Inca ruins, but made no discovery of importance. A first ascent was that of Cerro Pabellón de la Laguna Verde (5815m), on 17 March.

The Argentinian Antonio Beorchia led, as every year, a group to locate Inca ruins and ascended Cerro Amarillo de Zenta, only 3660m high, but located at the E end of the Andes of the province of Jujuy and facing the semi tropical forests. Large ruins, with well built staircases, were inspected on this occasion (30 July).

Central Andes. Operating on their side of the frontier peaks, Chilean and German climbers made new routes on the S faces of Cerro Sierra Bella (5230m) and Cerro de Orientación I (5005m) and on the N face of Marmolejo (6100m), all in January and February 1985. The Argentinians, on their side, climbed on 9 February the SE gully of Tupungato (6550m), a triumph that was paid with the lives of the experienced L Rabal and G Vieiro. The Swiss U Buehler climbing alone in the first days of the year, climbed the Yugoslav route on the S face of Aconcagua, an exploit he carried out in only three days.

Both Aconcagua and Tupungato mountains are now both Argentinian national parks. The legislature of the province of Mendoza created the Parque Provincial Aconcagua in April 1983 and the Parque Provincial Tupungato in September 1985. Bad weather has slowed down most operations to build facilities for tourists and mountaineers. A small helicopter rescue station, a library and a museum are contemplated.

Patagonia. One of the great problems of technical climbing in Patagonia, the NE wall of Cerro Murallón (2831m), was solved by three members of the Italian group appropriately named *i Ragni* (the spiders). The final climb was executed by the expert Casimiro Ferrari, a constant traveller to the Andes, with Carlo Alde and Paolo Vitali (14 February 1984). Four attempts, between 1979 and 1984, were necessary for this triumph.

Nearly unvisited last summer (January 1985), the Patagonian Andes had an unusual visitor in the Italian Giuliano Giongo who, in August (the Chilean winter), traversed N to S, the five plateaus of the ice cap. Complete details are lacking, but it is known that he began the traverse at the Pascua fjord and, with very light loads and marching even under bad weather, he took only 34 days to reach a fjord around 50°S. He had covered, according to his own estimates, some 550km and constantly at a height of 2000m.

Scottish Winter 1984-85

Ken Crocket

The Scottish winter season of 84/85 was one of the driest for decades with very little snow. Despite this several hard and classic rock climbs received winter ascents under mainly powder snow conditions. In the Northern Highlands some use was made of a build-up of ice, with routes such as Diamond Five (V) on one of the Horns of Beinn Alligin, by S Chadwick, G Livingston, and G Strange on 10 February. In January, C Maclean and A Nisbet paid a visit to the Fannichs, climbing the excellent Cuileag Corner (IV/V) on the right side of No 3 Buttress of Sgurr nan Clach Geala, and The Ramp Tramp (IV) in the Garbh Choire Mor of An Coileachan.

The Cairngorms gave a higher yield with several Grade VI routes. Tough Guy (VI) on Lochnagar was climbed over two weekends by A Nisbet. On 18 December, Nisbet and Maclean climbed the first three pitches before taking to an escape ramp. Returning on 26 December Nisbet and B Davison succeeded by way of an alternative start and the true finish. This is a fine sustained route with difficult route finding. The crux was a thin crack slanting leftward up an otherwise blank slab.

In the Northern Corries, Ventricle (VI) on Coire an Lochain by Maclean and Nisbet, climbed on 27 December, is perhaps the 'state of the art' for technical difficulty. Maclean led the first two pitches with several overhanging sections requiring much strength. But perhaps the most outstanding ascent in the Cairngorms was the ascent of The Needle on the Shelter Stone Crag later in the season by Maclean and Nisbet. Their ascent took 16 hours for 11 pitches, eight of which were 'very hard'. The most natural winter line was followed, the summer line on the Crack for Thin Fingers being impossible, the approach being very rounded with much ice. Similarly, Nisbet had to quit the Needle Crack at half-height because of verglas. The climbing was mainly by way of torqued axes in cracks, the Shelter Stone being most suitable for this mode of progress. Maclean led the crux.

Ben Nevis had a lean winter. Early in the season D Cuthbertson soloed Centurion in powder snow conditions. M Duff and J Tinker made a steep ascent on No 3 Gully Buttress on 16 March with Direct Route (V/VI), though the exact line is uncertain, the route starting up an icefall somewhere between Green Gully and No 3 Gully Buttress. Earlier in the winter, on 19 January, the same pair climbed Sod's Law (V/VI), taking the buttress left of the chimney of Route I.

Stob Coire nan Lochan in Glencoe saw a desperate ascent on 24 January with Maclean and Nisbet on Unicorn (VI). The corner was followed directly to below the last pitch. Here, darkness forced a left traverse to finish up a back-and-knee chimney. The cliff was under powder snow condition. Leftward on Summit Buttress, an alternative start was made to Spectre (IV) on 1 February by M Duff, M Garrett, and R Nowak. On the Buachaille Etive Mor, A Paul and D Hawthorn made an ascent of June Crack.

One point which follows on from recent developments in winter climbing is the possibility of rock damage due to the use of axes on routes climbed in summer. Picks are increasingly being used in cracks for progress, and it will be interesting to see whether summer ascenders will have reason to complain. Crampon scratches on rocks are of little event, but cracks may be splintered by picks. Some axes are not designed to take this sort of punishment in any case, and it may be that there will be 'a self-limiting effect'.

South Africa 1985

Michael Scott

Rock climbing developments here have tended to mirror trends overseas (particularly British) although usually several years later. We now appear to have reached the stage where the enthusiasm is for small crags or boulders, with short walks to get to a vertical gymnasium. There have however continued to be some notable achievements on the big walls, especially solo ascents.

South Africans have continued to perform reasonably well overseas and this last season included some visits to the Ruwenzori. One team, consisting of Armand Hughes d'Aeth, Rob Brand and Clive Ward, climbed a new route up 600m of grade 6 mixed snow and rock on the NE ridge of Savoia (4977m), a southern peak on Mt Stanley. They spent two days climbing it in a blizzard and declared it to be currently the hardest undertaking in the Ruwenzori.

Transvaal

The Magaliesberg kloofs continue to see frantic activity and new routes and aid eliminations too numerous to categorize. The number of new, hard climbers beavering away is very encouraging. At Blouberg, the searing hot cliff in the north, the Razor's Edge (G3) was completed by Smith and Mallory. It aims for a monster dihedral left of the top pitches of Big Corner and ranks as a major climb having taken several days to complete.

Many of the Blouberg classics were repeated by Mallory, Lomax, Haffner, Smith, Bradshaw and others, quite unprecedented numbers for an area so remote.

The Hanglip area also saw some activity, notably by Russ Dodding and Paul Fatti, who opened a variation to the top of Black Widow (G1. M2).

Natal

Steve Bradshaw opened Flames of Sunset at Monteseel. This was the first route to be graded H3 (Australian 26). His usual partner, Adrian Jardin, made the second ascent of White Rider — unrepeated since Mike Roberts opened it in 1981 at Australian 25/26. Jardin took 21 falls before getting through, which is indicative of the approach accepted by the top climbers to achieve these grades of climbs.

The Drakensberg peak, Mponjwana, had a solo ascent by George Mallory using Snelson's original route.

Cape

Andrew de Klerk completed a spectacular and prestigious season by soloing Renaissance (G3) on Du Toit's Peak in 4hrs 20mins. As someone once described Messner & Habelers' ascent of the Eiger — this was 'vertical running'. De Klerk had achieved an ideal earlier in the year by soloing Oceans of Fear (G3 M3) on the Klein Winterhoek Peak. His epic ascent took four days, through a chilling rain squall which left him exhausted. He had to abandon his pack on the last pitch and walk out with no gear. Lighter moments between these two events were the climb Heart of Darkness (H1) on the Lion's Head granite, spurred on by Aleck McKirdy's joke cardboard bolt and hanger glued onto an 'impossible' position, which prompted the route. Andrew's free ascents of Winds of Change (H2 and previously mechanical) and his new route Dream Street Rose (I1 or Australian 27/28) both on Elsies Peak, were accomplished after uncountable falls — a tribute to tenacity.

De Klerk, with Kevin Smith, opened God of Thunder at Krakadouw in the Cedarberg (H3). It overhangs 30m in 70m of climbing.

The Eastern Cape area has had a surge of activity, largely led by expatriate schoolteacher Keith James and some of his pupils. They have opened new climbs in the Swartberg Pass and in the Wolwerivier Gorge area.

Undoubtedly the premier climbing get-together this year was the centenary climb of Toverkop to commemorate Gustav Nefdt's climb. Some 14 people repeated Nefdt's route (F3) conventionally and several found it still a desperate pitch, while three hard lads soloed up and down it, and one climbed it in socks.

New Zealand 1984–85

Bill King

A wet December/early January thwarted the plans of many climbers except for a few stayers.

At Mt Cook, hard, fast solos came into vogue. The most notable was Paul Bayne's first solo ascent of the Balfour face of Mt Tasman in 2½ hours. This was one of New Zealand's most sought-after climbs on one of the country's premier ice test-pieces. Al Wood made a fast first ascent of the Central Gullies route on the S face of Mt Hicks in 7½ hours, which was repeated shortly afterwards by John Goulstone in 9 hours. This climb is undertaken on steep ice and rock and is both difficult and demanding. Greg Aimer continued the solo trend with a direct line on the S face of Malte Brun.

In early December the Caroline face of Mt Cook was climbed by two German guides working in New Zealand. One was later killed attempting to cross a swollen river.

One of the best new routes for the season was a ten pitch rock route on the Linda face of the Bowie ridge of Mt Cook by Kevin Boekholt and Nick Craddock. This climb was completed in rock boots and is reputed to have been some of the most difficult rock climbing to be found at Mt Cook.

There were also a number of important ascents of some of the more classic routes. The third ascent of the Frind route on Mt Sefton was made by John Nankervis and Jim Jolley. This completed 'Nank's' ascents of the 30 3000m peaks in New Zealand, a notable and still fairly rare achievement in New Zealand mountaineering. The second ascent of Nazomi (MacInnes ridge) to Mt Cook (S ridge) *integral* was made by Rob Hall and Gavin Tweedie.

It was also an important season for the re-emergence of New Zealand women climbers. Although women climbers have been making good ascents of New Zealand's hardest alpine routes for many years, it has generally been in the company of men who have been the dominant climbing partner. However, this season saw ascents of some of New Zealand's hardest routes by women-only teams. The most important ascents included 'White Dreams' on the S face of Mt Cook by Carol Nash and Lyn Bowering, and the Sheila face of Mt Cook by Ann Palmer and Carol Nash.

There were also many new ascents during the season in the Darrens and Mt Aspiring alpine regions.

Winter climbing in New Zealand's main alpine areas is still in its infancy. In fact many mountains still await their first winter ascent. Other than access problems because of deep snow and avalanches, long periods of bad weather make any winter ascent of the higher mountains a serious proposition. Although in recent years there has been a trend towards winter mountaineering, this did not live up to expectations this year and very few new ascents were recorded. However, Bill McLeod, who seems to have dedicated his life to first solo winter ascents, did Earle's route on Mt Cook and also managed to complete the second winter ascent of La Perouse. A somewhat controversial first winter ascent of the much sought after 'Black Tower' was made by Rob Hall and Bill Atkinson. The pair flew in to a hanging glacier on the N face of Black Tower by helicopter and completed a 15 pitch ice route to the summit before abseiling off and flying out again the following day.

The rock scene in New Zealand is alive and healthy. With an increasing number of participants in the sport, new crags are being opened up and climbing standards are improving to a high degree. New Zealand's best rock climbing crag at Whanganui Bay, Lake Taupo, had access problems during the summer months and was closed, except to those who had water access in a power boat. This probably had some beneficial effects in that it encouraged the development of new crags and pushed up the grades of new routes on existing crags. Roland Foster, after his European sojourn, managed to complete many high quality routes of grade 28 at the 'Bay' before it was closed. He also managed the second ascent of Charlie Cresse's test piece (Pet Cemetery) grade 29 at Auckland's Quarry.

With an increase in numbers now climbing in New Zealand, the standard of both alpine and rock routes is increasing, with a tendency now being directed towards hard, solo climbs and new winter climbs.

My thanks to — NZAC Bulletin, NZAC Journal, CMC News *for information on ascents.*

Mount Everest Foundation Notes 1984–85

Edward Peck

The following notes summarise reports from expeditions which have received the approval of the MEF and this is in most cases accompanied by a grant. MEF approval is generally an essential first step to seeking assistance, financial or otherwise, from other organisations. It should be noted that the MEF only 'sponsors' expeditions in exceptional circumstances, *eg* the 1981 Mount Kongur expedition.

Copies of the full reports of these expeditions are lodged, when available, with the Alpine Club Library and the Archives section of the Royal Geographical Society, and may be consulted in these places. Some expeditions will already have been described in the Alpine Journal and other journals.

The expeditions summarised in the following notes took place between August 1984 and October 1985 and these notes are based on reports received up to 1 December 1985.

North America, including Arctic & Greenland
84/32 *Anglo-Canadian Rocky Mountain Speleological Expedition (1983 & 1984)*

In August–September 1983 ten British speleologists joined a Canadian team to explore the limestone *karst* cave country in the Small River area west of Mount Robson. They surveyed ten significant new caves, the longest in excess of 1.3km. The following year (July–August 1984) seven British cavers joined Canadians in exploring sinkholes in the area of Bocock Peak south of Williston Lake in the Peace River district of British Columbia. Three caves were explored, one to a depth of 253m.

85/8 *Yukon — A winter journey (March–April 1985)*

Guy Sheridan's plans to traverse the full length of the Selwyn Mountains from Tungston, in the Mackenzie Mountains, to Dawson was frustrated by bad weather. Only two sections, from Tungston to Macmillan Pass and from the Ortell Camp down to Elsa Camp on the Stewart River, together with an excursion into the Tombstone Mountains north of Dawson were completed, a total of 812km on skis.

85/15 *Southampton University, Baffin Island Expedition (July–August 1985)*

The high cost of local rations from the Hudson Bay store at Pagnirtung limited the scope of this expedition, based at Summit Lake on the Weasel River in the Cumberland Peninsula. Sediment sampling from side streams was abandoned, but the glacier snout was mapped and there was some general exploration of the area.

85/39 *I M Marsh College Expedition to East Greenland (July–September 1985)*
Despite a (non-fatal) rockfall accident, this expedition climbed a number of peaks from a base camp at the junction of the Bersaekerka and Dunnottar Glaciers, including the SE face of Dunnottar, and also carried out glaciological and geological work in the area.

Andes
85/5 *British Peruvian Cordillera Expedition (June–July 1985)*
A major unclimbed route on the West of Milpocraju (5420m) was completed and filmed for the 'Mick Burke Award 1985' competition. More filming was carried out on Nevado Cayesh and Nevado Maparaju around the Quebrada Cayesh. Hinkes and Gore remained behind to make three new climbs: N face of Huandoy Deste, W face direct of Nevado Churup and S face of Nevado Pisco, as well as climbing three major peaks in the Cordillera Blanca.

85/18 *Cambridge Ecuadorian Andes Expedition (August–October 1985)*
This scientific expedition completed their studies of the thermal balance of the Caldera Glacier of El Altar and of the tree *Polylepsis Incana*, finding conditions warmer and wetter than expected. They also visited the area devoid of vegetation (the Limpio Pongo) round Cotopaxi to collect soil samples. Three members climbed Chimborazo.

85/25 *East Midlands Universities Peruvian Expedition (July–September 1985)*
Finding that their planned first ascents (Jurau D and Siula Grande W face) had been climbed, Ruddle and Ravenshill substituted two new routes, one on the W face of Trapecio (5653m), the other on the S ridge of Sierra Norte (5860m), but deep snow forced retreat at 5500m and 5600m respectively.

85/28 *Perth High Andes Expedition (June–July 1985)*
After climbing in the Ishinca Valley, making ascents of Nevado Ishinca (W ridge), N summit of Ranracalpa (E face) and Urus Este, the team successfully tackled Huascaran but were forced by bad weather to abandon plans for Alpamayo.

85/36 *Cordillera Apolobamba Expedition (July 1985)*
Tier and Curran succeeded in the first ascent of Palomani Tranca (5633m) not, as intended by the short steep N ridge, but by the 3km W ridge. A very mixed snow, ice and rock climb taking two days.

Himalaya
85/11 *London Shivling Expedition 1985*
This team's attempt on the unclimbed buttress of Shivling was abandoned at half height owing to bad weather and four members climbed the mountain by the original W ridge route.

85/32 *British Sickle Moon Expedition (August–September 1985)*
From a base camp on the Sarbal glacier this party, led by J.R Peart.

attempted an ice line on the NW face of the S ridge of Sickle Moon but heavy snow crushed Camp 2 at 5500m and continuous snowfall forced their retreat.

Karakoram

85/6 *Scottish Karakoram Expedition (June-September 1985)*

This party, under Cohen and Nunn, had as objective a new route on Gasherbrum III (7952m) by the SW ridge which they tackled from the upper coire between Gasherbrum IV and Gasherbrum III. After a bivouac on the ridge at 7400m, they pushed on (without bivouac gear) to c.7700m when high winds forced a retreat. In good weather another 3 to 4 hours would have been needed to cover the continuing difficulties to the summit which, although only 250m higher, was some considerable distance away. The third member of the party suffered frostbitten feet.

85/10 *British Masherbrum Karakoram Expedition (April-July 1985)*

This Anglo-Canadian team had the double objective of combining geological work round the Concordia area of the Baltoro Glacier with a reconnaissance of the formidable N face of Masherbrum. The extent of the geological work can be gauged by the fact that it took 8 porters to carry out 200kgs of rock samples. As for the mountaineering, Searle and Rex, after going as high as 6500m on the Abruzzi ridge of K2, set up camp to attempt, not the N face itself of Masherbrum where Japanese had been engaged for three weeks, but the long E ridge of Masherbrum. Atrocious weather and frequent avalanches made their ascent to a point on the E ridge, W of the Masherbrum La hazardous. They considered that to continue along this ridge in these conditions would have taken weeks, but in good conditions, this 'most spectacular unclimbed ridge' might have gone. They rounded off a useful month in the Karakoram with a look at Gasherbrum and the Trango Towers.

85/40 *Anglo Indian Expedition to Siachen & Rimo Range (June-September 1985)*

This expedition, combining Alpine Climbing Group members and Bombay Mountaineers, explored the S Rimo glacier, the Shelkar Chorten glacier and the S & N Terong glaciers, conducting some scientific work on the last. Venables and Saunders attempted Rimo I (7385m), but a dropped sack containing essential equipment forced a retreat at 6900m. Wilkinson and Fotheringham made the first ascent of Rimo III (7233m) crossing the previously uncrossed S col of Rimo I to the S Rimo glacier from which the summit was reached in two days on 14 July.

85/42 *Cambridge Ladakh Expedition (August-September 1985)*

This party carried out studies of the complex geology of part of the Zanskar range; in particular, the valley morphology of the Markha valley and its glacial morphology above Nimaling. They also researched the origin of the yellow silts in the Lamayuru basin.

Kenya

Peter Thexton Memorial Expedition to Mt Kenya (July 1985)

In addition to making several difficult ascents in good ice conditions on the S face of Mt Kenya (Diamond Glacier–Ice Window and S face direct), this 11-man team completed a scientific project into mountain sickness based on Two Tarn Hut (4490m), collecting data about the renin-angiotensin-aldosterene system (implicated in the genesis of acute mountain sickness) in accordance with a protocol extending over 18 days.

85/17 Imperial College Ruwenzori Expedition (July–August 1985)

As the E side of the Ruwenzori massif had been occupied by Museveni's National Resistance Guerrillas, this party had to abandon their plans for Ruwenzori. They substituted a visit to Mount Kenya on which they achieved a number of difficult ice climbs on the S faces (then in winter conditions) of the summit peaks. They also made three new rock climbs on Pigott and Midget Peaks including 'Hunting the Hyrax' (on the W face of Pigott) which they believe to be the first Grade 8 (E3) on the mountain.

Guidebook Notes

Compiled by Lindsay Griffin

Lindsay Griffin would welcome further information and new route descriptions for publication in these pages at: c/o 1 Lockerley Close, Newenham Road, Lymington, Hampshire.

The development on rock continues with the Mont Blanc Range again, almost exclusively, the focal point of creative activity. The majority of new ascents take the form of very technical but short (one recorded at 50m!) rock routes that in general have very easy access. Michel Piola has climbed over 20 new routes this summer and his Topo Guide to the massif should be available in Britain soon. In the main, climbs have fixed protection and belays on the open walls, whereas the cracks and corners are usually left clean. Abseil descents allow a lightweight approach.

Gabarrou still extracts routes of great length and apparent quality all over the Alps and during all seasons. This year (1985) his offerings include several steep and narrow couloir lines climbed during the winter months on the S side of the Mont Blanc–Maudit region, plus a 66 pitch rock climb up the NW pillar of the Petite Jorasses.

Dauphiné
Refuge du Promontoire   Few people now reach the Promontoire Hut by any other means than *via* the W branch of the Etançons Glàcier. The cables on the rock buttress beneath the hut are in a pretty poor state.

Refuge du Châtelleret   This was partially destroyed by an avalanche in spring 1985 and was being renovated and enlarged during that autumn. During this period the historic and famous boulder at the front of the hut was dynamited.

Pic Coolidge, NE Face Bizzare/Bonatti Route   Current descriptions of this climb do not give enough detail regarding the correct starting point. The line that appears to be most frequently climbed in error takes the obvious rock buttress on the L side of the face. This is easy and broken in the lower section but becomes steep and very difficult towards the top. There are a number of abseil pegs in place. The correct route lies in the depression/couloir to the R of this (not exactly 'the lowest section of the barrier of rocks at the base of the face') and gives easy climbing with several pitches of III.

Graians East
Gran Paradiso NE side from the Pol Hut. The route from the Colle Dell'Ape to the summit is misleadingly described in the present English guide. Phil

Bartlett writes: from the Colle Dell'Ape and just across the main ridge a loose rock ridge ascends towards the Roc (4026m). Climb this for 60m then make an easy and slightly rising traverse across the face on the left (traces of a path). Reach an obvious gap in the ridge above. Descend a steep snow slope on the other side for about 10m, cross a bergshrund and traverse easily to join the final section of the W flank (Gran Paradiso glacier) route. Follow this to the summit.

Mont Blanc
Pic Adolphe Rey   Another short rock route was made on the S face to the R of the Gervasutti route. The main difficulties involve some excellent slab climbing.

The route has been equipped to a certain extent and a convenient descent can be made by abseiling the adjacent Bettembourg route to the foot of the face.

(B Domenech and the Remy Brothers, 23 July 1985, 8h. 300m ED.)

Aiguille de Blaitière NW Ridge Direct   There are a number of hard rock routes on the steep pillar at the base of the NW ridge, first climbed in 1972 by the Japanese. The following climb takes an open groove system between the Japanese route and the line taken by the 1982 British 'Pilier Rouge' route.

Start 6m L of the British route and trend L up slabs to gain the base of the central grooves. Climb the grooves for 10m then traverse L to gain a series of discontinuous flakes (V+ sustained) then trend R up grooves (IV+) to belay just R of a large detached flake. Continue up for 4m to a horizontal ledge. Follow this L to a crack and climb this (a move of V), finally belaying below a small overhang. Climb the latter (V) then trend R up obvious grooves (V) to a stance below a slanting orange diedre. Climb the diedre (15m, V+) then make a hard exit (VI−) to reach the continuation grooves (V+). Climb these to more broken ground which quickly leads to a 10m high corner with a crack in the L wall. Climb this (VI−) to a belay. Trend slightly L up a crack in the slabs (IV+) then the corner which leads to a flake on the L (V). Surmount the flake and exit L to a belay. Take the obvious horizontal hand traverse L onto the arête and climb cracks and grooves (IV+) to the brèche. This is the junction with the Japanese and British routes. It is possible to make four abseils down the obvious couloir below the brèche on the W face to reach a ledge system from where an easy descent can be made.

An eight-pitch route with all runouts between 40m and 45m. No pitons used and no gear left in place. About British HVS/E1.

(David Simmonds and Chris Dale, 17 July 1984. 350m TD+.)

Aiguille du Grepon W face   A fine direct line has been climbed up the centre of this face. It gives some spectacular climbing on good rock.

Start in the middle of the face halfway between a large curving arch on the L and an obvious easy rake on the R. Above is an intermittent orange crack line. Climb the orange crack line boldly to a ledge (45m, VI sustained). Meander up the slab above trending L, to belay below an obvious flake system (45m, IV). Move R (awkwardly) to gain the furthest R system of flakes and follow these to a ledge (45m V). Move R into a flake crack and continue up this making a hard

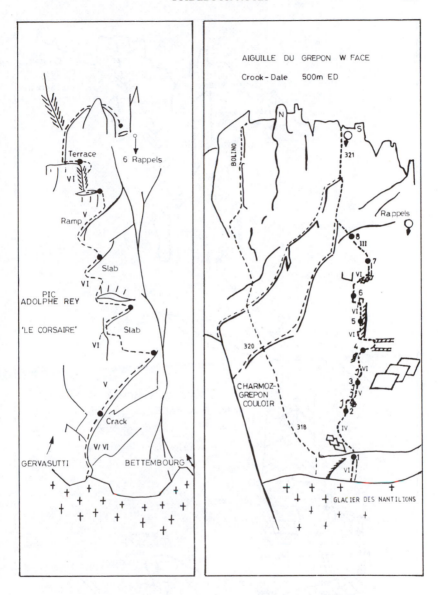

AIGUILLE DU GREPON W FACE

Crook - Dale   500m ED

exit to gain a ledge on the R (45m, VI). Move R along the ledge then move back L diagonally across the wall to belay at the base of an obvious diedre (20m V). Climb up on the edge of the L wall of the diedre, over a small overhang then back R into the diedre itself. After a few metres it is probably best to belay (15m, VI). Continue up the diedre to the overhang at the top then move L to a foot ledge on the arête. Reach a belay on the slab above, below a large overhang (45m, VI). Move up to the overhang then exit R on a series of short, easy

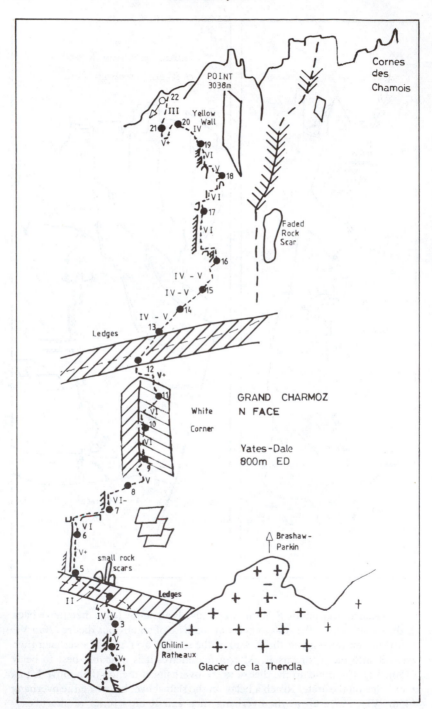

Cornes des Chamois

POINT 3038m

22
III
Yellow Wall
20
21 IV
V+
19
VI
V
18
VI
17
VI
16
IV - V
IV - V 15
IV - V 14
13
Ledges
12 V+
11
VI
White
10
Corner
VI
9
V 8
VI- 7
VI 6
V+
5
small rock scars
II
Ledges
4
IV V
3
V
2
V+ 1

Faded Rock Scar

GRAND CHARMOZ
N FACE

Yates-Dale
800m ED

Brashaw-Parkin

Ghilini-Ratheaux

Glacier de la Thendla

gangways to gain a wide crack. Follow this to a ledge (45m, VI−). From here it is possible to move L to gain Route 320 (Vallot) and so reach the summit. Or climb up the easy ramp on the R for two pitches to reach an abseil descent.

No pitons were used or gear left in place. However it is essential to carry a large selection of small wires RPs etc. The hardest pitches (in the diedre) probably equate to British E2 5C.

(Martin Crook and Chris Dale, 21 August 1985. 500m ED.)

Grand Charmoz Point 3038m N face   A long route giving some excellent and sustained pitches but unfortunately split by two ledge systems. A good bivouac site exists 5 minutes from the foot of the climb.

Start at the foot of the buttress leading down from point 3038m, halfway between an obvious monolithic corner and sickle-shaped groove. This is about 50m down and L of the start of the Ghilini/Ratheaux 1983 route. Climb the crack line with excursions rightwards at 15m and 20m to a ledge (30m V+). Move down awkwardly into corners and up these trending L to a belay (45m V). Climb the easy crack in the large corner trending R at the top (45m V). Slant up L to reach the ledges (45m, IV). Go along the ledges (II) to reach the base of a magnificent crack (initially bordering a corner). Climb the crack and flake, then continue up the crack to belay in a niche (30m V+). Continue over the overhang then trend R along a flake to a ledge (45m VI). Climb the corner above which is awkward at the top. Now trend R to a belay (45m VI−). Go up to a belay below the monolithic white corner (45m V). Climb this corner and belay in a chimney/cave (20m VI). Continue up the chimney crack to an overhang; surmount this, then trend rightwards up a finger crack, moving past a flake to belay in a cave — a superb and difficult pitch (20m VI). Continue up the crack then climb L across the cave to a ledge system (30m V+). Slant up R crossing short walls (V−) and ledges until below point 3038m, about 70m L of a faded yellow rock scar and below a R− facing orange (quartz) corner (150m). Layback the corner to a ledge, then move L over flakes to the base of another crack. Layback this, bold and sustained (45m VI). Continue up the crack above then trend R across several walls and cracks to make a hanging belay on a flake (40m VI). Move back L to gain a hanging flake and climb this, then the chimney that follows, to gain a series of short corners. Climb these to a ledge (45m VI). Move L along some ledges then climb a short wall to belay on an arête (30m IV). Climb down the wall for 15m into the couloir (V+). Reach the ridge below Pt 3038, easily in 45m (III).

DESCENT. Climb down the crest of the ridge to reach the brèche at its base (sections of III plus two abseils near the end). Continue down on the N side to reach the glacier and so regain the bivouac site.

No pitons used and the hardest climbing probably equates to British E2 5C.

(Chris Dale and Simon Yates, 24 August1985, 9h. 800m ED.)

The Pyrenees

Recent hot summers in the Pyrenees, especially on the Spanish side of the frontier, reached a climax in 1985 with the hottest, driest in living memory in the heart of the range. The effect on snowfields and glaciers has been dramatic; they are shrinking at an alarming rate. Those who regularly climb there will have noted the change that is occurring. On the northern slopes of Pic des Posets, for example, the Glacier de La Paül had completely disappeared from the steep valley in 1985, the only ice remaining being the glacial scarf draped immediately below the cliffs of the upper corrie. When Packe climbed here in 1861 the Glacier de Posets (in the E corrie) flowed over the Collado de La Paül and all the way down the valley into the Estos. It has now shrunk back some 2km and 700m vertically into the upper corrie below the E face.

Unless there is a radical change in climate in the near future, it will not be long before the Pyrenees are bereft of ice except in winter.

The Refugio de Estos (1835m) was destroyed by fire in 1979. This popular hut, base for climbs on the N side of Pic des Posets and owned by the Federación Española de Montañismo, has recently been completely rebuilt and enlarged, and was reopened in 1985. A full meals service is available during the season, and there is also a well-equipped kitchen for self cookers. The refugio can now accommodate 180 in its dormitories — which may not be such good news for those who loved the valley's former solitude.

NORWAY

Jotunheim

Galdhøpiggen NW Ridge   Galdhøpiggen (2469m) lies in the Jotunheimen region of central Norway and is the country's highest elevation. An unmade road from Hoft in the Boverdalen reaches the Spiterstulen Lodge due east of the peak. In late winter this road is easily and relatively safely crossed on skis or with snow shoes. Paradoxically the coldest conditions in Norway are found in the south where the mountain ranges are further removed from the coastal effects of the Gulf Stream than those further north.

From the Visdalen just below Spiterstulen at c.1000m follow the river course steeply to reach the base of the gently ascending Styggebreen (glacier). Follow this WNW then W keeping near the R side, round the foot of the NE ridge of Galdhøpiggen to reach the col between the latter and Vesle Galdhøpiggen. About 6½ hrs on snow shoes.

Begin on the E side of the sharp ridge and above its base where a diagonal slabby break leads rightwards towards the crest. Step off a large rock spike and climb a short awkward flake chimney to reach the break. Traverse this on snow, with a delicate step, to reach a short crack leading to slabs. Climb the steep buttress above by icy grooves trending R to a difficult exit onto a snow slope. Follow this easily to a snowy rock barrier. Trend R steeply then return L to reach a belay at the base of a snowy gully just R of the ridge crest. Continue up this avoiding the tower above by making an exit rightwards onto a subsidiary ridge. Follow this back L where the angle is much easier and climb more open ground on the R flank of the crest, avoiding another small tower, for several rope lengths to an abrupt exit on the summit.

Descend easily down the NE ridge in ½ hr.
(Chris Forrest and Lindsay Griffin, late Winter 1985, 3–4h Temperatures of
−17°C, c.250m, 9–10 pitches, Scottish 3–4.)

A number of excellent frozen waterfalls exist fairly close to the Visdalen Road
and were climbed at the same period.
(a) Skautafoss R hand route. Scottish Grade III
          L hand route (icefall). Scottish Grade IV.
(b) Glitrafoss Direct Route. Scottish Grade V/V+.

Romsdal
Forrest and Griffin climbed two routes here at the beginning of May 1985.
Existing guidebook descriptions are somewhat inaccurate and a bit misleading.

Norafjell c928m SE Pillar via the Grunero Route on the 'Great Slab'. (The
1978 Norwegian Route.)
Start at the L edge of the pillar where a steep black slab leads to a small
overhang. Climb the slab and easier rock to a small tree beneath an overhang at
15m (III). Climb over the overhang (IV) and continue up the grey slab to a
belay. Another long slab pitch, first R then L (III+) leads to a ledge and belay.
Continue up easy slabs to reach a steep wall with an obvious diagonal crack
sloping from L to R. A thin crack splits the overhanging wall on the R. Climb
this (VI−) then continue up easy ground to a high boulder-strewn terrace. The
next Buttress is split by a wide V chimney system. Layback the R crack (V−)
move R of a nose for a few metres then climb a roof crack on the L (one move of
VI) to reach the upper section of the chimney. Climb this (IV+ then III) to a
large terrace. Scramble up and across this to the base of the 'Great Slab'.
Towards the L of the slab where it steepens is a huge detached flake. Climb the
steep wall on the L of this (V−) on poor black rock to reach a smallish stance
below the impressive R− slanting crack. Climb the overhanging crack for 25m
(VI). Continue for 20m (V) to a ledge and flake. Follow the crack rightwards
(V) to the top of the slab. Easy scrambling up slabby buttresses interspersed
with vegetated terraces (pitches of II) gives way to a fairly steepish walk to the
Summit Cairn.
  Excellent rock, especially on the difficult pitches. Good protection and belays
throughout with climbing up to British E1. 5b. 5–8 hrs seems a reasonable
estimate.
  (B Ostigard, K Svanemyr and H Doseth, 1978. About 600m Grade VI−.)

Adelsfjell c.940m SE Pillar   The Eastern Slabs Route.
  Although this route provides some fine open slab climbing, the original
description is somewhat indistinct and in parts vastly over-graded. In fact the
hardest pitch may well be the steep crack and corner R of the Dirty Gully/Rake
mentioned in the description (V). No pitches of VI were encountered and the
climb was considered rather disappointing. Five to six hrs seems a reasonable
time for the ascent.
  (J Duff and J Brazinton, 1970. About 700m, Grade IV+/V−.)

KARAKORAM

Chogolungma Basin

Skari Lungma Snow Dome (c.5530m)

The fairly obvious snow dome at the head of the Sgari Byen Gang valley. From a camp on sand next to a stream L of the long rocky ridge which leads to the dome. Follow the ridge to the dome, loose and tedious but no problems until the distinctive black band at the base of the dome. This is steep and the rock is very very loose leading to the snow dome summit. 5½h. Views good. Descent via a long snow couloir to the glacier and follow the L side (heavily crevassed). 3h in descent.

Ron Giddy

'Aspirant Peak'

'Aspirant Peak' (c.6100m) is a rectangular shaped projection from the ridge defining the SE perimeter of the upper basin of the Haramosh glacier. From the Haramosh la, head SE into the basin, keeping well L to avoid the ice-fall, towards the obvious col at the end of the basin. When alongside the near shoulder of 'Aspirant Peak' (L shoulder, facing the ridge), break out L and climb directly up the increasingly steep slope to the foot of the steep summit ridge. Climb this (some Scottish Grade III) to the top. c.6h from the la.

Brendan Murphy

Central Peak at the head of the Boluche glacier (c.5600m)

From medial moraine camp, cross the W arm of the Boluche glacier to the base of a small glacier between the rock peak and the central peak (objective) opposite the camp. Climb up the L bank to the snow plateau (crevassed), cross to the S and get on to the broad easy ridge. Follow it to the snow shoulder and then the short rock ridge to the top. The rock is very loose and crumbly. Good viewpoint.

Ian Haig

Berganchu (c.5800m) — SW of the snout of the Chogolungma)

From the Arandu track on the S side of the Chogolungma glacier, climb to the snowline (2 days). Ascend over the ice dome, descend scree slightly and then ascend a series of snow domes and bowls (crevassed) and finish up the S side of the hogsback of Berganchu, large cornice.

N.B. To climb Sencho (an adjacent peak) another camp is needed between snowline camp and Berganchu. Excellent viewpoint for panorama of Karakoram peaks and Shigar valley.

Ian Haig

Chogolungma to Kerolungma and Arandu via Bolucho la (c.5700m)

The Bolucho la is shown on the Japanese Atlas Map, *The Mountain World — 1956/57*, p.169, Eric Shipton *the Six Mountain Travel Books* pp784–5, and the USA Army Series (1:250000). None of these are much help, the latter is misleading. Not a true pass but rather a name on the map. Unused locally and infrequently by mountaineers. Claims by porters at Arandu to know the pass should be treated with caution.

The Bolucho valley from its junction with the Chogolungma presents no problems. The path soon runs out. Follow the middle of the glacier. At the head of the cirque, towards the true L bank of the glacier and hidden behind a ridge, is a superb campsite on the shores of a small lake, off the ice and invisible from below; no firewood. From here there is a choice between a col above hanging glaciers R of the camp, and a col above an ice-fall and a plateau on the L. Take the left. Descend a short way from the camp across the glacier and follow an ice gully L of the ice-fall. Porters need to be roped up for about 60m. Threat of stones-fall from L. Above the ice-fall cross the plateau diagonally R (heavily crevassed). The parts of this glacier near the enclosing wall are under constant threat of stone-fall. Camp immediately below the col on the glacier (no water or wood). Climb 150m of rotten rock to the top of the col. From the col descend steeply towards the Kerolungma glacier about 300m over rotten rock and scree (porters have to be roped down) traversing R (stone-fall danger) to avoid bergshrund and crevasses. On the glacier cross diagonally to the true L bank to camp (firewood sparse). Follow the ablation valley to a path crossing lateral glaciers to another camp. Cross the main glacier to the R bank and up to the village called San Chu (= clean water). Follow a good path to the confluence of the Kerolungma with the Chogolungma and Arandu. 7 days including one rest day.

Ron Giddy

The Haramosh la   The Haramosh la (4800m on some maps, probably higher) provides a crossing between the Kutwal valley and the Haramosh glacier which is a southern tributary of the Chogolungma glacier. The Haramosh glacier approach is easy angled and uncomplicated but the Kutwal side presents a steep final slope about 2000m high with snow, avalanche runnels and extremely loose rock in the upper section. there is a rock platform campsite at the La which provides a good base for exploring the upper Haramosh basin.

Refer to the Polish map of the Karakoram 1:250000 and to the Japanese atlas maps of the Chogolungma area 1:150000.

From Arandu the stony snout of the Chogolungma glacier is crossed W to join a good path which follows lateral moraines and ablation valleys along the true L bank of the glacier. There are several good campsites along this section and the Bolouche glacier can be reached in two or three porter stages. Camp in the last ablation valley 1.5km before the Bolouche junction rather than the fairly unpleasant Dust Camp at the junction.

Here take to the centre of the glacier at the earliest opportunity or continue along moraines and more ablation valleys to the mouth of the Sgari Byen Gang which is opposite the Chogolungma-Haramosh confluence. Both routes head for a prominent ridge of red moraine and large boulders which issues from the W side of the Haramosh glacier and bends round into the centre of the Chogolungma glacier. Follow this moraine until opposite the serrated rock ridge just short of Cathedral Peak. The delightful Laila camp will be found on a grassy alp below the S end of the serrated ridge and a long way above the glacier (and water!); one stage from the Bolouche glacier.

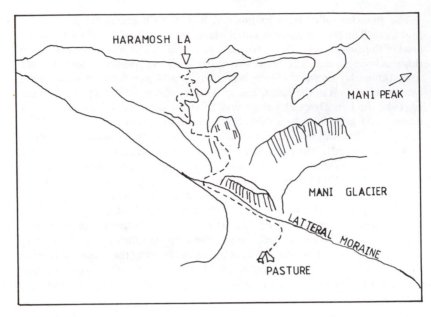

From Laila traverse steep vegetated slopes to rejoin the glacier just above the
ice-fall; in reverse care is needed to find the right point at which to leave the
glacier. A long gentle walk up the centre of the glacier leads through a final
crevassed area to the foot of a rock ridge descending from the N. The
Haramosh la is at the junction of snow and rock; two stages from Laila camp.

The first part of the descent to the Kutwal valley is uninviting. Start about
150m S of the camp platform and zigzag down through loose blocks and scree
terraces until a series of ridges provide a relatively safe descent. (Avalanche
runnels through intervening snow patches.)

Idyllic camping on pastures at the foot of the slope R of the Mani glacier.

The walk out to Sasli can be done in two porter stages by a variety of routes
taking in the villages on the N or S slopes of the Kutwal valley. Paths are good
and the forested area between Kutwal and Kutwal Sar is well worth savouring.

Lyn Noble

Askole to Hispar via the Hispar la   The Hispar-Biafo glacier system is the
longest continuous glacier system in the Karakoram, running for about 100km
in all, with the Hispar la dividing it roughly halfway. There are no real technical
problems on either side of the pass, although route finding on the lower
moraine-covered slopes of the Hispar glacier is difficult, and the going tedious;
the side walls are steep and limit views of the surrounding peaks. The going is
generally easier on the Biafo side, and the sides of the glacier less enclosed,
giving excellent views. The best map appears to be Shipton's 1939 map
published by the Royal Geographical Society.

From Askole to Hispar la is 6 porter stages although it can be done in a
leisurely 5 days. From Askole follow the path up the Braldu for an hour, then

turn NE up to the true R bank of the Biafo glacier, mostly on glacial moraine. Then follow bare ice towards the centre of the glacier and subsequently snow, except for deviations to campsites at the side of the glacier. There seem to be no major crevasse zones. Camp in ablation valleys on the R bank of the glacier, at Namla, Mango and Ho Bluk — good camping, water and firewood. Thereafter camp on snow, near the Sokha la and below the Hispar Pass. Soft snow limits progress after mid morning.

Hispar la to Hispar village is 6 porter stages (3 days in descent). From the pass, descend the upper glacier just R of centre, and follow a spur which avoids most of the crevasses down to the lower glacier. Camp on moraines just short of the Jutmara glacier. Then follow bare ice as far as possible (numerous open crevasses and ice ridges, and progressively encroaching moraine debris; the central river can be very difficult to cross). Take to the hillside on the L bank, to camp at Haigutum just W of the Haigutum glacier. Follow gradually improving herders' tracks, camping below Chandra Chish, before reaching Hispar on the third day. Similar paths on top of the lateral moraine of the R bank can be used also — both routes involve extensive labour in crossing side glaciers.

Steve Town

Askole to Shigar via the Skoro la   The Skoro la (5070m); can be used as a short cut between Skardu and Askole or a small trek in itself. It is best attempted in the months of July and August.

Hidden about 100m below Askole is an ancient intertwining rope bridge stretching for 60m across the Braldu river. Cross this with caution (many porters refuse to cross it with loads).

At Teste village on the other side of the Braldu, ignore the many paths going straight up the steep grassy mountainside. Skirt L round the village for about 1km. Follow a wide and well defined path which zigzags up about 900m to Teste Brook village. Guides can be hired here to show the exact way to the Skoro la.

From Teste Brook follow the only path on the R side of the stream for about 5km to the terminal moraine of 2 small glaciers. Here the path disappears and there are few cairns. Keep to the R edge of the rubble where there is green grass. Good camping.

The Skoro la is the middle of 3 passes at the head of the valley; the glacier up to it is heavily crevassed but safe on its R edge.

From the pass descend a steep rock gully carpeted with ice; care is needed to descend a track tending R which soon fades away into the gully itself. This is descended with caution for around 1200m to the valley. At the bottom of the gully turn L and follow the river down a gorge for about 16km to Shigar (several river crossings). Lifts to Skardu.

Tim Greening

From Chalt to Nomal, via the Daintar pass   The Hunza river is bridged at Chalt, where there is a primitive resthouse. A good jeep track leads up to Das, above the confluence of the Daintar and Bola Das rivers. The jeep track climbs up into the Daintar valley, but stops just above an inconspicuous footbridge, from which a path continues on the N side of the river, to and beyond the village of Daintar.

Below Taling the track re-crosses the river and continues up through the village (which is only occupied during the sowing and harvest seasons). Taling is wrongly marked on the Polish map; it is in fact on the true right bank of the Daintar river. Although there are good campsites near the village, it is advisable to continue up the valley for about 1½ hours, as far as a shepherds' encampment, because of the long day to follow. Above and to the SW of the shepherds' huts, steep wooded slopes are followed by grass, willow scrub and Juniper. Higher still are open scree slopes and moraine which are traversed W, passing below a small glacier. Then a glacier, with a crevassed zone not easy to see until you are in it, is crossed to a shattered ridge of loose rock and slate. This tottering heap, especially precarious near the top, is climbed to reach the pass, a shaly col with snow patches. 5–7 hours. A camp on the col is feasible, if uncomfortable, in order to climb Snow Dome to the SE.

The Daintar pass itself is at 4800m, and the route to it is not obvious from below on the Daintar side. From the opposite direction the line is clearer. Before August, the pass is likely to be snowed up, and there may be avalanche danger.

The descent is straightforward, down scree and snowfields to a good campsite in a grassy but woodless meadow by a stream, on a plateau above the Shani valley. Continuing along the cliff tops, a track is reached which winds its way down steep ground to reach the valley floor. A short day can be ended at Shiobar. The path runs through forest then an open valley to Upper Naltar, and the top end of a jeep track. In August 1985 a bridge below Lower Naltar was under repair, so there was no prospect of mechanised transport at all. Follow the track through a steep gorge to Lower Naltar, and bus to Gilgit. 4–7 days (map *AJ90*, p68).

Margaret Clennett

Book Reviews 1985

Compiled by Geoffrey Templeman

The Shishapangma Expedition
Doug Scott and Alex MacIntyre
Granada, 1984, pp 215 plus appendices (total 322), photos, sketch-maps, £12.95.
This is the account of the British expedition which succeeded in climbing Shishapangma (8012m) (or Gosainthan) in genuinely alpine style by its unexplored SW face at the end of May, 1982. The originator of the expedition, Nick Prescott, had never visited the Himalaya before, and wanted simply to do some mountaineering in Tibet. Permission to attempt the unclimbed face of an 8000m peak was the last thing he had hoped for. The result was that, while Prescott did much of the work which made the expedition possible and played a most unselfish supporting role when it got to the mountain, it turned into quite a different sort of expedition from the one he had intended. The leader, insofar as there was one, now became Doug Scott, and three of the five other members of the party were also climbers with outstanding records in the Himalaya and elsewhere — although one of these had to return home at an early stage for reasons of health. The remaining participant, Elaine Brook, although a climber herself, was invited mainly because of her interest in Tibetan culture, but little or none of this existed in the utterly desolate neighbourhood of their base camp; and she eventually made what must have been a brave decision, to leave the party and travel around in Tibet on her own.

Two acclimatization climbs, amounting to a total of only a few days, preceded the attempt on Shishapangma itself. Nevertheless, the ascent of the SW face, a wall over 2500m high, was achieved with just three bivouacs, plus another which occurred on the descent by a different line. This was clearly a remarkable and very bold achievement. Yet the paradoxical thing about this book is that the account of the climb may well be found one of its least interesting parts. It is difficult, for one thing, to tell how hard the route was technically; the most serious climbing clearly took place on the first day, yet it was possible to accomplish some 1000m of ascent before the party had to bivouac and on the second and third days there was apparently no need to use the rope at all until after the summit had been reached.

More absorbing, in fact, is the whole chaotic story of how the expedition came into existence, how it ever succeeded in getting to Heathrow, how, when it arrived in Peking, and later in Lhasa, it coped with the Chinese bureaucracy and (even more) how the Chinese bureaucracy managed to cope with it, how it ever got to Base Camp, with a few recalcitrant yaks as its sole transport and in spite of a totally obstructive liaison officer, how it survived the various strong tensions and disagreements which kept erupting between different members of the party. All traditional expedition rules seem to have been broken, and most conventions disregarded; indeed, one of the authors writes, admittedly only half seriously, of the party's 'reputation as the worst foreign expedition ever to reach Tibet'. Yet it is the fascination of the story that all this somehow works out successfully, and more or less happily, in the end. Among the expedition's other difficulties was the fact that the party simply could not afford costs of the order normally charged to western expeditions by the Chinese, a situation to which, once the authorities had grasped it, they seem to have reacted with a surprising degree of helpfulness.

The bulk of the text is written by either Doug Scott or Alex MacIntyre (who, sadly, was killed by a falling stone on the S face of Annapurna later in the same year), but occasional short sections are contributed by the other members of the party. This interrupts the narrative's continuity much less than might have been expected. It is clearly the book's intention to give an honest account of the expedition and not to gloss over the quarrels and clashes of personality which occurred, and this is admirable; but both the clashes and the reconciliations which usually followed them tend to become rather tedious and to detract slightly from one's enjoyment of an otherwise very intriguing book.

It is a pity also that there is no List of Illustrations; and the photographs themselves, which are all in monochrome, are not well reproduced. Doug Scott's Appendices, however, are a real contribution, especially I, 'Early Buddhism in Tibet', and (more surprisingly, perhaps) V, 'Expedition Medicine — A Personal View'.

David Cox

The Passage of the Alps
Edward Pyatt
Hale, 1984, pp256, many illustrations and maps, £14.95.
People have been crossing the passes of the Alps for many centuries in a multiplicity of routes and methods. A pass, as the author says in his Introduction, 'can be a trade route, carrying a much-used motor road or motorway, a scenic motor road used mainly by tourists, a saddle with only a path or a mule track or a notch in an ice wall or at a glacier head accessible only to the experienced mountaineer. A passage of a range can further be effected by a tunnel carrying a railway track or a carriageway, by a rack or other assisted adhesion railway, by cableway, or even in the air above the mountains. All will be treated hereafter.' That then is the scope of the book.

The Club's first publication was, of course, *Peaks, Passes and Glaciers*, each being given equal weighting in the title; but in recent years the literature on passes has been very sparse. This book makes up for the lean years as far as the Alps are concerned. The story starts in pre-Roman times with traders and raiders crossing the easier passes, but really gets under way with Hannibal's crossing of — was it the Col de la Traversette? — in 218BC. Although fully documented by de Beer and others, this crossing by foot soldiers, cavalry and elephants remains a fascinating and impressive achievement, always worth reading about.

The story continues via the Romans and their alpine routes, then the Dark Ages, to the building of the great hospices, one of which existed on the Simplon Pass as early as 1235. By the 16th century, travellers are crossing the major passes on tours of the Alps, but the real explosion came about in the'1700s when the Grand Tour really got under way. Further chapters cover the Napoleonic Wars, which in some ways echo Hannibal's campaigns, and the advent of road and rail traffic over and through the chain. The mountaineering side of pass-crossing is covered, and the story is brought up-to-date with the escapes over the mountains in the Second World War and events up to the present.

The illustrations are a feature of the book, and it is interesting to compare the 5-horse postal coach coming down the St Gotthard at full gallop with the acres of parked cars on the Stelvio today. Those horses must have been a wonderful sight!

The book ends with six appendices which list every conceivable pass crossed by road, railway and cableway, plus a selection of walkers' routes and glacier ways.

It does not say on the front endpaper how many books the late Ted Pyatt wrote but he must have been one of the Club's most prolific authors and this last work must count as one of his best. The amount of research needed was obviously enormous and it deserves a place on any Alpine-lover's bookshelf; it is a great pity that we shall see no more from Ted.

G.W.T.

Eric Shipton. The Six Mountain-Travel Books
Intro. Jim Perrin
Diadem/The Mountaineers, 1985, pp800, maps and photos, £16.95

Here is another sumptuous omnibus volume from Diadem Books and, like the Tilman one, how good it is. Shipton's Six Mountain Travel Books was an obvious choice for a successor to their Tilman saga, and how well it too comes over. Like Tilman, Shipton hardly ever changed his style; and like his friend, how versatile he was in his explorations. And yet, in his case, mountainous country was almost always at the heart of his explorations.

But the two men's styles of writing differed. Shipton's descriptions of his travels are full of romance and adventure. Tilman's play down the romantic streak in his nature, which was undoubtedly there, but make up for this by his laconic wit and flair for apt quotations. Of the two Tilman is possibly the better writer; but Shipton the more exciting and readable one for some people, perhaps. And yet I don't know! After all there is nothing much to choose between them. That is why these two volumes of their respective collective works complement each other so well. Surely no-one possessing the Tilman volume will like to be without this Shipton classic too?

Jim Perrin's otherwise interesting introductory biography is marred, at the end, by an intemperate and unfair attack on the old Himalayan Committee over the events of 1952 which not only is offensive but inaccurate over the way in which it deals with the infighting at the RGS over Hunt's election to the leadership on Everest in 1953. Particularly unfortunate, I feel, are his remarks about Claude Elliott's chairmanship of the Mount Everest Committee at that time, based upon the words of one contemporary observer whom he fails to name.

But what an extensive contribution Eric Shipton did make to mountain exploration and its literature! Two of his books I know almost by heart: *Nanda*

Devi and *Upon That Mountain.* The former I like for the sheer excitement of the
adventure; but also because it tells of his party's excursion to the Gangotri
glacier where I happened to have been the year before with Marco Pallis's
expedition. The latter perhaps my favourite, because in it he gives us so much
of his wise mountaineering philosophy. But with regard to the former, it is
quite extraordinary how few people had actually set foot on the Gangotri glacier
before we went there in 1933. Captain J A Hodgson was probably the first
European to do so and that was in the 1820s. It was only the more ardent and
ascetic of the Hindu pilgrims to Gangotri who pressed on to Gaumuck, the
place where the sacred river Ganges emerges from beneath the ice. One of the
important things to have been sorted out in this book is Shipton's explorations
in and around the Gangotri area. Birnie's col has now been properly identified,
as has the peak formerly known as Kunaling.

   Ken Wilson has done an important service for the mountaineering world
with the publication of this book. Research workers will be eternally grateful to
him for his own valuable historical appendix at the end on Shipton's Mountaineering Record. I have been asked, however, to point out an error in this
section, between 1962 and 1964/65 should come: *1963, Chile: Mt Burney and
Tierra del Fuego.* A season has been missed out.

   The publishers are to be congratulated on the nice form in which this most
acceptable book has been produced, printed and illustrated. It is good value for
money, and a worthy successor to their splendid Tilman volume which I
reviewed in the *AJ 89.*

Charles Warren

On Edge — the life and climbs of Henry Barber
Chip Lee
Appalachian M C, 1982, ppxxviii + 292, photos, $14.95.

The Breach. Kilimanjaro and the conquest of self
Rob Taylor
Coward, McCann and Geoghegan, 1981, pp254, photos and drawing, $14.95.
'Hot' Henry Barber has not been fortunate in his biographer. Chip Lee is an
admirer, uncritical to the point of sycophancy. The book started as a college
assignment and Lee's subsequent graduation does nothing for one's faith in
education. He completed the book hurriedly while engaged in other projects,
which may help to explain why the text is often repetitive, sometimes incohe-
rent and occasionally factually wrong. It is also in places incredible. Beery tape
recording sessions with Barber produced an unmanageable mass of information
— oral history which loses something of its heroic quality when imprisoned in
cold print. Paradoxically Lee serves his readers well in so far as he gives,
unintentionally perhaps, a 'warts and all' portrait of his hero.

   Barber emerged in the early 1970s as an outstanding rock climber with a
world-spanning reputation. He had opted out of the urban ratrace to become a
full-time rock climber — he climbed on 325 days in 1973. Unhappily he
substituted another sort of rat-race on mean cliffs rather than the mean streets.
He was intensely competitive and aware of the commercial value of well

publicized success. By concentrating on technical climbing he neglected to develop some of the traditional mountaineering skills and for this he was to pay dearly later. He tried to combine the roles of Superstar and One of the Lads. In this he was not always successful. His dynamism and lack of empathy made it difficult for him to build relationships with other people.

Fate caught up with him on a visit to East Africa with Rob Taylor. The last chapter of the book gives an account of the events before and after the near-fatal accident to Taylor, in what is the biggest mountaineering scandal at least since Maestri's imaginative first ascent of the Torre Egger. Barber by his own account emerges as an incompetent knave. Taylor's account supports this conclusion and labels him liar as well.

Barber put himself in a situation which illustrates the distinction between commercial and professional mountaineering. He had sold his story of the first ascent of Breach Wall before he left the States. Africa has a way of dealing with presumptuous young men. Administrative and communication hassles eroded his limited time. He was psyched by the wilderness. He was too self confident to make effective intellectual preparation for several days on a large and unfamiliar mountain — despite being the guest of the editor of the new guide book (which inconveniently gave details of three previous ascent routes on Breach Wall). His relationship with Taylor was strained and corrosive.

Nevertheless they reached the base of the great icicle which linked the Balletto ice-field and the Diamond glacier before noon on their fourth day on Kilimanjaro. They had avoided the problems of the lower tiers of the wall by traversing onto the ice-field from the Heim glacier. The icicle was rather 'vertical slush' according to Taylor who advised waiting for it to refreeze at night. Barber conceded that it was 'real unstable and dangerous' but pressed for an attempt. After all 'the whole financial success of the trip had come to depend on the climb'! Against his better judgement and stung by Barber's unconcealed contempt Taylor began to climb. At 7am he put in a solid ice peg. A metre or so beyond this he fell. Barber's negligence — Lee's phrase is 'normal brief inattentiveness' — allowed a fall of perhaps 10m onto the ice. Taylor smashed an ankle very messily. Incredibly Barber suggested continuing the climb — there was only about 100m of vertical difficulty to the Diamond glacier and about a kilometre of gently sloping ground to the summit. His claim that this proposal was based on the 'rescue possibilities and nothing more' does not convince me. Taylor insisted on going down.

To their credit they made an effective withdrawal to the snout of the Heim. Having made Taylor comfortable and 48 hours after the accident Barber set off to raise a rescue. Unladen he might have been able to descend the Umbwe route, familiar as their route of ascent, the same day. Instead he decided to traverse at a high level for some 13km across rough and unfamiliar ground in fog, to reach a hut on the tourist route up the mountain. Unladen this too could have been achieved the same day. Barber failed to rise to the demands of the situation. He had been six days on the mountain, four of them at over 4000m though conditions had enforced inactivity from about midday. He had been under stress throughout the trip to Africa. He was exhausted and did not have the hill skills required by the emergency. He was terrified by the prospect of being attacked by a leopard. Above all he lacked the commitment to his companion that would have released the resources he needed. Instead of leaving his gear he burdened himself with the bulk of it, significantly even taking Taylor's camera and film. He found a well marked trail leading to the tourist route but diverted off it descending to the Uweka Huts far below his chosen route. Having spent the night there it took him hours to get back to the traversing route. Incredibly he failed to follow it to the Horombo Hut where there was a wireless — he did not want to deal with any Africans! He rushed down the tourist track, lost it, thrashed about in the bush and did not raise the alarm until delivered to the Park Entrance at 7pm by some missionaries to whom he had been taken by a friendly helpful African. A pathetic performance by any standards, but for a superstar! Small wonder that he preferred to escape to a Houston Sports Convention rather than wait until Taylor was out of danger in hospital.

Back in the US he felt confident enough to call on Taylor's family assuring them that he had seen Rob comfortable and well cared for in hospital.

Taylor describes the hospital in graphic detail. An insanitary, uncaring hell on earth and is understandably bitter at being abandoned there; a bitterness compounded on returning home to find his family had been lied to by Barber.

For much of his book Taylor irritates. Parts are sentimental, parts contrived fantasy. There are trivial errors about mountains which a graduate in geography could have been expected to avoid. He invents a new name for Barber — Harley Warner, which seems to be pointless. Most damning he describes how Barber treats him like dirt on their trip and does not have the self-respect to quit. He pays a high price for his tolerance. Once his ordeal begins he reveals great physical and mental strength. He refuses to succumb to shock. He deals with his own leg, reducing and splinting the fracture thus making a rescue attempt possible. He controls his own descent, secured by Barber but little aided otherwise. Even after five days suffering he is able to help the rescue team take him off the mountain. The journey of self-discovery leads him to a spiritual satisfaction he might never have achieved had the climb been a technical success.

John Temple

Journey after Dawn
Bill Peascod
Cicerone Press, 1985, pp(14) + 174, photos. npq.

It was a tragedy that, so soon after the success of the *Lakeland Rock* television series and the completion of this autobiography, Bill Peascod should die from a heart attack on Cloggy. As we know from the book, he had nearly succumbed to a similar attack several years before, but the intervening years described towards the end of the book, when success as an artist, a happy second marriage and return to his beloved Lake District had all happened, seemed to combine to ensure a happy future, a new dawn indeed.

Bill Peascod was born into a mining family in Cumbria, and describes vividly his introduction to the life of a coalminer at the age of 14, and to the beauty of the fells when he was 17. This occurred after a night shift, when the following morning was so beautiful that he just cycled off through Buttermere, and was hooked from that moment. Many expeditions into the hills followed until, in 1940, he met Bert Beck and formed a partnership which added many new climbs to the guidebooks over the next seven or eight years. Eagle Crag, Buckstone How and others are described in detail.

Following a gradual change from coalmining which led to his being a lecturer in mining, the Lakeland scene suddenly lost Bill Peascod in 1952 when he emigrated to Australia. The next 28 years are not dealt with in great detail, but it was here that his reputation as an artist became established. He had numerous one-man shows, and particularly one in Japan which changed his life, as it was here that he met his second wife.

The final chapters describe his return to the Lakes, establishment of a new home and re-commencement of his climbing on his home ground. His paintings too were now being exhibited in London and, as I said earlier, all seemed set fair.

I found this a delightful book to read. Whilst possibly not of great literary quality, it has a directness and, if you like, a 'homeliness' which ring true and which give an excellent portrait of the author. The photos back up the text and are historically interesting. It can be recommended unreservedly to anyone who has not yet got a copy.

The Great Climbing Adventure
John Barry
Oxford Illustrated Press, 1985, pp4 + 252, maps and colour photos, £8.95.
I have not read any of the other books in the Great Adventure series, such as *The Great Railway Adventure* or *The Great Travelling Adventure*, but I doubt if they could compare with John Barry's tale. And it is a tale, a good old-fashioned adventure yarn which, just incidentally, is also John's climbing life story to date.

It starts with a Royal Marine posting to Singapore in 1969 which, the delights of climbing in Malaya quickly beginning to pall, turned into a mini-expedition to Mt Cook — successful — and then to Menthosa in the Himalaya. Adventures in the Alps and on British rock and ice follow, to end up with his disappointment at having an accident on Gauri Sankar, and a tremendous achievement on the E ridge of Mt Deborah. Stated like that, it may sound just another book of climbing reminiscences, but it is told with a raciness and humour that make it difficult to put down once started. It belongs to a 'Great Adventure' series alright.

Smythe's Mountains, The Climbs of F S Smythe
Harry Calvert
Victor Gollancz, 1985, pp224, maps, diagram & photos £14.95
In this study Professor Calvert reviews the career of Frank Smythe as a mountaineer, deliberately confining himself to the 'character that emerges from the literature'. Only in the first chapter does he touch upon any biographical detail, and only in the last upon the springs and motives of Frank's life. The

resulting sparseness of such material may disappoint some readers. The author obviously regards his subject with great affection and the book is prompted by his wish to repay the debt owed to the pleasure and inspiration he has found in the writings of F S Smythe.

The climbs themselves are divided into 11 chapters in chronological order. Most of them are also described in Smythe's own works, with which this book must inevitably bear comparison. Open any one of Smythe's volumes at random, as I have recently done after a lapse of years, and you will have difficulty in resisting the temptation to read on. One would have liked to be able to say as much for Professor Calvert, but his book contains too many passages in which the details of climbing and topography are piled into a catalogue which can mean little to a reader not himself familiar with the terrain. As a result much of the description makes heavy going. However, all the information about the climbs is there, and compressed into a volume sufficiently small for those prepared and interested to dig it out.

Chapter X, the 'Valley of Flowers', makes the most enjoyable reading. It includes good accounts of Mana Peak, considered by Frank the 'longest, grandest and hardest' of all his mountains; and of Nilgiri Parbat, his 'finest snow and ice peak', of which there is a lovely photograph. On that expedition, too, his mountaineering partnership with Peter Oliver was the 'happiest of his experience'.

The chapters on Everest and Kangchenjunga are not equal to Smythe's own accounts either in descriptive power or information, but that on Kamet brings out very well the conspicuous success achieved by a harmonious party of six Europeans in climbing the highest peak then attained by man. Frank Smythe's leadership and organization were the crux of that success.

The great but controversial climbs with Graham Brown on the S face of Mt Blanc are described in Chapter VI. The account adds little to the much already written. (See especially: 'T Graham Brown — A Footnote to Alpine History' by Lord Tangley. *AJ71*, pp51–57.)

A study of this book will certainly confirm to any reader Smythe's reputation and stature as a mountaineer of the very first rank. His expedition to Kamet; his solo traverse and descent of the Everest N face; his part in the Brenva face climbs and in the first ascent of Longland's route on Clogwyn du'r Arddu — any one of these would put him in such a category.

As a writer he is more difficult to assess, though not as a photographer where he again enters the top flight. Professor Calvert brings out the fact that Frank was the first climber to earn his living, and to need to earn it, by writing about mountains; and in that respect the first of those professionals so firmly established among us today. The appeal of his writings lies especially in their sensitive and lucid prose, untainted by even one of those four-letter words which besmirch today's mountain literature, and bent on telling us all, as none other save perhaps Winthrop Young, of the inner workings and insights of the mountaineer's heart and mind.

One other important point about Frank Smythe, one which this book does not fail to emphasize, was his 'notorious safety' on the mountains. Neither he himself nor any member of a party in his charge (including the Commandos he trained in wartime) ever suffered death or serious injury. As Frank put it in his own words: 'The measure of the worth of mountaineering lies not only in achievement but in the margin of safety over and above that achievement.' Not altogether a popular view today.

Edward Smyth

Wierchy — the Jubilee Issue
Ed W A Wójcik
PTTK, Warsaw/Cracow, 1983, npq.
The 50th volume of *Wierchy* (The Peaks) — beside *Taternik*, which has been published since 1907 — the most important Polish periodical of mountains and mountaineering, appeared in 1983. Its first volume was published in 1923 in Lvov by the local branch of the Polskie Towarzystwo Tatrzańskie (PTT, The Polish Tatra Association) and it was dedicated 'to PTT, as a mother association, on its half-century jubilee'. The Tatra Association was founded as the first Polish tourist society in 1873 in the Austrian — at that time — part of Poland (the word 'Polish' was added in 1918, when the country became independent). But *Wierchy* was not the first journal of PTT. In the years 1876–1920 37 volumes of *Pamiętnik Towarzystwa Tatrzańskiego* (The Tatra Association Memoires) were published.

The content and themes of *Pamiętnik* were criticized a few years before the First World War began. J G Pawlikowski, professor of Dublany Agricultural Academy, a member of the PTT management and chief of Tatra Mountains Preservation Section, wrote in 1913: 'the main part of *Pamiętnik* is full of reports; a few articles are added for decoration only'. In spite of this opinion the last volumes of *Pamiętnik* were published without any changes, in the traditional way. That probably made up J G Pawlikowski's mind to suggest at the meeting of the Lvov branch of PTT, that a new annual, entitled *Our Mountains*, be prepared. The PTT management in Cracow observed this activity and Pawlikowski's project with reserve; they were afraid that the new journal would be a competitor for their *Pamiętnik*, but after 1920 *Pamiętnik* was never published again. So, the members of the PTT had to wait for 3 years for a new yearbook, *Wierchy*. The annual was edited by J G Pawlikowski, A Chybiński — musician, professor of the Lvov and Poznań Universities, R Kordys — lawyer and journalist, pioneer of Polish mountaineering and skiing, and J Zborowski — ethnographer, for many years the director of The Tatra Museum in Zakopane. The next volumes were edited by J G Pawlikowski and W Goetel (later a professor at the Mining Academy in Cracow) and also by W Goetel and J A Szczepański (journalist); we encounter the name of B Romaniszyn once.

Wierchy was very soon accepted by the PTT management in Cracow and by 1933 had become the journal of the whole Association. Before the Second World War 16 volumes of *Wierchy* were published; the first post war (the 17th vol.) dated 1947 was printed in 1948. The articles had mainly been written before the war. On the first pages there were a list of war-casualties — names of Polish scientists, alpinists, skiers, guides and other people whose job and activity were connected with the mountains.

In 1950 The Polish Tatra Association (PTT) and The Polish Touring Association (PTK), est 1906, merged to form The Polish Tatra Tourist Association (PTTK) with management in Warsaw. The Mountains Tourist Committee of PTTK in Cracow became a successor of PTT traditions and it is still the official editor of *Wierchy*.

Immediately after the Second World War *Wierchy* was edited by W Goetel (chief editor), W Krygowski (secretary), B Malachowski, and J A Szczepański. From 1951, for over 25 years, *Wierchy* was edited by W Krygowski together with an editorial board, but its staff changed a few times. The next change took place in 1976 when M Sobolewski (professor at Jagiellonian University) became a chief editor with W A Wójcik as a secretary. Since 1983, after M Sobolewski's death, W A Wójcik has been a chief editor, and J Kolbuszewski (assistant professor at the University of Wroclaw) the chief of the new editorial board.

Wierchy records important facts and notes connected with the mountains and mountaineering around the world, especially the successes of Polish expeditions. The main objects of this yearbook are Polish mountains of course, and very often the nearest countries — Czechoslovakia, Romania, Bulgaria etc. Each volume is divided into three parts. In the first, there are articles, memoirs, scientific and historical notes, biographies, surveys etc. In the second (in the chronicle) we can usually find many chapters such as 'Scientific Research', 'In and near the mountains', 'Mountaineering', 'Rockclimbing in the Tatra Mountains', 'Touring', 'Speleology', 'Mountain rescue', 'Preservation of mountain nature', 'Historical notes' and — of course — 'Report of the Mountain Tourist Committee of PTTK.' Their make-up follows the yearbook tradition. The third part of *Wierchy* is filled by the 'Mountain bibliography' (Polish only) written by K Polak, obituaries and summary in five languages: Russian, English, German, French and Spanish. Many pictures (black and white only), some drawings and map sketches illustrate each annual, and a colour cover has appeared since 1976. Each number has usually over 400 pages and is distributed in 3400–3900 copies. The *Wierchy* yearbook is theoretically sold in bookshops, but practically, because of very small circulation and great demand, it has to be distributed mainly by subscription.

Jerzy W Gajewski

Parque Nacional Huascarán. Ancash-Perú
Jim Bartle
Dai Nippon, Tokyo, 1985, pp 40, 68 colour and 4 black & white photos, 3 sketchmaps, paper, large format. USA$8.
Adventuring in the Andes
Charles Frazier with Donald Secreast
Sierra Club Books, San Francisco, 1985, pp 262, 23 black & white photos, 9 sketchmaps, paper. USA$10.95
Parque Nacional Huascarán is a pictorial complement to the author's own *Trails of the Cordilleras Blanca & Huayhuash* (1981). In large format, 28 x 22cm, it is beautifully illustrated and well balanced with finely reproduced photographs of peaks, unclimbed walls, glaciers, lakes, flowers and highland people. The book

was originally designed to support conservation projects in the Peruvian Andes. Its text (Spanish and English) has therefore a slant on conservation. This second work by Bartle is an excellent composite picture of Peru's most imposing mountain land.

The purpose of the Frazier-Secreast guidebook is to indicate adventures that are possible within the realm of the old Incadom, today the modern nations of Ecuador, Peru and Bolivia. While it is true that some beaches, islands and jungles are also included, the major part of this book deals with the Andean highlands. Of its seven chapters, four cover the three Andean nations, the Galápagos Islands and the Amazonian basin; another, the regional human and natural history and two, with 50pp, the planning and undertaking of trips into the regions described. There are also two glossaries (Spanish, Quechua). Although basically a travel guide, it contains sections on climbing in the volcanoes of Ecuador and of Arequipa, as well as on high altitude pass crossing in the Cordillera Blanca and in the Ausangate area (Cuzco, Peru). But the book's greatest contribution to mountaineering lies in its many pages of excellent advice on solving problems of mountain travel in the central Andes. Information is both exact and practical and will make any other guidebook with the same geographical scope appear incomplete and outdated.

Evelio Echevarría

Modern Rope Techniques in Mountaineering
Bill March
Cicerone Press, 1985, pp 200, diagrams, £3.95 paperback.
This is the third revised edition of Bill March's essential manual, brought up-to-date to include the latest ideas in technique and equipment.

Medicine for Mountaineering
Ed J A Wilkerson
The Mountaineers, 1985, pp 446, diagrams, £8.95 softback.
Mountaineering First Aid
Lentz, Macdonald & Carline
The Mountaineers, 1985, pp 112, diagrams, £3.95 softback.
Both of these issues are also third editions of long-established standard text books on all the medical aspects of mountaineering.

Samivel des Cimes
Editions Hoëbeke, 1985, pp 104, illustrated.
Samivel's mountain illustrations have been known and loved by British climbers for many years, through his books such as *Sous l'oeil des Choucas* and *Contes à Pic*, but this is the first time that a representative selection of his work has been available. It is a beautifully produced art book, almost entirely of illustrations with minimal descriptions plus a bibliography, covering a selection of all his work from 1931 to 1984. Whilst the majority have mountain themes, a few of Samivel's illustrations to classic novels and children's books have been included to give balance. Whilst one or two of the subjects are a trifle 'twee',

there are some beautiful classic illustrations in this selection which can rival the
best in mountain pictures. The book can be obtained from Lionel Hoëbeke at
20, Rue d'Aumale, 75009 Paris 9, at FF175 + FF20 p&p. For the real
enthusiast, there is a limited edition of 100, with an original drawing, for
FF600.

The Glaciers of Equatorial East Africa
Stefan Hastenrath
D Reidel Publishing Co, 1984, pp xxiv + 354, maps, diagrams, photos, etc, npq.
During the last century the Lewis Glacier on Mt Kenya has decreased in
volume by about 75%. Mt Kenya has lost seven out of its 18 glaciers. It seems
probable that the mountain will be deglaciated by the mid 21st century.
Kilimanjaro's ice will last no longer. Only the Ruwenzori, notorious for its
cloud and rain, will retain its ice and that will be much reduced.

Professor Hastenrath has assembled and organized a mass of information and
photographs to provide a framework for his account of his own research. The
bibliography and photographs will be of interest to anyone who has visited the
area or who plans to. (Go now while the glaciers last!) His research methods will
be of assistance to anyone planning an expedition which, for financial reasons
perhaps, has a scientific objective.

He concludes that the dramatic decline of East Africa's glaciers is mainly due
to a reduction in precipitation of about 15%. The grim pictures of famine and
expanding deserts in Africa suggest that this is at least a continent-wide trend.

John Temple

Climbers and Hikers Guide to the World's Mountains
Michael R Kelsey
Kelsey Publishing Co. Available in Great Britain from Cordee
*2nd Edition 1984. pp 800. 380 black and white photographs. 377 maps. £15.95
paperback.*
Michael Kelsey feels, and he is probably right, that he has climbed more
mountains in more geographical regions of the world than anyone else. Almost
all of these trips which appear to flow into a continuum of travel beginning in
1970, have been made solo and include some impressive efforts, notably
(though illegally) reaching over 7400m on Masherbrum and 6000m on Tirich
Mir in 1975.

This book is a culmination of his experience and each individual mountain or
mountain area is given a double page format. The lefthand side details
information on how to get there, usually from the capital city or some major
town to the base of the mountain; weather seasons and useful equipment; some
indication of a trek in the region or an ascent of the peak by its normal route;
the length of time needed for the round trip; best place to buy food; last place to
buy food, get water, etc. Below this lies a black and white print of the peak or
area in question while the righthand page is devoted entirely to a map. The
maps, in every sense, are excellent — the photographs possibly the worst I've
seen in print; I am sure the originals were fine, but the reproduction . . .

Everywhere you have heard of and a good deal that you have not is dealt with in this book and, as one might expect of an author from Utah, the coverage of north, central and southern regions of the Americas is especially detailed.

A book packed with useful information to get one started on the road to some enticing and esoteric corner. A book offering a diversity of ideas together with food for thought to the discerning traveller. Pity about the photographs.

Lindsay Griffin

Expedicion Navarra al Himalaya '79. Dhaulagiri 8172m
Gregorio Arig
Pamplona, 1979, pp 104, photos, maps and diagrams, npq.
Buru Ilhun Lurruntsua. Euskaldurek Everest Mondian
Felipe Uriarte
Elkar, 1981, pp 320, photos and diagrams, npq.
Jannu. Una Primavera del Himalaya
Mari Abrego
Editorial Aramburu, Pamplona, 1983, pp 132, photos, maps and diagrams, npq.
These three books, presented to the Club by Sr Arig, detail the activities of Basque climbers in the Himalaya in recent years — Everest in '74 and '80, Dhaulagiri in '79 and Jannu in '81. All three books are very well produced, with excellent colour photographs, the Jannu volume including what must be one of the most stunning summit photos ever taken. It is only a pity that the double page spread effectively reduces its impact to zero. Whilst two of the books are in Spanish, the Everest volume is in Basque. Although this will make it unreadable to the great majority of members, it still remains one of the best photographic records of the 'normal' route up Everest.

Le Regard Intérieur
Marcelle Durieu-Zappelli
Michel, 1984, pp 72, photos, paperback in French, npq.
A small volume of thoughts on life in general followed by an account of climbs on various alpine peaks in the '50s.

Adamello Vol 1
CAI-TCI
Pericle Sacchi pp 388, maps, drawings and photos.
The title is misleading — it should be 'Adamello Group' — for the principal mountains in the range (Adamello itself, 3554m, and the slightly higher Presanella) are not included and are presumably left to Vol 2. The mountains and passes that do appear (310 of them) are dealt with thoroughly, eg 19 routes up Caré Alto are detailed, and there is a good ski section. The 100 pages of general information are comprehensive, as is usual with this series (*Guida dei Monti d'Italia*) of which this is the 46th volume.

Blackshaw's *Mountaineering* describes this group as 'Interesting mainly for novices or hill walkers' but the present reviewer recalls climbs up to TD grade and plenty of yawning crevasses.

WLR

Derwent Gritstone
Ed Geoff Milburn
BMC, 1985, pp 264, photos — some colour — maps and diagrams, £6.50.
The second volume in the Fourth Series of Peak District Climbs, covering the area from the big favourites in the north — Froggatt, Curbar, Gardoms — via the Cratcliffe groups and Black Rocks to the smaller crags in the south. A worthy successor to the Stanage volume, with reasonable photos and excellent diagrams.

Bibliography of Nepal. List and notes of Japanese Literature
Ed Prof Jiro Kowakita
Nichigai Associates, 1984, pp 10 + 470, photos, diagrams and map, Y9800.
The Japan-Nepal Society has produced this volume to mark the 20th anniversary of the founding of the society. It contains nearly 4000 entries of books, pamphlets and articles published in Japan about Nepal, covering all aspects of life there, politics, science, history, *etc* and including mountaineering. In Japanese.

Speak to the Hills
Ed Hamish Brown & Martyn Berry
Aberdeen University Press, 1985, pp xxx + 530, photos, £14.50.
This is an Anthology of Twentieth Century British and Irish Mountain Poetry, — and what can you say about it other than to urge people to buy a copy? Five hundred and thirty pages of 20th century poems about hills, from the sublime to the ridiculous, from Winthrop Young to Patey (without inferring anything ridiculous in the latter!), from Louis MacNeice to Anon, with a sprinkling by Hamish Brown himself. A marvellous anthology to dip into with many old favourites, but also many that have been culled from club journals and other not easily accessible sources. One's view of anthologies of this kind is often coloured by omissions or inclusions of personal favourites: many years ago I liked a little poem that appeared in Punch entitled 'Guard's Van to Wales', and cut it out to keep in a cuttings file. I did not expect to see it again but — p 16 — it's there!

Les Alpinistes
Yves Ballu
Arthaud, 1984, pp 468, paperback in French, FF98.00.
Yves Ballu has written a history of alpinists and alpinism from the earliest days — Mont Aiguille, 1492, — to the present, based on the lives and exploits of the individuals concerned. The book is, naturally, packed with facts, but is written in a chatty style, including such chapters as an imaginary interview with Mummery. All the major ascents and personalities in the Alps are included and the book includes a geographical list of major peaks in the Alps and Pyrenees with principal first ascents.

Trek the Himalayas
M S Kohli
Air India, nd (1972) pp 4 + 104, maps & illustrations, paperback, npq.
The Himalayas. Playground of the Gods
Vickas, 1983, pp xii + 244, maps and photos, paperback, npq.
In writing *The Himalayas*, Capt Kohli has attempted a trekking guide to the whole range, with chapters on India, Nepal, Pakistan, Bhutan, China and Afghanistan. In each area described, general information on permits, access, *etc*, is given, followed by detailed maps and descriptions of a number of treks in each district. *Trek the Himalayas* is an abbreviated booklet on various trekking routes, complete with adverts for hotels and airlines, written by Capt Kohli in his capacity as Manager for Tourism with Air India.

Medicina de Montana
Eusko Jaurlaritza
Gobierno Vasco, 1984, pp 414, photos and diagrams, paperback, npq.
Numerous papers, in Spanish, on mountain medicine.

Randonées Pédestres dans la Sainte-Baume
Alexis Lucchesi & Daniel Gorgeon
Édisud, 1985, pp 192, maps & photos, npq.
The indefatigable Alexis Lucchesi has sent us the latest in his Édisud guides — the second of the *Guides de Randonnées*. This one is to the Sainte-Baume area and is to the usual high standard. Eighty routes are described and a number of separate maps are included.

Haute Randonnée Alpine.
CAF
Édisud, 1985, pp 192, maps, diagrams & photos, FF60.
A further randonnée guide from Édisud, this time the high level route from Lac Leman to the Mediterranean at Menton, 1000km, in 50 stages, following the frontier between France and Switzerland or Italy.

Le Monoski
Pierre Raisson
Denoël, 1985, pp 142, photos, maps and diagrams, FF140.00.
This is a complete guide to mono-skiing, a cross between skiing and surfing. The author is obviously a keen advocate and gives a complete manual from learning to sit on a chair lift to descending the Vallon de la Meije.

A Chance in a Million? Scottish Avalanches
Bob Barton & Blyth Wright
Scottish Mountaineering Trust, 1985, pp vi + 120, diagrams, paperback, npq.
This book looks at the questions 'Is there an avalanche problem in Scotland?' — 'Where and when?' — 'Can avalanches be avoided?' and 'How can you survive one?' It provides the answers by studying the anatomy of snow structure and avalanche patterns, and relating them to specific happenings.

Advice on improving the odds and on survival and rescue techniques complete a most useful book.

North-East Outcrops of Scotland
Ed D Dinwoodie
Scottish Mountaineering Trust, 1984, pp 284, maps and diagrams, npq.
The three previous editions of this guide were published by the Etchachan Club, and covered only the coastal cliffs. The present edition has been enlarged to cover all sea-cliffs and ou crops north-east of a line from Arbroath to Inverness, but excluding the Cairngorms.

Bergell, Disgrazia, Engadine De Badile à la Bernina
Giuseppe Miotti & Alessandro Gogna.
Denoël, 1985, pp 240, maps, route diagrams, photos — many in colour, npq.
One of the latest issues in the *100 Plus Belles Courses* series which is so popular and of which the Club now has several volumes. (See *AJ89* for list.) This one comes up to the usual high standard and includes classic routes on the Badile, Bernina, Roseg and Disgrazia, among many others.

Le Massif Central
Annick and Serge Mouraret
Denoël, 1985, pp 240, numerous photos, maps and diagrams, npq.
One of the latest issues in the *100 Plus Bells Courses* series features the Massif Central, that vast area stretching from the Puy de Dôme near Clermont-Ferrand in the north, to the hills of the Cevennes and even closer to the Mediterranean in the south. This is a fascinating book, more varied than most in the series, in that the 100 are split up into 40 walks, 6 *passages Aquatiques* in the gorges, 30 rock climbs on the fantastic outcrops and gorges in the area, 7 nordic ski traverses, 7 alpine expeditions and 10 canoe expeditions on the famous rivers in the area such as the Tarn. Quite a mixed bag!

McMurdo Sound Area, Antarctica
Molenaar Maps, 1985, npq.
Not a book but a single folded sheet 'oblique-view pictorial landform map' published by Dee Molenaar in association with the AAC. The front of the sheet gives an excellent pictorial representation of the McMurdo Sound area, whilst the back has a summary guide to the region which itself contains as much information as a small book.

Mountain and Cave Rescue. 1985/86
Mountain Rescue Committee, 1985, pp 40, diagrams, £1.20.
The official handbook of the Mountain Rescue Committee, which not only gives the basic information on first-aid and mountain-craft as applied to safety in mountains, moors and caves, including notes on helicopter rescue, but lists every rescue post and rescue team in Great Britain and Ireland.

Cuadernos de Alpinismo: Chaltel. (Fitzroy)
Pyrenaica/SGIM, 1985, pp 48, numerous photos, maps and diagrams, Ptas 300.
Three years ago, Pyrenaica issued the first of their mountain monographs on
Aconcagua; this is the second on the Fitzroy group. The photographs and
general production are excellent and, as well as giving general descriptions and
histories of the various peaks, detailed topo-diagrams are included for each
major route. Text in Spanish.

A Guide to Trekking in Nepal
Stephen Bezruchka
Cordée, 1985, pp 352, numerous maps and photos, paperback, £8.95.
This is the fifth revised and enlarged edition of this excellent guide to Nepal,
covering not only the major trekking routes in the country but virtually all
information that any traveller there will want to know. Indispensible for anyone
going to Nepal.

Randonnées Pédestres dans la Sainte-Victoire
Alexis Lucchesi and Daniel Gorgeon
Édisud, 1985, pp 156, maps, diagrams and photos, paperback. FF50.00.
This is the third in the series of footpath guides edited and, in some cases,
written by Alexis Lucchesi, the two previous being to the Luberon and Sainte-
Baume. The area covered in this volume is not only Montagne de Sainte-
Victoire itself, but also Montagne de Concors and Montagne des Ubacs to the
north.

Back on the Piste
Barry Waters
Queen Anne Press, 1985, pp 96, drawings, £5.95.
This successor volume to *Piste Again* is rightly sub-titled 'A Guide to Armchair
Skiing'. With chapter headings such as 'Selecting your Stube' and 'Chalet-
maids and Chalet-mates' you know what to expect. If you want advice on how
to go skiing without actually setting foot on the slopes, this is the book for you.

**Northwest Discovery. The Stevens and Van Trump Ascent of Mount
Rainier, August 1870**
Northwest Press, 1985, pp 86, photos and diagrams, $5.00.
This is, in fact, the March 1985 issue (Vol 6, No 26) of the Journal of
Northwest History and Natural History. In it the editor, Harry Majors, puts
forward a detailed case to substantiate his argument that the actual summit was
not reached by Stevens and Van Trump in August 1870, but by Emmons and
Wilson two months later. A fascinating piece of detective work for anyone
interested in mountaineering history.

Dhaulagiri I. 8167m
*1985, pp 211 + xiv of English summary, maps, photos, diagrams and drawings,
npq.*
An account, in Japanese, of the Academic Alpine Club of Hokkaido Expedition

which climbed Dhaulagiri I in mid-winter 1982, with a brief summary in English at the end.

Sentiers de l'Himalaya
Bernard Germain and Henri Heidsiech
Limited edition, 1981, not paginated, drawings, npq.
This is a limited edition published by the authors of poems and thoughts of Nepal by Bernard Germain and drawings by Henri Heidsiech. It is accompanied by a typescript English translation by Linda Collinge, without the drawings.

Le Jeu de la Montagne et du Hasard
Anne Sauvy
Montalba, 1985, pp 284, paperback, FF75.00.
This is Anne Sauvy's second collection of mountain short stories — the first *Les Flammes de Pierre* having received excellent reviews on the Continent. In view of the fact that many of these 16 stories have their origin in mountaineering history, it is a pity that a British publisher cannot be found to allow their appreciation by a wider audience.

Rock Climbs: Glen Nevis and the Lochaber Outcrops
Ed Grindley
Cicerone Press, 1985, pp 130, photos, maps and route diagrams, £5.95.
Scrambles in Lochaber
Noel Williams
Cicerone Press, 1985, pp 152, photos and route diagrams, £5.95.
Two further guides from Cicerone, the first covering the modern crags in the area, the main ones being the Polldubh Crags in Glen Nevis, but also including Loch Leven-side, the Steall area, Glenfinnan and the Mallaig area amongst others. The second covers the major scrambling lines on mountains from Ben Cruachan in the south to the Saddle in the north, and out east to Ben Alder. Ben Nevis and Glencoe are, of course, in the middle, and such favourites as the Aonach Eagach ridge should make this a good seller.

Climber's Guide to the Cairngorms
Allen Fyffe and Andrew Nisbet
Scottish Mountaineering Trust, 1985, pp 364, photo-topos, route diagrams, npq.
Described as 'A Comprehensive Guide', this fourth volume in the new series of SMC guides is exactly that, covering in one volume what was previously intended to be five, and bringing up-to-date climbs which, in most cases, have not seen the light of day in book form for more than ten years. The authors give full descriptions for good routes and a summary of poorer ones, which can however be pursued in notes of further reading in the comprehensive first ascent list.

Turkestan Solo
Ella Maillart
Century Publishing, 1985, pp 334, maps, £4.95.
Scrambles Amongst the Alps
Edward Whymper
Century Publishing, 1985, pp xxii + 410, map and illustrations, £4.95.
Two paperback reprints in the excellent Century Travellers series, the first, telling of Ella Maillart's travels in 1932 from Moscow through Russian Turkestan, has an introduction by Julia Keay. *Scrambles* is the revised 1936 edition with extracts from Whymper's diaries, and has an introduction by Ronald Clark.

Skakki Podkrakowskie
Krzysztof Baran & Tomasz Opozda
PTTK, Warsaw/Cracow. Vol 1, 1983, pp 120, maps and topo diagrams. Vol 2, 1985, pp 112, maps and topo diagrams. Each volume zl 130.
These are the first two volumes of rock-climbing guides to outcrops in the Cracow area of Poland, produced by the Mountain Tourism Committee of the PTTK. Whilst comparatively few members will be able to follow the text, the numerous clear maps and diagrams will enable anyone who finds themselves in the area to follow the routes.

The Mountains of Wales
Terry Marsh
Hodder and Stoughton, 1985, pp 256, map and photos, npq.
Following his *The Summits of Snowdonia*, the author has now produced this walker's guide to the 600m summits of Wales which, personally, I think is a big improvement on his earlier book. The grouping is geographical from north to south, the photos are generally excellent, and the descriptions clear and concise.

Lakeland Rock
Adrian Bailey
Weidenfeld & Nicolson, 1985, pp 144, photos, many in colour, £5.95 paperback.
Most people will, I suspect, agree that the series on TV last year under the above title was the best rock-climbing TV-viewing yet, and there are probably more home videos still showing the series again as well! This, subtitled 'Classic Climbs with Chris Bonington' is the book of the film (we have not had the LP yet) and gives, in addition to written versions of the five climbs we saw, a layman's introduction to climbing in the Lakes, and Bonington's own climb 'Holy Ghost', which we did not see. The book is written by a layman, chiefly for laymen, but despite a few gaffes and a marked difficulty in distinguishing between Pete Whillance and Dave Armstrong, it is attractively produced, with some excellent photos. It is certainly worth having for the last, marvellous, portraits of Bill Peascod and Don Whillans.

Rock Climbing in Ireland
Ed Calvin Torrans and Dawson Stelfox
Constable, 1984, pp 260, maps, photos and photo-diagrams, £6.50.
Constable are doing a service to hill lovers everywhere in their uniform series of
walking and climbing guides. This current volume lists over 300 rock climbs in
all parts of Ireland and is a companion to the general hill guide by Joss Lynam.
Probably of greater use than the selective guides to the Lakes, etc., as the
average climber from Britain is more interested in having a selection presented
to him for a quick holiday visit.

Compte-Rendu de l'Expédition Française 1985 — Aconcagua — 7000m
Jean Paul Chassagne
Expedition report, maps, diagrams, and photo.
Report of the French expedition which climbed the SE pillar to the junction
with the 1954 French S face route.

A Delicate Wilderness. The Photography of Elliott Barnes. 1905–1914
Edward Cavell
Altitude Publishing, Whyte Foundation, 1983, pp 48, photos, npq.
Legacy in Ice. The Vaux Family and the Canadian Alps
Edward Cavell
Whyte Foundation, 1983, pp 100, photos, npq.
Two volumes of turn-of-the-century photographs. Elliott Barnes was a roman-
tic character who tried to establish his family in the wilderness close to Banff,
and in so doing took a number of excellent photographs. The Vaux family were
well-to-do Quakers who spent much time in the Banff area studying and
photographing the glaciers and mountains and making a number of ascents.
This book includes the scrapbook of the Glacier House Hotel, with a number of
entries by AC and ACC members.

Classic Walks of the World
Ed Walt Unsworth
Oxford Illustrated Press, 1985, pp 160, maps, photos — many in colour, £14.95.
This book, together with one on France, starts a projected 'Classic Walks'
series. Seventeen walks are included, the editor being responsible for six — the
Pennine Way, Tour de Mont Blanc, Via delle Bocchette, Kilimanjaro, Lidder
Valley in India and the Everest Trek. Dennis Kemp and Al Rouse deal with
Annapurna and Concordia, respectively, John Hunt with the Pindos Mountains, Hamish Brown with the Cordillera Blanca and Kev Reynolds with the
Pyrenees, among other interesting routes. One of the more unusual is Christopher McCooey's traverse of the North Alps in Japan, which shows that the
coverage justifies the 'world' title. The format is to give a description of each
route split into days' marches, with a sketch map and a mixture of black and
white and colour photos. It is essentially an armchair book for day-dreaming
about future possibilities.

Yorkshire Limestone
Ed Graham Desroy
YMC, 1985, pp 320, colour photos, maps and diagrams, npq.
The very much up-to-date and long-awaited guide to Yorkshire Limestone, including, of course, the major crags of Malham, Gordale and Kilnsey, as well as a host of less-frequented ones. Written with humour, and with excellent diagrams and photographs, the guide is one that the YMC can be proud of.

Yi Un Sang. Epic Poet
Jenifer Payne, 1985, photos, paperback in English and French, npq.
A small booklet of poems by Yi Un Sang, who was President of the Korean Alpine Club. Arising from an idea expressed at the UIAA Assembly at Seoul, it is hoped that this will be the first of a series of booklets on mountain poets.

Kamtschatka
Wadim Gippenrejter
VEB F A Brockhaus Verlag, 1985, pp 48 of German text and 91 colour photos, npq.
German edition of a Russian colour-plate book on the volcanoes, geysers, flora and fauna of the remote Kamtschatka peninsula at the far eastern end of the Russian continent. One of the very few books available on this fascinating area.

UIAA/Mountain Medicine Data Centre
Members should be aware that the Library has a folder of medical information leaflets on altitude sickness, frostbite, first aid kits, oedema, oxygen kits, etc, published by the Mountain Medicine Data Centre.

In Memoriam

Compiled by Geoffrey Templeman
Plates 88–93

The Alpine Club Obituary	*Year of Election*
Dawa Tenzing	Hon 1970
André Contamine	Hon ACG 1970
Donald Desbrow Whillans	{ 1967
	Hon ACG 1976
Rev Edward John Whiteley	1962
Gaston Rébuffat	1965
Roger Baxter-Jones	ACG 1976
Mrs Cicely M Williams	LAC 1942
Michael John Harber	1981
Michael George Geddes	ACG 1979
Edward Hamilton Marriott	1932
Edward Charles Pyatt	1957
John C Case	1926
Richard Cook	1959
Noel Peskett	1960

The 1985 In Memoriam list includes the names of a number of members who were notable mountaineers, none more so than Don Whillans. In view of Don's importance to British mountaineering I have included a number of tributes to him in an effort to build up a composite picture.

Sadly, notification of the last three names on the list came too late in the year to do anything about them, but John Atherton kindly sent me sufficient details on 'Charles' Marriott for a brief note to be included here. Full obituaries of each will appear next year.

Happily, to balance this, full tributes are included here for all those who were missed last year, namely Tom Brocklebank, John Bingham, Henry Booth, Mrs Evelyn Carr, Mrs Margaret Milsom and Hugh Pasteur.

One or two of the notices included here appeared in similar form in climbing magazines during 1985 — I make no apology for this as both the contributors and I thought them the best available, and the more magazines and journals there are, the harder it is to find original contributions!

Finally, my thanks again to the many who have helped.

Thomas Anthony Brocklebank 1908–1984

I know Tom's many friends would wish rather more about him to be added to the brief obituary which appeared in the *AJ90*. It was, I think, inevitable that he was best known as an oarsman. He stroked Cambridge to victory three times, stroked the winning crew at the Grand at Henley twice, and very nearly won the Diamond Sculls against the then finest sculler in the world. I think he

89   *André Contamine.*

88   *Sirdar Dawa Tenzing in the Yalung valley during the first ascent of Kangchenjunga, 1955 — then 53 years old.*

90 Don Whillans.

91   *Gaston Rebuffat.*

93   E. H. 'Charles' Marriot.

92   Roger Baxter-Jones.

was undoubtedly the greatest Cambridge oarsman in the period between the wars, light in weight but of immense stamina and determination. But when Tom was chosen to join the 1933 Everest team, he was very much more than 'the inevitable rowing Blue' whom Sandy Irvine had prefigured in 1924.

He had served a thorough and very well taught apprenticeship in guideless alpine climbing in the 1920s and early 1930s, thanks to the Eton masters who used to take promising pupils to their own favourite mountain districts, and put them through their paces. It was a terrible shock to Tom when three of them, Powell, Howson and Slater were killed on the Piz Roseg just when Tom was returning from Everest.

Competition to be chosen for Everest in those days was understandably fierce, but let there be no doubt that Tom Brocklebank more than amply justified his selection in 1933. As Hugh Ruttledge wrote in his book, 'His one idea was to be of service, and he never departed from it, now or later.' Tom Brocklebank, and his companion and friend 'Ferdie' Crawford were the essential link between the leading climbers and the support party of older and necessary specialists down the line. Hugh Ruttledge pays informed tribute to what they contributed. 'Crawford and Brocklebank began their great series of six ascents and descents of the North Col slopes, revictualling Camp IV and escorting porters. This hard work made the position of the higher party secure . . . the fact that it was carried through without a single accident reflects the greatest credit on both the skill and the energy of the pair.'

In the lost days between 21 and 25 May when through a conjunction of human failure and unlucky weather we forfeited our one real chance of reaching the top of Everest, Tom and Ferdie were putting in an immense amount of work, escorting parties up and down the North Col and keeping the long line of steps in order. When Camp V had temporarily to be abandoned, Ferdie and Tom were a tower of strength at the top of the ladder (over the ice bulge) roping up the invalid porters and lowering each man to one or other of us below. It was when the going got tough that Tom and Ferdie justified their selection to join the 1933 party.

Tom's contribution to Ruttledge's book, *Everest 1933*, included anonymously as 'Extracts from an Everest Diary', is one of the most human and revealing sections of the book. None of us who has been there will forget Tom's vignette of the great pyramid of town, monastery, fort of Shekar Dzong, wantonly destroyed by the Red Guards in the 1950s — 'The rock looks immense in the moonlight, and the clusters of ghostly white buildings seem to stand upon nothing at all.' Or there is the coming of spring to climbers chilled, frozen and debilitated by weeks of storm and cold on the upper mountain. 'When we reached Camp I, we found little tufts of grass all around the camp. The change is really wonderful; six weeks ago Jack and I were hacking through a young glacier with ice-axes to get water here.' Tom goes on to Base Camp, and tells, 'I slept in a Whymper tent all to myself, and it felt like bedding down in the nave of St Paul's.'

Our friendship, nurtured on Everest, continued, to my good fortune, till Tom's death in 1984, the night before Jane and he were coming to stay with us. After 1933, we did not climb much again together, but the occasions when we did perhaps have a certain significance. Between VE day and VJ day there were naturally readjustments in the plans for the future of the armed services. There was a real risk that the lessons learnt in fighting through mountain terrain might be lost in lowland Europe. I believe that the laboriously fashioned Mountain Division was employed in capturing the infamous island of Walcheren, which is mostly below sea-level. There seemed also a risk that the commando units might be scrapped in the expected rundown which peace would bring. Tom Brocklebank had, as an Eton beak and housemaster, organised two very successful mountain training courses for members of school cadet corps, in Snowdonia in 1944 and 1945. This gave us a certain leverage, and Tom recruited me to visit Leo Amery, a Cabinet Minister but also, most appropriately, a former President of the Alpine Club.

At the India Office, Amery listened sympathetically to our plans for the official and continued blessing on mountain training. It is not for me to say what degrees of results we can possibly claim. The facts are that the Commandos survived, mountain training gradually blossomed into the Mountain Leadership Training Board, the Outward Bound Schools grew and flourished, and bit by bit Adventure Centres emerged from encouragement by local education authorities and voluntary organisation, a long time before royal endorsement was gratefully received in the Duke of Edinburgh's Award Scheme. In these linked developments, Tom Brocklebank played an early and influential part, and many who do not know of this have cause to be grateful to him.

Tom was pre-eminently a Preux Chevalier, fortuned by birth, looks, talents. But he gave back far more than he received, and it is not only mountaineers who have cause to be grateful to him.

Jack Longland

Anthony Rawlinson and Alec Malcolm write:
Tom Brocklebank was a modern language master at Eton from 1936 to 1959, and a housemaster from 1946 to 1959, when he retired because of failing health. At Eton he is remembered as an aesthete rather than an athlete, but he was a highly successful rowing coach, and an intensely compassionate if sometimes moody housemaster.

He took part in parties of Masters and Old Boys which assembled at the Old Royal Hotel, Capel Curig, or at Pen-y-Gwryd, in the late 1920s and early 1930s.

John Sutton Martin Bingham 1908-1984
John Bingham was introduced to climbing while at Eton by the well-known Eton master and mountaineer, John Hills, climbing at first in the Lake District. At Oxford he was an active member of the OUMC, becoming, in due course, secretary of the club. Over a relatively brief period he climbed extensively in the Alps, also in Corsica, the Lake District and Scotland, climbing, often guideless, many of the better known Alpine peaks. However, soon after leaving Oxford, he became a land agent, a factor in a firm of which he, in due course, became senior partner and his climbing career ended.

William Younger

Tom Peacocke writes:
John Bingham was my contemporary at Oxford. He was Hon Sec and then President of the OUMC. I climbed with him in the Forno and Bernina Districts in 1929 on an OUMC meet. I also climbed with him on another OUMC meet in North Wales in 1931. He was a very good rock climber, but not so keen on ice and snow. He led six of us up the Holly Tree Wall which in 1931 was considered extremely difficult. Of course we were all wearing nailed boots. I know little about his Alpine ascents except that he climbed the Zmuttgrat in 1929.

I always found him a very pleasant companion though he did not suffer fools gladly.

Alec Malcolm writes:
John Bingham went up to Oxford where he became President of the OUMC and took a leading part in organising several club meets in the Alps. He then got a job as a land agent in Scotland. He joined the Black Watch as a Territorial and was made prisoner with the Highland Division at St Valéry. After the war he returned to Scotland and eventually set up his own firm of estate agents in Inverness.

He was a contemporary of Tom Brocklebank at Eton in his early days and took part with him in parties of Masters and Old Boys at the old Royal Hotel, Capel Curig, and at Pen-y-Gwryd, in the late 1920s and early 1930s, where they learnt the basics of rock-climbing.

Henry Booth d.1984

I first met Henry Booth at Oxford in, I think, 1920 or 1921 where he joined the Mountaineering Club which I had revived. His family owned the Booth Steamship Co at Liverpool.

In 1922 he attended meets of the OUMC at Pen-y-Gwryd in January and at Easter, and then at the end of June joined my parents and myself at Pralognan in the Tarentaise. With a porter, my father, Henry and I went to the Felix Faure hut, and Henry and I prospected the route up the Grande Casse. We were well trained by *Badminton* then. Next day, without the porter, we climbed the mountain and I remember cutting a lot of steps up snow in excellent condition. My father went back to my mother at Pralognan, but Henry and I left the Felix Faure hut and on the following day he and I went up a lonely glen and over the Col de la Laisse till we found a lovely campsite (I had a small tent with me that season) just below the Grande Motte, which we climbed the next day before going down to Val d'Isère. That week the same party climbed the Tsanteleina and the Grande Sassiere. Henry was also on the OUMC meet later that year, when we all went over to the Victor Emmanuel hut, and he was in my party on the Grand Paradiso.

Henry was elected to the Club in 1923, when he had a long season in the Alps, and I remember that he joined one or two of the Alpine Meets I ran in the later 1920s, but I fear I lost touch with him later on and never met him again.

Herbert Carr

Mrs Evelyn Dorothy Carr 1900–1984

Evelyn Ritchie, with her sister Brenda, was already an experienced rock climber with several seasons in the Lake District when, a classics student at St Hilda's Hall, she met her future husband, Herbert Carr whom she married in 1927, at an OUMC lecture. In 1925 he introduced her to the Alps and from then until the outbreak of war she climbed in the Alps every season achieving an impressive record of first class climbs, many of which she led, in addition to her climbs in Wales, the Lakes, Scotland and Skye. She resumed alpine climbing after the war but injuries sustained from a rock fall while she was leading near the top of the Trifthorn limited her later alpine visits to moderate glacier excursions. Sadly, the last few years of her life were under the shadow of a progressively disabling illness. We extend our sympathy to Herbert Carr and his daughter.

Frank Solari

Mrs Marjorie G Milsom d.1984

Marjorie Milsom's first Alpine season was in 1930 and her last in 1938; she never climbed after her marriage to Maurice, an unrepentant non-climber. She joined the Ladies' Alpine Club in 1934, served on the committee from 1937–9, had two spells as Editor and was President in 1950. Her presence at meetings and dinners (and she came often) always added to the friendliness and life of the evening. She was diffident in showing holiday slides not connected with climbing, but the few she did show were a delight to see and her commentary a model of brevity and point. Her earlier black and white photographs were very good.

Marjorie climbed in the Alps in 1930, 1933, 1935, 1936, 1937 and 1938, often with G R Speaker and usually in Switzerland. The Engelhorner made a favourite centre. Her last season in 1938 included the Obergabelhorn S face with a new direct finish, and the Matterhorn Traverse, up the Zmutt ridge and down the Italian. She was for a time a member of the Fell & Rock Club and walked and climbed in the Lakes, Scotland and North Wales.

After Oxford she worked for a time with the Woolfs at the Hogarth Press. Virginia, she found delightful but sometimes disconcerting: she liked to settle down to write in the Packing Room, oblivious to the confusion as people edged round her. Marjorie was Illustrations Editor to *The Listener* from 1936–45. She had three novels published; one went into a second edition.

I got to know Marjorie and Maurice well through the lucky chance of staying on after a Skye Meet. They also had a day in hand and we spent it together and became friends. We were never again in the hills together but met often. They were delightful hosts and guests. Marjorie had many interests; she was a good pianist and enjoyed painting.

The Ladies' Alpine Club owed far more to Marjorie than her brief record suggests and she kept alive her interest in the Club and afterwards in the Alpine Club until her death. She must have been good company in the mountains and it is sad that there is no one to report on this at first hand.

Margaret Darvall

Hugh William Pasteur 1899–1984

Hugh Pasteur inherited his love of mountains from his father Charles and grandfather Henri, and from the family's origins in Geneva, from where his grandfather moved to England in the 1860s. The writers of their obituaries in this journal used words which serve as well as any to describe the attitude to mountains which Hugh inherited. Alfred Wills wrote of Henri Pasteur, 'he was one of the best types of the true lovers of mountains, belonging to a class of which, as well as its great mountaineers and discoverers, the club may well be proud; of men whose souls are permeated by the beauty and grandeur and glory of the mountains and whose lives and characters are more or less moulded by their wholesome and invigorating influences', (AJ24). W B Carslake wrote of Charles Pasteur, 'he was indeed a mountain lover in the widest sense of that term . . . for him mountains became old friends', (AJ60).

The first entries in Hugh's diaries are of col walks on family holidays from 1910–13. After the war he was in the Alps most years between 1920 and 1936. At first there were the regular family holidays, when he and his brother Mits were introduced to Alpine climbing by their father, usually climbing with guides. Hugh's fourth climb in his first season was a traverse of the Matterhorn, up the Hornli and down the Italian ridge.

He acquired new climbing companions who joined these parties in the early '20s, notably Bill Carslake and Leslie Letts. In 1923–25, when he was working as an engineer at Winterthur, he was able to climb at week-ends in some of the lower ranges, sometimes with his life-long Swiss friend Robert Etienne. There were two excellent years in 1927 and 1928 when he climbed with Carslake and Letts without guide from Belalp, Zinal and Grindlewald. The best season must have been 1928 when in 12 days they climbed the Rosenhorn-Mittelhorn-Wetterhorn, Monch, Jungfrau, Eiger, Dreieckhorn, Weisse Nollen, Finster-aarhorn and Schreckhorn. This trio would also visit North Wales and the Lake District for rock-climbing weekends.

He became a member of the Club in 1924. His diaries are good on the record of routes and times, but without much comment apart from unusual incidents. Quite a number of these seem to concern either objects or people falling into crevasses; in 1911 it was Auntie Mary's butter dish on a walk from Breuil to Gressoney; in 1957 it was an English bishop near the Loetschenlücke.

He married in 1929, and his wife Grisell shared his love of mountains, accompanying him on the easier ascents in the early years, and on pass walks in later years. The family holidays continued in the '30s, the favoured areas, as in the '20s, being in the Valais, particularly Saas-Fee and Arolla. He only made two brief visits to Chamonix.

In 1948 he introduced his children to the Alps at Champex, taking them up some manageable peaks, with his father, then 78, also present, still walking up to the passes with measured rhythm and restraining the youthful enthusiasm to rush the pace. Hugh's last real climb was the Wildspitze in 1954 with myself. Then valleys and passes replaced peaks and glaciers, with favourite places for later walking holidays being Binntal and Fafleralp, usually with his brother Mark in the party. He lived long enough to see one of his grandsons, a fifth generation, show great promise as a climber.

His other interests were music, gardening and above all the family. Music was a pervasive influence and joy in his life, and he was a very competent pianist and accompanist. He inherited music, married into it, and passed it on. He was a successful and knowledgeable gardener, developing the garden of the family home at Fairseat in Kent, where he lived for just short of 50 years, and where he died peacefully. His favourites in the garden were rhododendrons and azaleas, and a pine imported from Arolla. There was a small corner for gentians and he was an expert with fruit. Almost his whole working life was spent with the old established firm of refrigeration engineers J and E Hall of Dartford. After the second war his successful work on the export side took him to many countries, from which came many life-long friendships.

He was never happier than when he was with a family party, whether of his immediate family, the wider family in England, which was very close-knit, or a visit from the Swiss branch, with which he maintained continuous links. Again the words of Alfred Wills of Henri Pasteur are remarkably fitting to describe how Hugh would receive family and friends at home: 'his manners were distinguished, with something of the courtly grace of an older time. There was a heartiness and sincerity about his welcome of a friend of which many must have felt the charm.'

David Pasteur

Dawa Tenzing d.1985

I first met Dawa Tenzing in Darjeeling in 1955 when he was our Sirdar on the Kangchenjunga expedition. He was already a close friend of Charles Evans, having been with him on Himalayan trips for the previous three years. In 1952 and 1953 he was his personal Sherpa and then in 1954 he was Sirdar to the New Zealand Barun Expedition. On Everest in 1953 he had twice carried loads to the South Col without oxygen and, from the South Col, had been fit and ready to go further if need be. He was tall for a Sherpa and had a more serious expression than most. In spite of his long service with climbing expeditions he had insisted on retaining the old traditions and still wore the pigtail and ear-ring.

When he joined us it was difficult to judge his age but he was thought to be between 45 and 50. We all took to him immediately and it was clear to us that here was an exceptional person.

Weeks later when Norman Hardie and I returned from the summit of Kangch to Camp 5 in a state of extreme exhaustion, it was those two great mountaineers Charles Evans and Dawa Tenzing who came up to meet us, sustain us and help us down. Although Dawa was putting on a brave face it was clear that he was preoccupied. We were soon to learn that news had just been passed up by radio from Base Camp that one of our young Sherpas, Pemi Dorje, had died. He had literally worked himself to death by exhausting himself on a carry to Camp 5 a few days earlier. He had never recovered from this. For Dawa Tenzing his death was a great grief for he was Pemi Dorje's brother-in-law. The loss of other close relatives on the mountains was something that was to dog Dawa over the years.

After the 1955 expedition Dawa came over to England for a while and many will remember the impact he and his young companion Chanjup made as they travelled around staying and climbing with their many friends — Dawa dignified and slightly aloof. He went on to be Sirdar of many expeditions after that, rapidly becoming one of the greatest Sirdars of all time. He was made an Honorary Member of the Club in 1970.

I next saw Dawa in 1976 when I passed through Duweche on the way to Everest Base Camp. I was very shocked at the state in which I found him. He had just lost his second wife and a son had been killed in a climbing accident and on top of this he had been accused of stealing items from a Monastery — something that was quite unthinkable to anyone who knew Dawa. It was later established that this was a false accusation resulting from a family feud but it had been taken very seriously by Dawa with the result that he had given all his money to the Monks in the hope that this would help him. He was drinking heavily. He was living in very poor conditions, and was being looked after, as best she could, by Nisha Llamu, his second daughter. He was convinced he had only months to live and wanted me to take his medals, including his Tiger Badge, and his papers and hand them to the Alpine Club. This would clearly have been an admission of defeat and so I persuaded him that he should hold on to his valuables and said that the Club would be honoured to have them in due course. His court case came up while we were there. I had in my team a very well connected Major of the Royal Nepalese Army who could see at once that such accusations against Dawa were clearly false and he insisted on remaining in the valley and going to court to speak for him. They both came up to Base Camp some days later with the good news that Dawa had been acquitted of the false accusations. This was to be a turning point for him. He flatly refused to accept charity but we did persuade him that he was more than deserving of a small pension after all he had done for so many expeditions and this we started to pay him straight away. Many of his friends contributed to this and it enabled him to live his last years free of financial worry. It was paid to him monthly through the Doctor at Kunde Hospital to ensure that he went there for regular medical checks.

I next saw him two years later. He had regained his strength and was much more his old self. He was married again, to a fine old lady who was the sister of Tashi, another of our Kangchenjunga Sherpas and an old friend of Dawa. Tashi had later gained fame by being the first to the summit of Nuptse with Dennis Davis. I stayed a few days with Dawa that year and late one evening, as he was reminiscing about his early expeditions, he said how he remembered as a boy being with a British Expedition to Everest which went into Tibet via Darjeeling and then two Sahibs disappeared high on the mountain. He was of course talking about Mallory and Irvine in 1924. Had he been even 17 then, Charles Evans' estimate that he was between 45 and 50 at the time of Kangchenjunga would have been correct and he would now be in his early 70s — very old for a Sherpa. But he now went from strength to strength. He moved house because he was convinced that the old one had brought him bad luck and settled down with his third wife to enjoy his late years. Those who met him during this time found again the same old Dawa — full of fun and always ready for a chat about the past and a drink or two.

Tragedy struck in February 1983 when he was on a pilgrimage to India with his wife and a large party of Sherpas from Solo Kumbu. The bus in which they were returning to Kathmandu left the road and plunged into a ravine. Thirty two people were killed and 20 others, including Dawa and his wife, were badly injured and admitted to hospital in Kathmandu. Another of his sons was killed in the accident. Dawa and his wife recovered sufficiently to be flown back to Solo Khumbu but Dawa was never to recover fully. He also lost all his valuables in the accident.

He spent his last years in Thyangboche, sometimes in the Monastery or with his daughter Nisha Llamu who was now married and ran a tea house just opposite. His right arm was paralysed and he seldom got up from his bed. He died peacefully in his sleep on 3 February 1985. He must then have been about 78. His wife had been to visit him a few days before.

And so we mourn the loss of a distinguished Honorary Member who had been a close friend to many of us. Dawa Tenzing will be long remembered as the great Sherpa personality of his era. With the changing times in which we live, there can never be another like him.

H R A Streather

André Contamine 1919–1985
André Contamine, Honorary Member of the ACG since 1970, died of a heart attack in March 1985, shortly after retiring from his work at the École Nationale de Ski et Alpinisme (ENSA), Chamonix-Mt Blanc. A man of remarkable warmth, he was always ready to help and advise climbers from his enormous knowledge of the Mt Blanc area, and will be missed sadly by his many British mountaineering friends.

He came from the mountain village of Feissons-sur-Salins in the Tarentaise. When in Paris, he met up with Pierre Allain and subsequently returned to the mountains with the Chasseurs Alpins, participating in the Liberation of the Tarentaise. As a guide he was an instructor at the École Militaire de Haute Montagne; and joined ENSA when it first started.

His influence on French mountaineering and skiing technical development through ENSA was continuous and profound. He climbed and ski'd with flair and technical perfection; and was able to demonstrate and teach his methods with great clarity and precision. He made a particular contribution in ice-climbing, with brilliant use of crampons on steep ground, exemplified by his direct ascent of the N face of the Triolet (with Louis Lachenal) and with the development of the *Super Conta* ice-axe, regarded by many as the best of its time. But he was also an initiator of the new French skiing methods of the 1950s and 1960s, particularly by *avalement*, seeming to float down through deep snow, like a bird on the wing. He became chief mountaineering instructor at the École, before eventually taking national responsibility there for French ski-teaching and for the training of mountain guides.

I first met him at the Envers des Aiguilles hut in 1952, when Roger Chorley, Geoff Sutton and I were there to do the East Ridge of the Dent du Crocodile. He was very helpful about the line of the route; and it was only much later that I heard that he had himself done this climb, together with the E ridge of the Plan, and most of the E face of the Caiman, in a single morning, before a storm stopped them!

He did about 1500 routes, including most of the major ascents of the time, with notable speed. Of these, about 40 were first ascents, and there is many a *voie Contamine*, for instance on the S face of the Dru or the W face of the Petites Jorasses, characterized by a directness and elegance of line and, originally, by a lack of pegs, which is still apparently found quite hard even 30 or more years later. He was very much tied to the École; but managed to get away for the successful Mustagh Tower expedition in 1956, with Paragot, Magnone and Keller.

He also made a major contribution to mountain rescue techniques, being responsible for the training of mountain rescue teams. He took part in about 60 rescues himself, sometimes at considerable personal risk. He was an early believer in the potential of the helicopter for rescues, demonstrating this by landing on the summit of Mt Blanc in 1955.

A fine photographer, he won first prize at the Trento Film Festival.

His links with British climbers were particularly close; and he was a regular source of information for the ACG Bulletin. He was a correspondent for Ken Wilson's *Mountain,* and provided reports of outstanding value and completeness about developments in the Mont Blanc group at a time of many major new winter ascents and solo climbs. His article 'Mont Blanc — the massif and its climbs' in *Mountain 43* gives an indication of his immense knowledge of the area.

Sad to say, he and his wife, Raymonde, suffered a deep personal tragedy with the loss of their daughter Arielle, French junior ice-skating champion, in a road accident.

I last ski'd with him at Lognan in January 1985, when he and Raymonde were about to undertake a post-retirement tour to Ceylon. It was a happy renewal of my earlier ski-ing with him, with André still demonstrating that skiing fluency, and love and enthusiasm for the mountains, combined with his customary humility and sense of humour, for which I will always remember him.

Alan Blackshaw

Donald Desbrow Whillans 1933–1985

Oration read at Don Whillans's funeral 9 August 1985.

Donald Desbrow Whillans was without fear of contradiction the most outstanding all-round mountaineer this country has ever produced. He excelled in every type of terrain; on the cliffs of Britain, in the Alps, in Patagonia with its ferocious storms, in the Andes, but most significantly in the Himalaya. The fact that he survived an unparalleled series of adventures and ascents in the mountains is perhaps the most telling aspect of his career, for only a climber with the soundest of judgement could have been so successful. But Don was more than a mountaineer; he was a legend, an institution beloved by us all.

Don was born in Salford in 1933 and therefore grew up in an era of austerity during and immediately after the last war. He hailed from a typical Northern city background, with a grimy environment, but a close-knit community which bred self-reliance, determination and a no frills attitude to life. Don when young was an excellent gymnast, and a fine rugby player. On leaving school he had to work hard at physically demanding tasks and eventually became an apprentice plumber. Young climbers today train to develop strength and fitness but in Don's youth it was physical employment which did this. He developed great strength, stamina and fitness beyond the norm.

He started hill walking and this naturally led on to rock climbing and a chance meeting at the Roaches with Joe Brown. This led on to the formation of The Rock & Ice Club in 1951, and the stage was set for one of the most outstanding partnerships in British climbing history. From the beginning Don carved out his own niche, for his first ascents were like his own character: bold, uncompromising and fierce, and were not often repeated in those days of almost unprotected leads. First on gritstone, then on the bigger rock walls in North Wales, the Lake District and Scotland, his brilliant climbs such as Sloth, Slanting Slab, Extol and Centurion presented a challenge that few could follow. Surrounded by an elite of young climbers, the halcyon days of the 1950s led Don to become an alpinist, and before the decade was over he was undoubtedly the country's leading figure in this field. First there were the early climbs with Joe Brown such as the third ascent of the W face of the Dru, and the first ascent of the W face of the Blatière in 1954, followed by many other great climbs which included early repeats in the Dolomites and the Mont Blanc Range, routes such as the Bonatti Pillar and the Cima Su Alto, culminating with an outstanding first ascent in 1961 of the Central Pillar of Freney. On this he shared the honours with Christian Bonington.

In 1957 Don visited the Himalaya for the first time, as a member of the Masherbrum expedition. This was a most significant experience for him, and although he failed narrowly to make the first ascent of this most difficult peak, and his close friend Bob Downes died of oedema, from that moment onwards he was held in the thrall of the highest mountains of the world. He could have continued easily to make rich pickings at home, in our homeland hills, but more and more the hostile environment and the adventures to be found amongst the remotest ranges was where he wished to place his effort.

Don married early and was extremely fortunate in his life-long partner Audrey, who stood by him through the vicissitudes of some of the greatest mountaineering adventures of all time. In Patagonia on the Aiguille Poincenot, on the Towers of Paine, in attempting the Torre Egger, in the Andes on Huandoy, in the jungle of Roraima, but most of all on the many Himalayan expeditions he undertook. On Trivor, on Gauri Sankar, the South Face of Annapurna — that trend setting, most technically difficult face route of its era — followed by the subsequent attempts on the SW face of Everest, and the many later expeditions such as Shivling and Broad Peak.

Don was an innovator as a climber, but he also brought to other aspects of our sport an enquiring mind. He developed the first modern type of sit-harness, which up until recently was the most widely used piece of equipment of its type in the world. He designed an alpine rucksack, a type of piton hammer (the famous Whammer!), he was forced to consider the inadequacy of tents in the high winds of Patagonia and came up with the idea on the Paine Expedition of 1962 of a 'Box'. These were later to prove a key factor in the successful Himalayan climbs of the early 1970s. Through all this Don remained unaffected by success or failure, and truly Kipling's poem 'If' could have been written about and for him. For triumph and disaster were equally well met by him; he hated cant, could not stand bull and remained true to his own standards and beliefs throughout his life.

Don kept up his friendships and in touch with his roots. He maintained an amazing network of contacts throughout the world, and in this country he must have had a resting place, a stop-over spot in almost every town and city in the UK. He worked at this, he kept up his communications and the roar of a motor bike engine outside the front door usually signalled the arrival of the Villain.

He had the physique of a pocket Hercules, and the stories of his brushes with bullies and over-zealous authoritarian persons will probably grow each year in their telling. Usually he managed to come out on top, and as in all the best stories the bullies were routed, though occasionally he did come out the worse, and on those occasions was not frightened of telling the story against himself.

Don was scrupulously honest about his climbing, and always saw things in a black and white fashion. He could not understand any reason why it should not be so. You described the climb exactly as you achieved it, with no frills into the bargain. In his earlier days he was possessed of such drive, physical energy and strength that lesser mortals such as myself found him a forbidding companion whilst waiting to climb, but once under way then you knew he would either get you to the top or organise a retreat in good order. And quite the opposite of his behaviour socially at that time, his patience with younger climbers was surprising. He once held my rope for half a day whilst I battled with Slape Direct. Retreat was not to be countenanced, he intended for me to be successful and if need be he would throw me to the top.

Over the years he mellowed. He continued with his interest in motorbikes and he was a safe and competent rider. In the Rock and Ice era he often managed to keep his bike up on its wheels when every other rider dropped their bikes due to bad road conditions. He became interested in matters as diverse as sky diving, sub aqua and breeding tropical fish.

My fondest recent memory of him was of his teaching my small girl to somersault — despite his accumulated girth — across our living-room carpet. The hardest of hard men, he had beneath the surface a soft centre. He retained throughout a common touch, and a quick wit. When young this could be hurtful, but over the years it was refined and it became loving, and it became a legend. He was truly a master of repartee and the one-liner. His lectures of his climbs were always punctuated by laughter, and this made him popular with a younger audience, and he became a cult figure although they had never seen him climbing at his peak.

We shall miss him so much, especially those of us who are no longer in the first flush of youth. For to know that Don was out there, indestructible and engaged in some titanic struggle or keeping his end up in the pub brought comfort. For it was a signal to us that you could just keep on trucking throughout this life.

The ancient Greeks believed that as long as you were being talked or written about, as long as you were in somebody's thoughts somewhere, you had immortality. Don is assured of this, for his memorials are his climbs and deeds. They will be talked about, written about as long as human beings set forth to take up the challenge set by our physical environment. In the telling they may become exaggerated, they may even become distorted. But we will be able to say truthfully to the enquiry 'What was Don Whillans really like?' simply the answer 'Absolutely unique.' I doubt if any of us will ever see his like again.

Dennis Gray

Chris Bonington writes:
He was wearing a cloth cap, was small, lean and obviously very hard. I recognised him immediately, and felt an excitement that was akin to awe. In 1958, Whillans and Brown were undisputed stars; many of their routes were unrepeated and their best climbs were at a standard on their own, considerably harder than anything that anyone else could put up. They had dominated the scene for a period of ten years, but in an age that today seems almost prehistoric, when there was no popular climbing media and climbing tales were passed haphazardly by word of mouth, their achievements and the activities of the Rock and Ice, inevitably, were embellished in the telling.

Hamish MacInnes and I, with the two Austrian climbers Walter Phillip (of Phillip Flamm fame) and Richard Blach, were bivvied on the Rognon below the Drus, about to attempt its SW Pillar. At the time it was the chief Alpine test piece and had only had four ascents, none of them British. Don Whillans and Paul Ross also wanted to try it out. On our first bivouac a crisis occurred when Hamish was hit on the head by a falling stone. We did not want to retreat, having just witnessed thousands of tons of rock, that had broken away from the Flammes de Pierres, go crashing down the gully we had climbed that morning. I do not think I could have got Hamish, in his concussed state, up that climb, and it was in this kind of crisis that Don came into his own. He hauled Hamish up the rest of the SW Pillar, looked after him and encouraged him over the next three days as we worked our way up and over the Pillar.

It was on the SW Pillar that I discovered that Don was much more than a superb climber and allround mountaineer. If things were going to get rough, you could not be with a better partner. He was totally dependable, never flapped and maintained a dry sense of humour that somehow helped keep the situation in perspective.

We spent the summers of 1961 and '62 laying siege to the North Wall of the Eiger, spending over a month in '61, living on £20 loaned us by John Streetley, waiting for the face to come into condition. We went onto it three times that summer but the conditions were never right, either too much snow, too much stone-fall or unsettled weather. Each time we returned to our tent and a diet of potatoes and eggs. Sharing a tent with Don was a matter of constant manoeuvre. He did not believe in cooking, washing up or doing any of the day-to-day chores. I was equally lazy and we would go for hours without cooking, each trying to wear the other down. Don usually won, commenting, 'The trouble with you Chris is that you're greedier than I am.' He was right.

He had been brought up in a hard school, and would often say, 'I'll meet anyone half-way.' This could make for a difficult relationship because it meant that his friends had to go slightly more than half-way to make the whole thing work.

In '61, we finally abandoned our Eiger vigil to go over to Chamonix to attempt the Central Pillar of Freney. We climbed it with Ian Clough and Jan Djugloz, hotly pursued by a Franco-Italian team comprising Desmaison, Julien, Poulet Villard and Piussi. It was the finest climb that I suspect any of us had ever climbed before or since. Don led most of the key section of the 'Chandelle', having one of his very few leader falls in trying to get into the overhanging chimney near the top, climbing free about 7m above his last piton runner. All I could see were his legs kicking against the rock 15m above me.

'I'm coming off, Chris.'

There was a long pause — not even a man as hard as Whillans resigns himself to falling. I hunched over my belay, wondering what the impact would be, whether his pegs would stay in. A mass of flailing arms and legs shot down towards me, the rope came tight with a sudden, but not over-violent jerk, and I found myself looking up into Don's face. He was hanging upside down a metre or so out from me, suspended from one of his pegs. He had fallen around 15m.

'I've lost me bloody 'at.'

He spun round a second time and the dreadful realisation came.

'Me fags were in the 'at.'

He was not worried that all our money was stuffed into his hat as well.

We raced back to the Eiger shortly after completing the Central Pillar, this time reaching the Swallow's Nest Bivouac, just beyond the Hinterstoisser Traverse, but the weather was unsettled, the stones whistling down even in the early morning, and we turned back. Our decision-making on the mountain was very easy. We thought along the same lines. It was a partnership, but Don was the senior partner, in age and experience, through the sheer force of his personality and his excellent, intuitive mountain judgement.

We spent the summer of '62 in the Alps with the Eiger once again our main objective. This time we had Don's bike, which we drove all the way up the narrow path to Alpiglen to find that the face was streaming in water. We went off to climb the W face of the Aiguille Noire de Peuterey, and then once again back to the Eiger. This time we reached the foot of the Second Ice-Field, were about to turn back because of stone fall, when some Swiss guides caught us up to tell us that two of our compatriots were in trouble at the other end of the Ice-Field. One of them, Barry Brewster, fell to his death, but we were able to bring Brian Nally back across the ice-field amongst a bombardment of stone-fall. It was certainly the most frightening thing that I have ever done and it was Don's totally cool, proficient presence that helped make it feasible.

I shall always be a little sad, even guilty, that circumstances dictated that we did not climb the North Wall of the Eiger together. Don had had to return to England earlier than I, the weather was perfect and I went for it with Ian Clough. It undoubtedly created a strain in our relationship; it was almost a repeat of the odd chances that had given his climbing partners better breaks than he had experienced — the way that Joe Brown had been to the top of

Kangchenjunga and the Mustagh Tower, when Don had given his all on Masherbrum and Trivor, but had not made it.

We went to Patagonia in the Autumn of 1962 to attempt the Central Tower of Paine. Throughout the earlier part of the expedition we tacitly avoided each other, climbing with other partners. It developed into a siege against the winds and weather which was compounded by the arrival of an Italian team determined to go for the same objective. It was Don who conceived our secret weapon, the first ever Whillans Box, prefabricated from timber and a tarpaulin found round Base Camp. It showed a practical strategic ingenuity that amounted to genius. It meant that pairs could take turns in sitting out the storms just below the Central Tower itself.

We were back at base camp one night when Don and I happened to go out for a pee at the same time. We stood looking at high cloud scudding across the moonlit sky. We looked at each other.

'You know Don, we've avoided each other up to now — I think we'd best get together.'

'Aye, I've been thinking along the same lines myself.'

A few days later we climbed the Central Tower of Paine a day in front of the Italians.

Except for a short spell on the Eiger Direct in 1966, we did not climb together again until 1969. I was planning the Annapurna South Face Expedition and Don was an obvious, indeed vital, choice but he seemed to have lost interest in British and even Alpine climbing; he had undoubtedly put on weight, not to the magnificent proportions of recent years, but he certainly was not as fit as he had been in the early sixties. We went winter climbing together in Scotland with Tom Patey and after an abortive attempt on Surgeon's Gully, did the first winter ascent of the Great Gully of Ardgour. Don had taken his time on the way up, was content to let Tom and myself lead the first two pitches, but at the foot of the third, an ice encrusted chimney that was uncomfortably wide, he said:

'It's my turn.' And he moved up it without any kind of protection with a complete certainty. I found it desperate to follow. He had lost none of his genius.

On the S face of Annapurna Don's forthright, single-minded approach undoubtedly complemented my own leadership style. His work out in front with Dougal Haston, culminating in their push to the summit, was a magnificent piece of mountaineering in the face of deteriorating weather.

It was a delight to climb with Don again in the *Lakeland Rock* television series shown in April 1985, when we repeated Dovedale Groove, the route he and Joe Brown had pioneered in 1952 (it was ten years before it was repeated). We had had our differences in the past, but we had also had some of the finest climbing together that either of us had ever had. No doubt both of us had mellowed with time and it was good to share a rope once again, to be at the receiving end of that shrewd, sharp, yet essentially kind, humour. Don had grown with the years, in every sense of the word, to be the best loved personality in British climbing. It is a reputation that will stand the test of time. He was both one of Britain's greatest climbers and characters.

Harry Sales writes:

Don Whillans was a splendid man. I use the word advisedly: if in doubt consult the OED, ignoring meaning 1. which is wide of the mark for Don. His splendour lay in his climbing and mountaineering achievements about which I am not competent to write. Fortunately others have done so, both here and in the many other mountaineering journals, at his memorial day and, even in verse, here at the Club.

I, like so many others, knew him better as a mere human. His toughness and potential aggressiveness masked one of the most kindly and loyal personalities. Again I use my words advisedly because not only did he decry the modern tendency to push oneself to the exclusion of others but he put his principles into practice throughout his life, caring for and seeking to sustain the lives of others in the direst of situations. Instances of this are legend.

He had the reputation for not suffering fools gladly: see, for example, Ronnie Wathen's poem if you can get a copy. But foolishness does not equate to not being a hard man: Don was equally at home with ordinary mortals like myself. He used to visit us when we were using that splendid house of Su and John Fowler at Sennen Cove, he happily enjoying all our facilities and we delighting in his company. Whillans stories are countless but now I cannot resist telling my own, which I properly refrained from using when we paid tribute to him at the Club, thus intriguing the President.

Don had been watching an old film on television of the murderer who was pursued everywhere, even into his bath, by the severed hand of his victim. The next morning he, Don, with a drinking friend, sauntered across from the Lands End Hotel to the rocks at the top of the Long Climb up the Hotel Buttress. By sheer coincidence Derek Walker, his daughter Jane and I were on that climb and I led through that last, easy pitch. My hand appeared on the final rock as Don approached and with horror he staggered back with the words, indelibly printed on my memory: 'Eee, there's an 'and 'ere.' Then, with a profound sigh of relief, 'Ooh, it's 'Arry's.'

Other stories are stronger, more sardonic or scathing. That of Chris, about the German climbers, is one of the best. The one about the noise in the Alpine hut is more succinct. What they all have in common is that they show that Don was never at a loss for words and that the words, though few and laconic, were always right for the occasion.

But this was just one part of his personality. He in the round, figuratively and literally, was a delight and a man one can be proud to have known.

John Barry writes:

I last saw Don Whillans at a rock'n'roll competition. He was the judge, taking his duties with great mock-seriousness, up on the stage and rolling his bones with the best of them. And the best of them were mostly 30 years his junior, which did not seem to matter to anyone. That was one of the things that always struck me about the man; how it was he bestrode generations, commanding instant attention, quick respect, no matter what age the audience; or who they were; or from where they came. When Whillans was doing the talking (and he usually was), others, all others, listened.

I saw that often, and wondered at it: Buxton conferences, Kendal film festivals, Alpine Club symposiums, lectures, bars — anywhere where climbers gathered. When he spoke they, great and small, young and old, tyro and tiger — they listened; and, as often as not, they learned. He was awesome — literally — and gave every impression that he enjoyed being it. Not that he exploited it particularly, but he was clearly at home before an audience. Which was just as well since that was where we all wanted him — before us.

I did not know him well (we all knew of him), but he seemed to be all we wanted, all we needed; some-time master of all the mountaineering games we play, a star in every climbing theatre.

In a way that is difficult to put a finger on, he was funny, very funny. I heard him say quite ordinary things that spoken by you or me would have met with stony silence. Uttered by Whillans the same few words had audiences falling about. His wit was acerbic, pithy, northern (or so northerners like to think). We, the audience, laughed or listened as he bid. He had a gift that is given to few. He could stand gravitas and levity side by side, word by word, so that laughter was succeeded by reflection; a happy knack that made him the most oft-quoted man in modern mountaineering.

He was special, perhaps unique, without peer or successor; recognised as king where there is no recognised kingdom; an image that will survive our iconomachy.

He died in his sleep, a good enough way to go and a tribute to his own judgement as a mountaineer. (On one of his retreats from the North Face of the Eiger, he passed two Japanese heading resolutely through the storm towards the mountain. 'Up, always upwards', they said. 'You may be going up mate but a lot 'igher than you think', Whillans warned.)

He was short, lean and mean when he began. At the end he was the short, fat, funny man who we all took seriously, partly because few dared not to, partly because he could squeeze more neat wisdom into the wit of one sentence than most of us manage in a lifetime.

There will be a rather bigger than average gap at tomorrow's festivals, conferences, symposiums and shindigs. Yes, and at the rock'n'roll competitions too.

Phil Bartlett writes:
'Dear Phil,
Many thanks for your letter re AJ article. I think that an article along the lines you suggest would not be out of place; I would write it from a personal viewpoint, that way it wouldn't be "heavy" in the way of attempting to tell anyone else how they should be doing things. Should have plenty of time to do it while I sit about in the Karakoram with Doug Scott this summer.
    Cheers the noo,
        Don.
PS "Taking Stock" seems a good title.'

I received this letter from Don Whillans some time before he died. The subject I had in mind is well indicated by the title the article was to carry — 'Taking Stock'.

Freedom is an unreasonable business; we go to the mountains to find it, but if a climber has talent and ambition it is forever threatening to slip away. Problems of sponsorship, of the media, of the subsequent pressures to 'get to the top', put decisions on a new level and can make a travesty of 'The Freedom of the Hills'. It is tempting to suppose that with regard to climbing in the greater ranges these problems are today greater than they have ever been before, though that must be arguable. What is not arguable is that Don Whillans was seen by the mountaineering fraternity as the man 'in charge' *par excellence*, one man who still had his freedom and made his own decisions. In this he had no peer, indeed, no equal. His climbing achievement was outstanding but his importance was much more than that. He was felt to represent a psychological achievement which was difficult to define yet clearly recognisable by everybody. Jim Curran referred in a recent obituary to his participation in the recent AC/ACG Himalayan Climbing Symposium and the effect his words had on all present. He was accepted as the man with the wise answers.

And when a journal editor wanted to commission an article with the title 'Taking Stock', not just of the writer's own career but of the whole state of mountaineering, there was absolutely no question of whom he would want to write it.

'Life is meeting' as John Hunt says, and so is mountaineering in large part. This issue of the AJ contains a number of appreciations by people who knew Whillans. But amongst the rest of us there is still an enormous feeling of regret. In terms of his insight and good sense Whillans was regarded as public property; and amongst all post-war mountaineers it is perhaps Whillans whom one most regrets not having met.

Edward John Whiteley, 1929–1984

John Whiteley started climbing as an undergraduate at Cambridge in 1952 with a group at King's which held regular meets in North Wales and the Lakes, and he first climbed in the Alps with members of this group in 1952. He became a member of the Club in 1962 after further seasons in the Alps in 1959, 1960 and 1961. In 1955 he was ordained in the Church of England. He first worked in an industrial parish on Teesside, and then for seven years was Chaplain of Marlborough College. After a further period of ministry on Teesside, he became Chaplain of Bishop Wordsworth's School, Salisbury. It was here that he was working when he died unexpectedly in January 1984 from a tumour on the brain.

In the early years Richard Morgan and myself were among his most regular climbing companions. He was a competent rather than an adventurous climber who appreciated the whole experience that mountains could offer. He was a delightful and stimulating companion, an excellent organizer, and completely unselfish and generous in all he did. As chaplain and teacher he introduced many boys at Marlborough and Salisbury to the hills in this country, and there were also school expeditions to the Alps on more than one occasion. As one who lived his life to the full and gave so much to all with whom he came into contact, he will be greatly missed.

David Pasteur

Gaston Rébuffat 1921–1985

Gaston Rébuffat, who died in Paris on 31st May after a long illness at the age of 64, was one of the outstanding French mountaineers who came to prominence at the end of the war. Following his first major Alpine climb, the N face of the Grandes Jorasses by the Walker Spur in 1941, he proceeded to acquire an international reputation by climbing many routes which were, in their day, in the first order of difficulty; his fame was enhanced through his books, lectures and films.

Gaston was born in Marseilles in 1921 and spent his boyhood in Provence. Throughout his life he retained the distinctive drawl of a Marseillais. Although his subsequent profession as a guide and his lecture tours took him far afield, he never lost his love for the Midi and, in later years, he spent a part of every winter with his family at their apartment in Cannes.

It was in Provence, on the limestone pinnacles of the Calanques, towering above the Mediterranean, that Gaston made his début as a climber. His description of his feelings on that occasion will find an echo in the memories of many mountaineers:

'Nous allons en silence. Au fond de moi-même je sens une joie, mais aussi un pincement de coeur. A ce jour-là, je n'avais jamais été encordé.'

His first Alpine climb, the traverse of the Barre des Écrins at the age of 17 was for him, as it was for myself at the same age, a revelation; there and then he resolved to make climbing his life and livelihood. At the early age of 21 he obtained his professional Guide's certificate and became, successively, an instructor at the École d'Alpinisme (later to be enlarged as the École de Ski et d'Alpinisme) and at the École Militaire de Haute Montagne.

Then came fame through his part, with two other Chamonix guides: Louis Lachenal and Lionel Terray, as a member of Maurice Herzog's triumphant expedition to Annapurna in 1950, which achieved the first ascent of an 8000m peak. Gaston's performance in escorting down the mountain the summit pair in a storm, both of them badly frostbitten and suffering from exposure after spending a night in a crevasse, was nothing short of heroic.

It was at that time, while serving with the Allied forces at Fontainebleau, that I first met Gaston at Chamonix. In the following few years we often climbed together, setting off from his châlet 'La Dy' above the town. Some of our climbs: on the Peuterey Ridge, the Ryan-Lochmatter ridge on the Plan and an abortive ascent of Mont Blanc on skis, were dogged or frustrated by bad weather. But to Gaston it never seemed to matter. For him, being with a companion on a mountain was enough. What mattered was, in his own words:

'L'amitié de deux êtres pour le meilleur et pour le pire.'

He was just as happy about the minor climbs which he, with my wife and myself, also did together, on the granite needles of the Clochers-Clochetons on the Brévent, and even on the sandstone boulders in the Forest of Fontainebleau. The summit was of far less importance than friendship on the steep places of the earth. For myself there was also the delight, as well as the lessons to be learnt, from watching Gaston's lithe agility, as he moved with relaxed elegance up vertical rock, or traversed a tilted ice face on his crampon points.

He was an obvious contact for supplying equipment from French firms for the 1953 Everest expedition. I recall that our 'Duvet' clothing, ice axes and crampons, *inter alia*, were obtained through his good offices.

Gaston was a gifted writer in the romantic tradition. Every mountain experience was for him: 'comme la première fois'; his books reflect this approach to his subject. It set quite a problem for myself and Wilfrid Noyce, who translated his first book *Étoiles et Tempêtes*, in which he recorded his experiences on six great north face climbs in the Alps, published in 1955. His other works included *Du mont Blanc a L'Himalaya* in the same year, and two instructional books: *Neige et Roc* and *Glace, Neige et Roc*, published in 1959 and 1970.

With Maurice Baquet and others as climbing companions and Georges Tairraz as photographer, he made a number of successful films, one of which *Étoiles et Tempêtes* was awarded the Grand Prix at the International Festival at Trento in 1958.

I counted myself privileged to have been invited by him to take part in another film, in which he recalled climbs with some of his many clients and companions over the years of his service as a member of the Compagnie des Guides de Chamonix; he wanted me to re-enact, with him, my own climbs on the Barre des Écrins which had been the source of his own inspiration for a lifetime. Prudence, and the excuse of other engagements dictated otherwise, but I retain a lingering regret that I did not avail of this last chance to climb with one of the leading mountaineers of my times; and, more important, with a valued friend who placed the meeting of men in relation to mountains, way beyond the creation of records and the pursuit of prowess.

John Hunt

Roger Baxter Jones 1950–1985
Born in London, Roger came north to Leeds in 1958 to study English at the University. It did not catch his enthusiasm, and he shifted into rock-climbing with the talented Leeds group of the day, living it up, working at Centresport and teaching dry skiing. A solid rockclimber, he knew from the extreme talent of some of his friends that he was unlikely to be tops. So he chose different ground.

After doing the major alpine routes in summer early in the 1970s, he soon turned to winter, trying the Super couloir on Mont Blanc de Tacul with Paul Braithwaite in 1972. His skiing was ever more developed, with a drive, enthusiasm and calculated risk well beyond the norm even among mountaineers. He had a practical side to his nature, securing his accommodation for three years of rather enforced mature studenthood in Sheffield by more or less completely refurbishing the old house in which he lived for its owner. He got his degree but the frustrations of study probably required such a release for volcanic energies. When he could not reach the Alps he made intense forays onto British mountains, especially in winter, where he was a formidable exponent of 'mixed' climbing. Perhaps most notable was his ascent of Red Slab on Cloggy with Paul Braithwaite in the winter of 1979, but whatever he did, he enjoyed.

He could hardly wait to escape from the claustrophobia of English existence, a trait which he perhaps shared with his sister, who worked for the EEC. He made the second ascent of the Whymper Spur Direct on the Grandes Jorasses with Nick Colton in the mid-seventies and in 1977 ski'd down the Vallée Blanche and across from the Dent du Requin to below the N face of the Aiguille des Grands Charmoz, made the first winter solo ascent of it, returned to Chamonix and ski'd down, again, for his skis. RBJ's hard work and talents were beginning to pay off in a field that suited his massive energies, stamina and calculated optimism.

An obvious candidate for the Himalaya, he joined Rab Carrington, Al Rouse and Brian Hall in their bold alpine style ascent of Jannu in 1978. In 1980, after trying the SE Ridge of Makalu with Doug Scott and Georges Bettembourg, almost succeeded in a solo ascent. In 1982 he played a notable part in the new route on Shisha Pangma with Scott and Alex McIntyre, again climbing in alpine style. In the following year came Broad Peak, with Jean Afanassieff as partner, climbing in two pairs with Andy Parkin and Al Rouse. He then made two attempts on K2. The first was foiled when Jean became unwell at high altitude. It was a mark of RBJ's determination that he then recruited a Spanish companion and again climbed alpine style beyond 8000m to be foiled by bad weather on the uppermost part of the route. It would have been the first alpine style ascent.

Meanwhile Roger picked off an impressive number of first winter ascents in the Mont Blanc Range and worked as an off-piste ski guide there. He picked up on inner game theories of sports performance and tried their application to skiing. One of Britain's leading mountaineers, a member of the ACG Committee for years, and certainly one of the strongest ever, he was a top off-piste skier, and a mountaineer of impeccable judgement, able to guide on routes of the highest standards with a considerable margin. He avoided the trap of expedition mania, which can prevent mountaineers from keeping up their 'bread and butter' climbing and enjoyment. In recent years he was a pillar of the Chamonix Franglaise. The place's cosmopolitanism and endless changes delighted him and fitted his temperament. He was a major performer in its raucous modern circus. At the same time his sympathies were ever more French, in language, tastes, and attitudes. In Autumn 1983 he married Christine Devassoux and they moved into a house in Rue des Sauberands, with her daughter Melanie. He took French nationality and became a member of the Guides Bureau. He became a part of Chamonix and could stand back from the crowds. It was somehow natural that, when a friend was badly injured in Switzerland in 1984, it was Roger and Christine who were at the centre of organizing help and relaying messages in Chamonix, coordinating the concern of French and British friends, and at the same time fed, accommodated and entertained them.

Of late he had avoided the Himalaya, though for how long one always wondered. He died with a friend client on 8 July 1985, when a serac fell on the N face of the Triolet, in a classic *Mort du Guide*.

Paul Nunn

Mrs Cicely M Williams d.1985
Cicely Williams joined the Ladies' Alpine Club in 1942 and she entered fully and enthusiastically into Club events. For nearly 30 years she gave invaluable help to the Hon Secretaries of the Club by duplicating and sending out the Club notices to members. She contributed many articles to the Club Journal, and she was the last Hon Editor and so produced the 1975 Journal with its memories and highlights of the Club's activities.

From her girlhood, Cicely had had a great interest in Switzerland and in the Matterhorn in particular, and from 1927 until her death in 1985, except for the war years, she had spent several weeks there every year, generally in Zermatt. Her climbing was done mostly in the Zermatt area and included the Riffelhorn, Rimpfischhorn and Zinal Rothorn, but it was not until 1953 that she achieved her great desire and climbed the Matterhorn.

From 1946 to 1978, her husband, Ronald, was the Chaplain of the English Church in Zermatt and this led to a close contact with many of the Zermatt people. Cicely's guide was Bernard Biner and the Biner family became her personal friends.

In 1953 she was asked to give a talk on the Swiss Radio and this she did under the title of *April in Zermatt*, having spent some weeks skiing there.

Although her climbing was confined to the Alps, Cicely had travelled widely, accompanying her husband on his many official missions abroad, after he became Bishop of Leicester in 1953. She had walked and scrambled in the lower hills of many countries including Israel, Turkey, Corsica, Germany and South California. On these journeys she made contact with many foreign members of the LAC.

Cicely was also a writer. She had contributed articles to *The Times*, the *Swiss Observer*, *Queen* and *The Lady*, mostly on some aspect of Swiss life, and she wrote five books. These included *Dear Abroad* describing her travels, *Women on the Rope* and a short history of the English Church in Zermatt.

Running through her writing is her love of Zermatt and her very lively interest in everything she sees and everyone she meets. She was, in fact, full of life and enthusiasm and humour.

Mary Starkey

Michael John Harber 1948–1985
Mike was one of the principal figures of the South Wales climbing scene, where he had been active for nearly 20 years. He visited the Alps frequently and had climbed many classic routes up to *TD* standard in a variety of areas. Mike was also an active rock climber and since the late seventies he opened up scores of new climbs on the N coast of Pembrokeshire.

One of Mike's main qualities was determination, which earned him success in his job as a medical researcher and in his other interests such as playing guitar. This determination would often manifest itself on a difficult climb, as once he got his teeth into something it was not in his nature to give up, and thus he acquired a certain reputation for being benighted!

In recent years Mike's climbing ambitions were focused on the greater ranges. Perhaps his best ascent was in 1982 when he and Tim Oliver made the first alpine-style ascent of the SW ridge of Huascaran (see *AAJ25*). His disappearance this summer whilst attempting Snow Lake Peak (6593m) in the Karakoram came as a shock to the small climbing fraternity in Cardiff, among whom he was a very prominent, enthusiastic and well-liked figure.

Pat Littlejohn

Michael George Geddes 1951–1985

I met Mike at University in 1970. We had both arrived in Cambridge from places well to the north and we both spent most of our university careers trying to hitch back to our particular brands of civilisation. He was an extraordinary enthusiast for the Scottish hills in all their forms and by the age of 17 had ascended all the Munroes and tops over 3,000ft. This experience he readily translated into ascents of the hardest snow and ice routes. He had a profound influence on my climbing, introducing me to the perverse and secret delights of the Scottish Winter Experience. His good judgement and impeccable route finding left a lasting impression on all who climbed with him.

In long weekends we hitched from Cambridge to Fort William, making second ascents, like the much feared Orion Direct. We saw through the myths a bit faster than many around us. Mike knew all of the background and carefully made plans of action while I provided added enthusiasm and a youthful long neck. We usually led through but he was the senior partner. He climbed with many other people as well, of course, completing routes like the first ascent of the modern form of Hadrian's Wall (also sometimes known at the time as Point Two Five).

He went on to climb in the Alps, completing several first British ascents, like the Zapelli-Bertone on Mont Maudit or the first winter ascent of the Rébuffat route on the Pointe du Domino. We nearly made a winter ascent of the Croz Spur in the mid seventies but were foiled by bad weather. He became a member of the ACG and went on to climb in Patagonia and Peru.

Living away from Scotland seemed to unsettle him and he returned to live in Fort William and get married to Helen, while working at the pulp mill. Here he climbed extensively with Con Higgens adding a fine series of first ascents like Galactic Hitchhiker on Ben Nevis. I occasionally joined forces for some memorable ascents, like the first ascent of Route 2 on Carn Dearg buttress. He was happy here engrossed in the culture and traditions of the Scottish hills. Perhaps my most memorable single moment was when after an 11am start on Route 2, for traditional reasons, we were caught by darkness at the end of the big traverse. A wind got up and spindrift was pouring down the uncomfortably steep looking pitch above. It was my lead but Mike asked if he could do the pitch. I agreed with a sense of relief. He smiled and said 'Let's just have a wee brew before starting.' Where-upon he delved into the depths of his well worn Tiso rucksack and produced an unexpected flask of coffee. He sipped the brew eyeing the snow covered rock above with quiet pleasure.

He died of cancer at age 34. Had he lived he would have undoubtedly carried on to become the leading authority on Scottish winter climbing.

Alan Rouse

Edward Hamilton Marriott 1906–1985
Edward Marriott, always known as Charles to his climbing friends, died in October aged 79. He had been a member of the Club since 1931, but was also a member of a number of other clubs, the Climbers' and Himalayan, but particularly the Lands End Climbing Club of which he was the first Chairman. His last known rock climb with the Lands End club was on Carn Les Boel in 1983, but his travels had taken him all over the world, most recently part way round Annapurna in 1985. Perhaps his most noteworthy exploits were the trips he made with Bill Tilman in 1955–56, 1961, 1964 and 1968. During the 1955–56 trip in 'Mischief', he crossed the Patagonian ice cap with Tilman.

Edward Charles Pyatt 1916–1985
I first met Ted Pyatt when I went to work at the National Physical Laboratory in Teddington in 1960. He was already a relatively old hand, having joined the Civil Service in 1947 after an 11 year period with the Telephone Manufacturing Company as an electronic engineer. We worked together in a newly formed Division of NPL, and I as a complete amateur so far as electronics are concerned profited considerably from his great experience in the development of a unique piece of apparatus which was to be the basis of my research work for some ten years. Later Ted moved on to assist another group, but it had not escaped his notice that I had an interest in climbing. I soon found myself gently persuaded to become the provider of area notes for North America for the Journal, on the basis of my slender experience of those regions. As a result of Ted's persuasiveness and good organizing ability, a variety of expertise and facilities available at NPL were on occasion discreetly diverted to the needs of the Journal!

Ted's love of mountains stemmed originally from a family holiday in North Wales in 1930, and was further inspired by a copy of the Abrahams' book *Rock Climbing in North Wales* found in the Islington public libraries. His rock climbing began on the Tunbridge Wells outcrops in 1936 and was followed by seasons in Skye in 1938 and '39, including a one day traverse of the Coolin Ridge. His Alpine experience was modest, consisting of two seasons in the Berner Oberland in 1946 and '47, but no doubt like many others his climbing activities were constrained by the war. He was involved in the 1960s in extensive explorations of West Country climbing, mainly on cliffs, in collaboration with K M Lawder.

He was elected to the Club in 1956, and his application shows an impressive list of sponsors, ie proposed by Bill Murray, seconded by Wilfrid Noyce and supported by Winthrop Young and Fred Pigott among others. However, prior to that he had already shown himself to be a keen club man. In 1938 he helped to found the Polaris Mountaineering Club in conjunction with Bernard Simmons. He became a member of the JMCS London Section in 1940 and was its secretary during the War years and later its President. He was assistant secretary of the BMC in 1945–47 and was elected to the Climbers' Club in 1945.

A few years after joining the Club he started to make significant contributions to its affairs, becoming Honorary Librarian in 1963, a post he relinquished on taking over the editorship of the Journal from Alan Blackshaw in 1971. In recent times, editors of the Journal have tended to come and go with some rapidity, reflecting the heavy demands the job makes on one's time. Ted was thus unusual in undertaking the task for a period of 12 years, handing it on to John Fairley in 1982. He thereby became the second longest serving editor of the *AJ*, overtaken only by Yeld, whose 31 year period as editor is surely unlikely to be remotely approached in future. Ted always had everything well under control, with a carefully organized network of delegated responsibilities for different parts of the Journal, and in the years that I was involved as part of the system, we were usually in the happy position of having extra copy 'in the box' ready for the following year. It is some measure of his forethought in these matters that I am writing these valedictory lines with the considerable aid of a brief but detailed *curriculum vitae* which Ted had thoughtfully prepared for this purpose, apparently in 1984.

Ted's involvement with writing was of course much wider than his work for the Journal. His first guide was published in 1947, *Sandstone Climbs in South-East England*. This was soon followed by *Climbers' Guide to Cornwall* (1950) with A W Andrews, and *British Crags and Climbers* (1952) with Noyce. Then came other detailed guides and also *Mountaineering in Britain* with R W Clark (1957), and *Where to Climb in the British Isles* (1960). The latter was my personal introduction to Ted's work, being received as a gift soon after I went to NPL, and led to my first realization that my new colleague was an author of considerable experience. He also wrote extensively about walking, producing a series of books for David and Charles Ltd and an HMSO guide to the Cornish Coast Path. His final works on mountains were the *Guinness Book of Mountains and Mountaineering Facts and Feats* (1980) and *The Passage of the Alps* in 1984.

Towards the end of his time at NPL, he wrote a fascinating history of Bushy House, and also an extended history of NPL itself (*The National Physical Laboratory — A History*, 1982). Ted was also responsible for setting up a museum at NPL before he retired, which involved the bringing together, restoration and display of various historic pieces of apparatus used in high precision measurements of fundamental constants at NPL over the years.

After passing on the editorship of the Journal, Ted felt free to move out of London, and he and his wife Marguerite moved to Hungerford about three years ago, partly to be near good walking country on the Downs. Sadly, Ted was the entirely unexpected victim of a routine operation which went tragically wrong; this caused him many weeks of suffering before his strong constitution finally gave up the struggle against acute septicaemia. His death is a great loss to the Club which owes him much, and an incalculable one to his family and friends. Our sympathy goes to Marguerite and to his son and daughter, Christopher and Gillian.

Tom Connor

Christopher Russell writes:
I should like to add a short tribute to Ted Pyatt with whom I worked for many years, at first in the Alpine Club Library and later, with my brother Jeffrey, as a contributor to the *Alpine Journal*.

We soon came to know Ted quite well and were both impressed by his boundless, almost relentless energy. As Editor he was always approachable, helpful, and generous in his acknowledgements. We never ceased to wonder at the amount of detailed work he completed each year, assisted by his wife and family.

It is nice to think that a lasting reminder of Ted Pyatt will be his 12 volumes of the *Alpine Journal*, which will surely retain an important place in the Library he knew so well.

Geoff Templeman writes:
Like Tom Connor, I was another who was gently persuaded to assist in the production of the Journal, and soon found myself doing book reviews and then organizing obituaries. As the person who introduced me to the Club, I have a lot to thank Ted for and got to know him well. He gave great service to a number of clubs including, of course, this one, but was not essentially a 'clubbable' man — the idea of struggling into a dinner jacket to attend an annual dinner not being his idea of pleasure! His knowledge of mountains and mountaineering was immense. Whilst he researched the material for his many books carefully, much of it was in his head, and you only had to mention a particular climb for him to say, 'Oh yes, that was first climbed by . . .', particularly if it was one of the more obscure crags of Britain, or Europe.

In later years Ted took to walking the long distance paths of Britain, and I shall remember his anecdotes about his trips — like the night he spent in a phone box near Llanthony when caught in foul weather on the Black Mountains — usually related in his deep voice with chuckling laughter on the train home from the Club.

One thing Ted and I disagreed on was the length of obituary notices. He thought they should be very short, so I will stop here.

Alpine Club Notes

Office Bearers and Committee for 1986

President	Sir Anthony Rawlinson, KCB
Vice Presidents	Lady Evans[1]
	Dr H G Nicol
Honorary Secretary	S W Town
Honorary Treasurer	R A Coatsworth
Committee: Elective Members	A D S Bankes
	P J O'B Ledeboer
	D J Lovatt
	W G Lowe, OBE
	Colonel J D C Peacock
	Professor E H Sondheimer
	Mrs Larsen
	G W Templeman
ACG Co-opted Members	A V Saunders
	S Venables
Honorary Librarian	R Lawford
Honorary Archivist	V S Risoe, MBE
Assistant Archivist	E H J Smyth, FRCS
Honorary Keeper of the Club's Pictures	Dr C B M Warren, FRCP
Honorary Editor of the Club's Journal	J M Fairley
Assistant Editors	P M R Bartlett
	G W Templeman
Honorary Guidebooks Editor	G L Swindin
Chairman of the House Committee	G W Templeman
Assistant Honorary Secretaries	
Annual Winter Dinner	Mrs Larsen
Candidates	A N Husbands
Lectures	J S Cleare
Meets	M Pinney
Trustees	M Bennett
	A Blackshaw
	J G R Harding
Honorary Solicitor	S N Beare
Auditors	A M Dowler
	R F Morgan

[1] *Lady Evans replaces Sir Anthony Rawlinson as President as a result of his death.*

General Meetings of the Alpine Club 1985

15 January	Garry Gibson, *First Ascent Essay*.
12 February	Jack de Coninck, *Wings over Everest*.
12 March	Jim Curran.
16 April	Bill March, *Canadians on Everest*.
14 May	Stephen Venables, *Alpine Climbs in France, Switzerland, and Afghanistan*.
17 September	Stephen Venables, *AC-IMF Expedition to the Siachen Glacier*.
15 October	Peter Bicknell and Dr. Charles Warren, joint meeting with the Turner Society, *Artists in the Lake District*.
12 November	Will Hurford, *From Greenhorn to Guide*.
2 December	Annual General Meeting: the President's Valedictory Address.

Climbing Meetings 1985

19–20 January	Lake District. FRCC hut, Brackenclose, Wasdale.
9–10 March	North Wales. Informal dinner with lecture by Tony Saunders, *Eiger North Face*.
6 June–29 July	East Karakoram. Joint AC-ACG and Indian Mountaineering Foundation expedition to the Siachen Glacier area.
19 July–2 August	Cornwall. CC hut, Bosigran. Family meet held jointly with Climbers' Club.
27 July–10 August	Berner Oberland. Joint meet with Climbers' Club and ABMSAC based at Grindelwald.
August	Karakoram. Meet based on Chogolungma glacier.
28–29 September	Lake District. Informal dinner with lecture by Mal Duff, *Muztagh Tower*.

The Membership Survey

Few would doubt these days the value of survey data as guidance for decision making — widely practised in commercial life even if, rather unfairly, this professional approach occasionally gets a blowback in terms of 'the opinion polls got it wrong'. For the Club the conducting of a membership survey in 1985 must be seen as a significant development in the process of management.

The object of the exercise was to obtain members' views on possible ideas for increasing the attractions of the Club, which the Committee had been discussing, and to take advantage of this vehicle to collect profile information about the membership as a whole. Almost 1000 questionnaires were sent out in late July, and by the end of September the response was 40% — quite reasonable, considering the time of year. Although in statistical terms this was not a representative sample, the results correlate quite closely with the known age breakdown of the membership, and the level of response may be taken as pretty representative. The main findings may be summarized as follows:

MEMBERSHIP PROFILE

Sex	We are still 90% male (even though one member preferred not to answer!)
Age	It is perhaps understandable that only 11% are under 35, but from then on age is fairly evenly spread through 15-year age groups. This may come as a surprise to some.
Duration of membership	35% have joined in the last 10 years and a further 25% in the last 20 years, so perhaps we are not so antique after all!
Area of residence	Nearly half the membership live south of the Midlands, and 15% in the mountain areas of North Wales, the Lake District and Scotland.
Visits to the Club	Roughly half the membership has not visited the Club in the last two years either for General Meetings or the Library, but distance from home evidently plays a part.
Visits to the Alps	As an indicator of activity, nearly 50% of members have paid at least five visits to the Alps or similar ranges in the last five years.

TIME SPENT IN NORTH WALES AND THE LAKE DISTRICT
Bearing in mind the visits to the Alps and similar ranges, it is interesting to note the time spent by respondents in North Wales and the Lake District in the last year:

	North Wales	Lake District
Nights spent		
Nil	44%	39%
*Under 10	31%	39%
By type of accommodation		
Hut	39%	24%
Own	24%	22%
Camping	11%	16%
Hotel, guest house, B & B	8%	16%
Other (includes a high proportion with friends or relatives)	18%	22%
	100%	100%
By type of activity (Total of days up to 10)		
Climbing	234	206
Walking	171	220

This represents the bulk of activities, excluding such exotic items as ballooning and water sports!

USE OF CLUB HUTS
A series of questions covered the use of other club huts with a view to assessing whether would be interest in an AC hut or cottage.

Membership of other clubs	
No other club	31%
1 other club only	45%
2 other clubs	18%

Use of other club huts
Less than half of the '1 other club only' members spent nights in their huts in
the last year, but these averaged 10 nights per member — notably members of
the Climbers' Club.
Possible use of AC hut/cottage
Proportion of respondents who would spend nights:

	North Wales	Lake District
Nil	58%	46%
1–10	32%	42%

This does not suggest great interest, bearing in mind that the occupancy level of
those who would use it works out at 10 nights per year per respondent,
exclusive of guests. Perhaps the 'hutters' have sufficient access arrangements
already.

CLUB FACILITIES
The remaining questions covered possible additional facilities that members
might like.
London accommodation
A possible arrangement with a West End club for bed and breakfast at £30 per
night was of minority interest, although some overseas members were attracted.
A few optimists preferred hut-type accommodation at the Club!
Other facilities
Suggestions were few — in fact nearly 70% of respondents had none. Those
suggestions that were offered had some interesting pointers, including more
arrangements for use of huts, regional meetings, improved Library facilities,
better pre-lecture refreshments and, last but not least, improvements to the
ladies lavatory!

So now you know.

Peter Ledeboer

The Club's Archives
In the 1973 Alpine Journal there appeared an article by N R Rice, the
Honorary Archivist at that time, entitled 'A Guide to the Archives of the Alpine
Club'. There was an introduction by T S Blakeney who had read a paper on the
AC archives at a meeting of the Club in June 1966. Rice died shortly after his
article had gone to print and I took over.

Rice's guide to the archives contained abridged lists of the more important
correspondence, letters and diaries in the archives. Since then, more material
has been found and more has been donated to the Club and it might be of
interest to members to have details of some of the more important recent
acquisitions. These are:
- The manuscript in three volumes of D W Freshfield's *Life of de Saussure*.
- Letters from Dr A M Kellas to J P Farrar about his climbs in Sikkim in
  the early part of the century and a paper written in 1920 entitled 'A
  consideration of the possibility of climbing Mount Everest'.
- Geoffrey Winthrop Young's Pen-y-Pass manuscripts.

- A bulky file of letters from W A B Coolidge to H F Montagnier written between 1908 and 1917.
- T G Longstaff's climbing diaries from 1894 to 1933 presented by his widow. There are 45 in all, covering climbs in the Alps, the Caucasus, the Himalaya and Karakoram, Canada and Greenland.
- H E L Porter's climbing diaries in three large volumes illustrated by photographs covering the period 1905 to 1966.

Among the Whymper papers, I recently came across an anonymous letter to him dated 25 August 1865. I reproduce it as an extreme example of the sort of anti-mountaineering hysteria which gripped some of the public following the Matterhorn accident. It appears to have been a response to an appeal for Michel Croz.

'Touched by your recent appeal I enclose what I believe to be the full damage actually sustained by society by the late loss of life on the Matterhorn or *Madder*-horn (?) peak. The view of *The Times* and the opinions lately expressed in that paper by intelligent "Swiss" coincide with my own and with the general opinion of the English public. *The Saturday Review* mistakes bravado for bravery and fool-hardiness for manliness. The fact is that the members of the Alpine Club are generally a *vain* set. As the "Swiss" say — the motive of these ascents is a base and corrupt one. Vanity — the love of notoriety — a morbid hankering for the applause of "stupid starers" and demoralised gobemouches is the prime and only motive. I never read the accounts of these rash adventurers and if the public only "mopped" the idiots of the Alpine Club by ignoring their existence and manifesting a cool indifference to their pranks the rash ascents would be unheard of. Prof Tyndall is an exception — he risks his life, and nobly, for science and truth. But what benefit do the ordinary mountain climbers confer on anybody? None — less than nil! Take my halfpenny for poor Croz and divide it fractionally so as to represent the value of the lives of those who perished suicidally on that occasion. I did not read your own "whimpering" account.

signed "Antihumbug".'

Although the letter was written from Winchester, F Morshead, to whom Whymper had shown the letter, did not think it could possibly have been written by a Wykehamist!

Bill Risoe

The Whymper Photograph
Among the Club's collection is a fine framed photograph of Edward Whymper in June 1865, with a tablet recording its presentation to the Club in 1911 by the then President, Sir Edward Davidson. This is the much-reproduced and well-known study of Whymper as a young man wearing a wide-brimmed hat and holding an ice-axe — clearly a posed studio shot. It was recently removed from the frame for copying when the following manuscript note was discovered:
Edward Whymper in June 1865

enlarged, from an original 'carte de visite' taken by Boissonnaz of Chamonix, and now in the possession of Dr Alexandre Seiler of Brigue and Zermatt, by Dr Charles

Atkin Swan, and presented to the Alpine Club by Sir Edward Davidson, President: January 16th 1911.
The platinotype enlargement was produced more than 45 years after the original 'carte de visite' which is now much faded, was taken.

Dr Atkin Swan (1863–1923) was a distinguished physician, an active mountaineer, and an outstanding amateur photographer of his time, becoming President of the Royal Photographic Society 1918–1920. He exhibited many alpine photographs at the Annual AC Photographic Exhibitions from 1906 to 1914 — his telephotographs were particularly singled out for favourable comment in the reviews in the *AJ* of several of the exhibitions (eg *AJ*25 649). On the outbreak of war in 1914 he was called to found the photographic section of the RFC, flew over the lines in France and was one of the first to take photographs from an aeroplane. Later the RAF claimed his medical expertise, and after the war he lectured on the effects of oxygen deficiency at altitude and was the author of a paper to the Royal Aeronautical Society on 'Physical and Psychical Effects of Altitude.'

Dr Atkin Swan's use of the platinotype process (in which platinum is used instead of silver) in copying the old and faded photograph of Whymper was doubtless because a print so made is far more permanent than any print having a silver image can be.

Frank Solari

Mountaineering Books and Ephemera in the Salerooms
Perhaps it would not be out of place, and even of interest to our members, to point out what has been happening in the sale rooms and rare book trade recently with regard to alpine ephemera, old photographs and early editions of the alpine classics, because some of this material has been changing hands at quite phenominally inflated prices to a few dealers bidding on behalf of wealthy collectors abroad.

Early books on mountaineering are much sought after these days and so have become quite good business for the specialist antiquarian book trade; and that is fair enough; but when such items turn up in the auction rooms collectors should beware, because the prices being paid for these are sometimes ridiculously inflated. Let me give an example or two of what has been happening, the first from a personal experience.

At a sale at Sothebys recently a Jane Austen item came up in which my wife was interested and we went to look at it, but in the catalogue of that sale I happened to notice another item of an entirely different kind which interested me. This was a 'lot' consisting of some personal effects of my friend Peter Oliver, the Everest climber who was with us in 1938, and so I had a look at it. But what a lot of rubbish practically all of this was — a trunk full of old magazines, bad photographs and old diaries, including one about Everest in 1938 which, however, was of no real interest because it consisted merely of day to day jottings of where the expedition had got to. But would you believe it? This load of indifferent material sold for £850! Indubitably this was a question of mis-advice on the part of the dealer to his client.

At an earlier sale a Bullock Workman miscellaneous lot of a similar nature, but much more interesting, fetched no less than £16,000. But what a pity it is for ordinary collectors of mountaineering books that a few very wealthy collectors should spoil the market for them by paying inflated prices for indifferent material. My advice to collectors of books on mountaineering would be: seek the help of a reputable specialist in the mountaineering book trade before you bid in the auction rooms. I have good friends in the book trade and at Sothebys and I am sure that they would always give fair advice.

Charles Warren

The UIAA Mountain Medicine Data Centre
The UIAA is the international federation which co-ordinates mountaineering activities in its 26 member countries and advises on mountain rescue, equipment safety, access to mountains and the environment.

The UIAA Medical Commission was established in 1980 with the object of collecting information about medical problems in the mountains and advising mountaineers about them.

The Mountain Medicine Data Centre which is funded by a small annual grant from the UIAA and the Mount Everest Foundation is an office whose purpose is to advise climbers and answer their questions about medical problems. Our specific areas of interest are:

Acclimatization, Acute Mountain Sickness
High Altitude Pulmonary and Cerebral Oedema and related problems
Frostbite and hypothermia
Expedition Medical Equipment
Injuries during mountaineering
Problems of extreme altitude
Medical problems of trekking and mountain holidays
Fitness to travel to high altitudes

The Centre is run on a voluntary basis by Dr Charles Clarke, FRCP who is a Consultant Neurologist and has wide knowledge of the problems of expedition medicine and high altitude research. The secretarial work is carried out on a part-time basis by Mrs Ann Tilley. Enquiries from many countries are handled regularly.

Any questions on medical problems should be addressed to the Data Centre. If it is necessary to see those with enquiries as patients, a letter from a general practitioner is usually necessary.

A reading list is available, together with specific publications by the MMDC. A reference list of articles of interest to climbers is kept up-to-date and literature searches can be undertaken for special problems.

The address is:
UIAA Mountain Medicine Data Centre
Department of Neurological Sciences
St Bartholomew's Hospital
38 Little Britain
London EC1

Please enclose a stamped, addressed envelope with all enquiries,

Charles Clarke & Ann Tilley

Alpine Avalanche Warning Service

Information about the likelihood of avalanches and the condition of the snow-cover in the Alps can be obtained by telephone by means of pre-recorded announcements from the following regional telephone numbers. These numbers give the code for calls from Britain. For calls within each country the international code (first bracket) must be replaced by the number '0'.

France

Haute Savoie	(010 33) (50) 531 711
Savoie	(010 33) (79) 070 824
Isère	(010 33) (76) 511 929
Hautes Alpes	(010 33) (92) 201 000
Alpes Haute Provence	(010 33) (92) 649 050
Alpes Maratimes	(010 33) (93) 723 133

Switzerland

(French)	(010 41) (22) 120
(German)	(010 41) (28) 120
(Italian)	(010 41) (93) 120

Germany

Bayern	(010 49) (89) 12 59 555

Austria

Vorarlberg	(010 43) (5522) 16
Tirol	(010 43) (5222) 196
Salzburg	(010 43) (6222) 196
Steiermark	(010 43) (316) 840
Kärnten	(010 43) (4222) 16

Italy

Cuneo Imperia	(010 39) (171) 66 323
Torino	(010 39) (11) 32 90 191
Val d'Aosta	(010 39) (165) 31 210
Novara Vercelli	(010 39) (324) 2670
Lombardia	(010 39) (342) 901 280
Bolzano (Italian)	(010 39) (471) 994 114
Bolzano (German)	(010 39) (471) 994 111
Trento	(010 39) (461) 981 012
Veneto	(010 39) (436) 79221
Friuli-Venezia Giulia	(010 39) (432) 208 633

Information from the International Alpine Mountain Rescue Commission, IKAR/CISR.

Errata

The following errors in *AJ90* have been noted:

p24.   The Chinese name for Broad Peak is Buwde. Gasherbrum I and II are known as Kiaxiu Buwma.

p28.   Galen Rowell was assistant leader of the ascent of Anye Maqen. The leader was Kim Schmitz.

p30.   Jialobaili is also known as Gyala Peri.

p31.   The most accurate elevation for Changtze is 7553m.

p32.   The Chinese-Japanese attempt on Gurla Mandhata was successful. The Chinese leader was Shi Zhonchun. Kailas is sacred to both Bhuddhists and Hindus.

p74.   This was not the second ascent of the Mustagh Tower. McNaught-Davis and Brown reached the W summit on 7 July '56. Next day, Patey and Hartog traversed the W summit to the E summit. Guido Magnone climbed the E summit from the SE on 17 July '56.

p157.   The highest peak entirely within British Columbia is Mt Waddington, not Mt Robson. Mt Fairweather on the Alaskan border is higher.

p282.   Tom Brocklebank was a schoolmaster, not a journalist. He was a housemaster at Eton for 15 years.

Plate 63.   This actually represents Nevado del Muerto, 6476m. Ojos del Salado is to the right of the picture. Ojos del Salado means 'Sources of the Salty River'.

Acknowledgements

Once again I am grateful to several people without whose help the production of this issue would have been impossible. Maurice Bennett, Margaret Clennett, Ashley Greenwood and Robin Robinson have all faithfully read and corrected manuscripts and proofs — a major task. (Errors and undesirable alterations, however, are all my fault.) Frank Solari has carefully converted endless colour pictures to black and white. My two Assistant Editors, Phil Bartlett and Geoffrey Templeman, have patiently gathered in a tremendous quantity of material. Peter Ledeboer has quietly carried out the unglamorous but necessary task of shepherding in the advertising which helps keep costs within bounds. And last but not least the friends who have dragged me out climbing despite the pressures of deadlines and my family who have put up with me through the last months.

This is the last issue of the *Alpine Journal* which I shall be editing. It has been an intensely satisfying and enjoyable four years and I am especially grateful to all who have encouraged me throughout this time.

Ernst Sondheimer, who has helped me on previous issues, kindly offered to take over the task. Please give him the support and encouragement that I have enjoyed — it makes all the difference.

John Fairley

Index

GUIDANCE FOR CONTRIBUTORS

The *Alpine Journal* has been published regularly since 1863 as 'A Record of Mountain Adventure and Scientific Observation'. At first contributions were accepted only from members of the Alpine Club, but today this is no longer the case. The Journal has always been a record of all aspects of mountains and mountaineering and although its main function is to record mountain adventure, articles on mountain art, literature, sociology, geology, medicine, equipment, etc., are all suitable.

Language Papers should be written in English whenever possible. Translation is usually possible from French, German and Italian but papers requiring translation must be submitted at least 3 months before the Editorial Deadline.

Typescript The complete typescript including the text of the paper, list of references, footnotes and captions to illustrations should be typed on one side of A4 paper, at double spacing and with 20–30mm margins. Authors should keep a spare copy.

Illustrations The number of colour photographs which can be printed is extremely limited and only top quality photographs will be accepted. Prints, half-tones or colour should be between 150 × 200mm and 220 × 300mm large and be printed on glossy paper. Colour transparencies should be at least 35mm format. A portfolio of up to 10 photographs should be provided. Maps and line drawings should be of a similar size to the prints and be finished ready for printing. Place-names appearing in the text, where relevant, should be marked on the maps also.

Each photograph should be clearly labelled with title, author and any copyright. This information should be typed on a separate sheet of paper attached to the photograph and not written on the back of the photograph itself. Routes of climbs should be marked on separate sheets of transparent paper.

Always take special care in sending prints through the post. Do include adequate stiffening to prevent folding and clearly label the cover, 'Photographs: Please Do Not Bend'. Do not include paper-clips or pins which could damage prints.

References Details of other publications referred to in the text should be given in a separate list and should include:
— the names of all authors,
— the title of the paper and publication as appropriate,
— the year of publication, volume number and first page number.

Units Metric (SI) units should be used throughout except when quoting original material which uses other units.

Deadline Copy *must* be with the Editor by 1 January of the year of publication.

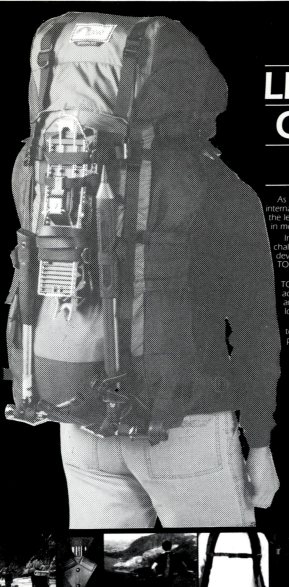

LEADERS OF THE PACK

As the originators of the large capacity internal frame concept, Lowe has provided the leadership which has set the standard in modern rucksack design.

In 1985, Lowe continues to meet the challenge for innovation and development, with the patented TORSO-TRAC system.

Designed by Greg Lowe, the TORSO-TRAC system offers immediate adjustment for maximum fit, comfort and responsive performance under all load carrying conditions.

Together with further refinements to the Lowe system, these features provide unparalleled comfort and load control. Take a close look at the 1985 Lowe range and better still try one on.

Then you'll see why we are **the** leaders.

NORWEGIAN EVEREST EXPEDITION

FACED WITH THE WORST CONDITIONS IN THE WORLD, ONLY THE BEST WILL DO.

The best research, the best design and the best quality made Mountain Equipment the automatic choice for both major expeditions to Everest in 1985.

Make your choice from the full Mountain Equipment range. It includes down and synthetic jackets (with optional Gore-Tex outers) specialist high altitude wear, and the most advanced sleeping bags in the world.

Mountain Equipment
SUPPLIERS TO 14 EVEREST EXPEDITIONS

Please send me your new 24 page colour catalogue. I enclose 40p to help cover post and packing.

NAME _____

ADDRESS _____

_____

_____ POST CODE _____

A J 86

Send to: Mountain Equipment Ltd.,
Leech Street, Stalybridge, SK15 1SD.
Telephone: 061-338-8793

 **00:04**

 **00:20**

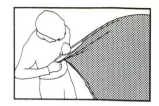 **01:03**

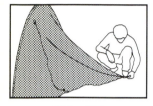 **01:13**

 **01:25**

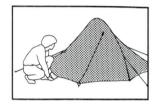 **02:28**

 **03:06**

 **03:24**

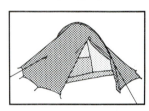 **03:35**

Easy.

Once you're familiar with pitching the Space-Packer you'll be amazed at how easily it'll go up.

We managed it in 3 minutes 35 seconds. We were, admittedly, trying to prove a point, but if it was getting dark and pouring with rain, you'd stand a very good chance of beating our time!

It pitches flysheet first, so you've got protection from wind and rain in a couple of minutes.

And once it's up it'll stay up.

The Space-Packer is made of high tenacity ripstop nylon, and is built to an aerodynamic shape that will withstand the most extreme weather conditions. Weighing only 3 lb. 14 oz., the Space-Packer is not only one of the lightest and strongest tents available, it's also probably the fastest.

SAUNDERS
TENTMAKERS